1994

GLOBAL CHANGE

GEOGRAPHICAL DIALOGUE:

SOVIET AND AMERICAN VIEWS

This unique series brings the results of joint research conducted by Soviet and U.S. scientists on global geographical issues to scholars of many disciplines. Volumes in the series are published simultaneously with Progress Publishers, Moscow.

SERIES EDITORS

George J. Demko, Director
The Nelson A. Rockefeller Center for the Social Sciences
Dartmouth College

Vladimir M. Kotlyakov, Director
Institute of Geography
U.S.S.R. Academy of Sciences

GLOBAL CHANGE

GEOGRAPHICAL APPROACHES

A Joint USSR-USA Project under the Scientific Leadership of Vladimir M. Kotlyakov and Gilbert F. White

UNIVERSITY OF ARIZONA PRESS

TUCSON · ARIZONA

AUTHORS

Roger G. Barry

Tatiana V. Bochkareva

George J. Demko

Aleksandr V. Drozdov

Nikita F. Glazovsky

Sergei P. Gorshkov

Samuel N. Goward

David E. Greenland

Julia A. Jones

Aleksandr N. Krenke

John R. Mather

James K. Mitchell

Sergei M. Myagkov

William E. Riebsame

Tatiana G. Runova

Galina V. Sdasyuk

Vladimir N. Solntsev

Andrei A. Velitchko

Thompson Webb III

Cort J. Willmott

EDITED BY

John R. Mather

Galina V. Sdasyuk

The University of Arizona Press

Copyright © 1991
The Arizona Board of Regents
All Rights Reserved

⊖ This book is printed on acid-free, archival-quality paper.
Manufactured in the United States of America

95 94 93 92 91   5 4 3 2 1

Library of Congress Cataloging-in-Publication Data

Global change : geographical approaches / edited by John R. Mather and
    Galina V. Sdasyuk.
        p.   cm. — (Geographical dialogue)
    "A joint USSR-USA project under the scientific leadership of
Vladimir M. Kotlyakov and Gilbert F. White."
    Includes bibliographical references and index.
    ISBN 0-8165-1272-8 (cloth : alk. paper)
    1. Man—Influence on nature.   2. Environmental protection—
Research—International cooperation.   3. Environmental mapping.
4. Landscape protection.   I. Mather, John Russell, 1923–   .
II. Sdasyuk, Galina Vesil'evna.   III. Kotliakov, Vladimir
Mikhaĭlovich.   IV. White, Gilbert F.   V. Series.
GF75.G56   1991
363.7—dc20   91-14025
                                                               CIP

Designed by Laury A. Egan

CONTENTS

LIST OF FIGURES

LIST OF TABLES

LIST OF ACRONYMS

AFRENA	Agroforestry Research Network for Africa
AVHRR	Advanced Very High Resolution Radiometer
CFC	Chlorofluorocarbons
CILSS	Comité Internationale de Lutte contre la Secheresse Sahelienne
CIMMYT	Centro Internacional de Melioracion de Mais y Trigo
CLIMAP	Climate: Long Range Investigation, Mapping and Prediction project
COHMAP	Cooperative Holocene Mapping Project
EIA	environmental impact assessment
EIS	environmental impact statement
EPIC	Erosion Productivity Impact Calculator
FIFE	First International Satellite Land Surface Climatology Project Field Experiment
GCM	general circulation model or global climate model
GEMS	Global Environmental Monitoring Program
GIS	geographic information systems
GISS	Goddard Institute for Space Studies
GOES	Geostationary Operational Environmental Satellite
HAPEX	Hydrologic Atmospheric Pilot Experiment
HNP	hazardous natural process
IBSRAM	International Board for Soil Research and Management
ICRAF	International Center for Research on Agroforestry
ICRISAT	International Crop Research Institute for the Semi-arid Tropics
ICSU	International Council of Scientific Unions
IGBP	International Geosphere-Biosphere Program
IIASA	International Institute for Applied Systems Analysis
IITA	International Institute for Tropical Agriculture
ILCA	International Livestock Center for Africa
ISCCP	International Satellite Cloud Climatology Program
ISLSCP	International Satellite Land Surface Climatology Project
KMA	Kursk Magnetic Anomaly
LTER	Long-Term Ecological Research
MSS	Landsat Multi-Spectral Scanner
NADP	National Atmospheric Deposition Program
NCAR	National Center for Atmospheric Research
NOAA	National Oceanic and Atmospheric Administration

OTU	operational territorial unit
PAM	portable automated mesomet
PAR	photosynthetically active radiation
SCOPE	Scientific Committee on Problems of the Environment
SIA	social impact assessment
SPOT	Système Probetoire d'Observation de la Terre
TM	Landsat Thematic Mapper
TSBF	Tropical Soil Biology and Fertility network
UNCOD	United Nations Conference on Desertification
UNEP	United Nations Environment Program
UNESCO	United Nations Educational, Scientific, and Cultural Organization
UNFAO	United Nations Food and Agriculture Organization
USDA	United States Department of Agriculture
WDC	World Data Center
WMO	World Meteorological Organization

PREFACE

Geographers from the Soviet Union and the United States of America have joined in a review of selected geographical approaches to the study of global change as part of the new efforts sponsored by the International Council of Scientific Unions under its International Geosphere-Biosphere Program (IGBP) to investigate major alterations in the world environment. The scientific leaders of the project—Professor V. M. Kotlyakov, the corresponding member of the USSR Academy of Sciences and director of the Institute of Geography of the USSR Academy of Sciences, and Professor Gilbert F. White, member of the U.S. National Academy of Sciences and foreign member of the USSR Academy of Sciences—took upon themselves a difficult task. Their goal was to create not a collection of articles but a joint, consistent monograph uniting the efforts of a selected group of Soviet and American geographers. These geographers were asked to discuss methodological approaches and techniques now available to geographers that could be used effectively for studying global changes, with the aim of finding ways to achieve a sustainable ecological-economic pattern of development that will result in the preservation of the earth as a living system.

After outlining the background of the IGBP, the authors conclude that global change cannot be fully understood without reconstruction of earlier landscape processes, more sophisticated modeling of the dynamics of present-day land-scapes, analyses of the causes and consequences of anthropogenic changes in specific regions, appraisal of the ways in which societies can respond to the knowledge of those changes, and a greatly enhanced geographic information system supported by detailed field studies. Geographers' knowledge of strategies for stabilization and improvement of the human environment is considered, and new geographical approaches to the assessment of territorial systems, structures, and dynamics are described. One suggestion is the creation of "red-zone maps" of critical ecological situations. These raise a warning flag when the threshold of irreversible change is approaching—change that will result in the loss of both resources and the regenerative capacity of the environment. This volume contains examples of several red-zone maps reflecting the locations of critical situations in both the USSR and the USA that have resulted from anthropogenic modification of water. These, as well as other regional samples included in the book, are limited to areas of the USSR and the USA only.

One of the unfortunate tendencies of our time is the growing impact of natural disasters on human populations. The development of scenarios of probable natural disasters with an optimum modeling of preparatory, rescue, and restoration operations is a complicated but solvable problem. We must understand the interaction of the major parameters existing in the narrow ecological corridor for life support on the earth. Special efforts should be made to predict potential changes in the biosphere in the coming century. This vital research must be carried out at all three major levels of spatial organization—local, regional, and global.

The findings of the participants of this joint project not only suggest how geographers may be able to contribute to the IGBP research initiative; they also serve as a call for new research and data collection to provide needed information to help understand environmental futures. The authors invite comments by other geographers as well as by scientists in related disciplines.

Principal contributors to each section of the book are listed below, although it must be understood that all those who assisted in the writing and editing of the different sections cannot be acknowledged by name. They all have the grateful appreciation of the editors.

1.0: V. M. Kotlyakov, J. R. Mather, G. V. Sdasyuk, and G. F. White; 2.1: C. J. Willmott, A. N. Krenke, and S. N. Goward; 2.2: A. A. Velitchko, T. Webb, and R. G. Barry; 2.3: R. G. Barry and C. J. Willmott, with Russian references by A. N. Krenke; 3.1: T. V. Bochkareva, S. P. Gorshkov, A. N. Krenke, and N. F. Glazovsky, with contributions by B. A. Alekseev and A. V. Vasilieva; 3.2: J. A. Jones (Concepts and Definitions); J. A. Jones, T. V. Bochkareva, S. P. Gorshkov, A. N. Krenke, and N. F. Glazovsky, with contributions by B. A. Alekseev and A. V. Vasilieva (Impacts on Deforestation); J. A. Jones (Impacts on Desertification, Impacts on Soil Degradation); 3.3: J. A. Jones; 4.1: S. M. Myagkov and W. E. Riebsame; 4.2: J. K. Mitchell; 4.3: W. E. Riebsame and T. G. Runova; 5.1–5.3 edited by G. V. Sdasyuk and G. J. Demko; 5.1: T. G. Runova and G. V. Sdasyuk, with contributions by M. Ya. Lemeshev; 5.2: A. N. Krenke, S. P. Gorshkov, and J. R. Mather; 5.3: V. N. Solntsev and S. P. Gorshkov; 6.1: S. N. Goward, with contributions by N. N. Kazantsev and Russian references by L. N. Vasiliev; 6.2: D. E. Greenland and A. V. Drozdov; 7.0: J. R. Mather and G. V. Sdasyuk.

J. R. Mather and G. V. Sdasyuk
Co-editors

ACKNOWLEDGMENTS
FOR THE U.S. EDITION

The U.S. editor would like to express his sincere appreciation to all the scientific contributors to this volume for their patience during the four years of negotiating with the Soviets over format and outline, collecting scientific material, and editing. The contributors are listed by chapter and section at the end of the Preface. In addition, many others contributed time and talents to the enterprise. It is not possible to acknowledge all who have contributed to making this project a success, but they all have my heartfelt thanks.

Special thanks must be given to Dr. Gyula Pauer, Director, Cartographic Laboratory, University of Kentucky, for his untiring efforts in redrafting many of the Soviet diagrams to bring them into conformity with those contributed by U.S. authors. Ms. Linda Parrish, Cartographer of the Department of Geography at the University of Delaware, also contributed her skills to the clarification of some of the diagrams.

I can never sufficiently acknowledge the work of Ms. Joanne Danoff who, with the assistance of Ms. Cyndi Timko, took charge of the typing, correcting, and retyping of the whole manuscript during many drafts. She had to wrestle especially with many versions of the extensive Russian bibliography. Ms. Bernice Williams oversaw the early development of the manuscript material and coordinated our efforts to meet with our Soviet counterparts to produce an outline and a workable time table. My sincere thanks go to all three of these indispensable colleagues.

To my Soviet coeditor, Ms. Galina Sdasyak, I express my warm thanks for her patience, her cooperation, and her many kindnesses while we conferred in Moscow, Washington, and Newark, Delaware.

John R. Mather
U.S. Editor

THE CONTRIBUTORS

Scientific Leaders

Vladimir M. Kotlyakov, Ph.D.   Director, Institute of Geography of the USSR Academy of Sciences; Corresponding Member of the USSR Academy of Sciences; Chairman of the Aral Research Center; People's Deputy of the USSR; specializes in glaciology and geoecology.

Gilbert F. White, Ph.D.   Gustavson Distinguished Professor Emeritus, University of Colorado; Member of the U.S. National Academy of Sciences; Foreign Member of the USSR Academy of Sciences; former Director, Institute of Behavioral Science, University of Colorado; specializes in water resources and environmental impacts.

Editors

John R. Mather, Ph.D.   Professor, University of Delaware; Director, University Center for Climatic Research; President, Association of American Geographers, 1991–1992; Secretary, American Geographical Society; specializes in applied climatology and water resources.

Galina V. Sdasyuk, Dr. Sci.   Leading Researcher, Institute of Geography of the USSR Academy of Sciences; awarded Przhevalskiy Gold Medal of USSR Geographical Society; specializes in regional development and planning, India, critical environmental zones, and global changes.

Other Contributors

Roger G. Barry, Ph.D.   Professor, University of Colorado; Director of the World Data Center-A for Climatology, National Snow and Ice Center; Cooperative Institute for Research in Environmental Sciences; specializes in climatology (synoptic, paleoclimatology) and Arctic snow and ice.

Tatiana V. Bochkareva, Ph.D.   Researcher, Institute of Geography of the USSR Academy of Sciences; Executive Secretary of Man and Biosphere II program; specializes in urban development, environmental management, and methodological issues of ecology.

George J. Demko, Ph.D.   Professor, Dartmouth College; Director, Rockefeller Center for the Social Sciences; Honorary Member of the Slovak Academy of Sciences; former U.S. Department of State Geographer; specializes in population geography, political geography, and public policy.

Aleksandr V. Drozdov, Ph.D.   Leading Researcher, Institute of Geography of the USSR Academy of Sciences; specializes in contact zones, landscape cartography, and fluxes of energy and materials.

Nikita F. Glazovsky, Dr. Sci.   First Deputy Director, Institute of Geography of the USSR Academy of Sciences; Professor, Moscow State University; specializes in landscape geochemistry, environment, and land and water use.

Sergei P. Gorshkov, Dr. Sci.   Associate Professor, Moscow State University; specializes in landscape dynamics, changes in human land use, and the noosphere.

Samuel N. Goward, Ph.D.   Associate Professor, University of Maryland; Director, University Remote Sensing Systems Laboratory, Laboratory for Global Remote Sensing Studies; specializes in remote sensing, numerical analysis, modeling, and climatology.

David E. Greenland, Ph.D.   Professor and Chair, Department of Geography, University of Colorado; specializes in climatology (micro, applied, and air quality) and environmental conservation.

Julia A. Jones, Ph.D.   Associate Professor, University of California at Santa Barbara; specializes in soil mapping and genesis, forest watershed management, and environmental analysis.

Aleksandr N. Krenke, Dr. Sci.   Head, Department of Climatology and Hydrology, Institute of Geography of the USSR Academy of Sciences; specializes in hydrology, climatology, glaciology, and humans' impacts on nature.

James K. Mitchell, Ph.D.   Professor and Chair, Department of Geography, Rutgers University; specializes in resource management, coastal and marine geography, and human response to hazards.

Sergei M. Myagkov, Dr. Sci.   Professor, Moscow State University; Head, Laboratory of Snow Avalanches and Mudflows; specializes in natural disasters, social-ecological impact, and long-term development.

William E. Riebsame, Ph.D.   Associate Professor, University of Colorado; Director, Natural Hazards and Applications Information Center; specializes in natural hazards, natural resources management, and climatology.

Tatiana G. Runova, Ph.D.   Leading Researcher, Institute of Geography of the USSR Academy of Sciences; specializes in environmental management, the Soviet Union, and regionalization.

Vladimir N. Solntsev, Ph.D.   Associate Professor, Moscow State University; specializes in landscape studies (theory and methods).

Andrei A. Velitchko, Dr. Sci. Professor and Head, Department of Paleogeography, Institute of Geography of the USSR Academy of Sciences; Awarded Litke Gold Medal of USSR Geographical Society; specializes in paleogeography and the history of evolution of human interactions with the environment.

Thompson Webb III, Ph.D. Professor of Geological Sciences, Brown University; specializes in paleoclimatology, Quaternary environments, and palynology.

Cort J. Willmott, Ph.D. Professor and Chair, Department of Geography, University of Delaware; specializes in climatology and quantitative methods.

GLOBAL CHANGE

1. INTRODUCTION

A momentous development of the past century has been the growing recognition, among people of all countries, of the effects of human activities on the global, interactive systems of the air, rock, water, and biota that sustain them. This deepening understanding has been nourished by scientific research. Advances have occurred through the identification of the complex ways in which flows of matter and energy link the earth's natural components together, and through an understanding of the social and economic bonds that explain human activities within and across national boundaries. This understanding is now being expressed in international environmental movements and in the International Geosphere-Biosphere Program (IGBP), sponsored by the International Council of Scientific Unions to examine the geophysical and biological changes that are now under way and that may occur in the future.

The Twentieth Century and Geography

With the rapid growth of technology, the activities of people have begun to affect our environment on a scale comparable with powerful natural processes. Until recently, science has been unable to make confident predictions of vital changes in many parameters of the earth, or to distinguish between natural and anthropogenic causes contributing to those changes. But in the 1960s this situation began to change.

It is now clear that people do not merely live within nature. They are gradually replacing its natural elements and objects by artificial, human ones. In doing so, they are creating a secondary environment. The principal object of geography—geographical environment—no longer exists in its natural form. There are no longer natural landscapes and natural geosystems. All of them have, in different measures, been changed by people, and we must now deal with natural-anthropogenic and natural-technical geosystems.

In the twentieth century, human civilization is the most important factor influencing nature. The interaction of society and nature takes place in the geographical environment where the laws of nature and society are interrelated in complex ways. This interaction gives rise to ecological problems in a setting where ecological laws are far from completely understood.

The interaction of society and nature is a field in which the interests and tasks of many sciences intertwine. These interests include improvement of technologies, economy and its management, and the working out of legal regulations and a system of control. Of similar significance are such aspects as rational use of natural resources; the dynamics of natural-anthropogenic and natural-technical geosystems; the efficient location of industrial production, agriculture, and settlement systems; geosystems monitoring; and the forecasting of the state of the natural environment under conditions of intensive development.

The task of harmonizing the interaction of society and nature requires that the earth and its human society be considered as a single system possessing a specific quality—spatial organization. Territory or landscape as a special type of spatial classification of resources becomes more important than material resources. The latter may be replaced by other natural or artificial substances; in contrast, landscape is an exhaustible and nonrenewable resource.

In the second half of this century, the course of development has led to a situation in which the human family and its individual members are faced with the necessity of working out a framework of thinking that considers the planet as a whole. The real threat of nuclear self-destruction and our unprecedented demands on nature make the "human-environment" problem a specific function of the survival of human society. In these circumstances, deepening our knowledge about the regularities of the earth's geographical sphere becomes a key task of geography.

The International Geosphere-Biosphere Program

The thirty-year experience of scientific studies within the framework of international programs has demonstrated the limitations of strategies of component and regional studies of the earth. The time has come to change from study of individual spheres to study of the planet as a whole. The urgent challenge is to obtain synthesized information on a global scale and to build integrated models of the system.

Since the early 1980s, wide circles of the scientific public have discussed the idea of creating a large international program aimed at understanding causes and mechanisms of global changes and searching for scientific methods of prediction of events in the twenty-first century. In 1986 the International Council of Scientific Unions approved the International Geosphere-Biosphere Program: The Study of Global Change, the largest truly international project to be started in the present century and planned to continue on into the next one (Malone 1986; Belousov 1987; Kotlyakov 1988; Kotlyakov et al. 1988a, 1988b). Priority will be given to understanding and predicting changes in the global environment on the basis of models of the earth system, using accumulated knowledge on global physical and biogeochemical processes. The IGBP expects to examine fundamental problems of the evolution of the earth's natural systems and changes caused by both natural and anthropogenic factors. The final goal of the program is to solve a basic problem of the survival of mankind.

As thinking turns to the means by which the IGBP's scientific program may be realized, it is important to consider its roots in the diverse fields from which it draws information, method, and theory. One of those fields—a uniquely integrative discipline—is geography. In this book we bring together, from two countries, a rich body of experience in shaping geographic approaches to environmental change.

Our aims are threefold. First, geographic studies help to illustrate the intricate and fundamental problems encountered in attempting to assess global change. Second, these studies emphasize some of the lessons learned in earlier efforts to examine interrelationships among natural systems at local, regional, and world scales. Third, a number of approaches are described that will need to be considered if the significant interactions of natural and social systems are to be understood and prudently managed.

This introductory chapter sketches the historical traditions contributing to the contemporary concerns and work relating to environmental modifications. It then outlines the principal systems of the human environment that are involved. Finally, it notes several of the distinctive roles that have been played by geographers in the past, and that will need to be exercised in the future if an integrated understanding and management of global change is to be achieved.

The decision to bring together the American and Soviet bodies of geographic experience in dealing with these matters was partly chance and partly the product of complementary activities. Growing out of the commitment by geographers in both the USSR and the USA to seek grounds for closer cooperative work, a number of scientific issues of common interest were canvassed by representatives of the two groups during 1986. One of the issues identified was the proposed organization of the IGBP and the extent to which geographers should participate. It is apparent that the questions the IGBP has raised have claimed the attention of both American and Soviet geographers for a long time, but with a somewhat different emphasis: namely, human-environment interactions. The time seemed right to appraise and compare this history of geographic research on "global change" with the objectives of the IGBP and to bring this work to the attention of other potential participants in the IGBP, in the hope that it would stimulate more innovative approaches among geographers as well as in related disciplines.

The materials that follow are in no sense intended to be comprehensive or fully representative of the geographic discipline. Rather, they were chosen to illustrate a variety of the methods and topics that geographers, in the past and currently, address which are relevant to the IGBP.

Historical Concerns

Prior to the intensified concern for global environmental matters that has occurred during the past twenty-five years, relatively few voices were heard calling for broad approaches to the questions relating to the global environment, development, and population. Some were biologists (Osborne 1953), and some were concerned with family planning (Vogt 1948); four stand out.

In the 1860s, G. P. Marsh was among the first to raise questions about the extent and long-term deterioration of soils and forests, chiefly in the ancient Mediterranean world (1864). Somewhat later, the Russian soil scientist V. V. Dukuchayev not only showed the close relationships among climatic, vegetation, water, and soils systems, but also initiated experimental investigations on how these systems were being altered by humans' activities (1892). Possibly more than Marsh and Dukuchayev, Russian geographer and environmentalist V. I. Vernadsky developed a global ecological conception of the biosphere. He felt that biotic matter not only permeated the upper lithosphere, the hydrosphere, and the lower atmosphere, it also acted as a force controlling matter and energy flows, linking together all the spheres of the earth into one integrated system.

Vernadsky's book *Biosphere* was published in 1926. In the following year, mathematician and philosopher E. LeRua, who had been strongly influenced by Vernadsky's lectures in Paris in 1922–1925, introduced the term *noosphere* to describe the developing state of the biosphere over historic time—a biosphere that was being influenced and modified by the activities of humans. Both Vernadsky and LeRua felt that the self-organizing capacity of the biosphere—its ability to maintain those geochemical and geophysical conditions suitable for life—had changed markedly under the growing impact of humans. Vernadsky referred to the anthropogenic modification of the biosphere as the entry into the noosphere—into a sphere of intelligence—not because human activities and natural processes were in harmony with each other, but rather because "with the growth of scientific thinking" and "social activities of mankind based on it" (Vernadsky 1973, 31), the biosphere had acquired new properties, many of which humans were only beginning to understand, often from bitter experience. Vernadsky pointed to some important peculiarities inherent in this period of transition from the biosphere to the noosphere. His concept of biosphere finally caught on in the UNESCO Man and the Biosphere program (1981).

In 1955, a biologist (M. Bates), a geographer (C. O. Sauer), and an urban planner (L. Mumford) joined in organizing a monumental interdisciplinary review entitled *Man's Role in Changing the Face of the Earth* (Thomas 1956), the first such review of its kind. An undertaking on this scale was not repeated until 1987, in a project jointly sponsored by the Clark University School of Geography, the International Institute of Applied Systems Analysis, and the World Resources Institute.

After the late 1960s a considerable number of appraisals were made of different sectors of the world environment as well as of the entire globe (Whittaker and Likens 1973; Woodwell et al. 1978, 1983b). These works presented evidence on specific types of deterioration; for example, in air or water quality, or forest cover. It was difficult for these researchers to appraise the effects of alterations in one place or sector on another. While the broad linkages had become apparent as a result of research during previous decades, more precise, quantitative assessments were lacking at many points. But the framework for a more searching analysis was now at hand.

Interlocking Systems

The achievements of the twentieth century made both scientists and political leaders aware that the magnitude of human alterations of the biosphere had become comparable to some natural processes (United Nations Environment Program [UNEP] 1982). As Vernadsky put it, humanity was now an agent of global change. There was an ever-growing list of areas where the environmental situation threatened to get out of control. Reliable predictions of the consequences of continuing at the present level were impeded by lack of accurate knowledge of the specific processes at work.

The earth's general system of components can be graphed schematically, as shown in Figure 1.1. The atmosphere, hydrosphere, and lithosphere may be viewed as layers through which matter and energy move. A thin *geosystems* mantle occurs along the upper limit of the lithosphere/hydrosphere, within which most life processes on earth are maintained in a quasi-stable state by processes of matter and energy transfer. These energy/matter flows are influenced by both external processes, such as the sun, and internal processes, including human activities. "A" cycles are maintained by solar and other external impacts below the ozone layer and above the lower lithosphere. "B" cycles are driven by endogenous processes from within the lithosphere, hydrosphere, and atmosphere, including human activities. When the two types interact, they produce very complicated "C" cycles in the geosystems mantle.

The magnitude of humans' impact on the biosphere is now increasing at an accelerating rate. The interaction between individual layers is thereby inten-

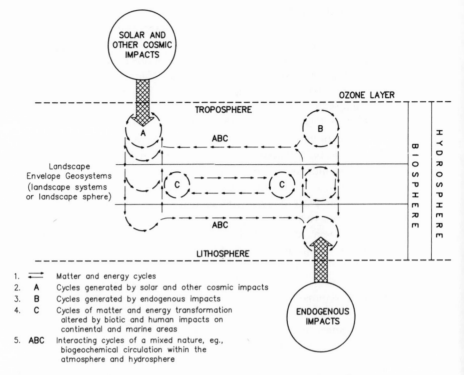

Fig. 1.1 The position and role of the geosystem cover in the system of geospheres.

sified, and earlier physical explanations of the resulting processes may no longer hold. Three classes of change may be under way at the same time. First, and underlying the other two, are the global evolutionary changes caused by external cosmic forces. These were evident in fluctuations in temperature, ocean level, and related phenomena before any humans were on the scene. A second class of changes includes those that occur at the global scale as a result of local actions; for example, volcanoes emit CO_2 and SO_2 and industries emit chlorofluorocarbons (CFCs) that affect the global atmosphere. Third, some local disturbances, such as accelerated soil erosion, may not directly affect the global layers, but they acquire global significance because they are widespread. While all are important, there is a special challenge in measuring the anthropogenic changes.

Geographic research is not directed toward describing a static situation, although a stereotypic view of geographers as mapmakers might foster this impression. In fact, the approach commonly is evolutionary. It seeks to identify the processes responsible for evolving spatial patterns and the human actions that affect them. Whether the aim is historical, descriptive, or predictive, the necessary analysis takes into account lithosphere, biosphere, atmosphere, and hydrosphere, as well as human society as affected by both external and internal factors. It is notable that much geographic analysis involves the interaction of natural and social systems and is interdisciplinary. Typically, geographic analysis draws upon methods and data from a variety of scientific fields, and geographers are accustomed to collaboration with scientists from those fields. The scientific leaders of this project have joined with the editors of this volume in summarizing our thinking on these matters in identical articles published in the proceedings of our two national academies of sciences (Kotlyakov et al. 1988a, 1988b). The following observations are drawn from those articles.

For the current IGBP effort to be genuinely productive, it needs to undertake vigorously at least five lines of geographic research: (1) analysis of landscape change dynamics; (2) examination of the evolution of geosystems of different scales; (3) analysis of factors, mechanisms, and effects of anthropogenic changes in geosystems and their socioeconomic and environmental causes and consequences; (4) appraisal of the human dimensions of forces generating these changes and of the conditions under which they may be guided or controlled; and (5) improvement of methods for simulating geosystems dynamics, including creation of a new generation of geographic information systems.

Investigations should involve intensive collaboration among disciplines, but our primary concern must be with the mode of analysis rather than with the discipline.

Modeling the Dynamics of Landscapes

The concept of developing a fully integrated numerical model of the earth stems from the success achieved by numerically modeling atmospheric and oceanic circulation of the planet (Washington and Parkinson 1986). Some progress has been made in developing local models of vegetation dynamics (Shugart 1984) and hydrologic systems (Camillo et al. 1987), but no global models of such phenomena have been developed. If truly interactive models of land phenomena are to be incorporated into integrated earth models, then much more attention must be given to developing analytical descriptions of land processes. Developing dynamic models of land phenomena is more difficult because simple concepts of turbulent energy/mass balance do not adequately describe the spatiotemporal evolution of land conditions (D. H. Miller 1978). Discrete and highly contrasting land conditions are maintained in close proximity over long time periods.

Landscape heterogeneity varies in space and time not only because of the diurnal, seasonal, and long-term variability of climate but also because of geologic events recorded in the topography and stratigraphy of continents. Additional effects of human activity on landscape heterogeneity date back several centuries, and their history is insufficiently documented to incorporate into a dynamic land model (Thomas 1956). An effective macroscale description of terrestrial biophysical processes is needed before progress can be achieved in global change studies. Derivation of such a description will scientifically challenge the IGBP.

Models of climate, biogeochemical cycles, groundwater and surface runoff all apply to global change studies. The effects of the various factors can be studied by linking them with resource and economic models. For example, existing statistical and deterministic crop-yield models have been applied to climate scenarios generated by global-circulation models to estimate possible implications of greenhouse gases (W. A. Warrick et al. 1986). By varying environmental factors with potential future climate conditions, the models simulate effects on future yields.

Unfortunately, certain weaknesses apply to most uses of simulation models in assessing environmental effects: (1) the environmental projections themselves may be unrealistic; (2) the impact models often assume constant human management and input, which could vary over time; and (3) the models may be particularly unreliable when used to project effects of environmental factors substantially altered from those under which the models were developed. Although simulation models cannot replace empirical impact assessment, they can help guide empirical impact studies and, perhaps, make them more efficacious.

Evolutionary Geography

A realistic assessment of the state of terrestrial landscapes and their future development must consider changes over evolutionary time scales. Spatial reconstruction of previous climates and landscapes helps illuminate regularities in the development of the geosystem's climatic fluctuations over time and individual components of landscape systems during those fluctuations. Reconstructions also provide a basis for ecological and climatic scenarios for the future. Such research may be called evolutionary geography (Velitchko 1985a).

Evolutionary analysis indicates that the present-day landscapes form a heterochronous system with strong inherited features, a polarized structure, and large instability. The response of these landscapes to new temperature regimes may involve quite different alterations in the zonal distribution of vegetation and moisture than those that have occurred historically. Scenarios from paleogeographical reconstructions must be corrected for rate differences in component modifications due to natural factors (thousands of years) and anthropogenic factors (decades).

Analysis of Anthropogenic Causes of Change

Causes of anthropogenic change in landscape variables deserve careful examination. Predicting where and how long human alterations may prevail involves cumulative empirical evidence. Identifying possible lines of corrective action or positive adaptation also requires knowledge of human activities as a process function. Experimental evidence suggests that sustainable management of anthropogenic-natural processes is possible if such management relies on a spatial framework consisting of complex, heterogeneous regional systems (nature-resource-ecological, demographic-social-ethnic, productive-economic) which are closely interconnected. This shifts the focus from tracing effects to regional analysis with full use of concepts of *resource cycles*, defined as the "sum total of transformations and spatial transfer of a certain matter, or a group of substances at all stages of its use by man" (Komar 1975). Principal cycles receiving attention from geographers are those of energy, water (Mather 1984; L'vovich 1986), and nutrients (Ryabchikov 1980). Closer linkage of analysis of global cycles with regional analysis is needed, as well as a recognition that each anthropogenic change, such as industrial waste generation, *originates* in certain regions and *affects* particular regions, and these are not necessarily the same areas.

Socioeconomic development of any region obviously depends to some extent on the environment. These constraints and opportunities may be identified only when the natural resource/ecological potential of natural biospheric subdivisions is known. Often, river basins serve as such subdivisions (Chorley 1969; S. P. Gorshkov 1982). The basin approach to resource assessment supplements the traditional physiogeographical landscape approach. The approach may suggest a matrix of landscapes and drainage areas within which change under an anthropogenic load and, in particular, in the process of materials migration can be investigated.

Regional Development and Environmental Quality

In many parts of the world an earnest search is under way for effective means of coordinating economic development with environmental conservation. Much research has been devoted to simulation of ecological systems at a local scale and economic systems at regional and world scales. Global modeling focuses primarily on economic and sectoral systems. Much less developed is thoughtful simulation of regional natural resource use. Building a single management model of a system as complex as a region, a city, or an agglomeration is extremely difficult. Yet a great deal of anthropogenic change is being generated in precisely these areas.

In these situations, the challenge seems to be to build interrelated models of social, economic, and ecological development. One obstacle is that no agreed-upon criterion of socioecological/economic efficiency presently exists. This lack is due to insufficient analysis and to incompatibility of those indexes that characterize economic and mostly social and ecological effects of nature conservation measures. One simplified approach by geographers confronted the possibility of climate change. The rapidly evolving field of climate impact assessment emerged in the mid-1970s from concerns over the grave consequences of climate fluctuations such as the Sahelian drought, recent El Niño episodes, and, of course, the potential for global climate change associated with the buildup of greenhouse gases. Climate impact assessment is, by definition, an attempt to assess social implications of global change and its regional and local manifestations, and the field is the most developed and broadly applicable area of global-change impact studies (Kates et al. 1985).

Coping with Environmental Change

Social consequences of environmental changes likewise deserve analysis to learn how societies perceive these changes as hazards and then cope with them. These matters have been approached tangentially by environmental and social impact assessments (EIAs and SIAS).

SIAS of global environmental changes are needed to evaluate humans' ability as a species to cope with change and formulate preventive or adaptive responses. Since the emergence of contemporary concerns for environmental quality in the late 1960s in the United States, the phrase *impact assessment* connotes efforts to measure the effects of specific events on the natural environment. The impact assessment process, of course, focuses on humans' effects on the environment, not vice versa, and the process is generally restricted to local or, at the most, regional effects extrapolated to about a decade. The process lacks clear-cut guidelines for measuring effects because the focus has been on forecasting results to make preproject decisions, rather than on measurement of actual signals. Both approaches are needed in global change studies. As now pursued, the EIA process only partly applies to studies of global environmental changes, their regional result, or their ramifications for social systems. But some EIA methods could be adapted for global-change impact studies, such as (1) the identification and monitoring of key species and other indicators or effects, (2) the use of impact matrices, and (3) methods for anticipating the interaction of multiple environmental effects (Munn 1980; Parry et al. 1988).

The field of social impact assessments has not focused on social implications of environmental changes, but rather on direct social implications of specific projects and development plans. Some topics, such as weather modification and large water-development schemes, the subject of SIAS (Kates et al. 1985), may in many ways emulate the effects of global environmental changes at the regional level.

The fields of environmental and social impact assessments offer guidance for assessing complex interactions between environmental and social elements, methods for extrapolating effects into the near future, designs of monitoring schemes, and approaches to handling large amounts of data. Properly appropriated, these methods will be useful as efforts begin to assess global changes.

At the request of the Council on the Problems of Conservation and Improvement of the Environment, of the Council of Mutual Economic Assistance Committee on Scientific and Technical Cooperation, geographers of socialist countries in 1981 prepared a report entitled "Methodological Recommendations on Economic and Extra-economic Evaluation of the Impact of Man on the Environment." These recommendations were based on an assessment of the social consequences of the effects on different economic sectors of specific projects in model regions, chosen by the countries especially for this purpose. The following conditions were examined in the step-by-step research: (1) the effect of human activity as a "trigger mechanism" of interaction, (2) change in geosystems due to this impact, and (3) consequences for human health and economic activity resulting from the altered environment. Methods were suggested for integrated study of the spatial unity of the interaction of people, economy, and nature (Committee on Scientific and Technical Cooperation 1986).

Natural Hazards and Risk Assessment

One disturbing tendency of our times is the intensification of hazards from extreme natural events and the increasing damage that results. Such events present concrete instances of how societies and individuals react when nature threatens their well-being. Geographers have tried to evaluate ways to reduce, prevent, and mitigate severe consequences and to classify hazardous areas systematically, and they have worked to refine methods of environmental risk assessment.

Much experience has accumulated in assessing impacts and responses to environmental extremes under the rubric of natural hazards research (Burton et al. 1978; J. K. Mitchell 1984; Heathcote 1985; Myagkov 1986; O'Riordan 1986). Demographic, technological, and political circumstances, errors in the assessment of natural situations, and mismanagement of production are among causes of social losses from natural hazards.

In associated studies, geographers have contributed concepts, models, and methods to the emerging interdisciplinary field of environmental risk assessment (Kates 1978; Whyte and Burton 1980; Kates and Kasperson 1983; Kasperson and Pijawka 1985; Kasperson and Kasperson 1988). Research on the human ecology of natural hazards established that the degree of threat experienced by a society is a function of four interactive variables: risk, exposure, vulnerability, and response. Subsequent research identified previously neglected alternative adjustments to hazard and focused attention on behavioral factors affecting risk assessment. Later work on technological hazards also established the interactive character of human, machine, and environment systems under conditions of failure, underlined the importance of accurate risk communication, and addressed various social constraints on risk assessment.

Methods of assessment for long-established local risks are already well developed; much is known about the natural risk components of dramatic events like earthquakes, storms, and floods, and, to a lesser extent, about drought, erosion, and other long-term, quasi-natural risks. Information about human exposure to risk and physical vulnerability is also widely available. Fewer studies of socioeconomic vulnerability have been completed, and even less has been published about the efficacy of available public and private responses to environmental hazards. Although only recently begun, the pace of research on assessment of new universal risks is accelerating rapidly. Pioneering work on the environmental consequences of nuclear war and climate impact assessment studies guide future work on other universal risks (Harwell and Hutchinson 1985; Kates et al. 1985).

Geographic Data and Information Systems

Unraveling the mechanism of global change in the coupled biosphere-atmosphere system and determining the direction and rate of such change require modeling studies and compatible, homogeneous global data sets for a variety of key terrestrial variables. Many, but not all, of these data may be gathered using remote-sensing technology. A continual need exists to conduct regional field studies to coordinate remotely sensed data as well as to collect data not acquired with remote-sensing technology. Over the long term there will be a need for consistent, quantitative global measurements of surface albedo, surface temperature, vegetation cover, moisture, snow cover (extent and depth), evapotranspiration, and precipitation (frequency and intensity) for terrestrial ecosystems, and ocean color, tropospheric gases, ocean topography, sea-surface temperature, sea ice, and wind stress for the oceans (Rasool 1987). Atmospheric and space observations should include solar flux (and spectral variability), stratospheric temperatures, stratospheric aerosols and ozone, and tropospheric aerosols. Cloud cover is not specifically listed, although it is a key element of the World Climate Research Program under the International Satellite Cloud Climatology Program (Schiffer and Rossow 1983). Recent remote-sensing research by geographers includes the estimation of precipitation rates from visible and infrared satellite images (Barrett and Martin 1981), the modeling of radiation in mountainous terrain from multispectral Landsat data (Dozier 1987; Kasperson and Kasperson 1988), analysis of the climatic significance of cloud cover (Barry et al. 1984), the estimation of large-scale net primary productivity (Goward and Dye 1987), and the remote sensing of snow and ice parameters (D. K. Hall and Martinec 1985), especially from passive microwave data (M. R. Anderson 1987; D. K. Hall et al. 1987).

Model building and data collecting are corequisites for any successful evaluation of the interactions between terrestrial biosphere and atmosphere. Sophisticated biosphere models (Mintz et al. 1983; Dickinson 1985; Sellers et al. 1986) are of little value without adequate observations and precise characterization of the near-surface environment. But, concomitantly, data that purport to characterize the biosphere are of limited value if (1) variables required by climate models are not sampled, or (2) the time or space scales of observations or statistical summary are inconsistent with the models' needs. For example, daily changes in plant transpiration in general cannot be adequately inferred from monthly climate data. Data collection and modeling efforts must not be conducted in ignorance of one another. This means that collected data should be representative at space scales of about 100 km^2, although this resolution will improve with faster computers and more efficient algorithms. Model time scales, by contrast, are much more variable and range from hours to millennia, again depending on the variable of interest and the model.

The conceptual bases for conducting regional and global studies with remotely sensed observations and computer-based geographic information systems are only now developing (Kushkarev and Karakin 1987). A major conflict currently exists between the concepts of raster and vector storage of geographic data in digital computers, and it has effectively halted the marriage of remote sensing and geographic information systems (Marble and Peuquet 1983). Vector data descriptions tend to preserve the precision of boundary definitions, whereas raster systems tend to preserve measures of spatial heterogeneity. Because remotely sensed observations are now viewed as contiguous, but discrete, observations of heterogeneous phenomena, such vectorization is not possible. Inasmuch as the IGBP fundamentally depends on the marriage of remote sensing to geographic information systems and global models, a solution to these conflicts should be a focus of early IGBP research.

Furthermore, research is needed on the interacting of different scale sizes. In some physical fields, such as numerical modeling of the atmosphere, this interacting has been approached by nesting of grids of various sizes. There might be a very high density array of data points existing within a sparser network. This approach often works for the atmosphere because of its commonly smooth gradients in values of the treated variables. In some cases this treatment might also work in earth-surface problems, but in others it would not (e.g., where great heterogeneity of land cover exists and distinct changes occur over short distances; the urban-rural boundary would be illustrative). Geographers need new methods for varying grid size—methods that do not necessarily treat the problem as linear in time or space. In mental or perceptual maps, for example, we have not been constrained by linearity. Nor should there be need for constraint in the present context, save only for the constraint of consistency and the adherence to physical and geometric laws.

Interpolation between locations implies that the way in which the particular observed phenomena change in space and time between the observations is understood. Any effort to map point information without that knowledge introduces unknown errors which may increase rapidly away from the observation point. The combination of remotely sensed observations and ground measurements has the potential to study these patterns, but carefully designed experiments over a period of several years are necessary. Preliminary experiments of this type are now being conducted under the International Satellite Land Surface Climatology Project (ISLSCP; see Ruttenberg 1983). Similar studies are needed to evaluate other types of land phenomena. In each case a major focus of such research should be the scaling question; that is, how do local phenomena aggregate to produce continental-to-global descriptions of land conditions and dynamics?

Full evaluation of terrestrial dynamics must include human activities. Greenland (1983) has suggested, in the context of resource management, that the number of indicators that can be developed is limited only by the imagination. In the IGBP studies we consider here, however, somewhat more restraint operates when studies rely solely on those variables monitored from space or air. There is no a priori reason why only remotely sensed data should be used to monitor socioeconomic indicators, although the consistency might be greater.

Need for Site Studies

From the foregoing, it is clear that the effectiveness of the data base for monitoring and predicting environmental changes will be greatly enhanced by detailed site studies. Initially, existing network and individual study sites should be used as representative sites. Long-term ecological research (LTER) sites and sites belonging to the ISLSCP immediately suggest themselves for use in these geographical studies. A significant contrast exists between LTER sites, which generally represent a particular biome with minimum human impact, and ISLSCP sites, which are chosen for the degree of impact already experienced (Callahan 1984).

Using N. I. Vavilov's ideas of maximum diversity and plant migration, Soviet scientists (Sokolov and Puzachenko 1986) developed a scheme for locating stations for integrated monitoring within continents and ocean surfaces. This scheme rests on an analysis of climatic zones, lithological orographic heterogeneity of continents, and ocean circulation. Areas with a maximum diversity of ecosystems as well as those with greater sensitivity to changes in thermal and precipitation regimes are identified. The number of such areas all over the planet would probably range between 150 and 200.

In areas bordering subdivisions of the biosphere (broadly defined as eco-tones), the main features of the structure and function of ecosystems change significantly—primarily under the influence of external factors. As for the slow self-development of ecosystems and their evolution in the purest form, they can best be studied not in the interfaces and not in zones of maximum diversity of environmental conditions, but rather in regions with the greatest homogeneity—that is, in the foci of corresponding areas.

Concluding Discussion

The following chapters draw upon extensive research in the Soviet Union and the United States to illustrate the current state of knowledge of interacting systems in the human environment and to suggest lines along which studies of its change may be productive. The studies reported have been selected to demonstrate the opportunities now available to improve global data sets, to identify the conditions in which future changes may take place, and to canvass the options societies face in dealing with them.

We look to further expansion and specification of the ideas and methods expressed here, and we hope that they will be carried out on a broader base, enlisting the imagination and experience of all relevant disciplines and of many national groups.

2. LANDSCAPE DYNAMICS

It is important to recognize that the earth's surface is a great mosaic of smaller areas, or landscapes, within which characteristic physical, biological, and social factors interact in complex combinations (Soviet geographers identify these as *geosystems*). Forest biomes, semiarid grassland regions, and river basins, for example, are not uniform. There is a long tradition of landscape analysis in geographical studies (Sauer 1925; Hartshorne 1939; D. L. Armand 1975; Solntsev 1981).

Landscape refers to a section of land or region that can be viewed as a whole. It consists of the lithosphere and soil elements, the biotic cover or vegetation assemblage, the surface and subsurface water resources, and the atmospheric elements that constitute the weather and climate of the area. Landscape is altered by both anthropogenic and natural activities that are manifested in that area. Landscape, then, is the result of internal and external processes of change, or, more succinctly, of *landscape dynamics*. The study of landscape dynamics is therefore necessary for explaining and forecasting landscape and its contribution to global change.

Widespread landscape change (e.g., cutting extensive forests or draining large marshes) affects global systems, and changes in global systems may in turn result in significant changes within landscapes. Landscape studies have revealed that the forces generating change are not entirely general: they are often characteristic of specific landscapes. Processes set in motion by human efforts to alter or adjust to environmental changes also are not everywhere the same: they affect both natural and social components differently from place to place.

The concept of landscape dynamics is thus a useful framework within which to examine both the causes and consequences of global change. This chapter defines the concept more precisely, outlines principles of analysis, and illustrates the utility of this framework in examining past landscapes. The chapter concludes with a discussion of how our knowledge of contemporary mechanisms of global change in a coupled biosphere-atmosphere system may be expanded and made more useful through increased surface and atmospheric observations—a significant goal of any geosphere-biosphere study.

2.1 Landscape Dynamics as a Unifying Principle

Landscape systems are complex and possess several peculiarities, including: (1) the existence of a complicated hierarchy of boundaries and networks, (2) interactions among complex sets of organic and inorganic compounds, and (3) marked and often discontinuous spatial variation. To describe such systems and to forecast their states as well as their spatial flows, it is necessary to understand certain fundamental concepts.

First, the terrestrial system as a whole and its separate subsystems, united by common properties and interrelated processes, can be defined as a set of landscapes of different taxonomic ranks, or scales, ranging from local to global. Important peculiarities of landscape include the continuous renewal of biomass and the biochemical and biogeophysical changes of nature necessary for its "metabolism," and an ever-growing intensity of economic activity.

Second, the functioning of such systems produces fluxes of energy and mass (e.g., gas, water, minerals, geochemical elements, and biological organisms) as well as of people and commodities. There are even fluxes of information. Many of these fluxes (e.g., of energy) occur predominantly in the vertical, while others (e.g., of gas and minerals) occur mainly in the horizontal. Horizontal fluxes also dominate flows of air, goods, human activities, pollen, seeds, and pollution. It is the horizontal fluxes within and among landscapes that are of traditional interest to geographers.

Third, spatial heterogeneity creates gradients and a hierarchy of boundaries (discontinuities). Boundaries also define relatively homogeneous landscapes. On a local scale, within homogeneous landscapes (the degree of homogeneity depends on the scale of investigation), continuous spatial variation (with gradients) often can be assumed. Equating integrated spatial gradients with electrical potential, spatial flow (E) within a continuously varying landscape can be written

$$E = PR^{-1},$$

where the potential for flow between locations a and b is

$$P \propto \int_{a}^{b} \left(\frac{\partial A}{\partial x} + \frac{\partial A}{\partial y} \right) \mathrm{d}l$$

The symbol A denotes any spatial field of interest, and R is the integrated spatial resistance along the path (l) of the flow. It should be noted that x and y are coordinates in a functional plane and may not be Euclidian. Such an approach breaks down along many boundaries because $R_B \gg R_A$, where R_B is the boundary resistance to flow across the boundary and R_A is the ambient resistance.

Boundaries, of course, have dissimilar resistance qualities to different phenomena. For example, watershed boundaries are impermeable to the horizontal flow of surface water but are easily crossed by animals. Forest-field boundaries are often easily crossed by water (perhaps a stream) but can be relatively impermeable to animals and seeds. Political boundaries are open to pollution flows but sometimes closed to trade and human migration. Boundaries may be barriers, but they can also be attractors. Seashores, for instance, are attractive to many people, while forest-field boundaries may be sites of biological diversity.

Fourth, landscape systems include not only heterogeneous areal parts within their boundaries, but also different kinds of networks such as rivers, transportation networks, and animal migration routes. Networks are characterized by $R_N << R_A$ where R_N is the resistance along the paths of the network in the direction of flow. Networks are very important means of horizontal transfer. Horizontal water movement, for example, is to the second or third power more significant through a river network than over the ground; the same is true of trade along railway or highway networks, but this relationship does not hold for ocean or air routes. Flow through a network is related not only to the potential but also to the functional distance of the exchange.

Landscape Dynamics and Global Change

Flows over the landscape often result in new states of spatial heterogeneity, which in turn give rise to new flow patterns at future states. It is the changing state of the landscape which must be coupled with atmospheric and oceanic systems if we are to obtain the understanding necessary to forecast the environmental consequences of human activity and humans' responses to global environmental change.

Landscape systems are linked to the oceans primarily through drainage-basin networks, shorelines, and vertical exchanges with the atmosphere. Water lost by evapotranspiration from agricultural regions, for example, may be advected and then later condensed and precipitated into the ocean. Important landscape/atmosphere interaction takes place across an extensive surface (29 percent of the earth's surface) of contact.

Landscape dynamics drastically affect all terms in the surface energy and water balances, and, consequently, the state of the lower atmosphere. This in turn alters atmospheric circulation and climate. Well-documented changes in albedo, for example, change the proportion of solar radiation absorbed by the landscape. Available soil moisture is known to have considerable influence on the evapotranspiration field (which may in turn influence downwind precipitation), and it too is affected by changes in landscape. Ecological policy should therefore consider human influences on (1) surface properties, (2) geographical boundaries, and (3) geographical networks. Landscape dynamics, including society's role, are an integral part of the global system. Thus the significant role of landscape dynamics in global change must be investigated. Such investigations are the province of the geographer.

In view of what has been said above, the development of landscapes should not be considered only as the result of the development of such physical, chemical, and biological properties as meteorological indexes, runoff, energy fluxes, biomass, soil acidity, content of humus and microelements, or diversity of animal and plant species. Rather, a most important index of landscapes' changes is a change in their structural indexes—location and properties of boundaries (e.g., snowlines) and appearance of new heterogeneous areas, or even their merger into homogeneous entities. New geographical networks can appear, become more or less complex, or even disappear. New sources, such as cities or industrial centers, can appear or disappear. These structural changes are superimposed on changes in other properties, including potentials in the continuous fields and on the linear elements of geographical networks, as well as on changes in the intensity of the sources.

Changes in natural processes resulting from anthropogenic impacts produce a related series of consequences. The change in evaporation from the ocean surface (e.g., by the blocking effect of an oil film over the ocean) or from the land (e.g., increased owing to the application of irrigation or decreased owing to the effect of desertification, deforestation, or plowing) introduces fundamental alterations in the structure of the global hydrologic cycle as well as horizontal redistribution of energy across the landscape. Human-induced changes may also alter the structure of landscape processes by shifting energy from one set of processes to another.

Energy characteristics also may be indicators of the state of more complex biogeochemical processes. Bowen's ratio of the heat expended for sensible heat exchange to the heat expended for evaporation ($H{:}LE$), for example, is related to the amount of precipitation and biomass production (Krenke and Zolotokrilin 1984). Biomass production is in turn related to the rate of physical and geochemical loss of matter from different landscapes. Hence, information on the intensity of vertical energy flows as well as on changes in their structure may provide measures of anthropogenic impacts.

Changes in landscape caused by natural and societal processes bring about fundamental changes in global energy and biogeochemical cycles. Several approaches to the investigation of such processes taken by geographers and others are reviewed below. Landscape dynamics occur over a range of space and time scales, and the long-term (evolutionary) patterns (section 2.2) set the stage for a discussion of what information must be obtained to permit a shorter-term contemporary analysis of landscape dynamics (section 2.3).

2.2 Evolutionary Analysis of Landscapes

Evolutionary Features of Modern Landscape Systems

As interest in questions of the variability of natural environments increases and our need to understand changes in possible future landscapes becomes more urgent, accurate predictions will depend to a large extent on how well we understand the physical processes that have been involved in the formation of present landscapes. The field of study that evaluates the place of the existing landscape in the continuum of geologic time and recognizes the dynamic properties that characterize the landscape development process can be called *evolutionary geography* (Velitchko 1985a, 1989a). It involves (1) knowledge of the history of the formation of present-day landscapes, both natural and natural-anthropogenic*; (2) establishment of the physical bases for landscape instability, both over the earth as a whole and regionally, over different time scales; (3) evaluation of the temporal course of global change and our current position in this continuum; and (4) forecasting future landscape development. Accordingly, evolutionary geography involves much paleogeographic analysis, particularly for the last glacial cycle (Porter 1983; Wright 1983; Velitchko 1985a).

Two main stages in the history of landscape can be distinguished: the first covers the first billion years of earth's history when the lithosphere, hydrosphere, and atmosphere were the primary forces influencing the landscape system; the second covers all later time and adds the biospheric component to create a qualitatively new terrestrial system. We will consider only this latter period as we investigate aspects of landscape development affected by climate and vegetation.

Evolutionary analysis reveals that, even in its current form, the natural zonality of current landscapes, which represents the highest level and apparently the most stable system of landscape organization, is only a transitory structure that changes over time with a certain regularity. For example, the natural zonal landscape structure may be shown to change with surface temperature and moisture variations. Mean annual winter temperatures in southern Russia have fluctuated over the last 200 million years (Velitchko 1987b) from approximately $+30°C$ in the Triassic to $-12°C$ in the cold epochs of the last million years (i.e., the Pleistocene; see Fig. 2.1). This temperature curve is unique because it covers a considerable portion of geologic time and was prepared from data collected for a particular region on a continental land mass.

---

*The term *natural-anthropogenic* is used in this volume to refer to those natural systems or processes that are being somewhat influenced or modified by human activities. As opposed to this, *anthropogenic* processes or systems are strictly under the control of human activities. The difference is a matter of the degree of human influence.

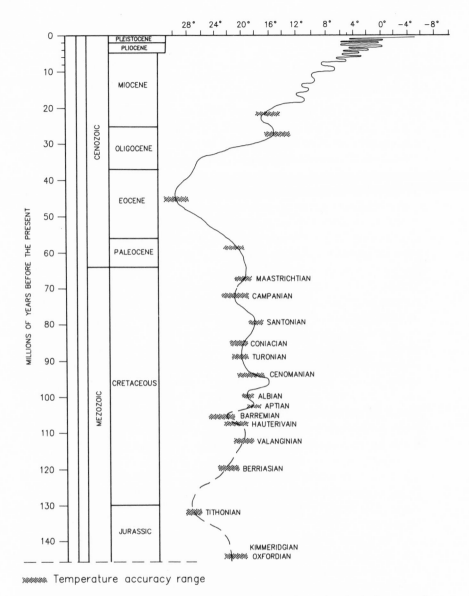

 Temperature accuracy range

Fig. 2.1 The curve of winter temperature fluctuations at the earth's surface for the last 150 million years according to data on the southern half of the Russian plain. (By A. A. Velitchko)

The Cenozoic cooling trend matches other land and ocean records (Barron 1985, Grichuk 1989). Globally, the Mesozoic era, which includes the Triassic, Jurassic, and Cretaceous periods, appears to have been significantly warmer than the warmest Cenozoic epoch—the Eocene. The processes involved in major paleoclimatic episodes, such as the Permo-Carboniferous and late-Cenozoic ice ages and the intervening Mesozoic–early Cenozoic warm interval, include changes in atmospheric composition, especially in carbon dioxide levels, as well as changes in continental positions and elevation resulting from tectonic plate movements (Barron 1985).

The Mesozoic period of elevated temperatures was characterized by long-period oscillations with a frequency of about 15–20 million years and an amplitude of 2°–4°C (Fig. 2.1). About 80 million years ago, a downward-trending regime with shorter-wave oscillations with a period of 2–5 million years and an amplitude of 2°–4°C can be recognized. High-resolution ocean and land records indicate the first appearance of quasi-periodic climatic oscillations about 2.5–3 million years ago, with periods of 20,000–200,000 years and temperature amplitudes of 3°–6°C. Some specialists think these oscillations are forced mostly by variations in earth's orbital geometry (Shackleton et al. 1988), while others (Velitchko 1973; Budyko and MacCracken 1987) consider the climatic oscillations to be the result of more complicated causes, such as changes in gaseous composition of the atmosphere and general input of solar energy. In any case, the climatic variations resulted in the alternating glacial and interglacial epochs that have been major features of Quaternary climates (Markov 1960). These variations have also resulted in changes in tropical landscapes due to periodic changes in monsoonal intensity (Kutzbach and Street-Perrott 1985). Dramatic changes in the structure of landscapes resulted from these relatively high frequency climatic fluctuations during this period of low temperatures. The present landscapes have developed within a warm, interglacial period during the last 10,000 years (the Holocene). During the current interglacial, the period of highest temperatures in mid-latitudes apparently ended 5000–6000 years ago, and we may be approaching the start of a new glacial epoch some 3000–4000 years in the future (Khotinskiy 1977). In Northern Hemisphere tropical and subtropical latitudes, the Holocene maximum of solar radiation occurred around 9000–10,000 years ago (Kutzbach and Street-Perrott 1985; see Fig. 2.2) and resulted in very moist conditions with high lake levels in the northern tropical zone between 12,000 and 5000 years ago (Fig. 2.3). In the northern extratropics, in contrast, most lakes were high from 30,000 to 13,000 years ago, but there were important regional differences in timing of high stands (Street-Perrott and Harrison 1985). During this time, the level of solar radiation was possibly reduced. Even the main Holocene climatic warm period (5000–6000 B.P.) did not coincide with the period of maximum solar radiation. The northern boundary of the forest zone shifted northward by 200–400 km at this time, while lake levels within the

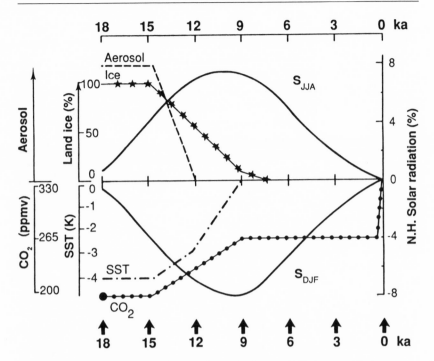

Fig. 2.2 Changing climatic boundary conditions for the past 18,000 years with the horizontal axis indicating time in Kyr BP (1000s of years before present). Aerosol indicates a qualitative measure of aerosol concentrations, Ice indicates global ice volume as a percent of the volume at the last glacial maximum, SST is the global average for sea surface temperature anomalies in degrees Kelvin, CO_2 is carbon dioxide concentrations in parts per million by volume, and S_{JJA} and S_{DJF} are solar insolation for June, July, and August (JAA) and for December, January, and February (DJF) as percent difference from radiation today. See COHMAP (1988) for references to the sources for the values graphed. (From Kutzbach and Street-Perrott 1985. Reprinted by permission from *Nature* Vol.317, p. 130. Copyright © 1985, Macmillian Magazines Ltd.)

tropics remained higher than at present (Khotinskiy 1977; Klimanov 1978; Velitchko 1987a).

Planetary fluctuations in thermal regime appear to be the dominant factor in the resulting structure and dynamics of extratropical landscapes, while moisture fluctuations control tropical landscapes. These fluctuations are primarily determined by the amount of energy received from the sun and its distribution over the surface of the planet as influenced by such factors as continental drift, the earth's orbital variations, orogenesis, atmospheric composition and circulation, and ocean circulation. The most significant feature of the landscape system is its ability to change its structure radically in response to fluctuations in the amount and seasonality of solar radiation (Fig. 2.4). Under warm condi-

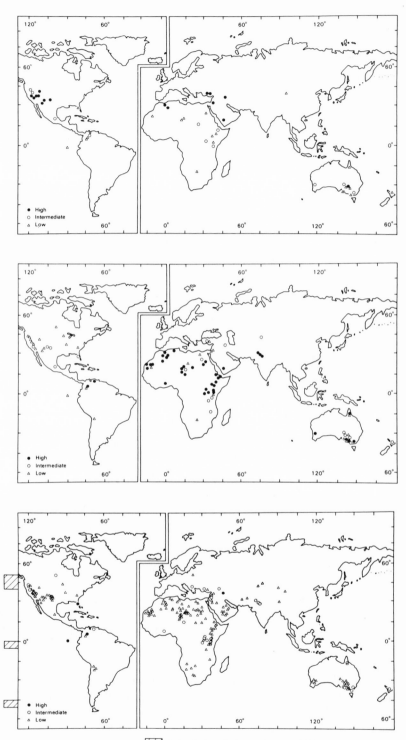

Latitudinal peaks in areal extent of lakes

tions (e.g., in the Triassic and the Eocene), warm, moist climates were found up to the present latitudes of the polar circles, and only near the poles did the climate change to subtropical and temperate (Ushakov and Yasamanov 1984). Forests appear to have been a dominant vegetation form for most land surfaces throughout much of these megathermal periods. Such a landscape distribution can be called a *thermo-hyperzonal* structure. However, major fluctuations of shorter duration did occur, as evidenced by variations in tropical lake levels during the Triassic (P. E. Olson 1986).

The transition from warm Mesozoic to moderate Cenozoic temperature conditions was accompanied by an equatorward shift of a number of vegetation belts. The zonal vegetation structure also became more complicated in the Cenozoic, with an increase in the extent of the temperate forest. A tundra belt formed in the Neogene in high latitudes. This type of zonal vegetation structure can be called a *polyzonal* structure.

High-amplitude temperature fluctuations during the generally cool Quaternary period resulted in the alternation of two types of zonal structure: the polyzonal type during interglacials and the *cryo-hyperzonal* type during glacial stages. Forests were greatly reduced and displaced during glacials in middle to high latitudes. The cryo-hyperzonal type was characterized by a prevalence of open landscapes: tundra-steppes, steppes, desert-semideserts, parklands, and savannas. Geographers have long been engaged in active studies of cold-climate processes and landscapes (Troll 1944; Peltier 1950; Grigoryev 1970; French 1976; Sher 1976; Romanovsky 1977; Volkova 1977; Barry 1983; Baulin 1985; Bradley 1985; Colhoun and Peterson 1986).

The repeated Quaternary alternations of polyzonal and cryo-hyperzonal structures are defined as a *transformational* (*pulsatory*) type of zonal structure. The present landscape exists within this transformational (pulsatory) regime and represents its polyzonal phase. If the natural course of thermal conditions is followed in the future, this regime should be replaced by a cryo-hyperzonal regime during the next glacial stage.

Latitudinal asymmetry that reflects planetary factors (e.g., peculiarities of land and sea distribution, the location of seasonally semipermanent high and low pressure systems, the position of storm tracks) is an important feature influencing the general structure of the earth's landscape. Different climatic controls within the same latitudinal belts in the Western and Eastern hemispheres may significantly modify the components of the landscape that result. This phenomenon of latitudinal asymmetry is especially noticeable during

Fig. 2.3 Maps indicating the status of water levels in lakes with black circles indicating high water levels, open circles, intermediate levels, and open triangles, low levels for 18,000 years ago (top), 6000 years ago (middle), and today (bottom). (From Street-Perrott and Harrison 1985, in Hecht 1985, *Paleoclimate Analysis and Modeling*. Reprinted with permission from John Wiley & Sons.)

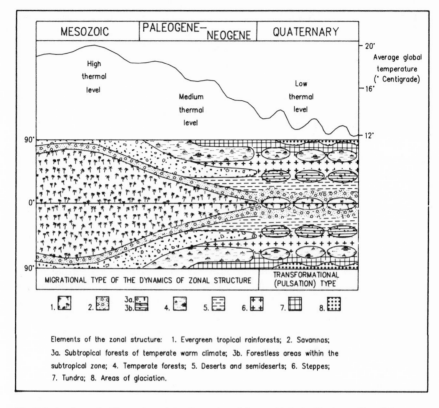

Fig. 2.4 A schematic illustration of the dynamics of the earth's latitudinal zonality of the landscape geosphere in Mesozoic and Cenozoic time. (Compiled by A. A. Velitchko)

glacial periods. For example, more extensive areas in the Eastern Hemisphere were covered by long-term permafrost than by glaciers during the last glacial maximum at 18,000 years ago (CLIMAP 1976). This picture was reversed in the Western Hemisphere. Palynological evidence has been used to produce maps of major plant taxa for eastern North America and Europe for the last glacial maximum and postglacial time (Gerasimov and Velitchko 1982; COHMAP 1988). Figure 2.5 presents maps for three time intervals and shows how well the patterns in relative abundance of pollen taxa 500 years ago (i.e., just before European disturbance of the vegetation) match the major patterns in the map of North American vegetation (Huntley and Webb 1988). Forb (Compositae and Chenopodiaceae/Amaranthaceae) and sedge (Cyperaceae) pollen dominate in areas of steppe and tundra, and tree taxa from spruce (*Picea*), to birch (*Betula*), pine (*Pinus*), hemlock (*Tsuga*), beech (*Fagus*), oak (*Quercus*), and hickory (*Carya*) pollen dominate in order from the boreal forest (taiga) to the mixed, deciduous, and southern conifer forests. The pollen maps show that vegetational patterns 18,000 years ago differed markedly from those of today. When the Laurentide Ice Sheet was at its maximum extent—covering much of Canada and the northern United States—the distribution of spruce and sedge pollen indicates growth of a spruce parkland south of the ice sheet. Forests of northern pines grew in the southeast, and oaks and hickories also grew in sparse amounts in the south. None of this vegetation was closely analogous to the modern vegetation. The modern vegetation patterns first appeared about 10,000 years ago when prairie vegetation, spruce forests, birch woods, and shrub populations became extensive. By then, oak and hickory trees were growing abundantly in the south, and forests were well established in the eastern United States.

A different pattern of vegetation distribution has been reconstructed for Eurasia during the last glacial maximum based on a large volume of paleobotanic data. Typical periglacial vegetation—tundra-steppe and steppe assemblages—are thought to have existed there at that time (Grichuk 1989).

Asymmetry is also revealed during interglacial periods. Prairie and steppe vegetation extended eastward in central North America during the peak of the most recent interglacial period (5000–6000 years B.P.; see Wright 1971; Webb et al. 1983), while this phenomenon was not observed in Eurasia (Velitchko 1985a).

Analysis of the development (evolution) of landscapes leads to the recognition of a variety of features in landscape structure (Velitchko 1973).

Heterochronism on landscapes is the coexistence of elements that originated at quite different times. For example, at the beginning of the Holocene, some types of forest vegetation redeveloped in local topographic elements which resembled forests that had first formed as long ago as the Paleogene. Tundra vegetation of today resembles that which first appeared in the late Neogene–early Quaternary (Hopkins et al. 1982), while the age of steppe formations dates back to the mid-Cenozoic.

Inheritance is the presence within landscapes of elements which, while part of the continuing energy-mass exchange, originally developed and were found to exist optimally under somewhat different conditions. The extent of long-term permafrost is now greatly reduced in area compared to that which existed in the preceding cryo-hyperzonal epoch, whose maximum occurred 18,000–20,000 years ago. The present glaciers and ice sheets are also much reduced in size from their size then, and also from their size during the Little Ice Age of A.D. 1450–1850.

Inertia refers to the ability of some past landscape elements to exist under present conditions although their disappearance might be irreversible; for example, modern pack ice in the Arctic basin, if destroyed, might not reform because of potential warming due to ice-albedo climate feedbacks (Budyko 1980).

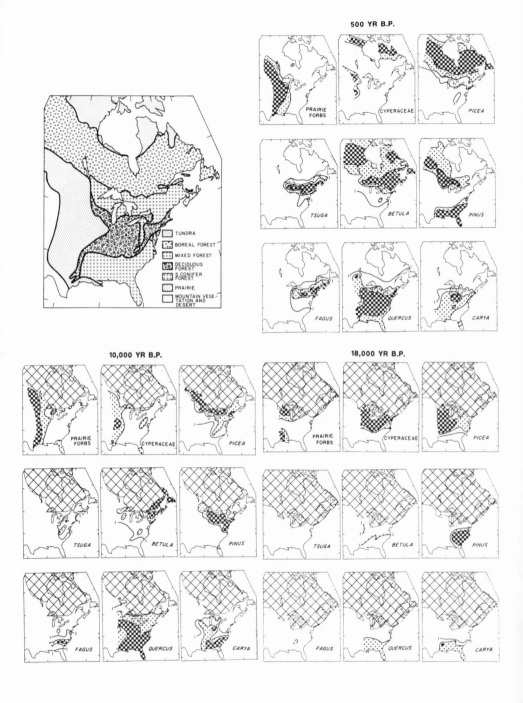

500 YR B.P.

PRAIRIE FORBS   CYPERACEAE   PICEA

TSUGA   BETULA   PINUS

FAGUS   QUERCUS   CARYA

TUNDRA
BOREAL FOREST
MIXED FOREST
DECIDUOUS FOREST
S. CONIFER FOREST
PRAIRIE
MOUNTAIN VEGETATION AND DESERT

10,000 YR B.P.

PRAIRIE FORBS   CYPERACEAE   PICEA

TSUGA   BETULA   PINUS

FAGUS   QUERCUS   CARYA

18,000 YR B.P.

PRAIRIE FORBS   CYPERACEAE   PICEA

TSUGA   BETULA   PINUS

FAGUS   QUERCUS   CARYA

Transitivity suggests that the same component may be capable of moving from a condition of being a zonal element to that of being a provincial or local element under different hydrothermal regimes. Thus, broad-ranging taxa in temperate-zone forests became local landscape elements under full-glacial conditions, and certain full-glacial vegetation elements today are much reduced in size (Huntley and Webb 1988).

Variability indicates that the apparent stability of existing landscapes is illusory; landscapes as a whole and their components change at different rates (Gerasimov 1985; McDowell et al. 1989). The climate, vegetation, and some components of the cryosphere (mountain glaciers) are the most variable elements. Data on the history of the last phases of the Pleistocene show the frequency and amplitude of climatic oscillations (and with them changes in the vegetation cover and the cryosphere) that resulted in the transitions from glacial ages to interglacials (Ruddiman and Wright 1987; Khotinskiy 1989; Klimanov 1989b). The replacement of glacial landscapes by periglacial ones during these periods took only 100–200 years. Because the present epoch may be transitional to a new period of glaciation, the variability of landscape regimes due to natural factors may increase.

The above discussion allows us to conclude that the present landscape exhibits both heterochronic and inherited features, has a polyzonal structure, and may change quickly in the face of future natural and human-induced variability.

Problems of Predicting Future Landscapes

The evolutionary-geographic approach and modeling form integral parts of any effort directed toward understanding those landscape regimes that might develop in the future (within the twenty-first century) as a result of both anthropogenic and natural changes. The construction of such scenarios must involve two stages: (1) the construction of scenarios derived from geologic and biologic data on the states of the landscape that correspond to assumed changes of global temperature and moisture, and (2) the development of landscape scenarios that are undergoing both natural changes as well as changes brought about by human economic activity.

Fig. 2.5 Modern vegetation map for eastern North America and maps showing the distribution of 9 major pollen taxa at 500, 10,000, and 18,000 years ago. Tree genera include spruce (*Picea*), hemlock (*Tsuga*), birch (*Betula*), pine (*Pinus*), beech (*Fagus*), oak (*Quercus*), and hickory (*Carya*). Herbaceous groups include sedge family (*Cyperaceae*) and prairie forbs (Chenopodiaceae, Amaranthaceae, and all Compositae excluding *Ambrosia*). Dark and light stippling indicates high and intermediate abundances as indicated by the pollen percentages. Cross-hatched area indicates the location of the Laurentide Ice Sheet. See Webb (1988) in Huntley and Webb (1988) for details. (Reprinted with permission of Kluwer Academic Publishers.)

Climate model simulations indicate a possible increase in global warming of $1° \pm 0.5°C$ by the beginning of the twenty-first century, and $2° \pm 1°C$ by 2025–2030 (National Research Council 1983; Budyko and Izrael 1987). Scientists at the Paleogeographic Laboratory of the Institute of Geography of the USSR Academy of Sciences have attempted to create paleolandscape and paleoclimate reconstructions based on scenarios having specified deviations of temperature from the present values of mean global temperature. These reconstructions can be used as possible models of conditions that may occur as a result of human impacts on climate in the coming decades. Such reconstructions have involved a mean global temperature increase of $1° \pm 1°C$ (Holocene optimum, 5500–6000 years B.P.) and $2° \pm 1°C$ (Mikulino interglacial optimum, 125,000 years B.P.; see Klimanov 1978; Velitchko et al. 1982; Khotinskiy and Savina 1985). Landscape reconstructions for times when global climates may have been warmer than they are today are especially important because they permit visualization of features that might develop in the near future. Studies of past landscapes also teach us how the complete climate-vegetation-landscape system operates and can highlight interactions between subsystems. Studies of past climates also indicate the possible causes of past changes and have shown that these causes differ from those predicted to bring about changes in the immediate future (COHMAP 1988).

The Soviet Institute of Geography reconstructions of hemispheric anomaly patterns of temperature and precipitation (i.e., differences from the present) show that high latitudes have experienced the greatest warming as average global temperatures have risen (Fig. 2.6). This effect is particularly significant for the time when mean global temperature may have increased by 2°C. Winter temperatures in northern Siberia may then have been 10°–12°C higher than they are today. With mean global temperature only 1°C above today's value, these high-latitude temperatures may have increased by only 2°–4°C (Fig. 2.6A). In both cases, positive deviations decrease rapidly as one goes southward, and essentially vanish in a belt centered at 45° N. From here to the equator, very weak negative deviations (by 1°–2°C) are estimated, interspersed with some small belts that have weak positive deviations as well. These reconstructions for the tropics, however, contrast markedly with indications of positive temperature deviations described by COHMAP (1988).

In eastern North America also, the map of mean July temperatures estimated from pollen data (Bartlein and Webb 1985) for the mid-Holocene warm period 6000 years ago (Fig. 2.7) shows a somewhat different pattern from that

Fig. 2.6a (above) Reconstruction of the temperature and precipitation patterns for the Holocene warm period approximately 5000 to 6000 years ago (on the basis of deviations from present values). **Fig. 2.6b (below)** Reconstruction of the temperature and precipitation patterns for the Mikulino (Sangamon) interglacial based on deviations from the present values. (By A. A. Velitchko)

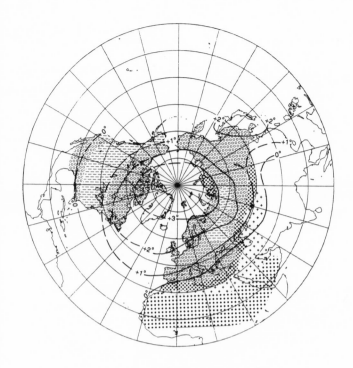

ΔP
▦ > 100%
⋮ 50 - 100% —— +2°—— Δt°C
▨ 25 - 50%
▨ 0 - 25%
▱ < 0

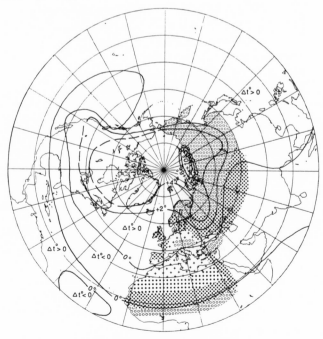

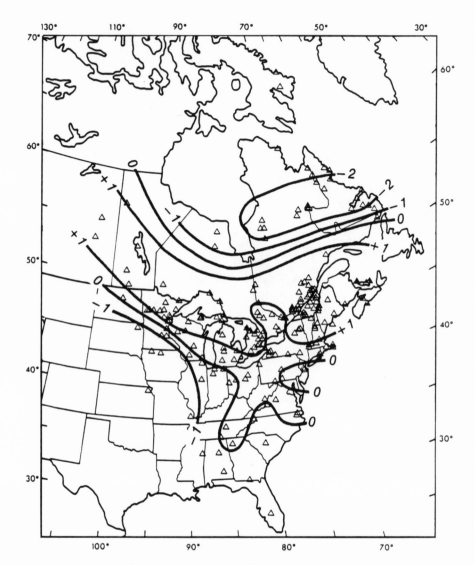

Fig. 2.7 Map of mean July temperature anomalies (°C) between 6000 years ago and today (pluses indicate higher temperatures 6000 years ago than today). Temperatures were estimated from the pollen data for 6000 years ago using multiple regression equations. See Bartlein and Webb (1985) for details.

shown in Figure 2.6A. Temperatures in eastern North America were higher than today mainly in a band from 40° to 50° N. In the far north they were colder than today's temperatures by as much as 2°C. In eastern Europe, the temperatures estimated from pollen data were generally higher than today by 1°–2°C north of 45° N, but were colder than today in the Mediterranean region (Huntley and Prentice 1988; Klimanov 1978). Although this general pattern in Europe agrees with that shown in Figure 2.6A, the specific mapped pattern differs in several regions (see the map in Huntley and Prentice 1988). These differences in the reconstructed isotherm maps for the mid-Holocene warm period provide a challenge to paleoclimatic researchers, and their reconciliation could be the basis for much future cooperative research between American and Soviet scientists.

Data on precipitation changes accompanying temperature changes are of great interest, although they are far less reliable than temperature data. Estimates obtained by scientists at the Laboratory of Paleogeography of the Institute of Geography indicate that for the Mikulino warm period, when the mean global temperature may have been 2°C higher than today (Fig. 2.6B), the precipitation values were higher than those today in all latitudinal belts in Eurasia (25–75 percent higher in the steppe and semidesert belts of temperate latitudes and more than 100 percent higher in the tropics). For the Holocene warm period, when the mean global temperature may have been 1°C higher than today (Fig. 2.6A), the effect of increased precipitation in the area outside the tropics was not as large, and in some places precipitation deviations were negative. In the Eastern Hemisphere, in a narrow belt from about 50° to 55° N, total precipitation either did not change or decreased by 25–50 percent; a considerably greater precipitation decrease in similar latitudes occurred in the Western Hemisphere (Fig. 2.6A).

Based on the paleogeographic data, it is possible to predict how the equilibrium of the zonal structure of the landscape system would respond to different changes in the hydrothermal regime. This process has been studied using data obtained from extratropical Eurasia. With a mean global temperature increase of 2°C—and northern Eurasia warming by 10°–12°C—the tundra zone would ultimately disappear, to be replaced by taiga forests. However, a time interval of at least several centuries might be required for thawing of the permafrost. In the temperate forest zone, broad-leaved forests would probably spread 500–600 km to the north. Forest associations might also move 200–500 km into the steppe region, where the climate might change to being supportive of a forest-steppe zone. With a mean global temperature increase of 1°C, zonal shifts should not be as great; the forest zone may still expand to the north, but the tundra zone would probably not completely disappear. The boundary between forest and steppe would probably remain near its present position.

Phytomass production over the Eurasian landmass may have increased during periods that were warmer than today (possibly up to 50 percent during the

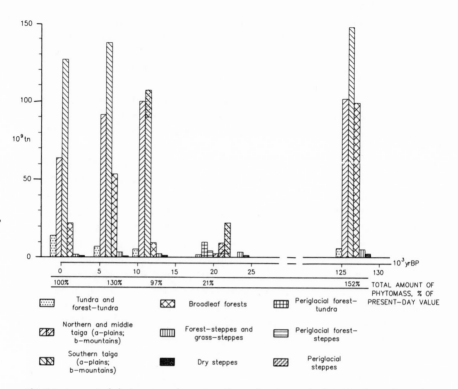

Fig. 2.8 Amount of phytomass under various thermal regimes calculated for the territory of the USSR north of the subtropics. (From Velitchko 1983)

Mikulino interglacial optimum and up to 15–20 percent in the Holocene optimum; see Fig. 2.8).

Landscape modifications that might accompany other changes in thermal regime have also been studied; these include a 0.5°C increase (minor Holocene optimum) and a 4° ± 1°C decrease (most recent glacial maximum). Because long-term global cooling may result from orbital forcing (Imbrie and Imbrie 1980), scenarios for such conditions should be considered.

Based on the data already available, it is possible to predict the following changes in the natural landscape system (provided the time is long enough to achieve a quasi-equilibrium state [Velitchko 1989b] and there are no anthropogenically induced disturbances):

1. 4° ± 1°C decrease in mean global temperature: possible transformation of the landscape from a polyzonal to a cryo-hyperzonal one;
2. 1°–2°C increase in mean global temperature: a poleward shift of natural zonal boundaries up to 300–400 km may occur;

3. <1°C mean global temperature increase (e.g., 0.5°C increase): the zonal landscape structure would not change appreciably, although the composition of vegetation formations (Huntley and Webb 1988) and the nature of the cryospheric and hydrospheric components might change.

The importance of landscape study in specific interpretations of the possible effects of climatic change is illustrated by Knox's (1983) work on river systems. He identified several regionally differentiated episodes of alluviation and valley cutting in the United States during the Holocene. Most significantly, he found that the response of river systems during the cool, moist late Holocene differed markedly from that during the climatically similar early Holocene, because the sediment yield of rivers is also strongly dependent on vegetation cover, which underwent major postglacial changes in composition and distribution.

Introduction of an Anthropogenic Factor

The scenarios outlined above, which are based purely on paleogeographic data, should not be interpreted as final equilibrium patterns just awaiting the introduction of humans; rather, they should be considered as indicators of tendencies that must be taken into consideration for specific projections of future conditions.

Two significant problems prevent paleogeographic data from being used directly for such projections, and both are related to anthropogenic factors. The first problem involves time. Paleoreconstructions are based on assumed equilibrium states achieved naturally by the landscape system in the course of long-term adaptation (over hundreds or thousands of years) to a new hydrothermal regime. Anticipated changes in atmospheric composition and in the mean global temperature of the boundary layer as a result of human activity might occur at a more rapid rate. Clearly, under the new human-induced conditions, the landscape system as a whole, as well as its individual components, would not approach an equilibrium state. This provides a new approach for landscape study (i.e., modeling the behavior of the components in the landscape system as a whole in particular time coordinates). Preliminary investigations suggest the need for a differentiated approach to the evaluation of rates of change of different natural components. A spectrum of curves characterizing the rates of transition to the quasi-equilibrium state can be established (Fig. 2.9). These rates vary from tens of years (for climate, snow cover, and sea ice), to hundreds of years (some vegetation types and ocean temperatures), to millennia (some relief types and ice sheets).

The second factor of importance is that the current landscape system is far from being in its natural state. Natural landscape systems are at present limited and primarily found in subarctic and tropical regions and selected mountainous

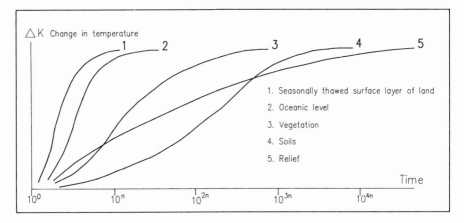

Fig. 2.9 A schematic illustration of the differentiation of major landscape components based on time required to achieve a new quasi-stationary state under a modified climatic regime. (By A. A. Velitchko)

and desert regions. Present landscape systems consist predominantly of mixed natural-anthropogenic systems.

With increasing human settlement of the earth, landscape has experienced local, regional, and global human impacts over the last 5000–7000 years; all three are occurring together at present. During this period, the manner in which humans have interacted with nature has also changed.

Three types of interactions may be identified. The first, the *migration* type, prevailed through the earliest stages of human existence. During this long stage, humans' reaction to stressful conditions was to migrate to more favorable regions (e.g., during glacial periods humans migrated toward the equator). This same reaction is still found on a local scale among some groups that practice primitive forms of agriculture. It is also found on a regional scale in areas where nomads live.

The second type of interaction mechanism is *adaptation*. Beginning with the late Paleolithic and the establishment of a primitive communal system, the socioeconomic potential of the hunting-gathering society allowed humans to adapt to the severe conditions of the periglacial zone, and later to the unstable conditions that prevailed during the transition to the Holocene (Neolithic; see Butzer 1975; Budyko 1980).

The third type of human-landscape interaction is *transformation*, which began with the appearance of agriculture and has become increasingly predominant up to the present. In this case, the economic potential is so great that rather than adapting to a certain landscape situation, humans have chosen to modify the landscape itself to satisfy their needs. The transformation mechanism has become most apparent during the last millennium. Having first occupied steppe areas, agriculture and cattle breeding then began to intrude into and destroy the forest zone. As a result, the natural terrestrial biomes have been disrupted or even eliminated and, for all intents and purposes, are no longer visible.

As far as the natural landscape is concerned, the most significant impact of humans can be seen in the elimination or reduction of forest zones (deforestation). Deforestation has accompanied human activity since the Paleolithic (Velitchko 1985b). Even though forest formations contain great amounts of biomass (phytomass), only small quantities of this phytomass can be assimilated by society for trophic purposes. By contrast, open spaces such as steppes, savannas, or artificially deforested areas make it possible to obtain biomass that can be utilized more efficiently by humans even though it is available in smaller quantities.

Considering future economic-demographic estimates, there is reason to believe that the process of deforestation may continue (see section 3.2). One might even anticipate the possible creation of an artificial anthropogenic landscape structure, which in turn would result in additional changes in different components of the landscape system. One of these would be an increased albedo, which would affect the global hydrothermal regime. One might also expect an increase in the importance of erosion-diluvial and eolian processes. The most active areas of landscape change might be expected to occur in the equatorial zone, which is especially sensitive to any modification in either the vegetation or soil covers. The tundra zone is no less sensitive, but it is not being exploited as intensively as the tropics.

All of the data obtained so far clearly indicate that realistic assessments of the current landscape system as well as predictions of future landscape changes are hardly possible without detailed understanding of the evolution of previous landscapes and the interaction of landscapes with human society.

2.3 Understanding Contemporary Landscape Dynamics

Modeling Global Atmosphere-Biosphere Interactions

Unraveling the more contemporary mechanisms of global change in the coupled biosphere-atmosphere system and determining the direction and rate of such change will require both modeling studies and the collection of compatible, homogeneous global data sets for a variety of key terrestrial variables. These key variables can be categorized as basic surface properties, derived physical variables, and fluxes (Table 2.1).

In view of the requirement for time-synchronous and spatially consistent data for the total global system, remote-sensing technology is central to the global change program. Over the long term, there will be the need for consistent, quantitative global measurements of surface albedo, surface temperature,

Table 2.1 Categories of key terrestrial variables and associated surface-atmosphere fluxes.

Surface properties	Derived physical variables	Fluxes
Vegetation, land use	Biomass, vegetation indices	Energy
Soil characteristics	Albedo, emissivity	Moisture
Snow and ice cover		Momentum
Topography	Slope, aspect, roughness	Aerosols, gases

vegetation cover, moisture, snow cover (extent and depth), evapotranspiration, and precipitation (frequency and intensity) for terrestrial ecosystems, and ocean color, tropospheric gases, ocean topography, sea-surface temperature, sea ice, and wind stress for the oceans (Rasool 1987). Atmospheric and space observations should include solar flux (and spectral variability), stratospheric temperature, stratospheric aerosols and ozone, and tropospheric aerosols. Cloud cover is not specifically listed, although it is a key element of the World Climate Research Program under the International Satellite Cloud Climatology Program (ISCCP; see Kondrat'yev 1982; Schiffer and Rossow 1983). Recent remote-sensing research by geographers includes the estimation of precipitation rates from visible and infrared satellite images (Barrett and Martin 1981), the modeling of radiation in mountainous terrain from multispectral Landsat data (Dozier 1980, 1987), the estimation of large-scale net primary productivity (Vinogradov 1982, 1984; Kondrat'yev 1986; Goward and Dye 1987), and the remote sensing of snow and ice parameters (Garelick et al. 1975; Kotlyakov 1981; Krenke and Menshutin 1984; D. K. Hall and Martinec 1985), especially from passive microwave data (Table 2.2; see D. K. Hall et al. 1987; M. R. Anderson 1987).

Theoretical and modeling considerations will be reviewed first in order to place the discussion of large-scale geographic data requirements, which follows, in the proper context. Global weather and climate are partially controlled by the fluxes of energy and mass emanating into the lower atmosphere from terrestrial and oceanic surfaces (Mintz 1984). While land areas comprise only 29 percent of the earth's surface area, their diverse and highly variable (in both space and time) surface characters dramatically influence the rates at which heat and moisture enter and exit the lower atmosphere (Mintz et al. 1983; Krenke and Zolotokrylin 1984; Sellers et al. 1986). This in turn affects the overall distribution of heat and moisture in the atmospheric system and, subsequently, global weather and climate (Mintz 1984). Fluxes of properties other than water (e.g., CO_2, methane, and aerosols) are also regulated by the nature and state of the terrestrial biosphere (Bjutner 1986; Borisenkov and Kondrat'yev 1988). The biophysical relationships between the terrestrial biosphere and the lower atmosphere must be modeled at the process-response level in order to understand how human-induced changes in the biosphere will affect global weather and climate (Terjung 1976).

Since the important fluxes flow into and out of the lower atmosphere across the surface of tangency between the atmosphere and the terrestrial surfaces, modeling these fluxes requires a focus on and understanding of this interface. The equations that govern the heat and moisture fluxes are well known in physical geography. They are:

$$Q^* = H + LE + G \tag{1}$$

where

$$Q^* = (Q + q)(1 - a) - I,$$

and

$$\partial w/\partial t = P + M - E - S \tag{2}$$

Equation 1 is the surface energy balance, and the fluxes are net radiation (Q^*), sensible heat flux (H), latent heat flux (LE)—the latent heat of vaporization (L) times evapotranspiration (E)—ground heat flux (G), beam solar irradiance (Q), diffuse solar irradiance (q), albedo, or the integrated reflectivity of the surface, (a), and effective outgoing longwave radiation from the surface (I). Equation 2 is the water budget equation, and its fluxes are precipitation (P), snowmelt (M), actual evapotranspiration (E), and surplus (S), which includes surface and subsurface runoff. Soil moisture (w) is the state variable. It is important to understand that, in nature, these equations are inextricably linked through the evapotranspiration process, and to account for this synergy they should be solved simultaneously.

With the exception of $\partial w/\partial t$, M, and S, each flux in equations 1 and 2 is usually stated as a differential equation in z (vertical). Variation in the horizontal also can be important, but for illustrative purposes the discussion will be confined to z. Letting any one of these fluxes (or the fluxes of trace gases) be represented by X, we can write

$$X \approx \frac{\chi(z_+) - \chi(z_-)}{_{z_-}\int^{z_+} D^{-1}\, dz} \tag{3}$$

which illustrates that in practice X depends on the "concentration" of χ at some location (z_+) above or at the interface $(z_+ \geq 0)$ and at some location (z_-) below or at the interface $(z_- \leq 0)$. It should be noted that X also depends on the conductance (D) or resistance

$$_{z_-}\int^{z_+} D^{-1}\, dz$$

of the biosphere or near surface with respect to species or energy quantity χ, and z_+/z_-. While equation 3 is but a simple steady-state representation of X, it underscores the importance of being able to evaluate χ above $(z_+ > 0)$, at

Table 2.2 Observational requirements for study of snow and ice.

Variable	Observation type	Accuracy	Resolution (km)	Time (days)	Data type	Platform	Available product level
Snow cover (continental scale)							
extent	percentage area	10%	50	7	vis/IR, μwave	sat.[a]	
thickness	area average	10%	50	15	μwave	sat.	research
density	area average	20%	50	15	μwave	sat.	research
water equivalent	area average	10%	50	15	μ wave	sat.	research
grain size	area average	10%	50	15	IR/μwave	sat.	research
albedo	area average	0.02	100	15	vis/IR	sat.	feasible
Snow cover (alpine scale)							
extent	percentage area	10%	0.5	7	vis/IR	sat.	feasible
thickness	area average	10%	0.5	15	μwave	a/c[b]	research
density	area average	20%	0.5	15	μwave	a/c	research
water equivalent	area average	10%	0.5	15	μwave	a/c	research
grain size	area average	10%	1	15	IR/μwave	a/c	research
albedo	area average	0.02	1	15	vis/IR	sat.	feasible
Sea and lake ice							
boundary	position (line)	10 km	10	7	vis/IR	sat.	current
					μwave, radar	a/c	research
concentration	area average	10%	50	7	μwave	sat.	research
					radar	a/c	research
ice type	percentage area	10%	50	30	μwave	sat.	research
					radar	a/c	research

motion	point displacement	1 km day^{-1}	10	7	radar	sat.	feasible
thickness	area distribution	1 m	25	30	sonar	sub.[c]	feasible
leads	percentage area, orientation	10%	50	7	sonar	sub.	feasible
surface roughness	area distribution	1 m	25	30	alt.[d]	sat.	feasible
ice surface temperature	area average	2 K	25	7	IR, μwave	sat.	feasible
snow cover	area average thickness	10%	50	7	vis	sat.	feasible
albedo	area average	10%	50	7	vis	sat.	feasible
ice islands	point location, size	2 km 100 m	same	7	radar	sat.	feasible
icebergs	point location, size	2 km 100 m	same	7	radar	sat.	current

After National Research Council 1985. Reprinted in part from "A Strategy for Earth Science from Space in the 1980s and 1990s" (1985), with permission from the National Academy Press, Washington, D.C.

[a]sat. = satellite   [b]a/c = aircraft   [c]sub. = submarine   [d]alt. = altimeter

$(z_+ \text{ or } z_- = 0)$, and/or below $(z_- < 0)$ the interface. As $\chi(z_o)$ and $\chi(z_-)$ are largely controlled by the type and state of the vegetation (e.g., Rauner 1972; Dickinson 1983; Sellers et al. 1986; Budagovsky 1986a; 1986b), soil (e.g., Denmead 1984), and snow cover (e.g., Krenke 1982; Willmott 1984), information about the form and function of these elements of the terrestrial biosphere is essential to the solution of equations 1, 2, and 3.

Investigations of the troposphere above the boundary layer where $z_+ > 0$ and $du/dz \approx 0$ (where u is wind speed)—with regard to its influence on $\chi(z_+ \geq 0)$—have been primarily conducted by atmospheric dynamicists and physicists, although geographers (mainly synoptic climatologists such as Dzerdzievsky [1975] and Kuvshinova [1987]) have also contributed to the predictability of the near-surface atmosphere from upper-air observations. The boundary layer $(z_+ \geq 0$ and $d\bar{u}/dz > 0)$, by contrast, is being investigated by a wide spectrum of researchers (e.g., meteorologists, climatologists, hydrologists, pollution engineers, biophysicists, and agronomists) because it is where most human activities take place. The subsurface $(z_- \leq 0)$ also is being investigated by scientists from many disciplines (e.g., geography, geology, geomorphology, soil science, plant science, and climatology). Geographers' roles in the modern exploration of the biosphere have been significant, and their main contributions have been in that critically important near-surface zone of the biosphere $(z_+ \to 0, z_- \to 0)$; that is, in the investigation of the vegetation/soil/soil moisture/snow-cover complex for purposes of predicting and explaining the biosphere's role in solving equations 1, 2, and 3.

Geographers have been investigating the near-surface climate for decades. Kuz'min (1937) and Thornthwaite and Holzman (1939), for instance, were among the first to recognize the importance of evaluating the fluxes into the boundary layer. Thornthwaite (in Wilm et al. 1944) also proposed the climatic water budget as well as the concept of potential evapotranspiration. Budyko (1956) mapped energy budget variables, while Chang (1958) was the first to consider the large-scale importance of ground temperature. Thornthwaite (1954) and later Terjung (1976) argued that geographers' overriding concern should be to solve the primitive equations for the near-surface environment. While geographers have already made notable strides in parameterizing and modeling equations 1, 2, and 3, most of the large-scale work remains to be completed.

Model building and data collection are corequisites for the successful evaluation of the interactivity between the terrestrial biosphere and the atmosphere. Sophisticated biosphere models (cf. Mintz et al. 1983; Dickinson 1983; Alexandrov and Svirezhev 1985; Sellers et al. 1986) are of little value without adequate observations and parameterizations of the near-surface environment. But at the same time, data which purport to characterize the biosphere are of limited value if variables required by climate models are not sampled, or if the time or space scales of observations or statistical summary are inconsistent with the models' needs. Consider that daily changes in plant transpiration in general cannot be adequately inferred from monthly climate data. It is paramount, then, that data collection and modeling efforts not be conducted in mutual ignorance.

The kinds of observations needed can best be understood if we know how near-surface data are used by the modeling community. A good introductory treatment of three-dimensional climate modeling has recently been written by Washington and Parkinson (1986). Other volumes have focused on evaluating the terrestrial biosphere for climate applications (e.g., Eagleson 1982; Hutchison and Hicks 1985; Rosenzweig and Dickinson 1986). The importance of general (atmospheric) circulation models (GCMs) lies in the fact that they are the only means by which the atmospheric redistribution of heat, moisture, and other species transferred into the lower atmosphere from the surface can be traced.

While climate modeling is a very active area of research, it is also very expensive, and at present there are only about twenty research groups in the world actively developing and refining GCMs (Alexandrov et al. 1983; Washington and Parkinson 1986). These models take several different forms, but the fully three-dimensional ones (e.g., Kalnay et al. 1983; Williamson 1983) evaluate fluxes at several levels in the atmosphere and at space scales approaching 100×100 km. Space scales on this order are sometimes referred to as "climate scale" (Andre et al. 1986). The time scales associated with these models vary considerably and depend on the variable in question as well as the model's purpose. Simulations of the seasonal cycle, for instance, require data resolved to the day or month, while paleoclimate simulations may require only a centennial or millennial resolution. It should be emphasized that so-called climate change experiments using climate models are sensitivity studies of the *equilibrium* response of the model to a change in forcing, even where a series of model experiments has been used to reconstruct temporal snapshots of climatic conditions (Kutzbach and Street-Perrott 1985). However, true climatic change experiments, where the model system evolves in a transient mode, are becoming possible for predictions of the short-term evolution of climate. This technique can be applied to the question of greenhouse gas effects, for example (J. Hansen, pers. comm., 1988).

If the data geographers collect are to contribute to a better understanding of global change, they should be compiled with an eye toward their potential utility to the climate-modeling community. This means that they should be representative at space scales of approximately 100 km^2, although this resolution will improve with faster computers and more efficient algorithms. Model time scales, by contrast, are much more variable and, once again, range from hours to millennia, depending on the variable of interest and the model.

Another general consideration is that data should be collected for at least one of two general purposes: to be used as initial conditions or parameters in

GCMs or other models which estimate climatically important variables; or to be used as evaluation data—that is, data with which model predictions can be compared. Crane and Barry (1988) made such a comparison for observed and modeled pressure fields in the Arctic using synoptic climatological techniques. Biosphere data that meet these criteria can be classified in three ways: (1) measurable properties of the near surface, e.g., leaf-area index, average canopy height, soil porosity; (2) derivable physical properties or variables, e.g., albedo, bulk stomatal resistance, and the thermal diffusivity of the soil; and (3) the fluxes to and from the interface described in equations 1, 2, and 3.

Geographers can make important contributions in data collection by making site measurements of important properties, developing transfer functions that use primary data (e.g., in situ or satellite observations) to derive climatically important observations, and measuring or modeling the energy and mass fluxes (equations 1, 2, and 3) in such a way that the results can be used to evaluate GCM estimates of the fluxes. While there is not yet a clear distinction between measurable and derived properties and variables, it is likely that more of the model data will be derived from boundary conditions in the not-too-distant future. Leaf-area index and albedo, for instance, will be derivable from more basic initial conditions (e.g., of vegetation and soil type) and algorithms that embody our knowledge of plant phenology and succession.

Vegetation and Land-Use Parameters

Geographers are currently making leading contributions to the store of global-scale terrestrial-biosphere data (Basilevich et al. 1970; Matthews 1983; M. F. Wilson and Henderson-Sellers 1985; Henderson-Sellers et al. 1986; Willmott and Klink 1986). Work accomplished over the last five years is well summarized by Henderson-Sellers et al. (1986).

Characterizing the terrestrial biosphere for climatic purposes has taken two main avenues: (1) archival data taken from vegetation atlases as well as other secondary sources have been synthesized and then interpolated to GCM-compatible grids (e.g., Matthews 1983; M. F. Wilson and Henderson-Sellers 1985; Willmott and Klink 1986); and (2) space-time series of vegetation indexes that describe the state of the vegetation have been and are being remotely sensed and archived (e.g., C. J. Tucker et al. 1985). Most of these data are encoded as annual or seasonal averages as well as at climate scale (i.e., approximately at a 1° latitude × 1° longitude resolution, or in a few cases at 0.5° × 0.5° resolution). In some instances derived parameters such as albedo (Matthews 1983) or roughness length (Henderson-Sellers et al. 1986) are also encoded at climate scale. Sparse in situ data exist, but their spatial and temporal resolutions are extremely poor and there is marked measurement and averaging inconsistency (see Cannell 1982).

While encoded global data bases are more readily available today than ever before, they continue to have several major deficiencies with respect to global systems study. First, most available biosphere data are given as annual means or maxima, making evaluations of the seasonal cycle or interannual trends impossible. Second, there is no indication of the subgrid-scale variability in the data; i.e., they are assumed to occur at the same level across the entire cell. Third, many climatically important biospheric parameters (e.g., field capacity and stomatal conductance) have not been measured or adequately estimated on the global scale. Before the biosphere can be adequately coupled to the atmosphere, many of these data deficiencies will have to be overcome.

Some of the properties of the terrestrial biosphere that have to be compiled include:

1. leaf-area vertical and spatial density distributions
2. leaf reflectivities, transmissivities, and absorptivities in the visible (*vis*) and near-infrared (*nir*) bands
3. stem-area properties and distributions
4. the spatial distributions of canopy heights
5. root-density vertical and spatial distributions
6. vertical, spatial, and temporal distributions of stomatal conductances as well as stomatal conductances as functions of ambient atmospheric conditions
7. information about those characteristic spatial scales over which within-biome vegetation associations tend to repeat themselves
8. soil depth and density profiles
9. distributions of soil porosity, mineral, and organic content
10. magnitude and distribution of soil diffusivities with respect to heat and water
11. the thermal properties of leaf litter, including reflectivity

These structural and thermal properties are necessary to guide the new generation of realistic biosphere models (e.g., Sellers et al. 1986) that are now being developed and used in GCMs.

A shortcoming of virtually all the current biosphere models used in GCMs is that they treat biospheric variation only in the vertical; once again, vegetation and soil properties are assumed to be evenly spaced across the grid cell. More realistic approaches (which will allow for vegetation clumping and local relief, for example) are possible, but they require information about the characteristic space scales (item 7 above) over which the vegetation ensemble repeats itself. Once these are established, three-dimensional parameterizations and calculations can be made for a basic vegetation unit. Ross (1968) and, later, Kimes and Kirchner (1982), for instance, have successfully used this concept and a ray-tracing algorithm to model albedo from vegetation structure. Rowe (1988)

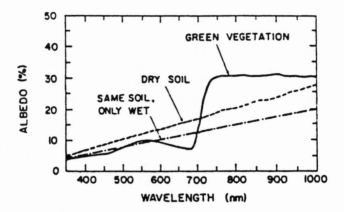

Fig. 2.10 Spectral reflectances for dry soil, wet soil, and a plot of blue grama grass. (From Tucker and Miller 1977. Reprinted, with permission, from *Photogrammetric Engineering and Remote Sensing*, copyright 1977, by the American Society for Photogrammetry and Remote Sensing.)

extended this work to the globe in order to ascertain the dependence of large-scale albedo on subgrid-scale vegetation phenology and structure. Such work also should be extended to canopy properties which affect the convective and longwave fluxes in equations 1, 2, and 3. Since subgrid-scale distributions of the important variables and fluxes are often nonlinear, they must be more fully measured, parameterized, and modeled.

Relevant biosphere data can be obtained by in situ (direct) measurements or compiled from secondary sources (e.g., atlases and journal articles) or satellite observations (Vinogradov 1983, 1988; Vasiliev 1988a, 1988b). Detailed in situ measurements for all the earth's major biomes and human-induced land covers are needed by climate-scale soil/plant/atmosphere models to determine which properties of the biosphere are most important, and as ground confirmation for satellite observations. They can also be used to develop transfer functions which convert satellite or secondary data into more useful biophysical data.

C. J. Tucker et al. (1985), for instance, have made a well-known land-cover map of Africa based on one such transfer function. This function is

$$I = \frac{nir - vis}{nir + vis} \tag{4}$$

where I is the normalized greenness index, *nir* is the upwelling near-infrared radiation, and *vis* is the upwelling visible radiation. Equation 4 exploits the facts that healthy green vegetation efficiently reflects near-infrared and absorbs visible irradiance (Fig. 2.10), and channel 1 of the NOAA-7 AVHRR scanner approximately records the visible band while channel 2 essentially measures *nir.* Many such transfer functions need to be developed to make full use of currently available and future satellite data. In situ measurements and satellite data in combination with plant/soil/atmosphere models should be the major source of such functions.

In situ measurements may also provide the data to develop functions that relate easily measurable properties to other biophysical properties that may be of more significant use to the modeling community. Reliable statistical functions that relate biome-specific tree heights and trunk diameters to leaf-area densities or rooting depths and densities, for example, would be very useful. Predictive relationships between ambient atmospheric conditions and bulk stomatal conductances, leaf-area densities, and the canopy green fraction would allow modeled canopy phenology to be interactive with the atmosphere. Experiments such as the First International Satellite Land Surface Climatology Project Field Experiment (FIFE; see Schmugge and Sellers 1986) and HAPEX (Hydrologic Atmospheric Pilot Experiment) (Andre et al. 1986) are important first field investigations into climate-scale relationships between the biosphere and the lower atmosphere.

Secondary sources (maps, atlases, data archives, and the literature) also provide measurements and data that can be used in the development of transfer functions. Rowe (1988), for instance, has used a biosphere radiation model to derive maps of albedo from secondary-source data compiled by Willmott and Klink (1986) and others. Properties such as leaf-area index also can be estimated (Fig. 2.11). The reliability of such estimated fields has yet to be determined, however. The literature contains a wealth of useful data and functions (many of which are published in obscure places), and therefore needs to be more fully investigated. The main problem with secondary-source data is that they were collected for different purposes and thus may not be usable in climate models or at climate scale.

Topography and Roughness Parameters

Terrain properties that are of significance for large-scale processes and surface-atmosphere interaction studies include the topography itself, relative relief, mean slope, aspect, and surface roughness.

Topography affects air motion by virtue of its orientation with respect to the air flow and the height, width, and shape of physiographic barriers (Barry 1981; Krenke 1982). For example, topographic maps have been used to estimate mean vertical motion for global and regional scales (Vianello 1985; Krenke and Mikhailov 1986). Slope and aspect are major determinants of the spatial variability of energy and moisture fluxes. On the global scale these factors are generally ignored, although this is partly because suitable data are lacking. When the data become available, methods for parameterizing topography at climate scale will have to be developed.

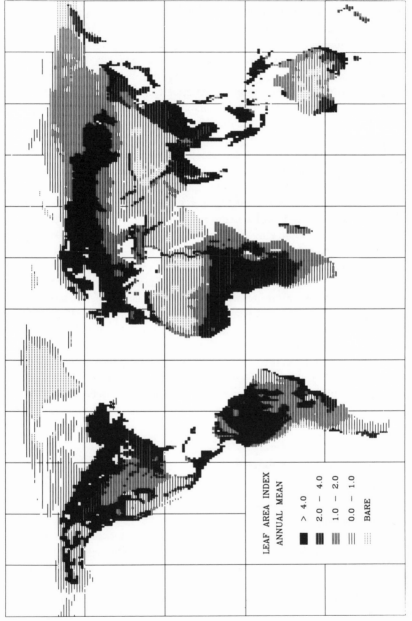

Fig. 2.11 Spatial distributions of annual average leaf-area index (*l*). (From Willmott and Klink 1986 with permission of the European Space Research and Technology Centre.)

LEAF AREA INDEX
ANNUAL MEAN

> 4.0

2.0 – 4.0

1.0 – 2.0

0.0 – 1.0

BARE

Surface roughness, which is determined by both small-scale terrain irregularities and characteristics of the vegetational cover, influences surface friction and thus the fluxes of momentum, heat, and moisture. The larger-scale relative relief also contributes significantly, through form drag, to the global-scale momentum flux between the atmosphere and earth.

Digital global data on topography are available with a spatial resolution of between 10 and 100 km and nominally 1 m vertical resolution. Although these have known errors, they are adequate for many global-scale studies, and indeed for climate-modeling purposes; such data are usually smoothed to a resolution of between about one and five degrees of latitude. Some atmospheric GCMs employ an "envelope" topography, rather than mean terrain heights, in order to treat orographic effects adequately on planetary wave structure. However, the benefits of an envelope representation for the simulation of subsynoptic-scale weather phenomena are uncertain. The treatment of terrain altitude in spectral GCMs in particular merits additional study.

For the United States, digital terrain data have been derived from 7.5-minute quadrangle topographic maps. Case studies in which attempts have been made to register Landsat radiance data to the terrain in mountainous areas of California (Dozier 1986) demonstrate that the spatial sampling introduced by the digital terrain data can lead to incompatibility problems when slope and exposure are correlated with radiance values for individual pixels. This question will need to be addressed in the context of overlaying data sets of differing resolution, and especially in the design of data collection programs for representative target areas.

A similar scale problem will arise in coastline studies concerned with changes in global sea level. Documentation of shoreline changes will require coastline data several orders of magnitude higher in resolution than those needed for climate-modeling applications.

Surface Albedo and Emissivity

Three-dimensional treatments of climate in GCMs require appropriate assumptions for surface albedo and infrared emissivity. Surface albedo is a complex parameter which depends on solar zenith angle (and therefore latitude, date, and time of day), cloud amount (which affects the spectral properties of the incident radiation), and the state of the surface itself. The term *albedo* properly refers to the integrated reflectance over the solar spectrum (0.150–4.0 μm), although measurements are often limited to a narrower range by the spectral properties of the sensor. Infrared emissivity is much less variable, and in most current GCMs a constant value is assumed. For natural surfaces, emissivity varies between approximately 0.82 and 0.99 in the 8–12 μm range.

Vegetation, soil, and snow-cover albedos are highly dependent on wavelength. Plants and soil surfaces typically have low albedos in the visible range and much higher values in the near-infrared, whereas the albedo of snow is very high in the visible and very low around 1.5–1.6 μm. The albedo of snow-free surfaces also depends on the vegetation canopy structure and the soil water content. For snow-covered surfaces, the albedo varies according to the age and depth of snow and its soot or dust content (Marshall and Warren 1987). For oceans, the albedo depends on the solar zenith angle (especially when this exceeds 60°) and the wave state. For sea ice, the albedo is a function of the snow cover or surface puddling (Scharfen et al. 1987).

GCMs treat the albedo of snow- or ice-free surfaces by (1) using a fixed value, (2) specifying albedo as a function of latitude, or (3) specifying a geographical distribution of albedo. There is considerable diversity in GCM formulations of albedo for snow- or ice-free and snow- or ice-covered surfaces (Table 2.3). Compilations of albedo and related values for the globe have been developed by several authors, and reviews are presented by Kondrat'yev et al. (1982), Henderson-Sellers and Wilson (1983), and Henderson-Sellers et al. (1986). More recently, Rowe (1988) has attempted to model global albedo as a function of vegetation structure.

Permanent and Seasonal Snow and Ice Cover

Snow and ice phenomena occurring on the earth's surface are collectively referred to as the *cryosphere* (Kotlyakov 1968). Although most prominent in polar regions, their significance in the climate-hydrologic system is global. Land ice, primarily in Antarctica and Greenland, contains enough water to raise world sea levels some 80 m and could furnish 75 percent of our global freshwater supplies. Typically, these ice sheets have ages of 10^5 years, whereas snow cover and most sea ice are essentially seasonal. Seasonal snow and ice are most extensive in the Northern Hemisphere, where they cover about 25 percent of the surface at maximum and 5 percent at minimum. Corresponding figures for the Southern Hemisphere are 12 and 6 percent, respectively.

The principal climatic roles of snow and ice cover relate to their high reflectivity (albedo), low thermal conductivity, water-holding capacity, and thermal inertia (Krenke 1974, 1982; Barry 1985a; Kotlyakov 1987). Typical albedos are: 0.8–0.9 for fresh, dry snow; 0.6 for old, melting snow and bare ice; and 0.3–0.4 for melting sea ice with puddles. These may be compared with the standardized model values (Table 2.3). Albedo changes due to snowmelt on Arctic sea ice have recently been mapped from visible satellite images by Scharfen et al. (1987), while the effect of surface cover type on the albedo of snow-covered land has been investigated in detail by D. A. Robinson and Kukla (1985).

Winter snow cover builds up a cold reserve that acts to depress temperatures in spring when energy is required to warm the pack to 0°C and then melt it

$(2.8 \times 10^6 \text{ J kg}^{-1}$; see Krenke and Loktionova, 1989). Snow cover can lower the surface air temperature over it by some 5°–7°C (Dewey 1977). This cooling is confined to a shallow layer due to the atmosphere's strong static stability (J. E. Walsh 1987), but effects on cyclonic activity resulting from the presence of snow cover and sea ice have been documented (Carleton 1987; Dewey 1987b).

Snow cover, especially fresh snow, insulates the ground surface from radiative and conductive cooling almost completely when it reaches about 50 cm thickness. Basal snowpack temperatures remain well above those at the snow surface, providing a vital microhabitat for small mammals in the Arctic tundra. Another effect on the energy budget is due to the virtual elimination of evaporative flux into the atmosphere. Snowpack sublimation is generally minor, except in windy environments where there is frequent blowing snow, which undergoes substantial sublimation losses (Dyunin 1963).

Available information on seasonal snow cover and sea ice has been reviewed by Barry (1985a, 1985b, 1986a, 1986b). Data on permanent land-ice cover (glaciers and ice sheets) will be available in the near future from the World Glacier Monitoring Service (in press). Data on ground ice and permafrost are fragmentary and, in many cases, not readily available because they are collected largely by private industrial and commercial agencies in North America (Barry 1988).

Paleoclimatic data from ice cores have received much attention over the last twenty years. Such cores provide long and detailed records of a suite of environmental variables with seasonal to annual resolution for several thousand years. The longest cores now span the entire last glacial cycle (Jouzel et al. 1987; Kotlyakov 1987) and permit rates of change in climate and other variables (gases, aerosols, temperature, precipitation, volcanic eruptions, and solar activity) to be determined.

Snow cover (Fig. 2.12), sea-ice extent (Figs. 2.13 and 2.14), and depth (or thickness) are highly variable seasonally, and there is substantial interannual variability as well. Consequently, additional questions arise concerning the appropriate spatial and temporal sampling intervals. Measurement requirements (Table 2.2) have been proposed for these variables by the Space Sciences Board, Committee on Earth Sciences (National Research Council 1985). The availability of homogeneous global data on seasonal snow cover and sea-ice extent is very limited. Records exist from 1966 (more reliably from 1973) in the case of Northern Hemisphere snow cover and from 1972–1973 in the case of Arctic and Antarctic sea ice. A Northern Hemisphere snow-cover climatology has recently been prepared by Dewey (1987a) using these data. The twenty-year records of hemispheric snow and sea-ice extent show short-term fluctuations on the order of 10 percent, but no apparent trends have so far been identified (Barry, in press).

Table 2.3 Surface albedos used in atmospheric general circulation climate models.

Example center (reference)	Model	Snow-free and ice-free surfaces	Snow-covered and ice-covered surfaces
Atmospheric Environment Service (Canada) (Boer & McFarlane 1979)	AES	no specific details but implied geographical distribution based on Posey & Clapp (1964)	follows Holloway & Manabe (1971), equation 5; see GFDL
Australian Numerical Meteorology Research Centre (McAvaney et al. 1978)	ANMRC	latitudinal variation based on Posey & Clapp (1964)	snow albedo prescribed as latitudinal variation of α. α of sea ice $= 0.07$
Computing Centre, Siberian Academy of Sciences (Marchuk et al. 1979)	CCSAS	$\alpha = 0.2$, bare ground; $\alpha = 0.1$, ocean	snow: $\alpha = 0.2 + 0.4d_{sw}$; $\alpha \leq 0.6$ (same as NCAR); ice: $\alpha = 0.6$
Geophysical Fluid Dynamics Laboratory (Holloway & Manabe 1971)	GFDL	geographical distribution based on Posey & Clapp (1964)	snow: equation 5; $\left. \begin{array}{l} \alpha = \alpha_1 + (0.6 - \alpha_1)d_{sw}^{1/2}\quad d_{sw} < 1\text{ cm} \\ \alpha = 0.6 \qquad\qquad\qquad\quad d_{sw} \geq 1\text{ cm} \end{array} \right\}$ (3); poleward of 75° lat., albedo for land and pack ice: 0.75
(Manabe & Stouffer 1980)	GFDL	geographical distribution based on Posey & Clapp (1964)	sea ice: 0.5 for lat. $< 55°$, 0.7 for lat. $> 66.5°$, 0.45 if top melting
Goddard Laboratory for Atmospheric Sciences (Halem et al. 1979)	GLAS	Feb.: geographical distribution based on Posey & Clapp (1964); Aug.: Charney et al. (1977) vegetated land, 0.14; desert, 0.35; ocean, 0.07	snow and ice: 0.70; Holloway & Manabe (1971), equation 5; see GFDL
Goddard Institute for Space Studies (Hansen et al. 1983)	GISS	land: 8 vegetation types have seasonally varying albedos for < 0.7 μm and ≥ 0.7 μm	snow-free ice: 0.45, ocean; 0.5, land snow albedo: $\alpha_s = 0.5 + e^{-age/5}$ ground partly snow-covered, albedo: $\alpha_1 + (\alpha_s - \alpha_1)(1 - e^{-d_{sw}/d_{mask}})$ two spectral regions

Institution	Code	Snow-free albedo	Snow/ice albedo
Meteorological Office, U.K. (Corby et al. 1977)	UKMO	5-level model: snow-free land values vary with latitude range, 0.150–0.223	snow: $\alpha = \alpha_1 + 0.38\, d_{sw}^{1/2}$ $\alpha \leq 0.6$ similar to Holloway & Manabe (1971), equation 5; see GFDL sea ice and permanent snow cover: $\alpha = 0.8$; $T_o < 271.2$ K $\alpha = 0.5$; $T_o \geq 271.2$ K
(Saker 1975)	UKMO	11-level model: land, 0.2; sea (where effective), 0.06	transient snow cover, 0.5; permanent snow cover, land ice, and sea ice, 0.8
National Center for Atmospheric Research (Washington & Williamson 1977)	NCAR	originally: geographical distribution based on Posey & Clapp (1964)	originally: snow or ice, $\alpha = 0.2 + 0.4 d_{sw}$ and $\alpha \leq 0.6$
(Dickinson et al. 1981, and unpublished)		third-generation model: two spectral regions $< 0.7\ \mu m$ and $\geq 0.7\ \mu m$; dependence on vegetation type and extent	third-generation model: snow albedo function of age and depth of snow; two spectral regions
Oregon State University (Schlesinger & Gates 1979)	OSU	geographical distribution based on Posey & Clapp (1964) and model's 9 surface types	fixed value
Rand Corporation (Gates & Schlesinger 1977)	RAND	geographical distribution based on Posey & Clapp (1964)	—
University of California at Los Angeles (Arakawa 1972)	UCLA	bare soil: 0.14, ocean: 0.07	snow-covered: 0.7; ice-covered soil or sea water: 0.4

Symbols: d_{sw} = the water equivalent depth of snow (cm); d_{mask} = the vegetation snow masking depth equivalent thickness of water (cm); α_1 = the snow-free land albedo.

Source: Henderson-Sellers and Wilson 1983. Copyright by the American Geophysical Union and reprinted with permission.

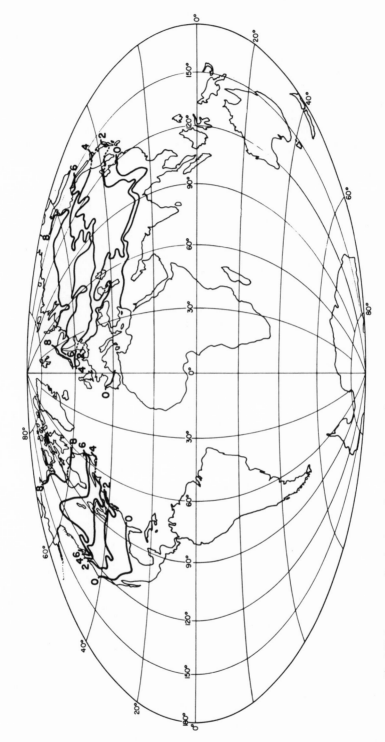

Fig. 2.12 Snow cover duration in months. (From Barry 1985b)

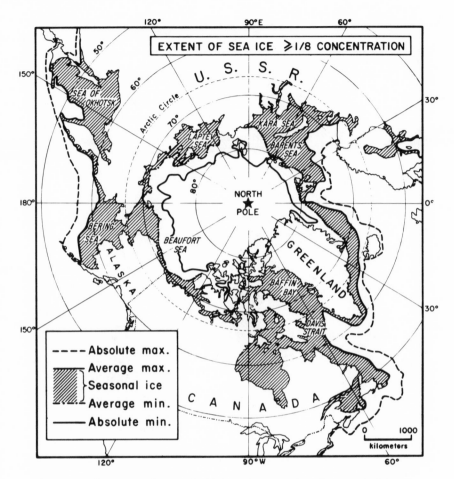

Fig. 2.13 Northern Hemisphere sea-ice limits at the seasonal maximum and minimum extent. (From Barry 1985b)

Soil Properties, Including Moisture

The large-scale spatial and temporal distributions of climatically important soil properties are even less well known than vegetation. Only two major attempts to characterize and encode the world's soils for climate purposes currently exist (M. F. Wilson 1984; Gildea and Moore 1987). In both instances data were taken from the UNFAO/UNESCO (1974) global soils archive. M. F. Wilson's (1984) archive contains information about soil color, texture, and drainage at a resolution of 1° × 1°, while Gildea and Moore's (1987) data set provides soil texture, slope, phase, and type, again at a 1° × 1° resolution. While these archives are important first steps, they do not provide direct infor-

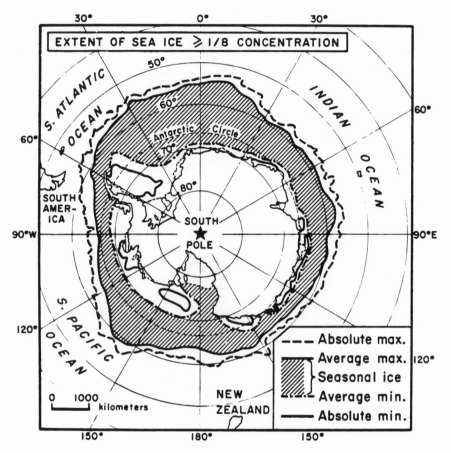

Fig. 2.14 Antarctic sea-ice limits at the seasonal maximum and minimum extent. (From Barry 1985b)

mation about soil thermal and hydraulic properties, soil depth, or field capacity. However, crude first approximations of important soil properties (e.g., hydraulic conductivity; see Fig. 2.15) can be estimated from these data. The global subgrid scale and temporal variability of climatically important soil properties are still unavailable. The relationships between large-scale soil properties and topography also await evaluation and specification at climate scale.

Soil moisture, perhaps the single most climatically important soil variable, also has been underinvestigated. It has been crudely estimated at climate scale from empirically based solutions to equation 3 (Fig. 2.16), but, as with most large-scale climate fields, the reliability of the derived fields has not been determined. In situ measurements of soil moisture at climate scale as well as

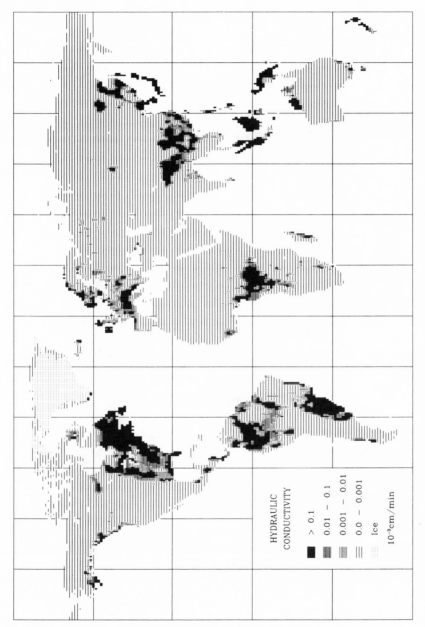

Fig. 2.15 Approximation of annual average hydraulic conductivity estimated from functions described by Clapp and Hornberger (1978) and data presented by Wilson (1984) and Willmott et al. (1985).

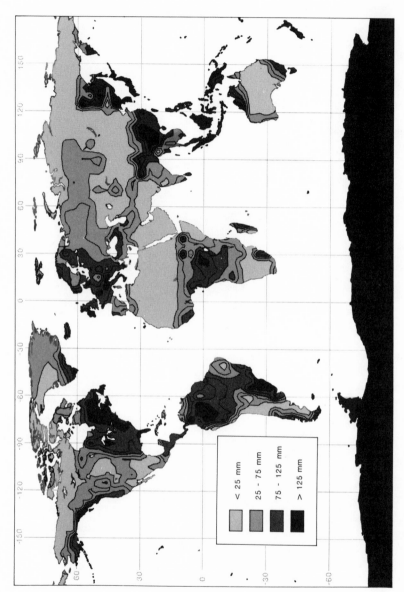

Fig. 2.16 Annual mean soil moisture (mm). Intermediate isolines of 50 mm and 100 mm are given within the second and third categories, respectively, to improve spatial resolution. (From Willmott, Rowe, and Mintz 1985. Reprinted with the kind permission of the *International Journal of Climatology* and the Royal Meteorological Society.)

< 25 mm

25 – 75 mm

75 – 125 mm

> 125 mm

satellite-derived estimates are needed to evaluate both empirically based and GCM solutions to the water budget equation (equation 3). Both climate averages and time series of soil moisture need to be compiled and analyzed.

Although some researchers believe that the soil exerts little influence on the important energy fluxes, Denmead (1984), for example, has suggested that soils can substantially affect these fluxes, even from beneath a forest canopy. Although the large-scale influence of soils remains a topic of speculation, it is clear that in situ observations, satellite data, and secondary-source data are needed to ascertain the climatic importance of the world's soils.

Evapotranspiration, Precipitation, and the Energy Balance

The terrestrial biosphere interacts with the lower atmosphere primarily through the regulation of the surface energy and mass budgets (equations 1, 2, and 3). Lush vegetation, for example, tends to reduce albedo and runoff while increasing evapotranspiration. It also has been hypothesized that an increase in vegetation may increase local precipitation and the uptake of anthropogenically produced CO_2. Quantitative information on these effects for the spectrum of biomes, however, are not available at climate scale (Mintz et al. 1983). Insufficient global water and energy budget data exist to make reliable inferences about the global space-time distributions of the pertinent energy and mass fluxes (Willmott et al. 1985a).

Empirically derived global water balance fields are needed for the initialization and verification of GCM predictions of near-surface climate and the validation of satellite-derived climatologies, as well as for bases of comparison in climatic change studies. Currently available data are inadequate because they are based on sparse data networks in many places (Willmott et al. 1985b) and they usually contain only climatic averages on monthly, seasonal, or annual time scales (e.g., L'vovich 1972; Wernstedt 1972; *Mirovoi vodnyi . . .* 1974; Jaeger 1976; Steinhauser 1979; Willmott et al. 1981). Where time series of the fluxes (precipitation only) are available (e.g., Spangler and Jenne 1984), the spatial density of the stations is low. Of the surface moisture fluxes, precipitation is the only one measured at enough locations to develop regionally reliable fields at climate scale. Before this can be accomplished, however, gauge biases resulting primarily from the surface wind field should be estimated and removed (Sevruk 1986). Transfer functions need to be developed to estimate the other surface moisture fluxes (i.e., evapotranspiration, snowmelt, and runoff) from other weather data (e.g., temperature and humidity), satellite data, and the form and state of the biosphere. Transfer functions also are needed to estimate large-scale radiation fluxes from satellite and site data because the station networks of solar, net, and longwave radiation are extremely sparse. Thus, we know very little about the large-scale spatial and temporal distributions of Q^*, $(Q + q)(1 - a)$, I, H, LE, or G, or about their subgrid-scale variability. The geography of climate remains to be measured, derived, and encoded for use in climate-model studies of global change.

Aerosols and Gases

Global climate and its evolution are significantly affected by the gaseous composition of the atmosphere and its aerosol content. Greenhouse gases (CO_2, CH_4, CFC-11, CFC-12, NO_x, O_3) and aerosols (mineral dust, sulphates, sea salts, and industrial aerosols) play major roles in the tropospheric and surface radiation budgets and are also involved in interactions with other components of the climate system (Karol' et al. 1983). Because many of these components exhibit important temporal variations and trends, an understanding of their reservoirs, residence times, and flux rates is essential for global change studies. Monitoring of CO_2 began only in 1957 at Mauna Loa, and for other trace gases and aerosols there are even shorter records (Wang et al. 1986). Proxy records derived from the gas content of air bubbles trapped in ice sheets are providing valuable evidence on long-term trends of carbon dioxide as well as of methane (Oeschger et al. 1985). Similarly, fluctuations in microparticles, heavy metals, and other atmospheric constituents have been determined from ice cores collected in Greenland, Antarctica, and high-altitude equatorial ice bodies (Thompson et al. 1984).

Field studies of gaseous fluxes have long been conducted by ecologists and biometeorologists, but the need for global-scale information has led to alternative estimation techniques utilizing global monitoring and modeling of atmospheric chemistry and biogeochemical cycles (Bolin and Cook 1983). The carbon cycle has been extensively investigated (Trabalka 1985; Bjutner 1986) in terms of the reservoirs in the ocean (marine biota, inorganic carbon, particulate and dissolved organic matter, and carbonate sediments), on land (terrestrial biota, organic carbon, and fossil fuels), and in the atmosphere, as well as in the exchanges between them. Uncertainty still exists, however, over the contributions of fossil fuel combustion, deforestation, agricultural expansion to CO_2 emissions, and their changes over historical time. Current estimates of total fossil fuel release (1860–1982) and net carbon flux from the land biosphere (1860–1980) are $150–190 \times 10^{15}$ g carbon and $90–180 \times 10^{15}$ g carbon, respectively. The recent airborne fraction of fossil fuels released may range between 0.5 and 0.8 (Solomon et al. 1985). Future trends, taking account of various energy scenarios, have also received much attention from geographers (J. Williams 1979; Budyko 1980; Jäger 1983). The geographical distribution of the estimated fossil fuel reserves, their type, and the likelihood of their exploitation are important aspects of these scenarios (Heede 1983).

Changes in other radiatively active trace species and their climatic roles are less well known (e.g., Karol' et al. 1983; Wang et al. 1986). Atmospheric methane is largely of biological origin, and important contributions to its increase appear to be caused by anthropogenic effects (microbial decomposition in rice paddies, enteric fermentation in cows, and biomass burning). Chlorofluorocarbons and many hydrocarbons are also of anthropogenic origin, the former as solvents, refrigerants, and spray-can propellants, the latter from industrial, domestic, and automobile combustion. NO_x, an important catalyst for reactions involving stratospheric ozone, is affected by fossil fuel combustion, including aircraft (Izrael' 1984).

The climatic effects of aerosols (Kondrat'yev 1976, 1980; Jaenicke 1981; Fejgel'son 1982; Tarasova and Fejgel'son 1982) are highly dependent on their physical properties (size distribution, optical cross section, and chemical composition), which vary widely in both natural and anthropogenically derived species. Climatic effects are also determined by their spatiotemporal distributions. These have received varying degrees of attention in terms of urban pollution by soots and sulphates, maritime aerosols (particularly sea salts), desert mineral dust, and Arctic haze. Urban pollution studies have been largely local, and extrapolation of results to global scales is problematic (Bach 1976; Bach et al. 1980). Model simulations of the type performed for global climatic effects of waste heat release by J. Williams et al. (1979) are needed (see Jäger 1983). Global climatic effects of aerosol loading have been studied principally in the context of nuclear war simulations (Stenchikov 1985). The radiative effects of naturally occurring aerosols have also been simulated, however, by Coakley and Cess (1985) and by Golitsyn and Ginsburg (1985). Arctic haze has now been extensively investigated with regard to its long-range transport from middle-latitude sources, its chemical composition (sulphates and elemental carbon), and its effects on the energy budget (Stonehouse 1986).

The response of climate to anthropogenically induced perturbations, especially those caused by increasing concentrations of greenhouse gases and aerosol effects such as Arctic haze, were topics specifically discussed at a recent meeting of American and Soviet experts on climate change (Budyko and MacCracken 1987). The group included geographers R. S. Bradley and H. F. Diaz, who have been prominent in recent research efforts to document the observational evidence for climatic changes on both short and long time scales (Bradley 1985; Bradley et al. 1985, 1987; Diaz 1986).

The understanding of contemporary landscape dynamics requires the collection of a broad complex of biospheric, topographic, oceanic, pedologic, hydrologic, and atmospheric variables. Some are currently measured routinely, while many others are only evaluated at special experimental sites or inferred from other data. One important contribution that geographers can make in the prosecution of the International Geosphere-Biosphere Program is to expand the data base of needed observations, especially in a form that can be easily adapted to global representation and analyses. The understanding and quantification of landscape dynamics processes must become a guiding principle for physical geographers involved in the IGBP.

3. TRANSFORMATIONS OF NATURE

I n the past two decades we have witnessed a major increase in academic and popular interest in land-use changes. Deforestation, desertification, and soil degradation are terms frequently heard, and increasingly used with alarm, because of their alleged relationships to biological diversity and species extinctions (Myers 1984; E. O. Wilson and Peter 1988), population growth and resource adequacy (United Nations Food and Agriculture Organization [UNFAO] 1979; Dregne 1983; Salati and Vose 1983; Berry 1985), climate change (Woodwell et al. 1983a; Bolin et al. 1986; W. W. Kellogg 1987; Parry et al. 1988), and famine and poverty (D. Johnson 1977; Spooner and Mann 1982; Glantz and Katz 1985; Gregory and Walling 1987; Douglas 1988). The actual relationships of these forms of land-use changes to humans and to the biosphere are rather poorly understood, however, particularly at the global scale.

Worldwide demands for energy and water resources are increasing rapidly. The vegetation component of the landscape is closely related to both local and regional energy and water budgets, so that transformations of the surface cover may significantly modify energy and material fluxes over vast areas. The concept of resource cycles can be introduced to aid our study of how changes introduced by human activity influence, for example, the reproduction of living matter, and hence the renewal of organic carbon in the geosphere.

Investigations of the structure and functioning of various landscape systems will provide increased understanding of local differences in the interaction between the atmosphere and the biosphere (especially local influences on the factors of heat and water exchanges). Furthermore, research on the role of turbulent energy exchange in the boundary layer also might make it possible to map the components of the local water budget and determine how they change with landscape type.

Deforestation, desertification, and soil degradation are complex forms of land-use changes taking place in time and space, and intimately interweaving human activity with the biosphere, geosphere, and climate. As such, they involve analysis, interpretation, and integration of data and theories at multiple spatial and temporal scales. Although there are many promising avenues for geographers to pursue in improving understanding of these issues, relatively few of the hypotheses suggested in the literature have been addressed by geographers thus far. This chapter examines not only human modifications of energy and material fluxes but also the processes of deforestation, desertification, and soil degradation with respect to the concepts and their definitions, an overview of key findings for each, and progress to date, including the state of empirical measurement of each process and theoretical models of the processes and their validation. The chapter highlights some promising areas for work by geographers that should contribute positively to understanding these global changes.

3.1 Human Impacts on Energy and Material Fluxes

Energy Flows

Natural processes are fueled largely by five energy factors: (1) solar and terrestrial radiation, (2) gravitation, (3) tectonic forces, (4) chemical energy (predominantly oxidation-reduction processes), and (5) biogenic energy (plant photosynthesis, chemosynthesis in bacteria, energy of food assimilation and oxidation in animals, biomass productivity, and respiration). With the increase in human population and activity, a sixth factor, anthropogenically produced energy, is becoming more important.

Our demands for energy have been doubling every fourteen to fifteen years (Ermakov and Uledov 1976; Darmstadter et al. 1977). By 1985, the annual production of primary energy required the equivalent of 10.3 billion tons of conventional fuel, divided as follows: coal, 30.3 percent; oil, 39.3 percent; natural gas, 19.7 percent; hydroelectric power, 6.8 percent; and atomic power, 3.9 percent. In addition, the equivalent of 1.7 billion tons of conventional fuel was produced from firewood, charcoal, and organic waste (mainly in developing countries). Based on one particular group of assumptions, a significant increase in the 1980 energy production has been forecast by the year 2000 (Landsberg 1979).

The volume of anthropogenic energy flows varies sharply with the type of economic activity. Society expends only about 10 percent of its total energy production on direct acquisition of biospheric products, whereas almost 90 percent is spent on maintaining and expanding the urban infrastructure, and mining and communications (V. G. Gorshkov 1981). Assuming that the extent of land area devoted to these intensive activities amounts to no more than 0.15–0.20 billion hectares, societal energy production on these areas is 350 to 500 times greater than on agricultural or forested land. Consequently, society's direct contribution to the total energy balance is about 150 MJ/m^2 per year, or 3–4 percent, and it is concentrated in a few areas such as cities.

Any estimate of the human-induced energy contribution also must include the indirect modification of the energy budget that results from humans' alterations of natural mechanisms. A poorly understood problem, for instance, is that of determining albedo fluctuations that result from temporal irregularities in the occurrence and melting of the snow cover. The seasonal snow cycle is sensitive to changes in atmospheric turbidity that result from natural (e.g., volcanic activity and natural fires) as well as anthropogenic pollution. Human-induced turbidity sources can be classified into three categories: (1) particulates and products of gas-to-particle conversions (especially sulfates) from cities, including those from industry and transportation; (2) organic volatiles and particulates from swamp and grass fires; and (3) mineral dust from denuded surfaces. Soot deposits in particular are known to lower the albedo of snow cover and thereby accelerate melting. Such pollution effects are apparent even in the Arctic.

Estimates of the contribution of different land-surface covers to heat losses through evapotranspiration reveal the important role played by moist tropical forests (Table 3.1). These are estimated to provide almost 30 percent of the terrestrial heat loss even though they occupy just 13 percent of the land. A much less significant role is played by cultivated fields—that is, they contribute only 12 percent of the terrestrial evapotranspiration while they cover 11 percent of the land. Removal of tropical forests followed by burning and cultivation, then, may lead to a reduction in regional evapotranspiration. This has been predicted to be followed by a change in atmospheric circulation to conditions similar to those found over arid lands and an increase in the heating of the surface layer.

Evapotranspiration estimates from different vegetation regions show considerable variability in the pattern of heat and moisture exchange between the biosphere and the atmosphere. Forests and deserts in particular act as energy-active zones emitting significant amounts of heat into the lower layers of the

Table 3.1 The contribution of various types of land surfaces to the global heat consumption for evaporation (according to Krenke and Zolotokrylin 1984).

Types of land	Area		Heat consumption for evaporation	Heat
	$10^6 km^2$	%	10^9 MW	%
Plowed fields	14.3	11	1.7	12
Meadows, pastures, steppes	30.6	23	2.8	20
Tropical moist forests	17.0	13	4.2	29
Deciduous summer-green forests	13.0	10	1.6	11
Taiga	12.0	9	1.2	8
Nonagricultural land	46.2	34	2.8	20

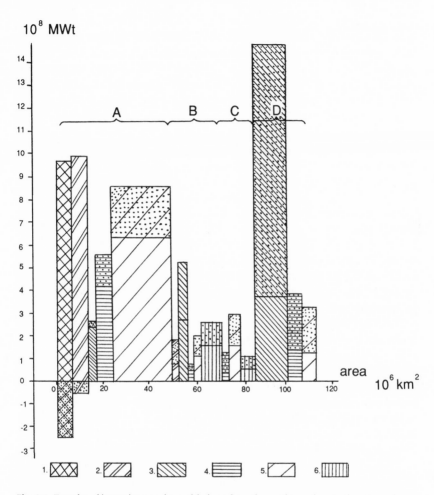

10^8 MWt

area 10^6 km^2

1. 2. 3. 4. 5. 6.

Fig. 3.1 Transfer of latent heat and sensible heat from the earth's surface to the atmosphere by vegetational and geographical belts. Geographical belts: A—forests; B—forest-steppe, savanas, forest-tundra; C—steppes, tundra; D—semidesert. 1—equatorial; 2—subequatorial; 3—tropical; 4—subtropical; 5—temperate; 6—subarctic. (From Krenke and Zolotokrylin, 1984)

atmosphere (Fig. 3.1). The principal zones of surface energy loss by evapotranspiration are the forests of the equatorial and subequatorial belts (A1, A2), while the tropical deserts and semideserts (D3) are largely responsible for energy loss through turbulent heat exchange with the atmosphere (Zolotokrylin 1986). Evaporative heat losses may exceed the rate of solar radiation influx over the moist forests. Horizontal advection provides a significant source of heat for evaporation in these regions. Annual evapotranspiration from different

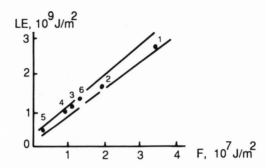

Fig. 3.2 Relation between transpiration (LE) and photosynthetic (F) (biologic production) heat losses in different vegetational zones. (1—tropical rain forests; 2—deciduous (summer-green) forests; 3—taiga; 4—meadows and steppes; 5—semi-deserts; 6—agricultural land)

vegetation formations appears to be related in a nearly linear fashion to the amount of annual precipitation (Figs. 3.2 and 3.3). Runoff ratios in the forest zones in different latitudinal belts vary only slightly.

These data show the importance of the vegetation component of landscape (particularly in forested areas) in water loss from land surfaces. Rainfall in forest landscapes accumulates in the vegetation and soil as if in a reservoir. Losses due to interception by the forest canopy and evaporation of intercepted water equal several millimeters a day. The typical time of water return to the atmosphere after interception by the forest canopy amounts to several hours, while the typical time of water return from the soil is approximately a month. In taiga areas, the snowpack in the forest may persist into early summer and greatly delay soil thawing (Rouse and Bello 1983). Evaporation from the soil surface in forests may average 10–20 percent of the total amount of water loss (Rauner 1972; Dunne and Leopold 1978). The remaining water reaches the atmosphere as a result of transpiration, which is controlled by the vegetation itself, and by the process of evaporation of intercepted water. These processes within the forest cover not only result in important thermophysical effects on the biosphere but also modify the water regimes of river basins (Krestovskiy 1986).

Evapotranspiration from a vegetated surface may be correlated with the rate of production of green phytomass resulting from photosynthesis. Equatorial and tropical forests are the most productive and transpire the greatest amounts of moisture. It should be recognized that natural changes in the terrestrial phytomass (and therefore in evapotranspiration) are characterized by a time period of one hundred years or more. This period is determined by the rate of tree growth and the formation of the whole plant community. Forest clearing and other human activities accelerate the process of green phytomass destruction in the different geographical zones. Further studies of the spatiotemporal variability of the heat balance over terrestrial surfaces will help to clarify the important role of landscape modification in climate change.

The effects of urbanization have not been considered here. Such effects do not yet influence the global scale, but the mesoscale effects are important both in terms of upward heat and water fluxes and in the amount of precipitation that occurs (Lipatov 1977).

Water Balance

Understanding the total water balance as well as its individual elements, including river flow, is of great importance in any analysis of the processes of water exchanges. Such investigations are largely based on water-balance relationships determined for typical landscape conditions (L'vovich 1945; Mather 1978; L'vovich and Belyaev 1982).

Investigations carried out during the International Hydrologic Decade (1965–1974) permitted scientists to expand existing knowledge of water-balance elements (including river flow) and evaluate freshwater resources by continent as well as over the whole globe (L'vovich 1974; Mather 1974, 1984). Published summaries reveal major discrepancies between global precipitation estimates that urgently need to be resolved (see Table 3.2). A next step in this work is to evaluate the different uses of water resources and obtain a quantitative description of the economic aspects of the water exchanges.

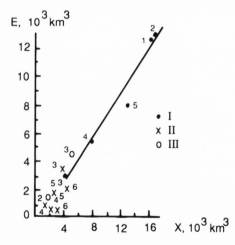

Fig. 3.3 Relation between annual precipitation (X) and evaporation (E) in different geographical zones of the earth. (1—tropical rain forests; 2—deciduous (summer-green) forests; 3—taiga; 4—meadows and steppes; 5—semideserts; 6—agricultural land. I—forests; II—steppes, forest-steppes, savannas, tundra, forest-tundra; III—semideserts)

Table 3.2 Global, terrestrial, and oceanic estimates of annual average precipitation (compiled from Mather 1969, 1974; UNESCO 1978; Jaeger 1983; and Kessler 1985; from Legates 1988).

Source	Year	Global (mm)	Terrestrial (mm)	Oceanic (mm)
Brückner	1905	940	819	994
Fritsche	1906	910	752	978
Wüst	1922	743	752	739
Kaminsky	1925	760	544	850
Brooks/Hunt	1930	975	665	1102
Cherubim	1931	880	752	925
Halbfass	1934	1000	671	1135
Meinardus	1934	1000	665	1141
Wüst	1936	780	665	822
Wundt	1938	880	665	958
L'vovich	1945	1020	719	1141
Möller	1951	832	665	897
Reichel	1952	810	671	872
Wüst	1954	830	671	897
Budyko	1956	930	671	1025
Mosby	1957	842	686	907
Albrecht	1960	940	671	1047
Knoch	1961	970	671	1097
Budyko	1963	1000	719	1119
World Atlas/Mira	1964	1020	725	1141
Strahler	1965	784	679	828
Kessler	1968	1000	671	1135
Nace	1968	820	671	883
L'vovich	1969	1020	732	1138
Mather	1969	955	712	1058
Baumgartner/Reichel	1970, 1972	950	671	1061
Budyko	1970	1020	719	1141
Marcinek	1973, 1976	931	670	1035
Baumgartner/Reichel	1975	973	746	1066
Manabe/Holloway	1975	1041	972	1077
Jaeger	1976, 1983	1000	756	1099
UNESCO	1978	1130	800	1270
Legates	1988	1123	820	1251

Table 3.3 River runoff control in water reservoirs, 1985 (L'vovich 1986; Avakyan et al. 1987).

	Number of reservoirs	Area ($\times 10^6$ ha)	Final volume (km^3)	Storage volume (km^3)	Ratio of storage to final volume (%)
Europe	517	90	616	330	54
Asia	577	121	1630	990	61
USSR	237	145	1170	575	49
Africa	105	35	885	530	60
North America	906	180	1810	1360	75
South America	179	60	511	310	61
Australia and Oceania	73	4	77	50	65
Earth as a whole	2360	470	5530	3480	63

Preliminary reports estimating the worldwide volume of water consumption and the quantity of effluent, or return flow (compared with available water resources), have been available for some time. Consideration of these early data has revealed the anthropogenic pressures (industrial, agricultural, power generation, etc.) that are limiting efforts to preserve and enhance water resources (Mather 1984). If unchecked, these pressures will eventually result in significant degradation of water quality. While this problem has been largely confined to economically developed countries, it will be only a short time before it touches literally all regions of the world.

Based on the early water-resources studies of the International Hydrologic Decade, indexes of water consumption for agriculture (irrigation and cattle breeding), industry, and power were developed for almost all countries of the world. Obviously, the variation in water consumption from country to country is quite large. Only a small portion of the earth's population has sufficient water for its needs (about 300–400 l daily per capita), while for 65 to 70 percent of the world's population, mainly on the African and Asian continents, water withdrawal is considerably less.

Globally, at present, annual water use for all needs constitutes about 10 percent of the volume of river flow. River flow, however, has two components—underground and surface flow—that differ from one another not only in kind but also in their economic roles. Underground flow to rivers is the most permanent and unchanging; thus it has greater economic importance. Surface flow (overland flow) requires some form of preliminary management (e.g., storage ponds) to make it a more viable resource (Table 3.3). Differences between surface and underground flows and their management significantly

Table 3.4 Characteristics of river runoffs, by continents.

	Natural stable runoff (subsurface) (km³ yr⁻¹)	Contemporary stable runoff (including controlled runoff) (km³ yr⁻¹)	Stable runoff increment (%)
Europe	1060	1406	33
Asia	3410	4310	26
USSR	1020	1580	55
Africa	1460	2000	37
North America	1490	2850	91
South America	3990	4300	8
Australia and Oceania	465	515	11
Earth as a whole	11,900	15,000	26

Source: L'vovich and White, in *Earth Transformed by Human Action*, B. L. Turner (ed.), Cambridge University Press, in press. (Reprinted with permission of Cambridge University Press.)

affect the global water balance (Table 3.4). It should be remembered that world water withdrawals are comparable to only about one-third of all underground flow. Changes in water flow may influence the sea-ice regime on a more limited scale (Krenke 1980).

Available data on the use of local river-flow resources (i.e., considering only those rivers formed within a given country's boundaries) are mapped in Figures 3.4 and 3.5, which show that economic needs require the use of 17, 16, and 11 percent, respectively, of total river flow in Asia, Europe, and North America. This is equivalent to 65, 46, and 38 percent of the underground flow in each case.

Quantitative studies allow us to evaluate the present condition of water resources (Fig. 3.6) and to consider changes over time as well (Losev 1988). Natural variability of runoff is one aspect of this question. Klige (1985) examined mean annual runoff on a subcontinental scale over the globe for three intervals between 1918 and 1956 and showed large-scale fluctuations of about ±5 percent from the long-term mean in most cases, with up to ±20 percent in a few instances. Most important, however, some information on the state of use and conservation of water resources through the middle of the twenty-first century can be deduced. One such future scenario suggests the continuation of current activities to conserve water resources and even suggests an increase in the effectiveness of methods to treat sewage effluent (L'vovich and Koronkevich 1974; L'vovich 1986).

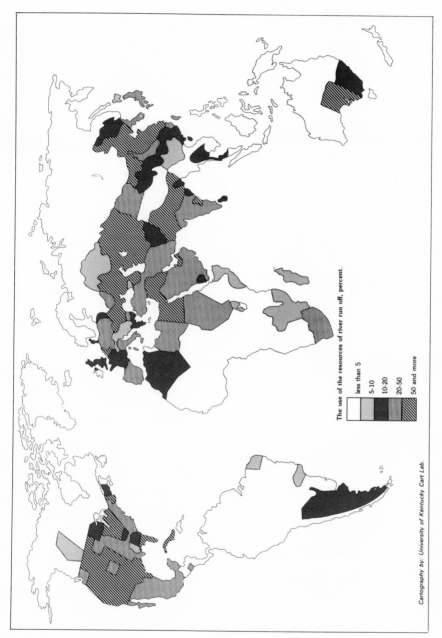

The use of the resources of river run off, percent.

less than 5
5-10
10-20
20-50
50 and more

Cartography by: University of Kentucky Cart Lab.

Fig. 3.4 Use of stream flow for economic needs. (Compiled by A. V. Balyaev)

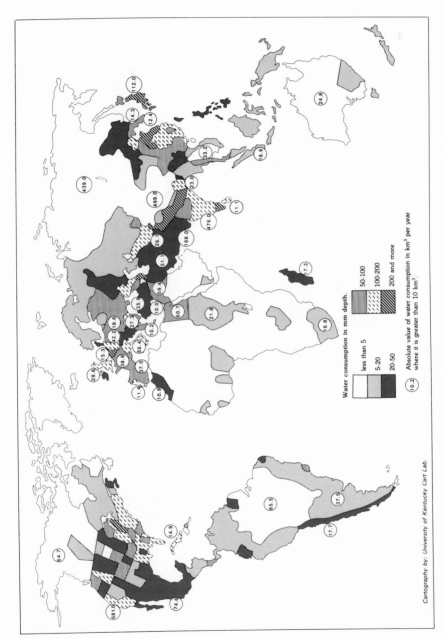

Water consumption in mm depth.

less than 5	50-100
5-20	100-200
20-50	200 and more

⑩ Absolute value of water consumption in km³ per year where it is greater than 10 km³.

Cartography by: University of Kentucky Cart Lab.

Fig. 3.5 Total water consumption by regions and countries.

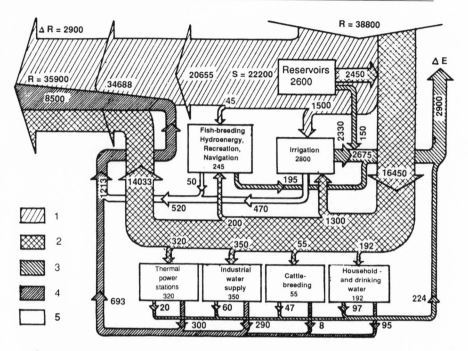

Fig. 3.6 Water circulation scheme for the earth's surface subject to artificial runoff regulation and economic water consumption. (1) Surface runoff, (2) Base flow, (3) Evaporation, (4) Sewage water and polluted river flow, (5) Return flow after irrigation. R = Total river runoff. (From L'vovich 1986)

Resource Cycles

Biogeochemical cycles have been studied by American and Soviet investigators (Vernadsky 1967, 1987; Perel'man 1972; Romankevich 1977; Ryabchikov 1980) and by many others as well. One of the most successful efforts was carried out under the auspices of the Scientific Committee on Problems of the Environment (SCOPE), and it involved the international cooperation of representatives from different countries (SCOPE 1975, 1979; Bolin and Cook 1983). Indexes characterizing some of the more important components of the geosphere are summarized in Table 3.5 (S. P. Gorshkov et al. 1980).

Organic carbon, which plays an important role in nearly all earth systems, is justifiably a focus of study. This most "vulnerable" biogeochemical cycle is closely connected with all other elemental cycles and combinations. Change introduced by human activity influences, in various ways, the reproduction of living matter, and hence the renewal of all organic carbon in the geosphere.

Table 3.5 Fluxes in the contemporary cycles of some of the more important components of the geosphere (million tons/year).

Indexes	C_{org}	N	P	Fe	S	Pb	Cd	Oil	Pesticides
Natural supply to earth's surface:									
from earth's crust	100	0.2^x	20	10	930	0.2	0.002	0.6	no
from the amosphere	—	47.6^x	—	—	—	—	—	—	—
involved in the biological cycle	86,300	1400	340	240	50	0.2	xx	xxx	xxx
anthropogenic release to the environment	6000	240^x	50	70	250	3	0.02	51	5

x = Compounds of nitrogen calculated against elementary nitrogen.
xx = Negligible quantities are involved.
xxx = When present in nutrients, it is utilized by organisms in particular food chains.

The chlorine-carbon branch of the carbon cycle has not been discussed much until recently. Leakage of artificial chloro-organic compounds into the atmosphere has resulted in their increased concentration in the troposphere (up to 3.5 ppb). While the contribution of chloro-organic compounds to the total carbon content of the atmosphere is still negligible, it poses a threat to the biosphere.

Modification of the sulfur and nitrogen cycles has resulted in the emission of their oxides and the regional spread of acid precipitation (Volkov et al. 1983). To a considerable extent this has been associated with changes in the carbon cycle, largely through the increased use of fossil fuel. Special consideration also should be given to the question of "ferrigination" of the earth's surface, since several billion tons of iron have been added during the last 150 years. A significant amount of lead and cadmium has also been added by human activities.

Releases of oil, oil products, and natural gas into the biogeochemical system create special problems. About 50 million tons of oil and oil products are lost annually in the process of extraction, transportation, processing, and use. Of this total, 25 million tons are deposited on land, 8 million tons in the oceans, and 17 million tons into the atmosphere. Of the oil products lost on land, about 8 million tons are carried by surface flow to the ocean, while the atmosphere acquires an additional 6 million tons by means of evaporation. Thus, up to 16 million tons of oil (in various forms) ends up in the oceans and as much as 23 million tons of hydrocarbons appears as vapor and gas in the atmosphere. Compared with the volume of oil that naturally moves into the ocean through crustal fractures, which may not exceed 0.5 million tons per year (Yermakov and Ryabchikov 1980), these figures are very large.

The anthropogenic material cycle is characterized by the presence of substances which either do not occur in nature (e.g., artificial radioisotopes, synthetic detergents, plastic materials, and pesticides) or are found in insignificant concentrations (e.g., mercury, chlorine, and fluorine). Such elements as gold, carbon, nitrogen, and helium, as well as many heavy metals, are considered the most technogenic (i.e., they are the elements most intensively involved in the anthropogenic cycle of materials in relation to their natural abundance; see Glazovsky 1975, 1982, 1987).

In their efforts to characterize regional differences in the geochemical effect, the Soviets have derived regional summary coefficients of the biospheric concentration (i.e., the ratio of the element content in industrial products to the mean content in the biosphere) for various industrial products by regions. Values of these regional coefficients can be used to generalize the geochemical effects of different industrial products (Fig. 3.7; see Glazovsky 1985). Further regionalization has been possible within the boundaries of large-scale economic regions on the basis of population density because the technogenic inflow is roughly proportional to the population density (Fig. 3.8).

Analysis of the transfer of technogenic products into the atmosphere further allows a determination of how the geochemical situation varies among different regions. Regions of convergence—that is, regions which accumulate or "draw together" element migration flows—are especially vulnerable.

Ideas concerning energy production cycles (Kolosovsky 1958) and biogeochemical cycles (Vernadsky 1987) allowed I. V. Komar to develop his concept of resource cycles. A *resource cycle* is a "set of transformations and spatial movements of a certain material or group of materials occurring at all stages of its use by society (including its location, preparation for use, extraction from natural surroundings, processing, consumption, return into nature) within the framework of a social element of the general cycle of a given material or materials on the earth" (Komar 1975, 75).

Resource cycles can be identified and analyzed at several scales (e.g., global, regional, and local). Study of their correlation with one another can help in analyzing characteristic space-time discontinuities. Analysis of resource cycles traditionally has focused on towns and urban agglomerations, where the concentration of activity is responsible for maximizing anthropogenic effects on natural systems (Bochkareva 1987, 1988). A similar concept of "resource-export cycles" has been suggested to analyze the problems of developing countries (Mashbits 1974). By analogy, one can also speak of "resource-import cycles." These concepts and their possible modifications might be utilized in investigations of anthropogenic effects within the IGBP framework.

Regional structures of the different resource cycles are mainly determined by social-historical development together with social-cultural and demo-

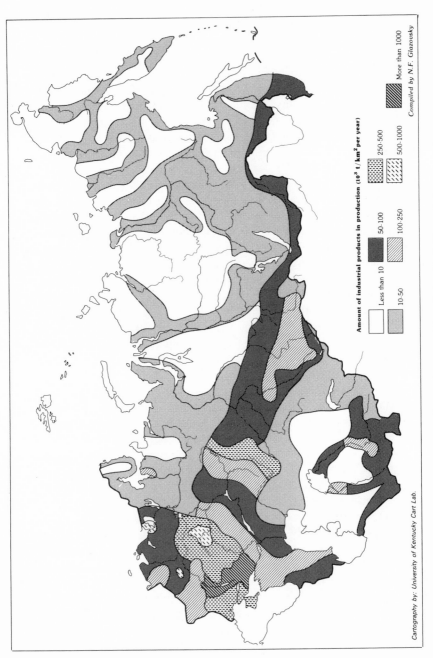

Cartography by: University of Kentucky Cart Lab.

Compiled by N.F. Glazovsky

Amount of industrial products in production (10³ t./km² per year)

| Less than 10 | 50-100 | 250-500 | More than 1000 |
| 10-50 | 100-250 | 500-1000 |

Fig. 3.7 Geographic spreading of technogenic geochemical sources. (Compiled by N. F. Glazovsky)

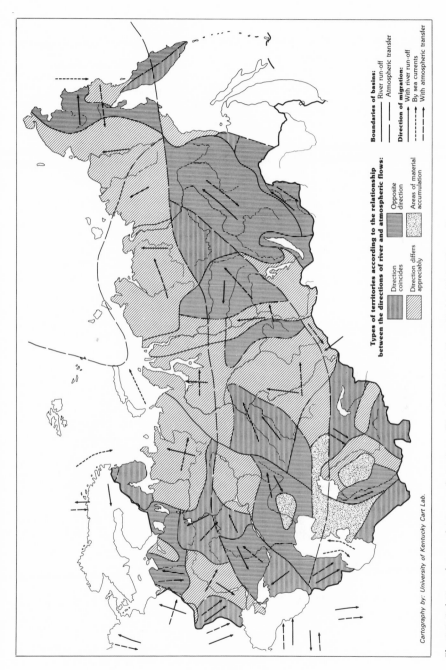

Boundaries of basins:

— River run-off
▬ Atmospheric transfer

Direction of migration:

⟶ With river run-off
- - → By sea currents
·····→ With atmospheric transfer

Types of territories according to the relationship between the directions of river and atmospheric flows:

▨ Direction coincides
▨ Opposite direction
▨ Direction differs appreciably
⬚ Areas of material accumulation.

Cartography by: University of Kentucky Cart Lab.

Fig. 3.8 Relation of atmospheric transfer and runoff in river basins. (Compiled by N. F. Glazovsky)

graphic processes. The concept of resource-export and resource-import cycles additionally allows analysis of the formation and change of national and international resource cycles.

Technology has a critical effect on the space-time dynamics of resource cycles as well as on the processes of social-historical development. The character of usable power and the possibility of its space-time concentration are decisive in the development of particular technologies. Current techniques and procedures for the use of oil and natural gas, and to a lesser degree carbon, form the modern "picture" of regional resource cycles as well as the peculiarities of their effects on natural systems. Increased understanding of the negative consequences of these processes contributes to the conflict between technological and ecological values. As a result, restrictions have been imposed on many economic activities, and the development of new ecocongruent technologies has been encouraged—along with efforts to understand possible consequences of their application. Analysis of the consequences of economic activity along with estimation of the risks of making uninformed decisions are prerequisites for control of negative ecological outcomes.

3.2 Human Impacts on Deforestation, Desertification, and Soil Degradation

Concepts and Definitions

Although apparently not recent phenomena, deforestation, desertification, and soil degradation are terms that have come into use in the mid to late twentieth century, often with vague and somewhat controversial definitions. In early comprehensive studies of historical land-use changes, Marsh (in Lowenthal 1965) and Thomas (1956) described processes of deforestation and soil degradation associated with human activity since pre-Christian times (see also Bondarev 1987; Khrisanova 1987). In contrast, Stebbing (1935) and Aubreville (1949) first applied the term *desertification* to describe a process observed in Africa in the 1930s. The term *soil degradation* has been used to describe the decline in soil productivity of ancient civilizations, and also was widely used in the 1930s to describe a range of processes associated with the Dust Bowl in the United States (C. E. Kellogg 1938; USDA 1938; Carter and Dale 1974). Thus, from their inception, all three terms have been applied to processes whose causes were not clearly enunciated and may possibly have been interpreted incorrectly.

While deforestation and soil degradation can be clearly linked to human modification of the land in order to increase food production (C. E. Kellogg 1938; Carter and Dale 1974; J. C. Allen and Barnes 1985), desertification refers to a process which, despite controversy, cannot be attributed solely either to humans or to climate (United Nations Conference on Desertification

[UNCOD] 1977a, 1977b; Babaev et al. 1985). Verstraete (1986) suggests that, in its early uses, the term probably was used to describe the effects of the 1910–1920 drought in Africa. Desertification has been used to imply a steady shift in isohyets over a large area—the "spreading deserts" idea (Winstanley 1976)—but no convincing proof of this process as distinct from drought persistence (e.g., P. J. Lamb 1982) has been produced (Dregne and Tucker 1988; A. Warren and Agnew 1988). Instead, many studies do confirm the existence of land degradation (loss of vegetation, soil erosion) concentrated in patches outside desert margins (Mabbutt and Floret 1980; Rapp 1986; A. Warren and Agnew 1988). However, other studies in semiarid and arid regions of Africa and the United States describe decreases in land productivity due to a decline in grasses and the invasion of thorny shrubs and succulents (Schantz and Turner 1958; Ludwig and Whitford 1981; Whitford et al. 1981).

Soil degradation refers to a wide variety of processes that reduce soil productivity, including leaching of nutrients, acidification, erosion, loss of organic matter by accelerated decomposition, and salinization (UNFAO 1979, 1980). These processes are also natural soil-forming processes, so the determination of degradation is a matter of degree. The best approach seems to be to define degradation as occurring when the process in question (e.g., erosion) exceeds some threshold level below which the soil remains at a steady state, called the tolerance level (Ross-Wight and Siddoway 1982; Skidmore 1982). For erosion, the threshold level is defined as the rate of soil formation (Alexander 1985). The implication of tolerance levels is that a nondegraded soil should have a more or less unchanging soil profile morphology (the type and arrangement of soil horizons). Thus, soil degradation by erosion can be easily identified by monitoring the depth and appearance of soil profiles over a period of time (Logan 1982; McCormack et al. 1982). Identifying significant changes in soil organic matter content, acidity, or leaching rates is a more difficult proposition. Soil salinization refers to salinity changes induced by artificial irrigation (UNCOD 1977a; Kovda 1984). However, areas that require irrigation have a natural tendency for an excess of evapotranspiration over rainfall, leading to the accumulation of salts in surface horizons. Furthermore, most irrigated soils in arid zones are formerly alkaline or saline soils that were reclaimed by drainage before they were cultivated (Brady 1984; Buringh 1986). Salinization has recently been redefined as a form of desertification (UNCOD 1977a).

Although they are widely used terms, deforestation, desertification, and soil degradation are not well defined in the literature, and they often refer to the same processes. Deforestation, which generally is interpreted as the loss of forest cover, can refer to such diverse transformations as impoverishment of a forest with regard to species without a change in its physical structure (e.g., Myers 1980, 1984), or to the complete clearance of forest and its conversion to another form of land use (e.g., UNFAO, *Production Yearbooks 1966–1988*; Persson 1974; Sommer 1976; Lanly 1982; Lanly and Clement 1982). Similarly, desertification is defined as natural fluctuations in climate (El-Baz 1983), human-induced changes in vegetation (Dregne 1984), or a combination of the two interacting with one another (Le Houerou 1976; Reining 1978). To add to the confusion, both terms have been applied to describe vegetation changes in ecosystems ranging from closed-canopy rain forest (Goodland and Irwin 1975; Glantz and Orlovsky 1983) to desert margins (Bovill 1921; Aubreville 1949; Dregne 1983), or even to desert interiors (Meckelein 1980). Soil degradation usually accompanies deforestation and desertification, and often a decline in soil productivity is the long-term undesirable impact of these other processes (Blaikie 1985; Blaikie and Brookfield 1987).

For the purposes of this study, deforestation and desertification are considered to be processes that result in a decline in actively photosynthesizing vegetation; and they, in turn, are associated with soil degradation or hydrologic and edaphic changes which reduce the capacity of land to be productive and to support human populations. Such a decline in vegetation in wet areas is referred to as deforestation, and in dry areas as desertification. Any changes that adversely affect soil productivity for supporting human populations are included as soil degradation.

Impacts on Deforestation

Deforestation was defined above as a process resulting in a decrease in photosynthesizing vegetation; namely, forests, especially in humid to sub-humid climates. It is of concern because it has a direct impact on the global radiation budget via the conversion of stored carbon to atmospheric carbon (Woodwell et al. 1978, 1983a; Houghton and Woodwell 1981; Houghton et al. 1983), and also because it has obvious effects on local and regional hydrology (Pereira 1973; Gentry and Lopez-Parodi 1980; Bosch and Hewlett 1982), climate (Potter et al. 1975), and soils (Raich 1983; J. C. Allen 1985).

With the emergence of humans on earth, the evolution of the biosphere entered a new stage of development. Forest ecosystems were among the first components of the biosphere to be exposed to anthropogenic impact. Ancient tribes and communities periodically set forests on fire when they hunted (Thomas 1956; Lowenthal 1965). In the Neolithic age, during the transition to an agrarian economy, forests were burned to create fields and pastures (Darby 1956). With the advent of the axe came a new type of forest destruction: trees were felled and shrubs were cut, while agriculturalists practicing shifting cultivation combined fire and cultivation. Industry and motorized transportation subsequently required wood as a fuel and raw material, and logging and road building had major impacts on forest landscapes.

Historical evidence suggests the early creation of a forest-field mosaic in the temperate zones of Europe and Asia (Darby 1956; R. P. Tucker and Richards

1983), followed by intermittent clearing and creation of forest-field mosaics toward the poles and the equator (Malaisse 1978). The spatial variability of forest-field mosaic landscapes is further increased by reforestation and regeneration in formerly cleared areas in boreal, steppe, and some small desert areas. Paleoecological evidence suggests that anthropogenic impacts have combined with climate changes to cause the disappearance of forests in Amazonia, the southwestern United States, Australia, and Africa (Livingstone and Van der Hammen 1978; G. Hope 1984; Liu and Colinvaux 1985; Kershaw 1986; Mac-Donald and Ritchie 1986; Spaulding and Graumlich 1986).

In the early stages of development of human society, so far as we can determine, human-induced deforestation was more than compensated for by natural regeneration. At some point, however, probably in the late 1800s, the global rate of deforestation surpassed the rates of regeneration and reforestation (J. F. Richards and Tucker 1985). As of 1989, most temperate industrialized countries are experiencing either no change in forest area or positive rates of reforestation, whereas most tropical developing countries are experiencing net deforestation as they pursue economic development (UNFAO, *Production Yearbooks 1966–1988*).

The term *deforestation* appeared in the world scientific literature only in the last few decades, but it is now as widely used as the terms *desertification* or *soil degradation*. However, there are many disagreements about the definition of the term, and these partially account for the substantial differences among estimates of deforestation rates (J. C. Allen and Barnes 1985; Melillo et al. 1985). As the definition of the physical structure of the forest undergoing transformation is broadened from "primary" forest (Myers 1980) to "forest-land" (UNFAO, *Production Yearbooks 1966–1988*), the estimates of deforestation decrease. For example, Myers (1980) includes as deforestation any transformation of forested landscapes considered to have been "primary." His estimates of deforestation rates as of 1980 are $16–27 \times 10^6$ ha yr^{-1} in the tropics, of which clearing for agriculture accounts for $10–20 \times 10^6$ ha yr^{-1}, pastures account for $1.35–2.0 \times 10^6$ ha yr^{-1}, and logging accounts for $1.7–2.9 \times 10^6$ ha yr^{-1}; these are among the highest published rates (J. C. Allen and Barnes 1985; Melillo et al. 1985). Moderate rates are reported by Lanly (1982) and Lanly and Clement (1982). In these studies, only those areas where trees cannot reappear are considered deforested; deforestation rates (11×10^6 ha yr^{-1} for tropical Africa, Asia, and Latin America) are calculated as changes in the cover of closed-canopy forest only. The lowest rates of deforestation (6.9×10^6 ha yr^{-1} in the tropics) are reported by the UNFAO *Production Yearbooks*, in which deforestation is the net loss of "forestland," which includes closed forests and other woody formations such as woodland, and even may include areas of shifting cultivation or agroforestry where some tree canopy and grass cover are present. UNFAO data also may be somewhat inaccu-

Table 3.6 Changes in forestland, by continents and regions, 1974–1983.

	Area of forestland (1000 ha)		Increase/decrease of forestland
	1974	1983	average annual percent
Australia	137,700	106,000	−2.6
Central America	77,999	69,892	−1.15
North America	116,771	591,317	−0.46
South America	967,010	928,643	−0.44
Africa	715,535	688,366	−0.42
Europe	152,920	155,292	+0.18
Asia	547,742	561,445	+0.28
Oceania	44,465	47,489	+0.8
Global average	4,180,192	4,068,444	−0.3

Source: UNFAO, *Production Yearbook*, 1984.

rate because they are official estimates of national governments, which may ignore the present condition of areas originally designated as forests (J. C. Allen and Barnes 1985).

Even the UNFAO *Production Yearbooks'* recent data (1974–1983) emphasize the continued net rate of global deforestation (Table 3.6, Fig. 3.9). Forestland has increased in nearly all European countries except the Netherlands, Austria, and France. In Asia, the apparent net increase in forest area is due to reforestation in the People's Republic of China and Vietnam, reported at 1.86 percent and 2.7 percent annually. However, over the same period, Thailand, the Philippines, Lebanon, and Malaysia experienced losses of forestland of 2.2, 1.3, 1.4, and 1.0 percent annually (UNFAO 1974, 1984). Forestland was reported to be declining at even higher rates in Costa Rica. High rates of deforestation also occurred over the period 1974–1983 in Ivory Coast, Gambia, Niger, and Nigeria (4.0, 2.3, 1.8, and 1.8 percent annual losses). Deforestation rates calculated from UNFAO *Production Yearbooks* data must be regarded with caution, as they were not intended for this purpose, and they differ greatly with rates reported from other sources. For example, the data in Table 3.7 show that continental rates of deforestation in Africa, Latin America, and Asia from 1968 to 1978 varied between 0.2 and 2.5 percent annual loss, depending on the continent and source. At the country level—in Brazil, for example—estimates of deforestation may differ by an order of magnitude (Fearnside 1982; C. J. Tucker et al. 1984; Malingreau and Tucker 1988; Booth 1989). Such

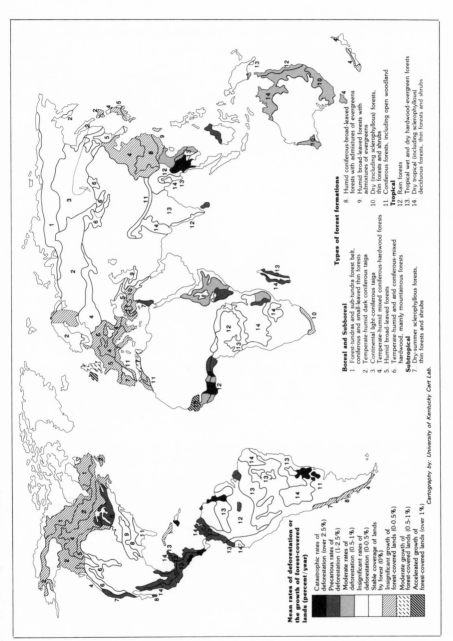

Mean rates of deforestation or the growth of the growth of forest-covered lands (percent/year)

Catastrophic rates of deforestation (over 2.5%)

Precarious rates of deforestation (1-2.5%)

Moderate rates of deforestation (0.5-1%)

Insignificant rates of deforestation (0-0.5%)

Stable coverage of lands by forest (0%)

Insignificant growth of forest-covered lands (0-0.5%)

Moderate growth of forest-covered lands (0.5-1%)

Accelerated growth of forest-covered lands (over 1%)

Types of forest formations

Boreal and Subboreal
1. Forest-tundras and sub-tundra forest belt, coniferous and small-leaved thin forests
2. Temperate-humid dark coniferous taiga
3. Continental light-coniferous taiga
4. Temperate-humid mixed coniferous-hardwood forests
5. Humid broad-leaved forests
6. Temperate-humid and arid coniferous-mixed hardwood, mainly mountainous forests

Subtropical
7. Dry-summer sclerophyllous forests, thin forests and shrubs

8. Humid coniferous-broad-leaved forests with admixtures of evergreens
9. Humid broad-leaved forests with admixtures of evergreens
10. Dry (including sclerophyllous) forests, thin forests and shrubs
11. Coniferous forests, including open woodland

Tropical
12. Rain forests
13. Tropical wet and dry hardwood-evergreen forests
14. Dry tropical (including sclerophyllous) deciduous forests, thin forests and shrubs

Cartography by: University of Kentucky Cart Lab.

Fig. 3.9 World forests and their rate of change, 1974–1984. (Compiled by B. A. Alekseev and A. V. Vasilieva)

Table 3.7 Deforestation by country, according to three different sources.

Country	(1) UNFAO Yearbook (1980a) Rank	Annual change[a] (%)	(2) UNFAO/UNEP (1982a, 1982b, 1982c) Rank	Annual change[b] (%)[b]	(3) Myers (1980) Rank	Annual change[c] (%)
Ivory Coast	1	− 3.70	1	− 5.40	1	− 5.3
Haiti	2	− 3.10	4	− 3.20	—	—
Togo	3	− 2.40	27	− 0.64	—	—
Philippines	4	− 2.20	22	− 1.02	8.5	− 1.25
Swaziland	5	− 1.90	—	—	—	—
Sri Lanka	6	− 1.80	18	− 1.89	5	− 1.8
Liberia	7	− 1.66	14	− 1.89	6	− 1.4
Niger	8	− 1.61	—	—	—	—
Upper Volta	9	− 1.56	—	—	—	—
Rwanda	10	− 1.46	10	− 2.13	—	—
Brunei	11	− 1.40	12	− 1.99	—	—
Ecuador	12	− 1.14	13	− 1.94	—	—
Somalia	13	− 0.94	32	− 0.22	—	—
Congo	14	− 0.90	36	− 0.10	—	—
Mexico	15	− 0.78	20	1.09	—	—
Malaysia	16	− 0.75	21	− 1.05	7	− 1.3
Thailand	17	− 0.54	6	− 3.15	2	− 4.3

[a]Average annual percentage change in forests and woodland over the period 1968–1978, using 1968 as a base year. Only complete removal of forest cover is measured. Forest and woodland refer to land under natural or planted stands of trees, whether productive or not, and includes land from which forests have been cleared but that will be reforested in the foreseeable future. Forests and woodland are not defined consistently in actual measurement practice by all countries or over all years.

[b]Average annual percentage change in natural woody vegetation in the form of closed broad-leaf, coniferous, or bamboo forest over the period 1976–1980. Excludes forest plantations. Only complete removal of forest cover is measured. Includes tropical countries only.

[c]Average annual percentage change in tropical moist forest over various periods. Includes all types of forest conversion, including logging. Tropical moist forest includes evergreen or partly evergreen forests, with or without some deciduous trees, but never completely leafless, up to 1200 m; forest savanna mosaic where forests are not confined to streamsides; and coastal savanna mosaic. According to the UNFAO Committee of Forest Development in the Tropics, interpretation of the term *tropical moist forest* should be left to individual countries. Conversion of tropical moist forest can range from marginal modification to fundamental transformation. Where Myers has no reliable figure for total forest area, UNFAO/UNEP estimates of closed forest or natural woody vegetation were used as a base to calculate deforestation rates.

[d]Average of deforestation rates rated by 1980 forest area of each country. This is a measure of average annual deforestation in each continent.

[e]Unweighted average of deforestation rates. This is an indication of the amount of disagreement among sources by continent.

Source: Allen and Barnes 1985. Reproduced with the permission of the Association of American Geographers.

Table 3.7 (Continued)

Country	(1) UNFAO Yearbook (1980a) Rank	(1) UNFAO Yearbook (1980a) Annual change[a] (%)	(2) UNFAO/UNEP (1982a, 1982b, 1982c) Rank	(2) UNFAO/UNEP (1982a, 1982b, 1982c) Annual change[b] (%)[b]	(3) Myers (1980) Rank	(3) Myers (1980) Annual change[c] (%)
Afghanistan	18	−0.50	—	—	—	—
Vietnam	19	−0.46	25	−0.71	—	—
Bolivia	20	−0.44	34	−0.14	—	—
Yemen PDR	21	−0.39	—	—	—	—
Costa Rica	22	−0.38	5	−3.19	—	—
Sierra Leone	23	−0.36	24	−0.75	—	—
Belize	24	−0.34	26	−0.65	—	—
Surinam	25	−0.34	37	−0.02	—	−0.3
Brazil	26	−0.24	29	−0.40	11	−0.3
Zaire	27	−0.23	33	−0.15	—	−1.2
Indonesia	28	−0.11	28	−0.47	8.5	−1.2
Nepal	29	−0.11	2	−3.68	—	—
Argentina	30	−0.09	—	—	—	—
Zambia	31	−0.08	19	−1.26	—	—
Paraguay	32	−0.08	3	−3.39	—	—
South Korea	33	−0.08	—	—	—	—
Bangladesh	34	−0.06	23	−0.83	10	−0.8
Jamaica	35	−0.01	11	−2.05	—	—
Madagascar	36	0.00	17	−1.50	4	−2.2
Benin	37	0.00	7.5	−2.83	—	—
Botswana	38	0.04	—	—	—	—
Kenya	39	0.05	16	−1.62	3	2.6
Uruguay	40	0.56	—	—	—	—
Ethiopia	41	0.68	31	−0.23	—	—
El Salvador	42	0.69	7.5	−2.83	—	—
India	43	0.40	30	−0.28	—	—
Guinea	44	0.50	15	−1.64	—	—
China	45	0.60	—	—	—	—
Burundi	46	1.60	9	−0.24	—	—
Cuba	47	2.83	35	−0.13	—	—
Weighted average[d]						
All countries	—	−0.25	—	−0.54	—	−0.8
Africa	1	−0.51	3	−0.47	2	−1.4
Latin America	2	−0.29	2	−0.51	3	−0.3
Asia	3	0.05	1	−0.66	1	−1.5
Unweighted average[e]						
All countries	—	−0.53	—	−1.52	—	−2.0
Africa	1	−0.77	2	−1.52	1	−2.5
Latin America	2	−0.62	3	−1.46	3	−0.3
Asia	3	−0.21	1	−1.59	2	−1.8

variation among estimates of deforestation rates increases the errors in derivative estimates of carbon release and other fluxes relevant to global change.

Deforestation may influence global change by other processes more important than changes in the physical structure of forests. Forests may be subtly but importantly altered by acid precipitation, environmental pollution, and changes in soils and local or regional climate (Pielou 1988). In turn, forests may modify biological diversity (Myers 1988; Raven 1988; E. O. Wilson 1988), hydrology (Lettau et al. 1979; Gentry and Lopez-Parodi 1980; Salati and Vose 1984; Sioli 1985), nutrient cycling (Herrera et al. 1981), carbon cycling (Wong 1978; Houghton and Woodwell 1981; Woodwell et al. 1983a), soils (N. J. H. Smith 1981; J. C. Allen 1985), climate (Bryson 1974; Sagan et al. 1979; Dickinson 1980), and landscape patterns.

Determination of these influences requires a better understanding than is currently available of the geographical variability of forests and their ecological processes. There is extreme variability among forest ecosystems with respect to net primary production, photosynthesis, and elemental cycling (Kozlowski 1978; Likens et al. 1981). Nevertheless, because of their large leaf area and the production of woody tissue, all forests can absorb solar energy and CO_2 in larger quantities and store larger amounts of biomass than other plant communities (Whittaker and Likens 1973). Forests occupy only one-third of the land surface, but they produce two-thirds of the dry matter (Lieth 1975). The large biomass per unit area of forest ecosystems means that the processes of energy, water, and elemental cycling associated with growth and decay are strongly self-reinforcing (UNFAO 1962; Likens et al. 1981). Thus deforestation results in a direct loss of organic matter storage, a direct loss of CO_2 uptake by vegetation, and a wide range of changes in energy, water, and nutrient cycles. At present, it appears that the losses of carbon can only be offset by reforestation (Marland 1988).

There is no doubt that the destruction of forest vegetation affects global biogeochemical cycles of the major biogenic elements, and must therefore affect the chemical composition of the atmosphere (Houghton et al. 1983; Woodwell et al. 1983a; Lockwood 1987). Indirect evidence in support of this hypothesis has recently been provided by C. J. Tucker et al. (1986) and developed by Goward et al. (1987) and Goward (1989a), who have shown a correlation between seasonal variations in photosynthetically active radiation (PAR; computed from satellite imagery) and atmospheric CO_2. Houghton et al. (1983) and Woodwell et al. (1983a) estimate that about 25 percent of the carbon flux to the atmosphere is from deforestation, while other sources (Seiler and Crutzen 1980; Rotty 1986; Dale 1989) generally agree that deforestation accounts for 10–50 percent of the carbon flux to the atmosphere from fossil fuels. Uncertain rates of deforestation and spatial variation in biomass are the major causes of the differences in such estimates (Dale 1989).

Forest clearing leads to marked changes in climatic conditions on local, regional, and perhaps global scales. These changes in climate are brought about through effects on components of the radiation and water budgets. A major hypothesis has linked forest clearing to increases in surface reflectance, or albedo (Sagan et al. 1979; Henderson-Sellers and Hughes 1982; Mintz 1982), and thence to surface temperature changes that could influence precipitation (Charney et al. 1975, 1977). However, attempts to link albedo changes to regional or global climate circulation models (GCMs) have so far failed to confirm the global importance of changes in albedo. In a study using the Goddard Institute for Space Studies (GISS) GCM of Hansen et al. (1983), Henderson-Sellers and Gornitz (1984) found that although they may have large effects on local precipitation, albedo changes associated with a deforestation of 4.9 million km^2 in the Brazilian Amazon will have little or no effect on regional or global climate.

Both models and empirical studies do suggest that an increase in albedo associated with deforestation in a wet forest will increase surface temperatures by decreasing evapotranspiration (Henderson-Sellers and Gornitz 1984). However, projected albedo changes may well be counteracted by vegetation regrowth in wet areas. In a long-term study of changes in albedo in mostly wet coastal areas of West Africa, Gornitz (1985) found a very small net regional change in albedo (0.4 percent) over the past hundred years.

Regional or global effects of deforestation on climate also are dependent on soil moisture and evapotranspiration anomalies resulting from the interactions between energy and hydrologic cycles (Rowntree and Vose 1983; Salati and Vose 1984; Sioli 1985). However, the response of evapotranspiration to vegetation change varies with forest type (McNaughton and Jarvis 1983). Moreover, long-term studies of catchment effects of deforestation and reforestation have demonstrated that soil characteristics and geomorphology, as well as the initial climate (particularly the type, amount, and distribution of precipitation) strongly influence the magnitude and direction of hydrologic response (UNFAO 1962; Pereira 1973; J. R. Anderson et al. 1976; Blackie et al. 1979; Bosch and Hewlett 1982; Hamilton and King 1983).

Deforestation also influences sediment budgets (Dunne et al. 1978; Dunne and Dietrich 1980a, 1980b, 1982) and nutrient cycles (Herrera et al. 1981). In the absence of other vegetation cover, forest clearing increases surface runoff, sheet wash, and sediment transport, so that soil loss on the most severely eroded 1 percent of plowed agricultural fields may reach 100–200 tons ha^{-1} yr^{-1} (American Farmland Trust 1984). When forests are cleared but replaced immediately by other vegetation, however, erosion effects are greatly diminished and may be negligible (see studies reviewed in Dunne and Leopold 1978; Blackie et al. 1979; Hamilton and King 1983). The effects of deforestation on nutrient cycles depend significantly on soil type, clearing method, the use of fire, and the type of subsequent land use (J. C. Allen 1985). These topics are discussed in greater detail in the section on soil degradation.

An additional aspect of deforestation causing increasing concern is its impact on biological diversity (E. O. Wilson and Peter 1988). Wet tropical forests are estimated to contain the greatest number of species of any biome—more than half the species in the entire world biota (E. O. Wilson 1988). Assessing the impact of deforestation on species diversity is complex (Lugo 1988; Myers 1988; Raven 1988), however, and conservation biologists have made only tentative progress toward predicting the effects of deforestation on biodiversity (Simberloff 1986; Soul 1986).

In sum, studies conducted over the past few decades increasingly demonstrate the interconnectedness between forest vegetation and energy, water, sediment, and nutrient budgets, but models and studies to date do not provide accurate predictions of the effects of deforestation at a range of geographically distinct sites; nor do they strongly link data on deforestation processes at the local scale to regional or global processes.

Impacts on Desertification

In this study, desertification is defined as the loss of photosynthetically active vegetation, particularly productive vegetation, in dry areas. It is a process that is believed to affect not only the margins of deserts but any portions of relatively dry areas where unproductive lands develop as the result of either climate change, human use, or both (A. Warren and Agnew 1988). Thus desertification, like deforestation, has impacts on energy and water budgets as well as sediment and nutrient budgets. However, many of these effects are distinct from those of deforestation in wet areas, and are so difficult to distinguish from cyclical climatic variations that the usefulness of the term *desertification* has been questioned (Verstraete 1986; Nelson 1988).

Desertification is difficult to measure (Rozanov 1984). Apart from trends in mean annual rainfall, vegetation cover, and surface reflectance, progressive desertification might also be occurring through increased rainfall variability (Parry 1986), adverse changes in the distribution of rainfall during rainy seasons (Dennett et al. 1985; Degefu 1987), or changes in the effectiveness of rainfall, such as by increased runoff from previously eroded soils (A. Warren and Agnew 1988). Most studies used as evidence of progressive desertification present one-time data (Hellden and Stern 1980; Olsson 1985) or pre- versus postdrought time sequences (Hellden 1984) showing land degradation. According to Gornitz (1985), studies by Aubreville (1949), Stebbing (1935), and Faure and Gac (1981) have interpreted historical trends in rainfall and related stream flow over the past hundred years as desertification. Other studies present misleading statistics (Grainger 1982; Dregne 1983) or make spurious comparisons such as confounding seasonal variation with long-term change (see, e.g., Lamprey 1975, critiqued in Hellden 1984). These problems are difficult to avoid because few consistent long-term data are available. In addition, the temporal and spatial variability of rainfall and the ephemeral nature of much vegetation (Western and Van Praet 1973; Karl and Koscielny 1982; J. E. Walsh et al. 1982; Karl 1983; S. J. Walsh 1987) make it difficult to establish or interpret time-series data in arid and semiarid regions.

The major hypotheses concerning desertification that have been debated and tested in the literature have to do with the radiation budget (e.g., potential albedo increases and their effects, including feedbacks that could prolong and intensify drought or arid conditions). Desertification is intimately related to climate, as both a possible effect and a cause of dryness (Hare 1977, 1983; Olsson 1983), because it modifies surface-atmosphere interactions (Anthes 1984; Nicholson 1988). The principal anticipated effect of desertification (vegetation removal) on climate is a change in surface temperature resulting from changes in surface reflectance (Otterman 1974, 1977; Idso et al. 1975); but changes in leaf geometry (Dickinson 1983), surface roughness (Lettau 1969), and evaporation (Mintz 1982) also have been suggested as modifiers of heat flux.

A rather spirited debate arose during the Sahelian drought of the mid-1970s as to whether consistent albedo changes and their predicted effects could be verified. Otterman (1974, 1975, 1981) and Otterman and Fraser (1976) showed that soils in the Negev had an increased albedo as vegetation cover decreased due to heavy grazing, and Henderson-Sellers and Hughes (1982) and Robinove et al. (1981) cited instances of increased albedo during droughts in the United States. On the basis of this somewhat fragmentary evidence, a number of authors suggested that increased albedo could decrease surface temperatures, leading to less lifting of air and less cloud formation, thereby reducing precipitation and creating a "biophysical feedback" (Charney et al. 1975) that would intensify aridity (Otterman 1974; Berkovsky 1976; Charney et al. 1977; Sud and Fennessy 1982). Where albedos increase, general circulation models confirm the predicted decrease in precipitation (Laval 1986), but field studies have failed to demonstrate that albedos increase by the amount required by Charney's model (about 20 percent; see Charney et al. 1975) over consistently large areas.

The biophysical feedback hypothesis depends on an initially dark (vegetated) surface becoming brighter with vegetation removal. The bare surface should have a lower surface temperature than the vegetated surface, as was found by Otterman (1974, 1975) and Otterman and Tucker (1985). However, evidence from the Sonoran Desert in the United States (Jackson and Idso 1975) and some portions of the African Sahel (Wendler and Eaton 1983) indicates that denuded surfaces have higher surface temperatures than vegetated surfaces. If pale-colored vegetation is removed, the albedo of a dark-colored dry surface soil may decrease and the surface temperature may increase, whereas recovery of dark-colored vegetation may lead to a decrease in both albedo and surface temperatures (Wendler and Eaton 1983). These paradoxical findings can be explained if the moisture balance is taken into account along with the radiation balance and surface soil color (Idso et al. 1975): the surface cooling anticipated to follow vegetation removal and increased albedo may be partially or wholly offset by decreased evapotranspirative cooling also resulting from vegetation removal. Thus, a decline in vegetation may lead to surface cooling, heating, or no change, depending on the site. Based on field studies, the positive feedback between albedo and air temperature exists only in areas where the biomass is below two tons per hectare. Thus, the biophysical feedback mechanism can develop in only rather limited areas (Zolotokrylin 1986).

The biophysical feedback mechanism (Charney et al. 1975) could explain the persistence of the mid-1970s Sahelian drought well into the 1980s (as documented by J. Walker and Rowntree 1977; Nicholson 1979, 1983, 1985; P. J. Lamb 1982; and Mensching 1985). However, increasing albedo during the 1967–1973 period was followed by decreasing albedo during the 1973–1979 period in the Sahel (Norton et al. 1979; Courel et al. 1984), suggesting that plant cover and albedo values follow vegetation cover, which varies seasonally and in response to rainfall (Olsson 1985; Nicholson 1985). Thus, the expected albedo contrast (between vegetated and unvegetated sites) depends on mean rainfall and vegetation type (Otterman 1977, 1981; Wendler and Eaton 1983), and probably on soil surface color as well, and these factors and albedo vary spatially (Rockwood and Cox 1978). As a result, remote-sensing studies have not produced conclusive evidence of secular changes in albedo or vegetation (Tucker and Justice 1986) and do not support the biophysical feedback hypothesis of Charney et al. (1975).

Spatial variation in reflectance and moisture is a major finding of field and remote-sensing studies of desertification. Thus a key objective of present research has been to incorporate spatially varying land surface and subsurface processes associated with desertification into numerical circulation models (Ellsaesser et al. 1976; Matthews 1983; Bolle and Rasool 1985; Neilson 1986; Nicholson 1988).

Impacts on Soil Degradation

In this study, soil degradation has been defined as any process that leads to a decline in soil productivity in its support of human populations. Soils are a critical component of the biosphere (Kovda 1977). It is estimated that they store an amount of carbon intermediate between that of the terrestrial vegetation biomass and fossil fuels (W. H. Schlesinger 1977; Kovda 1981; Post et al. 1982) in the form of organic matter and soil carbonates. Soils also store and cycle large pools of nitrogen, phosphorus, potassium, magnesium, sulfur, and other elements in organic and inorganic forms (Brady 1984). Processes of soil formation function to buffer acidity from atmospheric deposition, weather, and minerals. In the process, soils also release their constituent elements for consumption by plants and animals, moderate rainfall and runoff, decompose organic matter, and respire carbon dioxide (Knapp 1979). Soil degradation often is a consequence of land management by humans, and frequently it is associated with deforestation or desertification.

Soil degradation has been an unintended consequence of land management since the earliest human civilizations (C. E. Kellogg 1938; Carter and Dale 1974). In the 1930s in the United States, soil erosion and declining agricultural productivity in the Dust Bowl became a matter of national government concern (Dregne 1976). Since that time, the concept of soil degradation has been enlarged to include a wide range of interrelated soil processes that can reduce soil productivity.

Many soil-degradation processes are natural soil-forming processes, as elucidated by V. V. Dokuchayev and E. W. Hilgard (Brady 1984). According to Lal (1987), soil-degradation processes are adverse changes in soil characteristics in relation to their optimum levels for support of human populations. They include declining soil organic matter content, changes in soil temperature, changes in eluviation of clay and colloids, and leaching. Declining soil organic matter content decreases soil structure, buffering capacity, and biotic activity, and may lead to soil acidification or "nutrient imbalance" (Lal 1987). Certainly soil organic matter is increasingly recognized as critical for soil management and ecosystem functioning (Sanchez et al. 1982; Bohloon et al. 1989), and low soil organic matter is associated with low levels of soil phosphorus, nitrogen, and other plant nutrients (Sanchez 1976). Soil temperature can contribute to soil degradation by increasing or decreasing rates of soil organic mineralization and altering seed germination, crop establishment, and soil biotic communities (Lal 1987). Changes in clay and colloid eluviation and leaching in soil profiles can alter soil surface erosion, percolation, and subsurface flow, leading to changes in soil moisture and nutrient storage, structural stability, and buffering against acidity (Lal 1987).

In addition to these natural soil-forming processes, soil degradation may also include such "artificial" processes as irrigation, soil amendments with urban or industrial sludge, synthetic fertilizers, herbicides, or pesticides, and even particulate deposition from fossil fuel combustion (Brady 1984). These processes may have the most marked effects on soils in industrialized regions (Kovda 1976). Drozdov (1984), M. A. Glazovskaya (1976), and M. S. Sokolov and Glazovskaya (1979) suggest that the impact of synthetic chemicals and products of combustion on soils can be predicted by estimating regional rates of production, accumulation, and breakdown of pollutants. Dry and wet deposition of atmospheric pollutants from fossil fuel combustion have increasingly been implicated in stream, lake, and soil acidification in northern Europe, Asia, and the United Kingdom. A less well researched form of soil degradation is soil adsorption and release of radioactive elements accidentally emitted from thermonuclear power plants such as Three Mile Island in the United States or Chernobyl in the Soviet Union (Gee et al. 1983).

Like deforestation and desertification, soil-degradation processes can be examined with respect to their influence on energy, water, sediment, and nutrient cycling. By far the greatest emphasis in research on soil degradation has been placed on its influences on sediment and nutrient budgets, particularly wind and water erosion, and changes in soil chemistry, especially salinization (Rapp 1986). However, soil degradation also directly influences soil moisture storage and cycling (Dunne and Leopold 1978), and indirectly influences water and energy budgets via edaphic effects on vegetation distribution and recovery (Cairns et al. 1975) and the production of atmospheric dust (Rapp 1986). Energy fluxes may also be affected by changes in the reflectance, absorption, and radiative transfer properties of soils that have become degraded (Oke 1978).

Many soil-degradation processes may be the result or cause of soil erosion by water or wind (Rapp 1986) and the impact of erosion on soil nutrient and water status. Erosion contributes to soil formation under natural (undisturbed) conditions (Schumm and Harvey 1982; Woods et al. 1987) but also is associated with crop and livestock production. High rates of soil erosion by water are widely reported in the United States (Schumm and Harvey 1982), Africa (Rapp et al. 1972; Dunne et al. 1978; Christiansson 1981), Latin America, Asia, and Australia (El-Swaify and Dangler 1982).

The introduction of mechanized cultivation in place of hand cultivation has been implicated as a direct cause of soil erosion, decreased aeration, soil moisture infiltration and availability, and nutrient release contributing to decreased crop yields in the Amazon (Alegre et al. 1986a, 1986b; Alegre and Cassel 1986) and in Africa (Lal and Greenland 1979). In the United States, soil erosion, especially on sloping, bare, plowed fields, also contributes to reduced crop yields (American Farmland Trust 1984; Langdale and Schrader 1982). Soil erosion by water produces off-site effects of increased stream turbidity and reservoir sedimentation (Rapp et al. 1972; Dunne and Leopold 1978; A. R. Robinson 1979). According to estimates by Voitkevich (1983) and Lissitsin (1974), present global rates of sediment delivery to the oceans are thirty to forty times higher than over the preceding 3.5 billion years, suggesting major recent increases in global soil erosion.

Wind erosion in arid regions is equally problematic for cropping and range use at affected sites, and it also produces off-site effects (Skidmore 1982, 1986). Apart from its direct effects on soil profile truncation, which contributes to the soil-degradation processes described above, wind erosion produces atmospheric dust, contributes to soil formation and mid-oceanic dust deposition (Prospero and Carlson 1972; Yaalon and Ganor 1973; Parmenter and Folger 1974; Prospero and Nees 1977; Anthony 1978; Carlson 1979; Eriksson

1979), and may possibly modify processes of cyclonic storm development (Nicholson 1988).

Water and fertilizer use patterns for agriculture also influence soil degradation. Salinization—the accumulation of toxic levels of salts in the rooting zone of cropped fields—has been estimated to affect large areas (Hsu et al. 1977; Kovda 1983). Salinization is a natural soil-forming process, especially in arid basins, many of which have recently been irrigated for crop agriculture (Dregne 1976). Natural accumulation of salts by subsurface flow of soil water and groundwater into these irrigated, cropped areas of arid regions often exceeds salt removal by irrigation drainage networks, resulting in a buildup of salts that represents a serious threat to agriculture in many irrigated regions (Mabbutt and Floret 1980). Fertilizer use contributes to a decline in the native soil biota, and thereby indirectly may reduce a soil's capacity to decompose other chemicals or organic matter (Brady 1984). Surface application of chemical nitrogen fertilizers also leads to denitrification, the emission of nitrous oxides into the atmosphere (Brady 1984).

Our knowledge of the impact of soil degradation, especially soil erosion, on soil productivity in the United States has been derived from research on a relatively narrow range of soil types, notably the USDA soil orders of Mollisols, Alfisols, and Ultisols (Langdale and Schrader 1982). Yet different soil orders, and probably soil series, respond differently to management, implying that the type of soil-degradation processes that may be expected will vary depending on the geographical location. Some general patterns indicate that losses of soil nutrients are proportionately greater, and accompanying reductions in productivity are more permanent and more difficult to restore, on highly weathered soils such as Ultisols typical of the southeastern United States, and Ultisols and Oxisols typical of much of the humid and semiarid tropics (J. C. Allen 1985; Langdale and Schrader 1982).

The problem of predicting soil degradation or response to management is particularly difficult given the enormous spatial variability of soils and the fact that variability increases with increasingly larger-scale (smaller-area) soils maps. For example, a 1:15,000,000 soils map of the USSR contains approximately 800 soil units, but more than 10,000 soil series are distinguished on more detailed maps of smaller areas. In the United States, a 1:7,500,000 soils map contains 60 units (combinations of soil units at the suborder level of the USDA soil taxonomy), but more than 13,000 soil series are recognized in more detailed maps (1:24,000) of smaller areas (Brady 1984). Considerable research is being conducted on improved methods for soil management in recently deforested areas of the tropics such as Amazonia (see, e.g., Gonzalez-Enrico et al. 1979; Yost et al. 1979; Sanchez 1982; Sanchez and Benites 1987) and parts of Africa and Asia (Australian Centre for International Agricultural Research 1984; Offori et al. 1986; International Board for Soil Research and Management 1987a, 1987b). This work has provided initial indications of how soil degradation might be avoided or counteracted. There is still a clear need for an improved soil fertility reference base and nutrient dynamics studies to assist in identifying soil degradation (Lopes et al. 1987) as well as to improve methods for interpreting soil survey information (e.g., Manrique 1985; Breeuwsma et al. 1986; Young 1986) so that it can be used for predictions of soil response to management.

3.3 Geographical Research: Progress to Date

Measurement

The importance of the various human impacts on nature cannot be assessed without some idea of the spatial extent of the area affected and the rate of progression of the processes. Yet despite at least a decade of concerted efforts at measurement, considerable doubts are still attached to any figure cited. Four approaches have been used to capture the spatial and temporal extent of deforestation, desertification, and soil degradation: (1) maps, (2) change detection, (3) case studies, and (4) monitoring.

MAPS

Maps are models of spatial data (Goodchild 1988b). Maps of deforestation, desertification, and soil degradation would seem to be a natural starting point for the study of these processes, but they are the most abstract and least quantitative source of information. Construction of maps presupposes considerable spatial knowledge which is lacking for deforestation, desertification, and soil degradation, and furthermore compounded by unclear definitions of the concepts. Moreover, deforestation and desertification affect the nature and positions of vegetation boundaries or gradients over time, and soil degradation affects the nature and arrangement of soil horizons (soil morphology) over time. Therefore, maps of deforestation, desertification, or soil degradation require considerably more information than do maps of potential vegetation, soil maps, or surveys. Even existing maps of potential vegetation and soils are controversial, at least partly because of a lack of consensus on vegetation and/or soil classification and inventory procedures (Brady 1984; A. N. Strahler and Strahler 1987).

At the global scale, few maps that illustrate any transformations of nature have been attempted. A recent map made by the National Geographic Society (1988) attempts to depict areas of the earth at risk to a range of environmental problems, including deforestation, desertification, and soil degradation. In 1977 a world map of desertification was compiled (UNCOD 1977c), but the data sources used were highly variable in quality and coverage, and the map at best should be considered a "first attempt to establish areas of potential risk of desertification" (Rapp 1986). Because of the perception that multilateral funding might materialize for desertified areas, the units on this map may also have been the result of political compromise (Mabbutt, pers. comm.). In any case, the map units do not distinguish among areas according to the specific desertification process under way. Other global-scale maps have attempted to illustrate factors imputed as causes of these phenomena, such as fuelwood scarcity (UNFAO 1981).

All attempts to map deforestation or desertification are limited by the lack of accurate maps of present vegetation cover. At present, the best available indication of world vegetation cover is based on a vegetation index calculated from composites of satellite images (Goward et al. 1985, 1987; C. J. Tucker et al. 1985a, 1985b; Goward and Dye 1987).

Some maps have been constructed at the continental or regional scale. Gornitz (1985) has reconstructed the history of deforestation and desertification in West Africa based on historical records. A map of desertification hazard or soil degradation has been constructed for North Africa and the Middle East (UNFAO 1980; Rapp 1986). Its units, however, appear to represent subjective judgments about processes (e.g., water or wind erosion, salinization, loss of vegetation) that might be occurring in particular areas based on maps of topography, soils, and vegetation as well as anecdotal information. Such an approach to map construction risks enshrining guesses as facts. At the present time it is not possible to construct a map of actual deforestation, desertification, or soil degradation for any region (except possibly the United States or Europe) because of the lack of systematic surveys of ecosystem statuses conducted throughout any continent or region. The recently completed natural resources inventory (USDA Soil Conservation Service 1981; American Farmland Trust 1984) is one of the few such data sets available that could be used for the production of a map of soil degradation or desertification hazards (e.g., water and wind erosion and salinization). An alternative approach to mapping is to construct an index and then map that index consistently over continents or the globe (Goward 1989b).

At the local level, maps showing deforestation and desertification can be derived from soil survey and aerial photographic information, but few attempts have been published (see Rapp et al. 1972; Christiansson 1981). Local maps can also be constructed based on the sequential examination of satellite imagery, while other researchers have utilized a case study approach.

CHANGE DETECTION

The lack of believable or coherent maps of the processes of deforestation, desertification, and soil degradation is at least partly symptomatic of the lack of accurate information about long-term changes in land use. Because synoptic coverage of the earth by earth resources satellites began only in 1972, changes in global land cover prior to that time must be inferred from historical photography of point locations, tabular data on land uses, or historical aerial photography. None of these provides objective or complete coverage of the globe. Sequential historical photography of selected locations in southern and central Africa from 1920 to 1957 (Schantz and Turner 1958) confirms a trend from closed woodland to woodland-savanna mosaic in wetter areas (deforestation) and invasion of thorny shrubs and succulents in the grasslands of semiarid and arid areas (desertification), but does not confirm any significant trend toward a decrease in total vegetation cover over the period.

Despite strenuous efforts by a number of researchers, the accuracy of tabular data, especially historical data, is impossible to verify (Chernavskaya et al. 1986) because the data were often collected from a range of anecdotal or location-specific sources (see, e.g., Zon and Sparhawk 1923; UNFAO, *Production Yearbooks 1966–1988*; Persson 1974; Sommer 1976; R. P. Tucker and Richards 1983; Gornitz 1985; J. F. Richards and Tucker 1985). Such data are rife with unverifiable errors; documentation of definitions and methods of data collection are often lacking or inconsistent; and data have been aggregated or reorganized so that the original data and data collection methods are obscured (J. C. Allen and Barnes 1985). Moreover, changes in the particular data categories used in tabular data (e.g., fields, forest, barren land, wilderness, etc.) were, on the whole, not intended for answering questions about the rate or spatial distribution of deforestation, desertification, or soil degradation. The assumptions necessary to interpret these data to answer current questions lead to wide discrepancies among vegetation change rates calculated from various tabular data sources (Grainger 1983; J. C. Allen and Barnes 1985; Melillo et al. 1985). Rates of deforestation, desertification, or soil degradation calculated from tabular data also are difficult to reconcile with rates estimated by other methods, such as change detection using aerial photographs or satellite imagery.

In the past few decades more rigorous efforts have been made to detect land-use changes, but the success of these efforts is questionable. Aerial photographs and, since 1972, imagery from earth resources satellites are the primary data sources available. At the local level, aerial photographs provide the most detailed spatial information on vegetation and land use and, where sequential coverage is available, can be used to derive local estimates of deforestation, desertification, and surface soil degradation.

A number of researchers have attempted to use sequential aerial photography to document land-use changes over periods preceding the launch of earth resources satellites. Nosseir (1983) documented changes from forest to field in Ohio from 1938 to 1976; Pla (1980) studied changes in forest cover from 1946 to 1975 in Venezuela; and Frey and Dill (1971) used aerial photographs to monitor land-use changes in the Mississippi Valley from 1959 to 1969. Rapp et al. (1972) and Christiansson (1981) used historical aerial photographs to detect land-use changes, landslides, and soil erosion in various parts of Tanzania. Although aerial photography provides coverage of areas rather than points, and is more objective than anecdotal or tabular data, such studies still represent mere points with respect to global changes, and errors can be introduced both by the technology (camera angle, altitude, film, etc.) and by the interpreter. Logistical problems that bias aerial estimates (e.g., differences in scale, print quality, and distortion), combined with the difficulty of consistently interpreting and distinguishing vegetation and land-use units, raise serious questions about the validity of statistics derived from sequential aerial photography analysis.

Where classification accuracy is not an issue, as for relatively unambiguous features such as drainage networks (R. P. D. Walsh et al. 1988), aerial photographs can be fairly reliably used for the detection of changes. However, attempting to generalize or interpolate among localized sampling from aerial photographs raises other thorny issues because of the lack of consistent coverage, particularly in recent years in many developing countries. Yet it is on the basis of partial aerial photograph interpretation that some of the most frequently quoted and authoritative estimates of deforestation (Myers 1980; Lanly 1982) have been made.

Because it offers potentially complete coverage of the earth at regular intervals and digital data (from a consistently calibrated radiometer), satellite imagery appears to offer a solution to the problem of change detection encountered with aerial photographs (Hutchinson 1986). Remote sensing is a valid source of information on general surface conditions in areas where deforestation, desertification, or soil degradation may be occurring, and has been used to map soil degradation (C. W. Mitchell 1981), vegetation cover (Griffiths and Collins 1981), land use (Bardinet et al. 1978), crop cover (Yates et al. 1984), fire (Milne 1986), wetlands (Gilmer et al. 1980), and even surface and subsurface water (Latham 1981; Schneider et al. 1985). But satellite imagery is being used much less than it could be for change detection (Booth 1989). Furthermore, technical and interpretative errors have been discovered which raise questions about this approach.

Satellite imagery provides information that is both spectral (surface reflectance in a number of spectral bands) and spatial (each image is composed of pixels of a specified size corresponding to the field of view of the sensor). The digital satellite imagery used in change detection consists of a single value for each pixel for each spectral band. A number of satellites provide digital imagery, but the imagery from four satellites has provided most of the data used for change detection:

1. Landsat Multi-spectral Scanner (MSS): 80×60 m pixels; repeat interval 16–18 days; 4 spectral bands: $4 = 0.5–0.6$ μm (blue-green), $5 = 0.6–0.7$ μm (red), $6 = 0.7–0.8$ μm (reflective-infrared), $7 = 0.8–1.1$ μm (near-infrared); available since 1972;
2. Landsat Thematic Mapper (TM): 30×30 m pixels; repeat interval 16 days; 7 spectral bands: $1 = 0.45–0.52$ μm (blue), $2 = 0.52–0.60$ μm (green),

3 = 0.63–0.69 μm (red), 4 = 0.76–0.90 μm (reflective-infrared), 5 = 1.55–1.75 μm (mid-infrared), 7 = 2.08–2.35 μm (mid-infrared), 6 = 10.4–12.5 μm (thermal infrared); available since 1982;

3. Advanced Very High Resolution Radiometer (AVHRR), a meteorological sensor: 1.1×1.1 km pixels; 1.4 km^2 nominal resolution; repeat interval twice daily; 5 spectral bands: 1 = 0.58–0.68 μm, 2 = 0.725–1.10 μm, 3 = 3.55–3.93 μm, 4 = 10.5–11.3 μm, 5 = 11.5–12.5 μm (Jensen 1986; Markham and Barker 1987);

4. Système Probetoire d'Observation de la Terre (SPOT): resolution 20 down to 10 m. Imagery from SPOT is increasingly available, but the literature contains few references to change-detection studies using SPOT.

The principle of change detection using satellite imagery is to juxtapose two or more rectified sequential images of the same area for comparison by a number of different techniques. Rectification must be both geometric, so that pixels representing the same points are being compared, and radiometric, so that a given spectral reflectance (digital number) represents the same reflectance on the ground in both images. However, image rectification has proven difficult because of sensor calibration errors and differences in image products among various satellite sensors. Manipulations may be necessary to standardize the imagery before change detection can be attempted, and the magnitude of the resulting change estimates may depend on the correction or standardization procedure used (Nelson 1985; Musick 1986; Markham and Barker 1987). Time of day and year of sequential imagery may also produce errors. For example, Musick (1986) found that variation in shadow size due to time of day accounted for all the short-term variations in an albedo index for 1973–1983 in the southwestern United States.

Following geometric and/or radiometric rectification, five basic approaches have been utilized in satellite image interpretation for change detection: (1) simple ratios or differences between individual or composite bands of raw images, by pixel; (2) comparison of two or more classified images (on the basis of a set of rules); (3) comparison of images that have been preprocessed with a filter or vegetation index; (4) principal components analysis (and modifications thereof); and (5) change vector analysis.

By far the greatest number of change-detection studies have used Landsat MSS data, because of the longer period of coverage. Principal components analysis has shown that most single-date, four-band MSS imagery decomposes into two major axes of spectral information—greenness and brightness (Kauth and Thomas 1976; Lodwick 1979). All five of the change-detection approaches cited above, when applied to deforestation, desertification, or soil degradation, seek to identify and measure either (1) decreases in greenness, assumed to imply decreases in vegetation cover; or (2) increases in brightness, assumed to imply increases in bare soil (albedo), or both. C. J. Tucker (1979), Curran

(1982), and P. L. Warren et al. (1985) have shown that a ratio of MSS bands 6 (infrared) and 5 (red) is sensitive to vegetation, while Eliason et al. (1981) showed that a ratio of MSS bands 5 (red) and 4 (green) is sensitive to bare soil and rock.

Difference images have been widely used for change detection—both differences in brightness, that is, "albedo differences" (Nualchawee et al. 1981; Robinove et al. 1981; Musick 1986), and differences in greenness, often in the form of a band ratio (Griffiths 1988; Howarth and Wickware 1981; Frank 1984a). Ratios of individual bands, especially MSS bands 5 (red) and 7 (near-infrared), of sequential images also have been used (Weismuller et al. 1977; Jensen 1981), as have differences between covariance images (Coiner 1980). While expedient for automated image processing, difference and ratio images have been criticized as being too simple because they cannot discriminate various forms of change (Jensen 1981).

Postclassification change detection has been even more widely attempted than difference or ratio images (Joyce et al. 1980; Stow et al. 1980; Howarth and Wickware 1981; Jensen 1981; Nelson et al. 1987), but this approach often produces erroneous results because of classification errors and boundary overlay problems (Joyce et al. 1980; Stow et al. 1980; Jensen 1981; Nelson et al. 1987). Some of these problems are inevitable because at different levels of spatial resolution either scene noise or mixed pixels are likely to confound classification (Markham and Townshend 1981). Nelson et al. (1987) used postclassification change detection with stratified multistage sampling for detecting deforestation in the Brazilian Amazon, where, despite their belief that clearings were being classified with high accuracy (Hawley 1979; G. Johnson et al. 1979), classification errors, and consequently the accuracy of the estimates, are unknown.

Comparison of sequential images preprocessed to compute a vegetation index from AVHRR data have produced results in good agreement with seasonal and annual changes in vegetation cover (Goward et al. 1985, 1987; Goward and Dye 1987). This is especially encouraging because the vegetation index from AVHRR is correlated with net primary productivity (Breast and Goward 1987).

Principal components analysis has been used in a variety of change-detection applications (Byrne and Crapper 1980; Byrne et al. 1980; J. A. Richards 1984; Ingebritsen and Lyon 1985), where principal components images calculated from pooled (two or more) image dates show different kinds of changes. In an interesting twist on this approach, Switzer and Ingebritsen (1986) used principal components analysis and minimum/maximum autocorrelation analysis to separate spatially uncorrelated registration and other errors from spatially autocorrelated changes. Change vector analysis has been cited as a promising way to identify and discriminate changes in greenness and brightness (Malila 1980; Colwell 1981), but it has not been widely used.

Despite a rich literature on change detection using satellite imagery, the range of applications to deforestation, desertification, and soil degradation is disappointingly narrow. A number of studies have attempted to address desertification using remote sensing (e.g., Carlson 1979; Rapp and Hellden 1979; Latham 1981; Otterman 1981; A. S. Walker and Robinove 1981; Hellden and Olsson 1982; Hellden 1984; Olsson 1985; P. L. Warren et al. 1985), but Bartlett and Hamilton (1986) describe satellite image coverage for desertification as "disappointingly patchy, variable and incomplete," and characterize the use of satellite imagery as "fragmentary and unsystematic." Several promising studies (e.g., Nelson et al. 1987) have investigated deforestation with remote sensing. Dale (1989) identifies remote sensing as the only tool able to provide the information necessary to assess land-use changes at the global scale, despite the small area of the globe so far studied.

Several obstacles stand in the way of the routine use of satellite imagery for deforestation, desertification, or soil-degradation studies. The effective use of satellite imagery for change detection is limited by the logistical difficulties and high cost of acquiring good-quality sequential imagery (each digital tape of an MSS 185 × 185 km scene costs $700 before interpretation; TM and SPOT imagery are four to eight times that cost). Much of the earth's surface of interest has variable or poor coverage for both MSS and TM data, either due to cloud cover or because the satellite was turned off during an overpass. These factors make it difficult to acquire two sequential images taken at the same time of day and the same season for a given site. The task of acquiring, processing, and interpreting a complete global set of MSS, TM, or more detailed imagery in order to produce a complete inventory of world vegetation involves formidable logistical difficulties (Woodwell et al. 1983a).

The vegetation index calculated from AVHRR data (mentioned above) is probably the most successful application of satellite data to global change so far. Although it has been demonstrated to be related to net primary productivity (Breast and Goward 1987) and correlated with seasonal carbon dioxide emissions (C. J. Tucker et al. 1986), the vegetation index of Goward et al. (1985) is a measure of cover by photosynthetically active vegetation only. Deforestation, desertification, and soil degradation, however, are broad concepts that include subtle changes in vegetation, physical structure, and species composition; habitat fragmentation by the appearance of small clearings or bare patches in previously homogeneous vegetation stands; and changes in subcanopy and subsurface soil characteristics, as well as changes in parameters more difficult to quantify, such as resilience and economic productivity. Thus, satellite imagery may not contain sufficient information to infer the progress of deforestation, desertification, or soil degradation. Ahlcrona (1988) was unable to detect critical changes in shrub and grass species composition using satellite imagery in the Sudan. Moreover, surface soil characteristics, where visible, may not convey the necessary information about soil productivity.

Detecting changes in albedo is a major application of satellite imagery in studies of desertification to date. However, increased spectral albedo is not an exact measure of total albedo, nor is it directly synonymous with desertification, because the albedo of a surface depends on atmospheric effects as well as on the amount of dead vegetation and soil moisture content (Jackson and Idso 1975; Wendler and Eaton 1983). Plot-scale spatial variations in ground-measured albedo and changes in albedo with sun angle also add to the difficulties of interpretation of soil brightness changes (Musick 1986). Moreover, the satellite image coverage available may not correspond to the period of vegetation change (e.g., Musick 1986). In addition to the technical difficulties, there is the problem that increases in bare soil area may not all be indicative of desertification; cultivation and road construction are possible examples.

Like all forms of change detection, the use of satellite imagery ultimately relies on correlating remotely sensed parameters (such as reflectance or transformations of reflectance) with the actual conditions on the ground: vegetation cover and its health and composition. Field sampling for verification has been weak or nonexistent in many change-detection studies using satellite remote sensing (but see Musick 1986). Moreover, in most areas of interest on the earth's surface, no field data on vegetation cover, composition, or condition are available for earlier dates (even for the 1970s). Such data are essential not only to calculate first-order changes but also to understand higher-order changes, especially those associated with such historical events as drought, war, or technological innovation. Therefore, the rates of change that can be calculated from remotely sensed data remain speculative. The dramatic advances that have been made in image interpretation techniques will not be applicable to change detection of deforestation, desertification, or soil degradation until they are matched by high-quality data collected over the long term on the ground.

CASE STUDIES

Maps, aerial photographs, and satellite imagery at best indicate the distributional changes and perceived risks to visible physical features in the environment associated with deforestation, desertification, or soil degradation. Consequently, these techniques have focused almost exclusively on changes in vegetation or surface features. However, deforestation and desertification are of interest largely because of their actual and potential adverse impacts on human activity and the biosphere, including human health, quality of life, economic activity, soil quality, ecosystem resilience, water supplies, and climate. None of these can be directly assessed from spatial data sources such as maps, aerial photographs, or satellite imagery. Accurate quantitative estimates of changes must therefore include field observations and interpretations from a range of individual sites. Moreover, the relationships between the processes of deforestation and desertification, human activity, and the nonhuman system are complex and poorly understood, and may occur rapidly at a single location. Case studies of defined locations provide the opportunity to examine rapid temporal change on the ground, and to integrate the obvious physical and less tangibly expressed aspects of deforestation, desertification, and soil degradation into a single study. An excellent series of case studies of desertification (Mabbutt and Floret 1980) illustrates the value of this approach, but it also demonstrates the enormous quantity of data necessary to define and measure desertification and related processes.

Case studies of Tunisia and Chile (Mabbutt and Floret 1980) thoughtfully describe how the improved education of pastoralists in the near-desert zones increased their expectations for a higher standard of living, leading to expansion of cultivation in desert margins. This raised the short-term productivity of the ecosystem and produced incomes superior to those obtainable by pastoralism, until soil erosion and denudation destroyed the newfound productivity, leaving a landscape in which the native perennial vegetation has been unable to reestablish itself easily even in wet years.

Case studies of Niger, India, and Australia emphasize the role of grazing in desertification (Mabbutt and Floret 1980). The case study of Niger illustrates how the establishment of mechanized pumping from deep boreholes in the north of Niger resulted in areas of overgrazing and complete removal of plants in circular areas around the wells. During drought and dry seasons this barren area became so large that the distance between the water source (the well) and the palatable pasture grew to exceed the range that the animals could travel, so they weakened and died. Recent work by S. Jones (pers. comm.) notes that animals' reliance on fodder from trees during dry seasons and droughts is associated with widespread tree death and subsequent catastrophic erosion in the highlands of Eritrea (northeastern Africa). Both pasture grazing and forage production from trees can lead to the creation of desertlike patches of land well within regions not formerly considered deserts. A major factor necessary to reverse the process of patch creation from grazing is the maintenance of deep-rooted perennial grasses and shrubs that are more resilient and palatable forage plants. Two other important factors are the achievement of sustainable production of forage through the use of native trees and shrubs for browse (Le Houerou 1980) and the identification of locations for wells based on the productivity of the surrounding area (Mabbutt and Floret 1980).

Case studies from Iraq, Palestine, Australia, and the Colorado River basin in the United States (Mabbutt and Floret 1980) illustrate how seepage from poorly constructed irrigation channels and excessive irrigation have raised water tables and resulted in soil salinization, leading to sudden abandonment of farming. The case studies discuss the complex problem of combatting the natural tendency for soil salinization when irrigated crops that demand large quantities of water (especially cotton) are introduced into an arid region. The modifications to irrigation systems, extensive land-leveling operations, elaborate drainage systems, and water reclamation that are necessary to counteract salinization are also discussed.

The case studies described by Mabbutt and Floret (1980) graphically illustrate the enormous amounts of data on soils, geomorphology, native vegetation, crops, pastoral practices, herd sizes, farming practices, incomes, diet and nutrition, land tenure, social relationships, demographic patterns, and other factors that are necessary to reach an adequate understanding of the complex processes so deceptively summarized by the term *desertification*. The lack of data in many of the areas most affected by desertification represents an opportunity for geographers.

Case studies tend to emphasize the importance of drought or long periods of below-average rainfall rather than presenting evidence of general secular trends in rainfall. They focus on the importance of effective rainfall, or the soil water balance, showing that changes in infiltration or soil water-storage capacity due to erosion can outweigh the adverse effects of changed surface albedo and surface heat which have been emphasized by most of the modeling discussed below (Mabbutt and Floret 1980; R. P. D. Walsh et al. 1988). More important, case studies point to the importance of demographic, political, economic, and social factors, and their indivisibility from the physical environment (Mabbutt and Floret 1980).

Unfortunately, few case studies have examined the postdrought recovery stages of desertification (A. Warren and Agnew 1988), which are equally important, if less spectacular, than the crisis period. There is virtually no case study literature on vegetation and herd recovery in the late 1970s and after 1984 in the Sahel, although such recovery clearly took place (Wendler and Eaton 1983). The recent study of the Sudan by Ahlcrona (1988) is a welcome exception. The decline in literature and press coverage of desertification during the late 1970s and the post-1984 periods occurred despite evidence of persistent drought from 1960 to the present (Nicholson 1979, 1983, 1985; P. J. Lamb 1982; R. P. D. Walsh et al. 1988). A misplaced emphasis on research that documents trends in physical resources rather than case studies of these trends with reference to migration and other human cultural adaptations may explain this failure. Clearly, a great deal remains to be learned from careful case studies by geographers.

Case studies that address deforestation directly are rare; relevant studies usually focus on specific causes, consequences, or attempts to counteract deforestation rather than providing comprehensive overviews of deforestation in particular areas. The study of deforestation has tended to rely more on compendia of statistics of dubious value than on in-depth examinations of deforestation as a process. For example, much valuable information from selected locations was collected by Myers (1980, 1984), but he presents too little explanatory information to give a case study perspective on any of the countries. Two thorough case studies of fuelwood scarcity and tree planting are available for the northern Sudan (Hammer 1982) and central Tanzania (Skutsch 1982), while a range of reforestation and social forestry projects is described by Barnes and Allen (1982). In general, studies of deforestation in specific sites lack the interdisciplinary perspective necessary to understand the process. Consequently, there is considerable latitude for valuable contributions by geographers in this area. Geographers in the United States, at least, have tended to move away from case study approaches since the "quantitative revolution" of the 1960s. Nevertheless, it is certainly possible to conduct rigorous hypothesis testing and to use quantitative methods, if desired, within the framework of a case study.

MONITORING

A number of international organizations have established programs to monitor deforestation, desertification, and soil degradation. The UNDP/UNFAO Global Environmental Monitoring Program (GEMS) is one of the most active of such programs (Lanly 1982). CILSS (the Comité Internationale de Lutte contre la Secheresse Sahelienne) also maintains monitoring activities. United Nations regional agricultural research organizations, such as the ILCA (International Livestock Center for Africa, Addis Ababa), the CIMMYT (Centro Internacional de Melioracion de Mais y Trigo [International Center for Corn and Wheat Improvement], Mexico City), the ICRISAT (International Crop Research Institute for the Semi-arid Tropics, Hyderabad), the ICRAF (International Center for Research on Agroforestry (Nairobi), and the IITA (International Institute for Tropical Agriculture, Ibadan), maintain active research programs including monitoring. The World Meteorological Organization is active in providing data from climate networks. Soil-monitoring networks have only recently been established, notably the IBSRAM (International Board for Soil Research and Management 1987a, 1987b). Some international efforts such as the Desert Locust Control Program (a consortium of Sahelian countries) have been weakened or paralyzed in recent years because of political instability and regional conflicts.

Monitoring methods range from descriptive or anecdotal reports to quantitative, replicated experimentation. The usefulness of monitoring activities in the past has been limited by the lack of long-term or objective measurements at defined sites. Over the past decade there has been a marked trend toward more rigorously quantifiable monitoring by international organizations. This process involves (1) the identification of a network of sites, and (2) the selection of agreed-upon experimental protocols. Notable examples include the recently established Tropical Soil Biology and Fertility (TSBF) network and protocols, the Agroforestry Research Network for Africa (AFRENA) established by the ICRAF, and a set of replicated experiments being conducted by the ICRISAT. It is hoped that these experimental networks will provide not only data on changes in soil and vegetation at a range of geographically distinct sites, but also indications of the potential for various innovations to counteract deforestation, desertification, and soil degradation.

Models

A number of diverse models have been proposed that relate to the processes of deforestation, desertification, and soil degradation. This section describes four types of models. The first stage of model building is the conceptual framework, which relates sequences of causes and effects and feedbacks in space and time, but without a specified spatial or temporal scale. The second set of models are simulation models, which formally characterize climatic, hydrologic, demographic, or other processes related to deforestation, desertification, or soil degradation. Simulation models usually have a spatial dimension, a temporal dimension, or both, and a single specified spatial scale. The third class of models are optimization models that are or could be used to identify possible management solutions to deforestation, desertification, or soil degradation. These models can operate in space and time but require the formalized expression of relationships from simulation models as well as the definition of one or more suitable objectives. Usually an optimization model is limited to a single spatial scale. The fourth class of models are the least well developed but the most promising and the most needed, as they would relate local spatial processes to global or regional models (i.e., one spatial scale to another, in time), via formalized hierarchical relationships, perhaps assisted by geographical information systems (GIS) technology.

CAUSE-EFFECT MODELS

Both deforestation and desertification were initially studied as phenomena that at least partly resulted from human actions. Considerable effort has been expended, for example, in attempting to deconvolve human from climatic influences on desertification (Verstraete 1986). Similarly, many studies have attributed deforestation to various land-use activities, including agricultural land clearing, grazing, tree plantations, road construction, colonial-induced changes in building practices, fuelwood collection, war, migration, or population growth (J. C. Allen and Barnes 1985). Such hypotheses at the conceptual level are not amenable to rigorous testing. Conceptual difficulties and the lack of suitable data to characterize most of the imputed causes led to weak levels of significance and circular arguments in lagged regression analyses of the causes of deforestation (J. C. Allen and Barnes 1985). At the highest level of generality, population growth is the most frequently cited cause of deforestation and desertification (J. C. Allen and Barnes 1985), but this variable is strongly correlated with almost all measures of economic and social change.

Olsson (1985) failed to show any relationship between population growth and desertification in the Sudanese Sahel. Although there is an obvious benefit in understanding causes before attempting management, generalized causal models tend to distract attention from the highly diverse, often avoidable, local circumstances that lead to deforestation, desertification, or soil degradation. Case studies (e.g., Mabbutt and Floret 1980) underscore the uniqueness of most sets of local circumstances. Moreover, conceptual models of the causes and consequences of deforestation and desertification tend to be highly personal, reflecting the biases and experience of the author (Verstraete 1986).

Great effort also has been expended in the literature in identifying the effects or implications of desertification, deforestation, and soil degradation. A large number of studies have examined the influence of vegetation clearing on portions of the hydrologic cycle such as interception, stemflow and throughfall, infiltration, evaporation, transpiration, and the timing and magnitude of storm runoff and water yield in a wide range of vegetation types around the world (e.g., J. R. Anderson et al. 1976; Dunne and Leopold 1978; Blackie et al. 1979; Hamilton and King 1983; Ponce 1983; O'Loughlin and Pearce 1984). Examination of the combined conclusions from these studies indicates that the effects can be small or large, positive or negative, depending on the geography of the site and how it is managed. Since the 1970s, many studies have debated the influence of deforestation, desertification, and soil degradation on climate, particularly increased drought (Charney et al. 1977; Hare 1977, 1983; Nicholson 1988). A similarly large number of studies have examined vegetation-clearing effects on soil physical, chemical, and biological properties (summarized in J. C. Allen 1985). Finally, considerable attention has been focused recently on the probable consequence of cumulative desertification and deforestation for biological diversity (E. O. Wilson and Peter 1988). Again, examination of the conclusions from these studies reveals a wide range of different, even opposing, results of deforestation and desertification, depending on the location. These varying results underscore the need for concerted efforts by geographers to delineate geographical units that respond to disturbance in a predictable fashion.

Cause-effect models of deforestation, desertification, and soil degradation are unidirectional and somewhat simplistic. Greater emphasis needs to be placed on identifying recovery and resilience in these complex systems. Examination of cause-effect models also makes clear the impossibility of separating physical from economic, social, and political causes and consequences of desertification, deforestation, and soil degradation (Blaikie 1985; Blaikie and Brookfield 1987). An excellent example is the occurrence of harvest failures coincidental with war and social disruption in Ethiopia, Somalia, the Sudan, and the western Sahara since the early 1970s. Other examples include the deforestation attributable to large-scale resettlement in Indonesia, and tax incentives for land clearing and migration in Brazil.

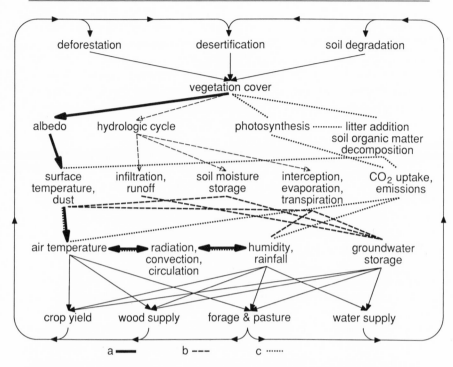

Fig. 3.10 Diagram of causal relations in the three major hypotheses regarding deforestation, desertification, and soil degradation from the literature. Solid lines indicate positive feedback loops common to all three hypotheses; bold solid lines indicate hypothesis A; dashed lines indicate hypothesis B; and dotted lines indicate hypothesis C referred to in the text. (Compiled by J. A. Jones)

SIMULATION MODELS

Simulation exercises relevant to deforestation and desertification have been conducted in the past two decades. Simulation models ask the question "What if . . . ?" given assumptions about cause-effect interactions. These assumptions may be deterministic or stochastic, but most models that have dealt with deforestation and desertification have incorporated deterministic assumptions. The models and their validations explore a number of the dominant hypotheses about the consequences of deforestation, desertification, and soil degradation diagrammed in Figure 3.10. Hypothesis A (bold solid lines) shows how deforestation, desertification, and soil degradation disrupt the energy balance. They involve loss of vegetation cover and increasing soil exposure, which increases surface reflectance (albedo) and atmospheric dust, thus changing surface temperatures and modifying radiation, convection, and circulation patterns in the atmosphere. This has consequences for rainfall and temperature which cause persistence of drought and continued vegetation decline. According to hypothesis B (dashed lines), deforestation, desertification, and soil degradation disrupt the hydrologic cycle. Loss of vegetation cover modifies interception, infiltration, evaporation, transpiration, soil moisture storage, and runoff, causing changes in groundwater storage and local humidity, which in turn affect convection, circulation, and rainfall, and thereby contribute to continued vegetation change.

One other major hypothesis is gaining momentum in the literature but has not been explored at any great depth in modeling exercises. According to hypothesis C, deforestation, desertification, and soil degradation disrupt the global carbon cycle through their effects on vegetation and soils. They involve loss of vegetation cover and reduced photosynthesis, resulting in a changed pattern of CO_2 uptake and emission. The loss of vegetation also changes patterns of litter additions to soil, causing a change in soil temperature and moisture regimes and consequent changes in soil fauna and decomposition processes, leading to changes in carbon turnover in soils. These changes in carbon cycling in vegetation and soil may modify global air temperatures and circulation patterns and change rainfall.

The changing albedo hypothesis (A) was advanced by Otterman (1974) and Charney et al. (1975), who detected increases in albedo in cleared areas near protected exclosures and inferred that this would lead to decreased surface temperatures and decreased convection, resulting in decreased rainfall and drought persistence. Additional work by Berkovsky (1976), Ellsaesser et al. (1976), and Hare (1977) further explored the idea of feedbacks. The positive feedback concept was contradicted by measurements made by Jackson and Idso (1975). The discrepancy appears to be due to the differences in albedo of differently colored vegetation (living and dead) and bare soil, rock, and so on, in different ecosystems.

Subsequent modeling efforts using one-, two-, and three-dimensional climate models, including a GCM (Hansen et al. 1983), indicate that albedo changes alone may result in locally decreased precipitation but will have little effect on global climates (e.g., Lettau et al. 1979; Norton et al. 1979; Henderson-Sellers and Gornitz 1984; Gornitz 1985). A related "feedback" phenomenon incorporated in simulations of climate is the generation of dust associated with desertification (Kershaw 1986; Seiler and Crutzen 1980), which is proposed to influence surface temperatures and thereby reduce convective rainfall.

The computational complexity of large climate-simulation models results in great compromises in spatial detail (Henderson-Sellers and Hughes 1982). Major unexplored areas in climate simulation modeling are the influence of land surface–atmosphere interactions (Dickinson 1983; Nicholson 1988) and the influence of spatial scale on model outcomes. Geographers can make important contributions in research which assesses the influence on model predictions of the spatial scale at which land surface–atmosphere interactions are represented.

Disruptions of the hydrologic cycle (hypothesis B) have been studied for decades using field experimentation and monitoring of catchments (e.g., Pereira 1973; Bosch and Hewlett 1982; etc.). However, researchers have only recently attempted to generalize the influence of deforestation or desertification on hydrologic processes to scales larger than small catchments. Salati and Vose (1984) proposed that up to 50 percent of the water in the Amazon Basin is recycled locally via evapotranspiration, with turnover rates as short as 5.5 days. R. P. D. Walsh et al. (1988) have presented regional evidence from the Sudan of declining soil moisture and groundwater tables associated with a secular drying trend. However, as with climate simulation of albedo effects, there has been little exploration of the question of how to characterize spatially variable hydrologic properties as input to small-scale (large-area) water balances. This is a potentially fruitful area for geographical research.

The global carbon budget hypothesis (C) has only recently emerged in the literature. Only highly aggregated calculations have been made of global carbon pools in vegetation and soils (e.g., W. H. Schlesinger 1977; Budyko 1979; Post et al. 1982; Brown and Lugo 1984). However, C. J. Tucker et al. (1986) have presented convincing evidence linking seasonal photosynthesis (using vegetation indexes from AVHRR data) with CO_2 emissions, thus indirectly supporting hypothesis C. While attention has focused on the unexplained excess of sources over sinks and the possible role of the oceans as a CO_2 sink, current carbon budget models (e.g., Woodwell et al. 1978; Houghton and Woodwell 1981; Houghton et al. 1983) nevertheless incorporate considerable uncertainty about the terrestrial carbon budget (Idso 1984; S. P. Gorshkov 1986; Borisenkov and Kondrat'yev 1988). Regional carbon budget data are also being developed (Delcourt and Harris 1980; P. C. Miller 1980). Accumulating evidence suggests that regional soils and vegetation communities, especially in the tropics, may have unexpectedly high rates of carbon cycling (J. A. Jones 1990). Such analyses, which require the collection and interpretation of large sets of data on soil and vegetation characteristics (e.g., R. L. Jones 1988), are clearly needed to pin down carbon budget components. There is a clear role for geographers to assist in the assessment of these spatial and temporal trends.

On the whole, simulation models applied to deforestation and desertification processes suffer from a lack of adequate validation at various spatial scales, given the known dependence of the processes on spatially variable conditions of soils and vegetation. Geographers could make valuable contributions to improving the characterization of the spatial variability of soil and vegetation properties related to energy, hydrologic, and elemental cycles for input to simulation models.

OPTIMIZATION MODELS

Optimization models have only rarely been applied to issues related to deforestation and desertification, but they have great potential value. Since op-

timization models ask the question "How to best achieve . . . ?" with respect
to a stated objective, they could be applied to a number of management problems that influence deforestation and desertification. As such, optimization
models might be best predicated on the idea of counteracting or reducing
deforestation, desertification, or soil degradation. Since the causes of deforestation, desertification, and soil degradation include land clearing for agriculture, grazing, and fuelwoods, optimization models could address the following
questions:

1. How should trees and shrubs (indigenous or exotic species) be planted to
   provide wood in order to counteract deforestation and CO_2 emissions?
2. How can CO_2 emissions be reduced by reducing petroleum-based fuel
   usage?
3. How should land be allocated to improve yields from cultivation and grazing while minimizing soil erosion?

   J. C. Allen (1985, 1986) has applied multiobjective linear programming to
the problem of scheduling planting, harvest, fuel product choice, and distribution decisions to meet fuelwood needs in a sustained fashion in central Tanzania. Church and Migereko (1986) used location analysis to demonstrate that
considerable fuel savings could be obtained from small adjustments in the
location of coffee marketing and storage centers in Uganda. Work in progress
is exploring the use of mathematical programming to allocate tree planting in
order to compensate for CO_2 emissions.
   Many problems involving spatial decision making that affect deforestation,
desertification, and soil degradation could be formulated and solved as optimization problems by geographers. This is not to underestimate the formidable
assumptions that must be made in order to select parameters and formulate
objectives and constraints. However, the principal advantage of optimization
models over simulation approaches is that the former allow for the explicit
incorporation of human activities that could mitigate the undesirable aspects
of deforestation and desertification. Optimization models could be used to
consider broader and more essential aspects of global energy usage and food
production related to deforestation, desertification, and soil degradation.
While the data necessary to formulate accurate constraints and objectives may
be lacking in many cases, optimization modeling could provide evidence of
the range of options open to humans, given current knowledge of deforestation, desertification, and soil-degradation processes.

HIERARCHICAL MODELS AND GIS

The existence of data, simulated processes, and objectives at disparate
scales is a significant obstacle to progress in understanding deforestation, desertification, and soil degradation. Obstacles arise partly from the lack of workable techniques by which spatial data at different scales can be examined and

compared (Goodchild 1988a). The current development of geographical information systems, specifically the concept of data structures (Burrough 1986), directly tackles this problem. Considerable progress is being made in theoretical assessment of error propagation and the influence of various forms of data storage (Goodchild 1988a). Apart from the improvement of data management techniques, much more work also is needed to determine the degree of scale dependence of all of the processes implicated in deforestation and desertification. It has been clearly demonstrated in various fields that increased scale (smaller study areas) leads to increasing complexity in classification and process. A vital question for analyses of deforestation, desertification, and soil degradation, then, is how much does the loss of accuracy attendant on selection of increasingly smaller scales (larger areas) for study and modeling compromise the accuracy of model results being used for decision making?

Geographers have used a wide range of techniques to summarize and condense data, but it is not clear which of these techniques, if any, are adequate for study of deforestation, desertification, and soil degradation. For example, should different vegetation classification systems be used for assessing watershed impacts of deforestation compared with soil fertility changes? What form of land-cover data is most appropriate for incorporation into a general circulation model of Sahelian climate? Should different soil classification systems be used for assessing agricultural potential and conservation of genetic diversity? At what scale should soils and vegetation be classified, if at all, for identifying and responding to the impacts of deforestation, desertification, and soil degradation?

Contemporary Challenges

Deforestation, desertification, and soil degradation pose three major challenges for geographers. First, the present inadequacy of spatial data bases is a significant constraint to progress in testing hypotheses about the implications of deforestation, desertification, and soil degradation. Second, spatial data sets need to be integrated with global- and regional-scale models through characterization of regional variation of properties of interest and their significance to the energy balance, the hydrologic cycle, and global biogeochemical cycles. Third, the empirical testing of geographic theories (both descriptive and normative) needs to be continued and intensified.

Geographers today are in a strong position to contribute to research on human impacts on the land, especially deforestation, desertification, and soil degradation. The most valuable geographical research contributions will integrate landscape ecological theory on the relations between pattern and process with land unit definition and land evaluation, to provide spatial information useful in the prediction and management of vegetation and soils and their response to human activities.

4. HAZARDS, RISK, AND SOCIAL

IMPACT ASSESSMENT

The IGBP seeks to investigate physical and biological dimensions of global
environmental change (Liverman 1983, 1987; Clark and Munn 1986). The
program is motivated both by concern about the risks that such change poses
for society and by the need for improved detection, warning, and response
capabilities (International Council of Scientific Unions [ICSU] 1986). Up to
now, however, the focus has been on identification and measurement of environmental change. IGBP plans have failed to address issues of hazard, risk,
and impact assessment directly or to plan for the use of scientific findings in
policy responses. Much of the practical value of the new scientific information
that is expected to emerge from the program will be lost if these plans are not
altered. Indeed, it is doubtful that a feasible long-term management program
for the global environment can be created without direct consideration of associated risks and without definite plans for applying the scientific information. Fifty years of hazards research have clearly demonstrated that society
and environment, as well as hazards and resources, are inextricably inter-
twined. Moreover, in the absence of specific measures for encouraging use of
research findings, valuable scientific information about hazard reduction frequently remains unapplied.

Selected geographic contributions to the analysis of global changes as natural hazards are presented in section 4.1. Risk assessment (section 4.2) is one
of the approaches that geographers have found helpful in managing the broad
array of implications of environmental change. While the methods of risk
assessment are being refined by economists, engineers, medical scientists,
and sociologists, as well as by researchers in other disciplines, geographers'
experiences with estimating and managing the risk from exposure to natural
and technologic hazards yield important lessons.

Assessments of social impacts of global climate change (section 4.3) are
needed to evaluate society's ability to cope and to formulate preventive or
adaptive responses. Several lines of research and applications under the broad

rubric of climate impact assessment can be used to address the problem, as discussed in section 4.3.

4.1 Natural Hazards

Hazards as Part of Human Ecology

Geographers have developed considerable understanding of social systems under environmental stress through natural hazards research (Burton et al. 1978; Heathcote 1985; O'Riordan 1986). Although the focus of hazards work has been on short-duration, extreme events rather than on cumulative environmental changes, it provides at least three useful perspectives on the interaction of society and changes in the global environment: (1) an explicit definition of hazards as the result of the interaction of physical extremes and social vulnerability, thus demanding a conjoint social-physical analysis; (2) a recognition that people respond to the environment as perceived rather than as defined by physical scientists; and (3) even slow, cumulative changes in the environment may be interpreted and responded to as discrete, extreme events.

HAZARDS AS INTERACTION

The first useful perspective offered by hazards work is the conceptualization of hazards as occurring, by definition, only where and when natural extremes and social systems interact (Kates 1971), and the field's insistence on conjoint analysis of environmental and social systems. This "human-ecological" perspective was codified in a model constructed by Kates (1971) to show hazards-society interaction as a cybernetic system dominated by negative feedbacks between vulnerability, impact, adjustment, and changing vulnerability and impact (Fig. 4.1).

Kates later applied the ecological model to climate change (Fig. 4.2) to show that the impacts of climate were determined by both the nature of the fluctuation and the vulnerability or resilience of the affected social system (Kates 1985). Because vulnerability varies between societies and through time, so, then, will the effects of climate change.

Unfortunately, the fact that societal vulnerability changes over time has been neglected in most impact assessments. Only rudimentary efforts have been made to incorporate dynamic adaptation into impact projections (Parry et al. 1988), mainly because projecting social vulnerability is more difficult than simply projecting impacts on a static society; there are no widely accepted guidelines for predicting social change. Thus, impacts projected over several decades assume static societies, which means that the resulting threat may be over- or understated as social adaptation and change occur.

The human-ecological formulation of climate-society interaction (Fig. 4.2)

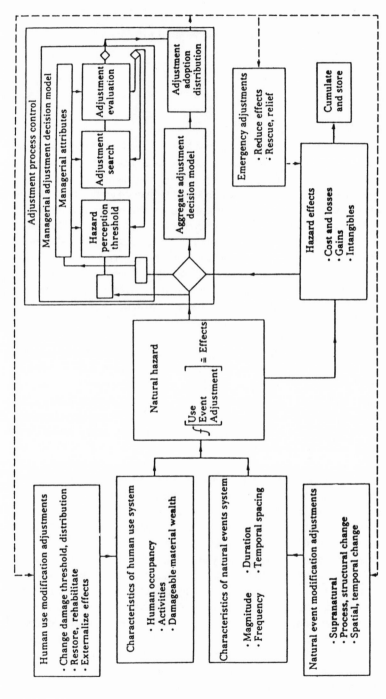

Fig. 4.1 General systems model of human adjustments to natural hazards. (From Kates 1971. Reprinted with permission of *Economic Geography* and Clark University, copyright 1971.)

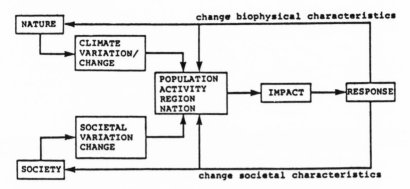

Fig. 4.2 Interaction model stressing feedback to underlying physical and social processes and structures. (From Kates, 1985. Reprinted with the permission of the Scientific Committee on Problems of the Environment—SCOPE—of the International Council of Scientific Unions.)

does, however, incorporate a "black box" of social evolution that must be explicated by the researcher. It is broad enough to encompass many different theories of how society actually works. The social systems box can subsume the major social-structural and process paradigms, including the Marxist or materialist perspective on differential vulnerability (Hewitt 1983a; Watts 1983), the structuralist perspective of institutions and social constraints (Giddens 1984), and the behavioralist perspective of individual perception, choice, and hazards management (Whyte 1986). These processes and structures produce more or less social vulnerability through time.

Yet the inclusivity of the ecological model is also a weakness. It offers no formulation for integrating the different hierarchical levels of constraints and opportunities that guide social processes or maintain structure. Hazards ecology is seen as isolated from the everyday world of social discourse, when, in reality, hazards are part of "normal" affairs in many places (Hewitt 1983a). Palm (1990) offers an integrative framework that maps social structure onto the traditional hazards framework and provides a template for linking different scales of environmental and social processes, a critical need in the face of global change.

HAZARDS AS PERCEIVED

The focus on humans' perception of hazards offers a second useful perspective for geographical analysis of global change. A great deal of attention has been paid in hazards research to exploring the effects of the truism that people respond to the environment not as it is but as it is perceived (J. K. Mitchell 1984). Thus, to understand people's behavior with regard to the environment, one must first understand how they perceive it.

Hazards researchers have been especially interested in how the filter of people's perceptions might result in suboptimal adjustment to hazards (Saarinen et al. 1984), or in how local understanding allows an accommodation for hazards (Whyte 1986). Although this work has illustrated some relevant factors (e.g., the roles of experience, tradition, and professional training in choice of adjustment), it has been criticized for its inability to define perception unambiguously and link perceptions to actual behavior (Bunting and Guelke 1979; Gold and Goodey 1984). Yet, within limits, it would seem that perceptions, or what may best be called "expectations," of climate and climate change among policymakers and other resource managers will affect how they respond to global change. Thus, this perspective also should be explored in global change studies.

HAZARDS AS EXTREME EVENTS

Besides comprising a human-ecological web interpreted by human perceptions, hazards can also be seen simply as extreme geophysical events with certain characteristics that threaten social well-being. This definition is, perhaps, the one most likely to be transferred to global change research because it is the easiest to operationalize through measures of physical events. By definition, global change, especially climate change, will alter the nature of extreme environmental events—in terms of frequency, magnitude, and spatial and temporal distribution. Surprisingly, however, most climate change research to date has focused on changes in average conditions, partly because the higher moments of statistical distributions (e.g., variance and extremes) are difficult to measure and model.

Hazardous Natural Processes

Soviet geographers have developed considerable experience in the classification of hazards as discrete events. Under the rubric of research on "hazardous natural processes and phenomena" (HNPs; see Table 4.1), they have built generalizations about HNP interactions based on relationships between sets of hazards, as follows:

1. HNPs that are incompatible in time (e.g., abundant rains and forest fires).
2. HNPs whose probability decreases when considered in relation to another HNP (e.g., the freezing of winter crops and abnormally high spring floods). It is possible to differentiate variations in the causative links between the occurrence of one and the absence of another HNP, or even their negative correlation, for points 1 and 2, while point 2 also includes those cases where, having occurred at the same time, one influences the other or the two develop independently.

Table 4.1 Genetic types and some kinds of hazardous natural processes and phenomena (HNP). HNPs that can initiate other hazardous phenomena are italicized.

	Recurring HNPs		
Occasional	Perennial (cyclic or seasonal)	Single HNPs

1. Lithospheric (geological-geophysical) HNPs

Earthquakes, volcanic eruptions, tsunamis, great rockfalls	certain *landslides*	Ground subsidence, deformations of subsurface work

2. HNPs on the boundaries of lithosphere, atmosphere, and hydrosphere (geomorphological, exogenous)

	pulsation of glaciers, mudflows, soil erosion deflation, ravine erosion, deformation of riverbeds, abrasion	Subsidence of perennial frozen ground

3. Atmospheric-hydrospheric HNPs

	hurricanes, floods, wind-induced flood surges, extreme precipitation, frosts, droughts, hail, glaze, soft rime, etc.	

4. Biotic HNPs

	forest and steppe fires, desertification, mass reproduction of pests, epidemics, epizootics, etc.	

Sources: Aristarkhova 1971; Chalov 1979; Dzyuba et al. 1984; Flejshman and Petrov 1976; Gorbunov 1984; Gulakyan et al. 1977; Kaplina 1965; Kotlov et al. 1967; Kyuntsel' 1980; Larionov et al. 1984; Lukashov 1987; Anonymous 1987; Popov et al. 1987; Rozhkov 1981; Sapunov 1985; Sovershaev 1987; Tushinsky 1970, 1971; Zolotarev 1983; Zolotarev et al. 1987.

3. Independent HNPs (e.g., earthquakes and droughts); there are occurrences of both mutual weakening and strengthening HNPs when they occur together.
4. Combinations of HNPs that increase each other's probability, assuming that one of them does occur (e.g., glacial surge and glacial mudflows [Krenke 1974]). Incidents to be distinguished include those having unidirectional (glacial surge and mudflow) and bidirectional (avalanches and rockslides) influences as well as those lacking any sign of direct influence (avalanches

and floods in Soviet Georgia; the common reason being abnormal precipitation). In case of mutual influence, different HNPs may increase each other's intensity.

5. HNPs that occur only with other HNPs: unidirectional (e.g., storm winds and blizzards) and bidirectional (e.g., extreme floods and ice dams in Siberian rivers).

A similar classification can be applied to spatial combinations of HNPs as well. This serves as a possible basis for mapping the intensity and probable incidence of HNPs. From a geographical viewpoint, a spatial classification of HNP sets is probably more useful than a temporal classification. The spatial classification may be used for planning the future development of an area and for evaluating the probability of HNPs after different global change scenarios (Legasov et al. 1984; Myagkov 1984; Voskresensky et al. 1987).

The degree of risk to both life and economic activity in an area depends not only on the likelihood of different HNPs taken separately and on the correlations mentioned above, but also on the probable damage caused by each of the HNPs (e.g., probability of death of each person, amount of material damage) separately or in combination. One should bear in mind the possibility of synergism (sometimes antagonism) not only in the intensity of several HNPs but, possibly, in the damage resulting from their combination.

It is also important that the evolution of hazards over time be included in any classification schema. For instance, three factors might increase future hazards: (1) the general growth of population and production pressures, as well as increased urbanization; (2) the use of more extreme natural environments for the location of settlements and industrial units; and (3) the growth in communications problems that will accompany the increasing complexity of industrial links along with the great increase in energy consumption. Estimating the hazards caused by climatic changes is still difficult because the changes themselves are uncertain (Myagkov 1989a). Yet this factor may turn out to be more important than many others. Nevertheless, on the whole, the potential damage from HNPs should increase in the next decade at a faster rate than the productivity of the world's economy (Myagkov 1986, 1989b).

The United Nations has already initiated a straightforward way to deal with this situation by establishing the International Decade of Natural Hazard Reduction (National Research Council [NRC] 1987a; J. K. Mitchell 1988). Experts from different branches of science, technology, and industrial management are joined together in this work, and geographers are already playing an essential role in the program.

It is important to emphasize that suggestions concerning possible changes in HNPs must accompany any general prediction of changes in natural environmental and regional production systems. Methods for such predictions are being developed (Lipatov 1977; Saf'yanov 1978; Yermakov and Ryabchikov 1980, 1982; Dulov 1983; Zvonkova et al. 1985; Koshin and Myagkov 1986; Chistov 1987; Zvonkova 1987). Still lacking is a technique for linking global change to environmental modifications caused by industries or operations with particularly hazardous technologies.

A useful contribution of the geographical approach to the understanding of HNPs would be the production of an atlas. The first section of such an atlas might include maps of natural factors that account for the distribution and regime of HNPs. These maps would then provide the foundation for the second section, which would map the distributions of the spatiotemporal and physical parameters of the most important HNPs, both at present and as expected under global change scenarios. This information is necessary for selecting possible protection measures. Beside maps of individual types of HNPs, it is necessary to have maps of types of combined HNPs.

The third section would include maps of the social-economic significance of HNPs. These maps would show various economic risks related to HNPs, including the increased costs in the construction and operation of different units requiring protection from HNPs now and in the future.

Atlases of this kind are needed on a world scale. For individual countries they should be executed in a more readable manner with recommendations affixed to suggest how humans might protect themselves from natural disasters. Is such an atlas possible? A review of publications of the Problem Laboratory of Snow Avalanches and Mudflows (Vashalova et al. 1984; Okolov and Myagkov 1987; Vashalova 1987) shows the significant progress that has been made in the techniques of mapping HNPs. The work of S. A. Rakita (1975, 1983) stands out among Soviet studies for its integrated approach to methods of mapping HNPs and unfavorable natural conditions. It provides maps for over half of the Soviet Union that are useful for engineering-climatic and engineering-hydrological regionalization. This series is supplemented by maps that show different transportation schemes optimized on the basis of costs.

Japan is also well advanced in HNP mapping. A systematic recording of HNPs and their damage was started there in the late 1940s. The data obtained have been integrated into a series of large-scale maps covering the country. These reflect the distribution and characteristics of HNPs that account for 80 percent of the average annual economic loss from natural disasters (e.g., typhoons, extreme rainfall, earthquakes). Other countries—the USSR, the USA, Switzerland, and Norway, for example—have produced survey maps for their countries (or significant portions thereof). These reflect the most important HNPs as well as their regional combinations.

The experience already gained provides a good starting point from which joint international scientific teams may undertake detailed analyses of the natural disaster problem within the framework of global change.

Natural Hazards and Global Change

Finally, it can be argued that social systems will respond not to slow changes in mean conditions but to extreme events and changes in the frequency with which critical thresholds are surpassed. Thus we will respond to individual, worsened "storm surges" rather than gradual sea-level rise, to "droughts" on the Great Plains rather than cumulative drying, and to "heat waves" rather than gradually warmer summers.

This tendency must be carefully analyzed and monitored as societies adjust to global change. It may be that "fixes" applied to extreme events may not be sufficient or efficacious in dealing with cumulative trends, and "crisis response" is not likely to be as efficient a way to adapt to climate change as more careful, proactive planning would be. This lesson is only slowly being learned in natural hazards mitigation (NRC 1987a), and the persistent gap between scientific understanding (e.g., we know a lot about how and where floods, earthquakes, and other hazards occur, and how to mitigate their impacts), and our ability to reduce their finite negative impacts (losses continue to increase as regions develop) is worth contemplating as we move forward with research to define global change. One disturbing prospect is that of a great outpouring of hard-won new knowledge on global environment with little application to social development and well-being.

4.2 Risk Assessment*

Dimensions of Risk Assessment

Virtually no human activity is without risk, and it can be assumed that individuals have been making informal assessments of known risks for thousands of years. During this time, priests, seers, and other selected citizens have also been given formal responsibility for assessing some kinds of risks (Covello and Mumpower 1985). Despite these venerable precedents, a professional field of risk assessment has arisen only in the past twenty years.

The field of risk assessment is still evolving, and research adds new insights on an almost daily basis. Not surprisingly, a clear consensus about terminology and concepts is lacking. For example, the words *risk*, *hazard*, and *uncertainty* are often used indiscriminately and interchangeably, or are defined differently by different authors. Given the fact that different formulations tend to reflect the distinctive needs of particular user groups, it is unrealistic to expect that a common vocabulary and common definitions will soon be adopted.

*This section is an abbreviated version of J. K. Mitchell, *Risk Assessment of Global Environmental Change*. Working Paper No. 13, Environment and Policy Institute. Honolulu, Hawaii: East-West Center, January 1989.

Risk assessment, risk evaluation, risk analysis, and risk management are increasingly recognized as major subdivisions of the field.

Risk assessment includes the identification, measurement, and characterization of threats to human welfare. It incorporates the investigation of both the risks themselves and their impacts on human societies. Various procedures are employed to canvass a spectrum of threats that exceed minimum impact thresholds, to determine when and where they are most likely to occur, to compare and estimate the consequences, and to assess possible courses of action. Many people regard risk assessment as a predominantly scientific activity that should be undertaken before decisions about management strategies are made. Choices among management alternatives should be informed by the best available information about risks and hazards.

Risk evaluation is a sociopolitical process that involves bringing together available information about risks and hazards from expert and lay sources for the purpose of making a policy decision about appropriate responses. In addition to the scientific assessments of risks, laws, customs, ethics, values, attitudes, and preferences are among the many factors that may be taken into consideration. The weighing of risks and benefits associated with specific actions is an important component of risk evaluation.

Risk assessment and risk evaluation together constitute *risk analysis*. Outputs from risk analysis become inputs to the process of *risk management*, which involves the use of policies and techniques to influence the generation and impacts of hazards. Individual hazards may occasionally be prevented by eliminating the agents of loss (e.g., smallpox), but avoidance or reduction is more often achieved by improving preparedness and by modifying risks, exposure, and vulnerability, as well as by cushioning losses via effective relief-and-recovery measures. Various models of the risk-management process have been published by public agencies and researchers (Kates and Kasperson 1983; U.S. Council on Environmental Quality 1985). American geographers have developed interactive models of natural risk management and technological risk management that have gained considerable acceptance in the United States and elsewhere (Burton et al. 1978; Kates and Kasperson 1983). Comparative international risk management studies have begun to illuminate the importance of different modes of implementation of risk-management measures among countries, but there are as yet no meaningful measures of success in hazard management.

A word of caution is in order here. The preceding characterization of risk analysis and risk management is essentially a pedagogic device rather than a portrait of reality. Sometimes the process of analyzing and managing risks follows the enumerated sequence and there is significant interaction among the components. At other times the tasks of assessment, evaluation, and management are pursued separately—out of sequence and with varying degrees of thoroughness. Moreover, the assessment, evaluation, and management components may not be equally weighted. Some decisions are made without securing any scientific information; others ignore or misuse available information. Given the unequal distribution of risks and rewards among affected populations, the evaluation of risk is open to varying interpretations. In many cases the assessment process is influenced by a premature commitment of decision makers to a particular management alternative or an abbreviated range of alternatives. Clearly, the value of risk assessment as an aid to improving human safety depends to a great extent on how it is used in making decisions about risk. Studies of the use of risk information to change public policies and private behavior are relatively few, but the available evidence is not always encouraging. Many observers are pessimistic about prospects for persuading public leaders to pay more than lip service to slow-developing environmental threats. Clear-cut success stories are few, partial, and slow to emerge. For example, a decade of high-visibility risk assessments of ozone depletion indicated the need to curtail global production of chlorofluorocarbons (Downing and Kates 1982) well before the Montreal protocol on phasing out CFCs was initiated in 1987.

The emergence of risk assessment as a formal field betokens deep-seated misgivings about existing approaches to the management of natural hazards and hazardous technologies. Crisis response is no longer regarded as an adequate or appropriate strategy. In the face of mounting evidence that old hazards are beginning to worsen and new hazards are emerging rapidly, there is increasing emphasis on anticipatory public policies. Risk assessment is an important element in this process. The shift from reactive policies toward anticipatory policies is not yet far advanced, and it will never be total because unforeseen threats are always possible. Nonetheless, the trend toward policies that favor preparedness, mitigation, and prevention of hazards seems to be growing.

Formal risk assessment is the latest in a group of analytic procedures that have been developed over the past forty years to assist public decision making. Among others, this group includes benefit-cost analysis, technology assessment, and environment impact assessment. These procedures are designed to provide ways of comparing and integrating diverse, often seemingly incommensurable, information about one or more alternative policy choices. They are intended to supply yardsticks for the selection of alternatives that are, respectively, economically most efficient, technologically most appropriate, and best fitted to their environments. Risk assessment adds another dimension to the evaluation of policy choices by integrating information about probabilities of disruption in natural systems, probabilities of failure in man-made systems, and likely consequences. But, like the other evaluation techniques, risk assessment has the potential to be something more than an aid to bureaucracy. It provides a means of highlighting issues of safety and survival that were previously ignored, neglected, subsumed, or camouflaged in decision making. As information about risks—and the process by which they are evaluated—is made available to the public, the prospect of a more representative debate about the global future increases, and with it the likelihood of achieving effective policies for avoiding or preventing the breakdown of life-support systems.

Methods of Risk Assessment

The modern field of risk assessment was pioneered mainly by engineers, biologists, and health scientists in North America and the United Kingdom. Behavioral scientists and human ecologists, including geographers, have also made important recent contributions to the field (Lowrance 1976; Kates 1978; Whyte and Burton 1980; Fischoff et al. 1981; Kates et al. 1985). Disasters and accidents frequently provided stimuli for the initial formal studies of risks; and these in turn laid the groundwork for development of risk-assessment procedures and institutions. Separate methods were devised for different types of risks, and separate systems of risk assessment were often adopted by different public and private organizations. Despite this diversity, three broad methods of risk assessment can be identified: (1) extrapolation from historical data, (2) heuristic modeling, and (3) reasoning by analogy (R. Wilson and Crouch 1987).

NATURAL RISKS AND PHYSICAL VULNERABILITY

Earthquake risk assessments illustrate approaches and methods used to assess local risks that have cumulative global effects. Earthquake risk is not a standardized concept, and there are many ways to measure and display the risks. One approach confines attention to the measurement of physical risks and the vulnerability of buildings to seismic shocks. Investigations of this type have led to the identification of "seismic gaps" and differential earthquake risk zones of subnational proportions, as well as to the preparation of microzonation maps and other devices that illustrate loss potential (Foster 1980, 1984; Terwindt 1983; Nakano et al. 1986). Complex computer simulations of building damage have been developed for use by the insurance industry and by national and local land-use planning and development agencies (Office of the UN Disaster Relief Coordinator 1979; Petak and Atkisson 1982; Friedman 1984).

Physical vulnerability is only one aspect of overall societal vulnerability. Unfortunately, some hazard-reduction programs appear to assume that physical vulnerability subsumes all aspects of vulnerability and that mitigation can be achieved by public awareness programs citing regulations and building controls (Barazangi and Rouhban 1983). A more complete assessment of hazards requires taking account of socioeconomic vulnerability.

ASSESSMENT OF SOCIOECONOMIC VULNERABILITY

Earthquakes that disable or destroy key economic facilities can have a disproportionate impact on affected regions. A good example is the earthquake that struck Ecuador in 1986. Relatively few people were killed, but the export of oil was halted, roads used for carrying commodities to coastal ports were severed, and the entire economic system was thrown into turmoil. It is widely believed that a major earthquake in southern California could severely impair computer networks that are used by international banking and investment institutions, thereby causing backups in international financial operations that might eventually bring global economic transfers to a halt.

Although the methodology required to assess economic vulnerability is not substantially different from the methodology used for physical vulnerability assessment, relatively few studies of economic vulnerability have been undertaken (Cuny 1983). After more than a decade the National Oceanic and Atmospheric Administration's early studies of earthquake losses in San Francisco and Los Angeles are still representative in the United States (U.S. Department of Commerce 1973a, 1973b). In view of the importance of the economic development process as a force for the addition of new loss potential, assessments of economic vulnerability may be valuable tools in making development planning sensitive to environmental risks (J. K. Mitchell 1988).

The concept of social vulnerability is still evolving. Some analysts apply it specifically to disadvantaged social groups such as the elderly, women with young children, the handicapped, the ill, and ethnic, racial, linguistic, or religious minorities (Pankhurst 1984). Such groups are more likely to be severely affected by disasters because they lack access to decision-making forums and have few resources to deploy on their own behalf. Other observers are more concerned about the impairment of social institutions that provide support networks before, during, and after disasters. These include families, communities, clans, and nongovernmental organizations (Cuny 1983). Institutions may be vulnerable to disasters themselves, or they may be susceptible to poorly conceived assistance programs and redevelopment activities that undermine local coping capabilities. The ultimate result may be institutionalized dependence on governmental programs that eventually become overloaded, underfunded, and ill equipped.

Finally, there is a growing belief that broad socioeconomic and political forces may push large numbers of poor people to the spatial and economic margins of society where they are at the mercy of even small-scale natural risks (Susman et al. 1983). In many developing nations, hazard loss potential is concentrated among poorer residents who occupy steep, unstable slopes and gullies, badly drained hollows, and similar marginal areas. From this perspective, there is reason to question the practice of labeling such hazards "natural" (Wijkman and Timberlake 1984). Unless enlightened actions are taken to redress the plight of people in these places, they are in danger of becoming perpetual hostages to hazard.

Methods for collecting and integrating data on social vulnerability with data on physical risks and physical vulnerability are at an early stage of development. Slowness to incorporate information about social vulnerability in risk assessments recalls the slow evolution of social impact assessment methods in the field of environmental impact assessment. One example of a partially integrated earthquake risk assessment is provided by Kolars (1982), who combined information about five levels of seismic risk in Turkey with data about population potential, road-transportation accessibility, and levels of socioeconomic development in urban and rural areas. This enabled him to show that 6 percent of the nation's population—residents of poor rural districts in eastern Turkey—have the greatest loss potential, despite the fact that 95 percent of all Turkish citizens live in earthquake risk zones.

As the preceding example demonstrates, generalized social vulnerability assessments can be carried out on a national scale, but many dimensions of social vulnerability probably are best observed at local scales of analysis. Patterns of social relations and social disadvantage are often fine-grained, and individual buildings or individual sites may contain diverse populations that exhibit many different kinds of social vulnerability.

Taking Response Capability into Account

One other aspect of risk and vulnerability assessments requires comment. This concerns the degree to which they take account of existing and possible measures for the reduction of risk and vulnerability. Many of the studies to date have assumed that risk and vulnerability are passive or fixed states represented by conditions at the moment of the survey. Clearly, this is a misleading interpretation. Human responses, including preparedness and mitigation activities, help to shape the risk, hazard, and vulnerability experienced by people. Responses may be few or many, relatively inconsequential or highly effective, stable or changing. The full range of existing alternatives may not have been adopted, and new alternatives may yet emerge fortuitously or through a program of planned development. Hence, risk and vulnerability are highly dynamic states. Assumptions about the current status of risk and vulnerability and the factors that will influence them in the future are usually implicit in risk assessments, but they need to be uncovered and subjected to careful analysis.

It is clear that risk assessment should take account of the potential for improving reduction of risks and vulnerability. This does not mean that such potential will or can be realized by the specific populations at risk. A great deal of work will be necessary to identify and develop measures of "realizable potential" for different groups and areas. Decisions about such matters involve considerations beyond the topic of risks per se, including the economic dimensions of public policy and the subject of economic development.

Russian geographers have done pioneering work on relationships between environmental constraints and economic investments (Kozhukhov 1982). Many of these studies have been carried out in support of northern development schemes involving mining, transportation, and housing projects. There have been recent systematic evaluations of the extra costs imposed on urban construction by the aggregate effects of climate, relief, subsoil, permafrost, waterlogging, avalanches, mudflows, glaciers, seismicity, and a variety of other adverse environmental factors. In one study, limiting environmental parameters for buildings and infrastructures were established on the basis of observations in sample localities, and cost increments were estimated for actual construction projects. These standards were then applied to the 305 physiographic regions that cover the entire Soviet Union. The results show that adverse environmental conditions impose only small extra costs on construction in the relatively benign lands of the European plain, but the cost of building may be doubled or tripled in the Arctic islands, the provinces of central Asia, and much of eastern and northeastern Siberia (Fig. 4.3).

It has become increasingly apparent that there are close connections between the process of development and vulnerability to disasters—both natural and human-made (Cuny 1983). Unfortunately, there is little evidence that hazard reduction is a prime consideration for the organizations and individuals responsible for initiating and managing the economic development process (J. K. Mitchell 1988). If risk assessment is to realize its potential as an aid to responsible environmental management and development activities, it will be necessary to ensure that information about the costs of hazards and protection programs—and the benefits of hazard mitigation—is fully integrated into development decisions.

Technological Risks and Impacts

Whereas the global impact of natural hazards is mainly the aggregate of local effects, many of the risks that will face the world in the twenty-first century involve unforeseen environmental impacts of new technologies that quickly become global in scope. These risks pose difficult problems for the developing field of impact assessment (see section 4.3). Undesirable modifications of the atmosphere have attracted widespread attention from impact assessors. Climate impact assessments are distinct from climate change assessments, which seek to establish the nature of physical changes in the atmosphere. Unfortunately, our understanding of the global dynamics of human systems is limited, and it is not possible to predict changes in the human component of climate change beyond a few years into the future (Bolin 1986; Jäger 1986). The entire

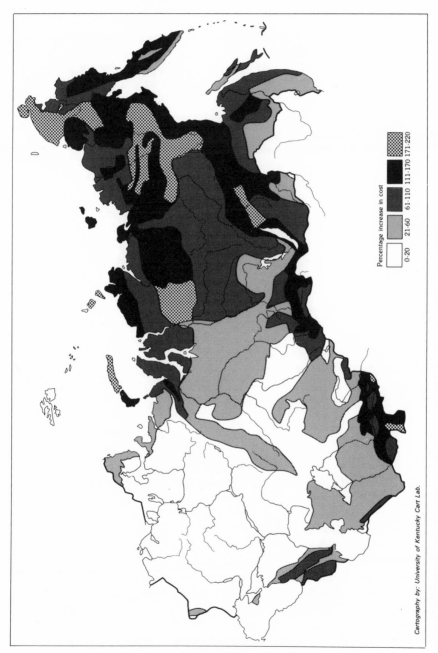

Cartography by: *University of Kentucky Cart Lab.*

Percentage increase in cost

171-220
111-170
61-110
21-60
0-20

Fig. 4.3 Rise in urban construction costs due to environmental factors, USSR. (From Kozhukhov 1981)

enterprise of climate change prediction is subject to major uncertainties. As a result, investigators have pressed ahead with studies that focus on physical, biological, economic, and sociopolitical impacts and implications of climate change (Chen et al. 1983; R. A. Warrick and Riebsame 1983; Kates et al. 1985; see section 4.3).

There is somewhat less overlap between natural science research and social science research in the field of climate assessment than in the field of natural hazards assessment. Assessments of natural hazards and natural hazard impacts are carried out at all scales, but most of the detailed work on climate change assessment has been carried out at global levels of analysis, while most of the work on climate impact assessment has been subglobal (Parry 1986; Gleick 1987). This contrast reflects differences between measures of risk and measures of vulnerability. Most of the risks of global climate change are universal and lend themselves to analysis from a top-down perspective. Earthquake risks, on the other hand, range from local to subcontinental in scale and may be examined from both top-down and bottom-up perspectives. In contrast, measures of vulnerability take account of densely patterned societal variables such as age, gender, and economic status. Vulnerability to earthquakes and climate change varies widely even within small areas, thereby favoring a local scale of analysis and a bottom-up perspective in vulnerability and impact assessments. These observations bear on the general issue of choosing appropriate scales and perspectives for risk assessments of global environmental change. Both the limitations of global analyses of climate change and the demand for information about risks that is useful to public policy makers underscore the importance of local field research.

Issues of Scale and Perspective

The cumulation and interaction of many separate risks creates a risk mosaic that varies widely from place to place as well as through time (Zeigler et al. 1983). Private decisions and public policies are formulated in response to prevailing environmental conditions in different parts of the mosaic and in consideration of the range of available courses of action. Hence, risk assessment must be carried out from the bottom-up perspective of resource managers in specific localities as well as from the top-down perspective of scientists who use the techniques of global modeling. The IGBP represents a top-down approach to the analysis of global environmental change (Schneider 1986, 1987) because it is primarily concerned with developing and refining global models of environmental systems that integrate previously separate models from the earth and atmospheric sciences and the biological sciences. The focus is on physical systems and risk, not on human ecological systems and exposure, vulnerability, and responses. The IGBP research strategy (IGBP 1988) makes little provision for exploring the local dimensions of physical environmental changes, nor does it address the coupling of natural systems to society.

It is inappropriate to apply the top-down risk-assessment methods derived from global modeling to worldwide environmental changes that are composed of accumulated local risks. There is more apparent logic to applying top-down approaches to universal risks, but the impacts of such risks are likely to vary from one place to another, so it will undoubtedly pay dividends to combine top-down and bottom-up approaches. In addition to being the most direct approach to the nexus of environmental processes that affects specific places, a bottom-up perspective facilitates the acquisition of information suitable for practical application by environmental management institutions and citizens at risk. A bottom-up perspective is also consistent with the intellectual thrust of geographical research (Hewitt 1983a; Abler 1987; Cutter 1988; O'Riordan 1988). It emphasizes the diversity of places in which change occurs and the great range of natural and human factors that create this diversity; it focuses on direct human experience and favors fieldwork; it encourages the use of dynamic interactive models of human ecological adjustment and adaptation; and it places a premium on the skills of interdisciplinary collaboration, synthesis, and integration.

Risk Assessment as an Aid to Managing Global Risks

What does this analysis of risk assessment tell us that might be helpful in the task of managing global environmental change? First, it suggests that concepts and methods are sufficiently developed and reliable to allow risk assessment to be more widely employed as a public decision-making tool. Certainly, the capabilities to assess different types of global risk are not equal. We are better equipped to assess sudden-onset threats than slow-developing ones. We are also better able to assess universal risks that affect near-term extreme events than longer-term changes that bring significant shifts of environmental means. Much more is known about risks and risk management in more developed nations than in the less developed nations where most of the world's population lives and where there is the largest potential for catastrophe. Nonetheless, risk assessment is a rapidly developing field. The concept of risk is being broadened. Techniques for assessing physical and natural components of risk are being joined by techniques that take human exposure and human vulnerability into account. There are increasing prospects for developing measures of different types of vulnerability—both individual and collective. Using the tools that are already available, and with the prospect of more to come, assessment of global environmental risk is a feasible proposition.

Second, it is clear that more is known about risk assessment than is put into practice in support of public policies and environmental management programs. Valuable means for reducing losses are being overlooked, especially in the less developed nations that are most at risk. Prospects for enhancing human well-being would be assisted by efforts to (1) acquaint decision makers with risk assessment, (2) perfect techniques for feeding risk information into public and private decision-making processes at appropriate times and places, (3) encourage public leaders to commission risk assessments and to take account of the results, and (4) provide incentives for the adoption of effective risk-management strategies.

Third, despite all our advances, risk assessment is still an incomplete set of procedures. In particular, the components of risk assessment are not fully integrated and there is no systematic means for taking account of independent contextual factors that influence risk. There is no easy solution to these problems, and they underscore the need for broad-based approaches to the analysis of risk and the development of risk-management systems. No single theoretical or methodological approach is likely to be sufficient; a hierarchy of investigative strategies is more appropriate, but these will have to be chosen with care (see below). Close collaboration among existing producers and users of risk information will enhance the integration of assessment and management. So too will measures that strengthen links between investment and development groups and organizations that have responsibilities for protecting society against undesirable risks.

Fourth, because risk assessment is a young and rapidly changing field, there has not been sufficient development of detailed guidelines for the use of different perspectives, methods, and techniques. As a result, methods have sometimes been misapplied and there are disputes about the accuracy of specific assessments. These problems are particularly acute if cross-cultural interpretation is involved or there is borrowing of assessment models across spatial and temporal scales (Land and Schneider 1987). Global risk assessment teams that are both international and interdisciplinary in composition offer one possible way to avoid such pitfalls.

The outlines of a program for assessing risks of global environmental change can now be sketched. Organizationally, it should be collaborative, integrative, and dynamic. Researchers from different disciplines and countries should be involved in interactive association with policymakers, managers, representatives of nongovernmental organizations, and affected publics from around the world. Assessment of risks of environmental change should become a permanent, ongoing process rather than a specific activity that follows emergencies.

From a methodological standpoint, risk assessments should adopt a predominantly bottom-up perspective that emphasizes the multifaceted environmental conditions that humans experience directly. The burden of global risk should be determined by aggregating the joint local products of risk, exposure, vulnerability, and response. This means that global modeling approaches to global risk assessment can offer only limited assistance to risk assessors. It also places a premium on the synthesis of local field data concerning many different environmental changes within broad conceptual frameworks that accommodate both environmental processes and human behavior. This view is in harmony with the emphasis placed by geographers on landscape dynamics and the delineation of areas especially significant in terms of landscape change.

In order to facilitate implementation, risk assessment should be tied firmly to the needs of policymakers and resource managers for information that can—where possible—be used by existing institutions. While it is necessary to emphasize hazards that are associated with global change, it is also necessary to be mindful that the impacts of global change will vary and may be beneficial for some areas and some groups. Policymakers must design appropriate mechanisms for taking these differences into account.

4.3 Assessing Social Impacts of Environmental Change

Impact Assessment Approaches

Since the emergence of contemporary concerns for environmental quality in the late 1960s, "impact assessment" has come to connote efforts to anticipate and measure the impacts of specific development projects on the natural environment. Useful guides to the environmental impact assessment (EIA) process are provided by Munn (1980) and Westman (1985). The EIA approach was created to anticipate environmental impacts of facilities like power plants, hydroelectric dams, and irrigation schemes, and activities like disposal of hazardous materials and storage of radioactive wastes. It is codified in national environment laws such as the 1969 National Environmental Protection Act in the United States, which requires an environmental impact statement (EIS) for any project involving federal action. Some form of environmental impact assessment is now required in at least twenty-nine countries (Westman 1985).

The EIA process focuses on humans' impact on the environment, not vice versa, and has generally been restricted to local or, at the most, regional impacts extrapolated over a few decades. Thus, as typically pursued, the EIA process is only partially applicable to research on changes in the global environment, their regional manifestation, or their ramifications in social systems. Yet, some EIA methods, with modifications, will be useful in global-change impact studies; for example, the identification and monitoring of key species and other indicators of impacts, the use of impact matrices, and methods for anticipating the interaction of multiple environmental impacts (see Munn 1980).

Environmental impact assessment is complemented by social impact assessment (SIA) to project the economic and social implications of development projects or other human activities. Finsterbusch and Wolf (1977) defined social

Table 4.2 Socioeconomic impact categories.

1. Demographic impacts: rural depopulation; suburban growth; etc.

2. Economic impacts: income, employment, and taxes; the affected parties; impacts on business and large property owners; increased short-term and long-term employment; the "boom and bust" pattern of project construction; problems of local inflation and short-term changes in supply and demand patterns.

3. Impacts on social values and attitudes:
   (a) Community cohesion; the social integration of the community and the mechanisms by which individuals and groups within a defined area maintain functional ties with one another;
   (b) Life-style, a perceptual and behavioral dimension, referring to accepted values and day-to-day behavior in the affected communities, as well as to outsiders' views of these values and behavior.

Source: After Munn (1980). Reprinted with permission of SCOPE, Scientific Committee on Problems of the Environment, International Council of Scientific Unions.

impact assessment as any attempt to measure and anticipate the impacts of technological development, environmental development, or any planned environmental intervention on society. As such, the field has not focused on the social implications of environmental changes, but rather on the direct social implications of specific projects and development plans. Some of the indicators commonly included in SIAs are listed in Tables 4.2 and 4.3. Some "interventions," like weather modification and large water-development schemes, subjected to SIA (see Farhar-Pilgrim 1985), may emulate the impacts of global environmental changes at the regional level. Like EIAs, however, SIAs typically focus on predicting future impacts so that project decisions can be made. Few empirical or comparative studies have been conducted, and despite provisions in environmental laws for monitoring impacts after projects are in place, most assessment methods have not been tested in retrospective analysis (i.e., postproject audits). The approach thus lacks an empirical base. But some longitudinal analyses have been conducted, and they are beginning to show both the weaknesses and the strengths of impact assessments.

Empirical Analyses: Two Case Studies

Appraising a particular ecological situation involves understanding the combined impact of at least the following three factors: (1) the type and amount of anthropogenic impact on the environment; (2) response of the environment to this impact, and its transformation; and (3) the impact of this transformation on different human activities—economic, social, aesthetic, and demographic. Two cases, the Kursk Development Impacts Study and the Colorado River

Reservoir Impacts Study, illustrate integrated approaches to impact assessment and their strengths and weaknesses when applied to large-scale environmental and social changes.

KURSK DEVELOPMENT IMPACTS

One assessment approach employed by Soviet geographers draws on the concept of ecological regionalization and the preparation of a series of interrelated maps. The first stage involves compilation of a map of anthropogenic (including technogenic) *impact* on nature, while the second includes the production of a map of the anthropogenic *transformation* of nature. The third stage results in the development of an "ecological map" based on standard

Table 4.3 Indicators of rural household economic status.

Surveys of economic stratification. Household is unit of analysis.

Land ownership
    Quality of land
    Intensity of cultivation and types of crops
    Land outside sample area
    Tenants and landless

Ownership of capital equipment and consumer durables

Income
    Agricultural income
        Sale of crops
        Rent
        Hired labor
        Marketing and processing
    Nonagricultural income

Ownership of livestock

Ownership of nonproductive property
    Housing
    Furnishings and consumer goods

Access to fuel

Ceremonial expenditures

Diet, nutrition, and health

Education

Household size and composition

Source: Farhar-Pilgrim (1985). Reprinted with permission of SCOPE, Scientific Committee on Problems of the Environment, International Council of Scientific Unions.

evaluations of the role of human-caused changes in natural parameters. Thus the changes in the chemical composition of air, water, and soils are estimated by concentration of pollutants in relation to the maximum permissible levels; to evaluate the changes in a forested area, one must consider the functions of forests in the region (e.g., environment conservation, recreation areas, timber resources); to evaluate the changes in water supply, it is important to know such things as the ratio of available resources to water requirements. In cases where these criteria and standards are not available, are too general, or do not take into account regional specifics, indexes of a "permissible pressure" may be employed. These indexes are determined by the resilience of a given natural complex. For instance, standards of tree harvesting in the USSR have been developed on the basis of the resources and growth rates of timber in different zones; the same applies to the standards for commercial fishing and hunting. Regional standards of permissible pollutant discharge are under development. The levels of permissible pressure may be defined by calculations based on previously known relations. Thus, based on known rates of river flow, it is possible to define the permissible level of pollutant discharge; similar relationships have been developed for calculating the rate of pollutants' dispersal into the atmosphere.

Based on a methodology of ecological regionalization developed at the Institute of Geography of the USSR Academy of Sciences, two regions differing in natural environment and economy were studied: the Kursk region with its intensive agriculture, iron ore mining, and nuclear power plant, situated in a chernozem region of the country; and the Perm region with its developed forestry, mining, chemical, and oil industries, indigenous agriculture, and animal husbandry, in a nonchernozem zone.

The Kursk Magnetic Anomaly (KMA) region is a vivid example of the growth of a potentially critical ecological condition at the local level, as illustrated by the degree of the air pollution in the Kursk region (Figs. 4.4 and 4.5), particularly where the mining industry centers are located. There, under conditions of intensive agricultural development and dense population, the development of large-scale mining of iron ores and ferrous metallurgy has resulted in the appearance of sharp discrepancies among the interests of the various industries with regard to the use of the land, air, and water resources.

Fieldwork and data analyses have revealed certain chain reactions resulting in decreased ecological potential as a result of mining activities (Fig. 4.6). It is precisely these enterprises that form the centers of almost total anthropogenic-industrial transformation of nature and newly created landscapes (such as technogenic waste dumps for tailings, hydraulic-mine dumps, sludge-dumping ponds, settling ponds, and drainage mines that form the centers of groundwater draw-down cones). The anthropogenic-industrial effect on the ecological potential of the region weakens as one moves outward from these centers (Fig. 4.6), but a very noticeable change in the ecological potential of nearby regions

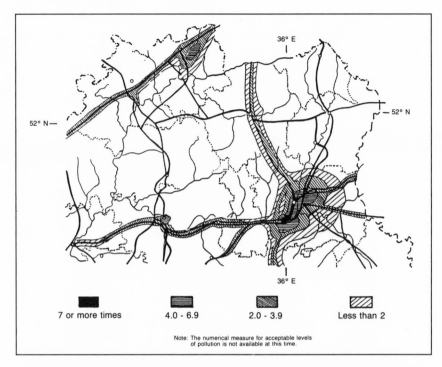

Fig. 4.4 Air pollution in the Kursk region. Shaded areas indicate by how much pollutants (SO_2, CO, NO_x) exceeded admissible atmospheric concentrations. Note: The numerical measure for acceptable levels of pollution is not available at this time.

is seen as a result of lowered groundwater tables and increased atmospheric pollution. The landscape is becoming more arid in character, and the groundwater supply to rivers is decreasing due to widening of the groundwater drawdown cone.

Geographers in socialist countries prepared a series of methodological recommendations resulting from an economic and extra-economic evaluation of the impact of man on the environment (Committee on Scientific and Technical Cooperation 1986). The recommendations were based on an assessment of the social consequences of the impacts of specific projects on different economic sectors in selected regions (including Kursk). The following conditions were examined in the step-by-step research: the impact of human activity as a trigger mechanism of interaction, landscape changes due to this impact, and consequences for the health of people and for economic activity as a result of feedbacks from the changed environment. Methodologies were suggested for integrated spatial study of the interaction of people, economy, and nature in order to devise a plan to preserve and improve the environment.

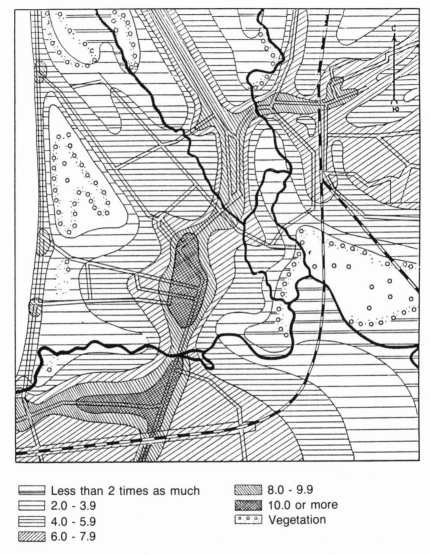

Less than 2 times as much   8.0 - 9.9
2.0 - 3.9   10.0 or more
4.0 - 5.9   Vegetation
6.0 - 7.9

Fig. 4.5 Degree of atmospheric pollution in Kursk in relation to admissible atmospheric concentrations.

COLORADO RIVER RESERVOIR IMPACTS

Another example of empirical and projective impact assessment illustrates the difficulties of following a comprehensive, step-by-step procedure to integrate impacts between physical and social systems. Fortunately, in this case a post hoc audit has been conducted. The National Research Council (1987b) recently reviewed the environmental studies conducted in 1978 by the U.S. Bureau of Reclamation to assess impacts of large impoundments on the Colorado River (Fig. 4.7).

The post hoc assessment team used an integrated template developed for the original studies (Fig. 4.8) to identify weaknesses and strengths in the assessment. Among their major conclusions were: (1) preproject baseline data were inadequate; (2) synergistic interactions and feedbacks between the major elements (Fig. 4.8) were either poorly understood, neglected, or simply could not be anticipated in the project design; and (3) management recommendations for reducing impacts were too vague for project designers and operators.

Some of these problems are likely to show up in a priori assessments of impacts and response to global change. For example, one goal of the original impact-mitigation component on the Colorado River was to achieve maximum density and diversity of floral and faunal assemblages in the river basin. This implied, to the managers, efforts to increase the number of plant and animal species, even though some effects in this regard—such as growth of exotic species—could be considered negative. Without further guidelines on appropriate actions, the vague criteria of increased "density and diversity" allowed some negative trends to be considered positive effects.

The review team also found that certain decisions on how to organize the original studies had negative consequences on subsequent project decisions. In particular, spatial and institutional boundaries placed on the original studies hampered the integration of data, and trends outside those boundaries were later shown to be relevant to the project and its impact. As with many impact studies, the original "scope" of the assessment was too narrowly drawn.

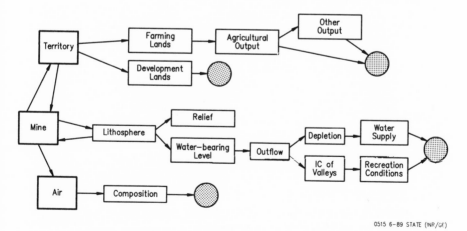

0515 6-89 STATE (INR/GF)

Fig. 4.6 Regional model of chain reactions leading to ecological change (as a result of mining activities).

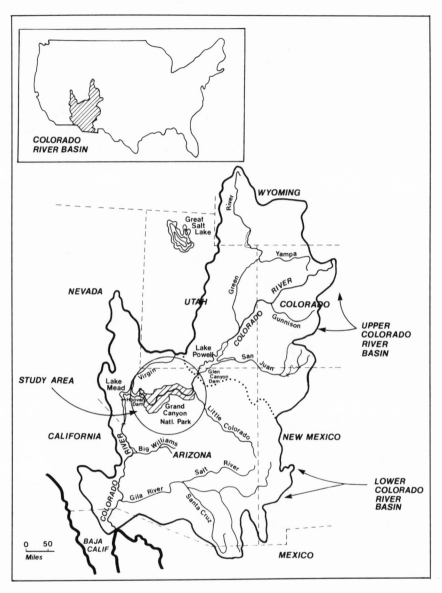

Fig. 4.7 Location map of the Colorado River basin. (Reprinted with permission of the National Academy Press, Washington, D.C.)

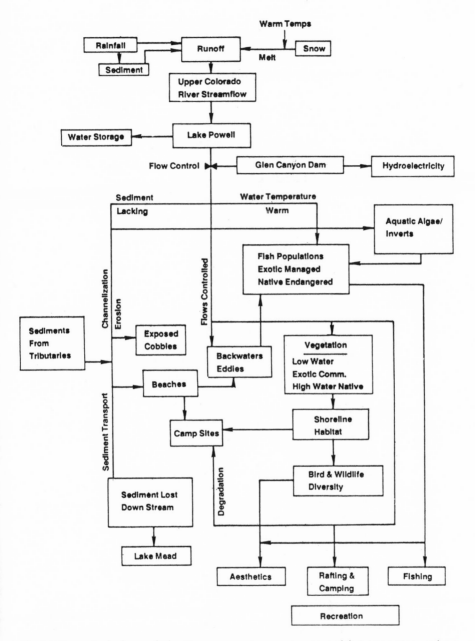

Fig. 4.8 Conceptual scheme of Glen Canyon ecosystem components and their interactions under present operations of Glen Canyon Dam. (Reprinted with permission of the National Academy Press, Washington, D.C.)

Despite such weaknesses, experiences with EIA and SIA will prove useful in designing a global-change impact study by offering guidance for assessing complex interactions between environmental and social elements, methods for extrapolating impacts into the near future, designs for monitoring schemes, and approaches to handling large amounts of data. Properly modified, these methods will be useful as we begin to assess global change impacts.

Assessing the Impacts of Climate Change

Concerns over the social implications of global change are driven chiefly by the potential effects of rapid climate change associated with global warming. Climate pervades essentially all natural resources and affects, subtly or more dramatically, many human activities. Thus, no single method will suffice to assess the effects of climate change on society. A wide range of approaches—from review of previous studies not originally conducted under the global change rubric to new field studies of perception, impact, and response—will be needed to assess social vulnerability to climate impacts. Flexible methods are necessary to accommodate large differences among studies in terms of goals, units of analysis, data availability, physical linkages between environmental elements, and socioeconomic settings. Yet such a methodologically untidy approach requires that impact assessors clearly define the scope of their analyses and be aware of the ramifications of their definitions and study choices. Some general themes that should be addressed in climate impact studies are now suggested.

CHOICE OF IMPACT UNITS

The first step in any assessment is to identify and clearly define the units of analysis; that is, the affected groups under consideration. As Kates (1985) notes: "Whatever the choice of events for which impacts are to be studied, an impacted group, activity or area exposed to those impacts must be selected. In general the focus is on individuals, populations . . . or species; activities in the form of livelihoods; specific sectors (in more differentiated economies); or on both groups and activities found within a specific society, region or nation-state."

Choice of affected units, scale, or the region or groups to be monitored is not always obvious or amenable to objective decision. The area to be studied is often bounded not by natural or cultural boundaries but by arbitrary political frontiers. The units to be studied may be determined largely by the goals of the impact assessor and will vary greatly between different natural resource and economic activities. For example, agricultural impacts might be studied for individual farms or at national or international scales of production and trade, or the assessor might choose to trace impacts as they ripple across these scales (Fig. 4.9). Assessments of natural resources such as forests may be

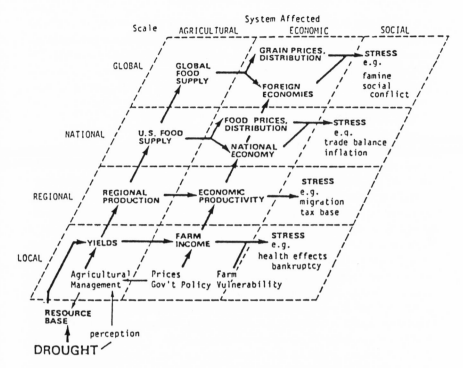

Fig. 4.9 The cascade of impacts of a drought in the United States Great Plains. (From Warrick and Bowden 1981, with permission of the University of Nebraska Press.)

delineated by ecosystem, or, in the case of water resources, by topographic boundaries. Here, the applications of "landscape dynamics," discussed in chapter 2, would help identify key analytical units. Studies of impacts on water resources might tend to focus on individual, integrated water systems operated by a central authority, while assessments considering, for example, rangeland livestock production might focus on more changeable impact units (e.g., pastoralists who frequently shift location).

Once the analytical units have been selected, the assessor can apply a step-wise analysis that begins with sensitivity analysis and then proceeds to empirical case studies and to the application of future climate scenarios to projective studies.

SENSITIVITY ANALYSIS

Social development trends bring about changing climate sensitivities in human systems. At least initially, most environmental-change impact studies will focus on particularly sensitive groups and regions; these can be roughly identified from previous research and theories of nature-society interaction.

Two basic principles apply. First, sensitivity to impacts from environmental changes is greatest where human activity and well-being rely most directly on immediate environmental inputs (e.g., self-provisioning or mixed agricultural societies) and where the range of possible adjustment (e.g., alternative food sources) is limited either environmentally or socially.

Second, vulnerability may be heightened in societies undergoing rapid change, especially where the traditional social institutions and processes are being replaced by industrial or market mechanisms and where this change fails to provide for future resilience (Watts 1983). The range of adjustments or alternatives available in the face of environmental stress is determined chiefly by social forces. In theory, the more options a society has in meeting human needs and wants, the less sensitive that society is to negative impacts from the environment. Enumerations of potential responses to environmental changes, drawn up by evaluating previous research or by conducting field surveys, help the impact assessor to identify particularly vulnerable activities or groups that might require aid to ameliorate impacts or need concerted efforts to reduce vulnerability—especially in developing countries (see section 4.2). If an impact assessor can ascertain adjustment gaps and the viability of available adjustments before large environmental changes occur, then impacts may be anticipated and plans for their amelioration formulated. It would be especially useful to identify social trends that reduce resiliency.

EMPIRICAL CASE STUDIES

Case studies are needed to provide empirical data on the social impacts of climate fluctuations. Some studies already conducted under other programs (e.g., desertification and natural hazards research) should be evaluated in light of the global climate change issue, and new studies should be organized to take account of our growing understanding of the potential patterns of climate change. Case studies of environmental changes might be selected from various rosters of environmental problems (see, e.g., Holdgate and White 1977) or from well-known and memorable episodes of obvious impacts (e.g., a particular climate fluctuation such as the Sahel drought or cumulative problems such as groundwater depletion, soil erosion, or woodland loss to fuelwood gathering). If the goal is to analyze the impacts of historical environmental changes, then results can be made more credible if some control is applied to data collection and analysis. For example, the impact assessor might compare indicator variables (e.g., fuelwood use, crop yields, farm income, nutrition) in a region undergoing a demonstrable environmental change with activities in a similar, but environmentally stable, region nearby. Such a "case-control" approach can isolate environmental impacts from the multitude of other physical and socioeconomic factors (e.g., market variations, war) that might affect the social well-being of a region. Among the indicators that should be analyzed are those suggested for monitoring desertification impacts (Table 4.4).

Table 4.4 Socioeconomic indicator categories for desertification.

1. Land use
   a. Irrigated agriculture
   b. Dry-land agriculture
   c. Pastoralism
   d. Cutting and removal of vegetation for fuel and construction
   e. Mining
   f. Tourism and recreational use

2. Settlement pattern, especially in rural populations and in relation to energy sources
   a. New settlement
   b. Expansion of settlement
   c. Diversification of settlement
   d. Abandonment of settlement

3. Human biological parameters
   a. Population structure and rates
   b. Measures of nutritional status
   c. Public health indices

4. Social process parameters
   a. Conflict
   b. Migration
   c. Redistribution patterns
   d. Marginalization
   e. Cash versus subsistence

Source: Reining (1978). *Handbook on desertification indicators based on the Science Association's Nairobi Seminar on Desertification,* reprinted with permission of the American Association for the Advancement of Science.

Where such case-control analysis is not feasible, the assessor may be able to devise a longitudinal design to compare impact indicators as environmental changes occur. A set of key impact indicators (e.g., the ratio of inputs to crop yields or relationships between fuelwood use and availability) should be documented for a period long enough to illustrate trends. Case studies might be strategically arrayed along or across environmental gradients. Examples include Heijnen and Kates's (1974) analysis of drought impacts along a moisture gradient in eastern Tanzania and the recent series of IIASA/UNEP (International Institute for Applied Systems Analysis/UN Environment Program) climate impact studies chosen to reflect conditions at the cold and dry margins of agriculture (where, it is expected, the impacts of climate change will be first and most seriously felt; see Parry et al. 1988).

Collaborative case studies focused on particular regions should be organized to assess impacts of interacting environmental changes such as climate fluctuation, soil erosion, groundwater depletion, desertification, deforestation, and coastal erosion. Large-scale comparative studies have been proposed in climate impact studies, such as matching the North China Plain and the North American Great Plains, or the Baltic Sea and the North American Great Lakes—areas that exhibit broad similarities in many environmental elements and human activities. The Working Group on Socio-Economic Impacts, convened at the 1985 Villach Conference on the Greenhouse Effect (see World Meteorological Organization [WMO] 1986), also proposed collaborative case studies in the Baltic, Zambezi Basin, and Amazonia. Other case studies might be organized by ecological zone (e.g., the world's large grasslands) or by social systems (e.g., pastoralism or dry-land farming).

Integrated assessments in selected regions would seek to identify impacts on, and feedbacks between, agriculture, forestry, water resources, raw materials processing, manufacturing, and secondary and tertiary economic activities like transportation, recreation, and government. Regional economic and resource allocation models (e.g., industrial input-output models or other econometric algorithms) will be useful in such studies, but there exists as yet little experience in their application to environmental change. In one recent study, G. D. V. Williams et al. (1988) assessed the economic impacts of a climate change in Saskatchewan, Canada, by linking climate, crop yield, and farm and regional economic models. But they did not assess soil erosion, pollution, or other changes associated with agricultural growth or decline.

The data and analytical requirements for such impact studies are large, and before embarking on them as part of global change research we should evaluate regional sensitivities, data quality, and, of course, the availability of methods and people to conduct integrated studies. Because no single impact assessor can possess all of the requisite insight to develop comprehensive assessments, case studies are best organized as broadly collaborative efforts that draw on the resources of multiple government agencies (e.g., meteorological services, agricultural bureaus, economic development offices, etc.), nongovernmental organizations, and university researchers. Some coordinative mechanism, perhaps similar to the World Climate Impacts Program coordinated by the UNEP, is necessary to establish and maintain the links and momentum needed to marshall the resources required for comprehensive global climate change impact studies.

Projecting Future Climate Impacts

Global-warming impact studies have been initiated by many national governments and by several international bodies (UNEP 1987). These studies indicate that anthropogenic climate change may result in significant shifts of vegetation zones, crop yields, freshwater runoff, sea level, and many other environmental factors during the next several decades.

Climate projections based on a human-enhanced greenhouse effect are compelling because they offer rough indications of the likely direction and magnitude of future climate trends. Current projections of the greenhouse climate are too uncertain to be used as regional predictions per se (Katz 1988), but they are useful in helping impact assessors to identify a range of possible costs and benefits, as well as policy options that are likely to help society cope with, or even benefit from, future climate changes.

SCENARIOS OF FUTURE CLIMATES

Scenarios of future climate are the first ingredient in impact-projection studies. It is prudent to explore more than one type of climate projection, and three general approaches have been used: (1) historical analogs, where past climate conditions are assumed to recur in the future; (2) modeled climate conditions based on statistical or dynamic models with altered radiation conditions; and (3) arbitrary scenarios. Each approach has weaknesses and strengths that must be weighed in choosing a method applicable to the impacts problem at hand (P. J. Lamb 1987). Historical analogs offer great detail but may not capture the full range of potential future climate changes. Climate models differ in their ability to simulate climate elements accurately. While most global climate models produce similar temperature patterns under greenhouse forcing, they yield precipitation changes sufficiently different between models to cause large differences in impact projections (M. E. Schlesinger and Mitchell 1985). Model output data are also too coarse to be applied to local impact assessments because entire regions are represented by single grid points in the model.

Alternatively, arbitrary scenarios consistent either with past fluctuations or with predictions based on model simulation (or both) have several useful characteristics. Impact assessments based on convenient ranges of climate values (e.g., 1°–2°C warming with 10 percent less precipitation) are easy to work with and relatively insensitive to changes in projections as models are refined. Arbitrary scenarios may also facilitate intuitive impacts estimation because they are less intimidating when presented to resource managers; greater detail or implied precision of analog or model scenarios may suggest more reliability than is warranted. However, arbitrary scenarios are simply that—arbitrary—and cannot emulate the empirical/theoretical consistency of the other approaches.

TRANSLATING CLIMATE SCENARIOS INTO IMPACTS

Once credible climate projections are selected, many of the approaches to impact assessment described earlier can be used to translate them into projected impacts. Relationships between climate and natural resources can be expressed as simple qualitative statements of the sign of impacts, rough rankings of impact magnitudes, or more formal statistical or physical simulation models; all of these can be applied to extrapolate impacts from scenarios. In light of the uncertainty of future projections, perhaps the most valuable use of scenarios is in sensitivity studies based on a range of future conditions rather than on a specific prediction.

Simulating Future Impacts

The great problem in projecting future impacts is that, for lack of better theories of social change, analysts often assume static social and technological conditions. It is difficult to predict future technological innovations and economic and social changes that might enhance or reduce impacts. One partial solution to this problem is simply to lay out the broad trends apparent now, and then to evaluate and rank their implications for future vulnerability. Impact assessors should consider whether there are indications now on trends in, for example, energy systems, water management, health care, demographics, settlement, and urban development that will increase or decrease society's ability to cope with projected climate changes.

A comprehensive assessment of potential future climate impacts affecting essentially all climate-sensitive activities is under way in the Great Lakes region of Canada and the United States. Cohen (1986) created a template for assessing elements of, and links between, the major economic activities likely to be affected by changes in climate and lake levels (Fig. 4.10). Such a template would be a useful guide to comprehensive studies elsewhere. Its construction is also the first step in assessing regional sensitivities, and work is under way to assess changes in the Great Lakes basin that might increase or decrease future climate impacts.

One promising approach to extrapolating the impacts of future environmental changes is the use of linked simulation models. A guide to computer modeling of environmental problems published by the Scientific Committee on Problems of the Environment noted that models

> are needed for integrating the information available about natural and economic systems—information that may often appear indigestible and incoherent—into usable form, and for predicting changes due to natural and man-made perturbation. . . . A simulation model imitates the behavior of a complex system in some different medium—most commonly a computer—so that the behavior of the model can be studied far more quickly, cheaply, and simply than that of the real system, and conclusions drawn from the former can be applied to the latter. (Frenkiel and Goodall 1978, 1–2)

Models of crop growth, vegetation dynamics, groundwater, and surface runoff are all applicable to global change studies. Social impacts can be simulated

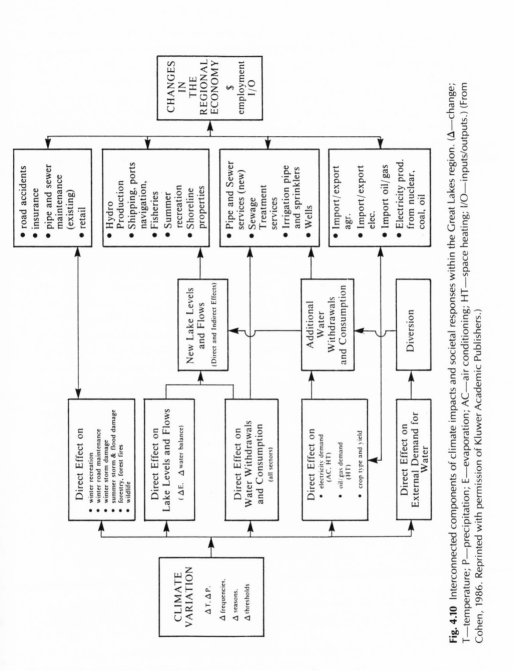

Fig. 4.10 Interconnected components of climate impacts and societal responses within the Great Lakes region. (Δ—change; T—temperature; P—precipitation; E—evaporation; AC—air conditioning; HT—space heating; I/O—inputs/outputs.) (From Cohen, 1986. Reprinted with permission of Kluwer Academic Publishers.)

by linking these models with resource and economic models. For example, existing crop-yield models have been applied to climate scenarios generated by global circulation models (see W. A. Warrick et al. 1986). Both statistical and deterministic crop models have been used; empirical-statistical models typically are based on multiple regression equations relating climate conditions (perhaps for specific phenological periods) to crop yields over a historical time period with matched climate and crop yield data sets. Deterministic models use mathematical formulas to simulate the physical processes by which environmental, chemical, and biological factors interact to produce crop yields. By varying the environmental factors in accordance with potential future climate conditions, the models simulate future impacts on yields.

Statistical models have been developed for most of the world's major crops, but they are not easily transferred from one regional setting to another because of changes in environmental constraints or technological treatments of fields. Thus, an impact assessor should try to use a proven, locally developed model where possible. Most models of this sort are built for short-term yield forecasting or for research purposes, but they can be modified to project future effects of climate changes. An excellent example of linking global climate to crop-production models is Rosensweig's (1985) careful analysis of potential CO_2 effects on North American wheat production. She first assessed the environmental requirements for wheat production (sensitivity analysis) and conducted a validation run of the model with base conditions, and then applied the output of the model with doubled CO_2.

G. D. V. Williams et al. (1988) used linked simulation models to project the regional effects of greenhouse climate scenarios for the Canadian Great Plains. They began with crop-yield changes estimated by linking climate and crop models, and then used these as input to farm-level production models. They then tied farm-sector production changes to a regional input/output economic model.

Hydrologic simulation models have often been applied to historical sequences of climate conditions in order to test the impacts of droughts or floods on water systems, but only recently have they been used to project the water impacts of future climate scenarios (e.g., Gleick 1986). Some progress has also been made in simulating future soil erosion impacts. Crosson (1986) used the U.S. Department of Agriculture's Erosion Productivity Impact Calculator (EPIC) to project impacts of soil erosion on future agricultural production and farm income; and Nix (1985) described how the model might be modified and linked to economic models to assess climate impacts on the farm sector. Similarly, classification models of terrestrial vegetation have been linked to climate models to assess the impacts of climate change on vegetation distributions. An analysis based on CO_2 doubling showed dramatic shifts in forest boundaries, especially in the high latitudes (see Shugart et al. 1986). Less work has been conducted on models of grassland production, energy, or fisheries, but all of these sectors can, theoretically, be modeled and linked to global changes.

Impact Studies and Global Environmental Decision Making

If they are to be useful in formulating social responses to global changes, impact studies must not only be as accurate and credible as the state of the art allows, they must also be effectively interpreted and translated into information on which public policy can be based. Unfortunately, we lack experience with communicating information on global change to decision makers, and we lack institutional structures for acting on this information. This section briefly raises some of the problems and opportunities associated with environmental management as more detailed data and better projections of future global changes become available.

The problem of translating global-change impact assessments into useful policy guidelines has been best addressed with regard to the climate change issue. The need to formulate social policy with the greenhouse effect in mind is now a standard component of climate change assessments (see WMO 1986). Clark (1986) suggested that the greenhouse problem must first be located within the context of related economic, political, and environmental issues that vie for attention, and then treated by policy analyses that focus on the risks it poses for society (risk analysis) and on potential social responses (policy exercises). Implicit in his suggestion is the assumption that policymakers are more likely to grapple with the problem if it is made somehow comparable to other, perhaps more familiar, issues. The idea of a "policy exercise" also implies that the uncertainty and novelty of the problem requires some form of awareness-raising activities involving decision makers. Both ideas hold promise, but more approaches are needed.

A comparative approach implicit in Clark's suggestion might be fruitful. With improved impact assessments, the potential costs associated with environmental changes might be better defined and compared with related problems (soil erosion or groundwater depletion) that have already elicited formal public policies. Before conducting climate-change policy exercises, however, it might be useful to conduct a set of detailed policy case studies to determine how issues like acid deposition and coastal erosion (themselves linked to the global change issue), which have already elicited explicit public policy, proceeded through the policy cycle. If we know more about how policymakers have responded to similar problems in the past, then their reactions to evidence for, and predictions of, global change can be more accurately anticipated.

5. REGIONAL DIMENSIONS OF

GLOBAL CHANGE

The relationships between socioeconomic development and changes in natural systems, and between regional processes of development and global change, have been poorly studied despite the fact that they are problems of some priority which deserve attention from many specialists, particularly geographers (Lavrov and Sdasyuk 1988; Sdasyuk 1988a, 1988b). All global-scale, human-induced changes originate from local activities. Some have direct global effects (for example, the release of chemical pollutants), while others (e.g., deforestation, accelerated soil erosion, and desertification) may begin as local disturbances and take on global significance because of their expansion. An increasingly noticeable feedback process also develops: global changes have direct impacts on development processes of countries and regions, and on the activities and health of people.

5.1 Regionalization and Sustainable Development

Regionalization, an important and classic method of geographical research, requires new refinements and innovative applications for use in analyzing global change (Lavrov et al. 1985). Such regional research is indispensable to achieve sustainable levels of development for different regions. Furthermore, a regionalization approach is critical for the stabilization of the current global situation.

In many parts of the world there is a continuing effort to find an effective means for coordinating economic development with environmental protection. Considerable research has been devoted to the simulation of ecological systems at local scales and economic systems at regional and world scales. Global modeling has focused primarily on economic/sectoral systems such as demography, agriculture, and manufacturing. Accurate simulations of regional natural resource use are much less developed; it is extremely difficult to build a single model of a complex system such as a region, a city, or an urban agglom-

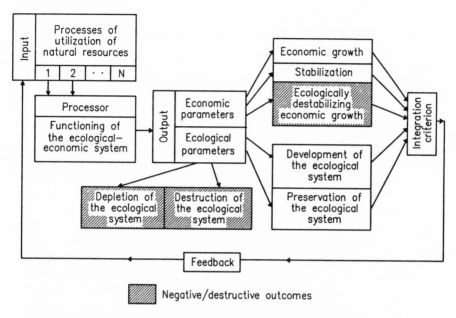

Fig. 5.1 General management model of a regional-economic system. (From Lemeshev 1986)

eration. Yet it is at such scales that much of the anthropogenic change is being generated. Under these conditions, the only reasonable approach is to build complex interrelated models of social, economic, and ecological development. The methodology for such an approach will require long time horizons and projections for the management of social development and environmental conservation within individual regions (Fig. 5.1).

At present there is no accepted criterion for socioeconomic efficiency, and this is a major obstacle to building accurate models. This situation derives from a dearth of analytical studies and the incompatibility of indexes that measure the economic, social, and ecological effects of conservation policies (Lemeshev et al. 1986). Detailed simulations of the socioecological aspects and interrelations of real and hypothetical decisions made by societies and smaller groups when responding to a changing environmental situation are sorely needed.

Geographic studies of natural resource consumption conducted at the Institute of Geography of the USSR Academy of Sciences have led to the idea that environmental management, which is at the junction of socioeconomic and natural systems, must utilize and be based on the inherent territorial (spatial) structure that reflects both systems. This means that the regions, zones, and areas delineated for managing the environment are not spatially coincident with the boundaries of economic, administrative, or natural regions, but rather form their own regional structure reflecting anthropogenic stresses and modes of natural resource exploitation (Privalovskaya and Runova 1980; Privalovskaya 1985; Runova 1985a, 1985b, 1987).

Clearly, the environmental management system, like socioeconomic and natural systems, is hierarchical and is exposed to the impact of specific factors at every regional (spatial) level. At the top of the hierarchy for the entire country there is a distinct natural-macrozonal structure reflecting climatic belts and orographic rainfall regimes which determine the existence of moderate, normal, and extreme technical-economic and natural conditions for the exploitation of natural resources (at a given level of development). These conditions in turn are prerequisites for the development of certain regimes or types of resource utilization overall, or for selective development and utilization within a specific territory.

The second level of the territorial hierarchy, which is most clearly observed in the temperate belt and under normal conditions, is a zonal-regional level that is the result of combinations of types of resource-intensive economic activities (e.g., agriculture, forestry, fishing, hunting, and recreation). Combinations of such resource exploitation within the same natural zone give rise to regions that differ in economic, social, and ecological character as well as in productivity, intensity, and types of problems.

The next level of territorial organization of environmental management is the network-nodal level, which evolves within an area with systems of industrial concentration, population density, and a high degree of infrastructural development. At this level there is a mosaic of resource-utilization types and regimes associated with variations in industrial centers, towns, and their populations.

Finally, a local level of environmental management may also be distinguished corresponding to the level of individual industrial centers, towns, agricultural enterprises, and similar activities, which create low-level cells in the territorial structure consisting of highly specialized resource-utilization nodes.

The schema described above establishes a series of hierarchical levels at which ecological and economic problems emerge; it clarifies the transition from one level to another and permits determination of the role of socioeconomic, technical, natural resource, and other factors in the creation and solution of these problems. The schema also helps to determine the level at which the state must step in with controls and regulations.

At the natural-macrozonal level one can address issues of national strategy in terms of resource use or in selecting major specializations for macrozones and regions and determining key objectives for each. It should also be noted that identification and selection of ecologically pristine and undisturbed natural areas are important for the conservation of the planet's gene pool and to ensure stability of global, continental, and other geographic-biospheric processes. At this level one can designate major regions for intensive environmental management as well as regions of risk which require a wide range of measures for conservation and environmental improvement. If all the above measures fail to ensure rational (i.e., ecologically, socially, and economically optimal) environmental management, then a structural reorientation of the economy is in order to find a new strategy of socioeconomic development that will ensure a radical solution to ecological problems. In such a case, national problems can and should be coordinated and reconciled with multinational and global problems and programs.

The regional-zonal level can and should be used to ensure stable (long-range) functioning of primary economic activities, agriculture, and forestry, and to preserve and enhance renewable properties of resources. At this level a combination of types of environmental management may be optimal for each region. This will establish the proportion of intensively and extensively used lands, as well as the proportion of unused land and water bodies to be protected. This approach is based on judgments about the optimal degree of such factors as forest cover and sown areas, the appropriate shelter-belt area, optimal application of fertilizers, and conservation of natural ecosystems. These assumptions raise the question of the necessity to identify, preserve, and strengthen the ecological core of territories with specified dimensions and locations that are unique for every region. Such an ecological core, which comprises all natural systems, including farmland, will help not only to preserve and increase the productivity of intensive types of environmental management but also to neutralize their negative consequences and preserve the uniqueness and variety of natural phenomena typical of each region, including their basic gene pool.

When cities, industrial centers, and their agglomerations are studied and compared at the network-nodal level of environmental management, problems of resource and energy conservation can be solved more rationally. Thus one can more comprehensively apply the concept of an integrated system of raw material and fuel use from major sources and promote joint and cooperative efforts to utilize by-products and wastes from industrial production. Joint analysis of industrial agglomerations and major settlements will permit identification of areas where the problems of resource conservation and waste reduction have the highest priority and the best prospects for successful implementation considering all conditions.

At this same level, remedies, programs, and ideas regarding a polarized biosphere and the establishment of compensation zones in the vicinity of large industrial and urban centers can be applied (Rodoman 1974; Vladimirov 1982; Vladimirov et al. 1986). These programs depend on a thorough understanding of the self-restoring properties of natural systems through the establishment of a reasonable territorial balance and the relative locations of enterprises in industrial-urban and surrounding natural-anthropogenic and natural systems. Such combinations allow, on the one hand, the neutralization of the residual contaminating effect of industrial production and urban impact, and, on the other hand, the restoration of water, heat, and oxygen budgets in these territories. Such programs will not only ameliorate conditions in current urban systems, but will also prevent the expansion of human-induced disturbances into adjacent territories.

At the local level (the level of individual industrial centers and microregions), technological and planning decisions may be efficiently applied to reduce environmental pollution. Environmental quality can be preserved at this level through a clear-cut functional-territorial zonation and by establishing limits for effects on natural systems.

The decisions and approaches that are presently used as the basis for physical planning schemes and spatially integrated schemes for nature conservation can also be implemented within the framework of current spatial-sectoral structures of environmental management and are effective at both the local and nodal levels of environmental management.

Macrolevel Approaches

Another approach to ecological-economic regionalization is the use of economic activities to identify different major processes in landscape systems. Such processes can be called "technogenic transformations." The particular combination of technogenic transformations in a certain region reflects local interactions of socioeconomic and natural systems. From this viewpoint, an ecological-economic region is a territory with a specific combination of technogenic transformations, and ecological-economic regionalization is a procedure to identify and delineate such regions (Yermakov et al. 1982).

It is necessary to study and map the diverse technogenic transformations of the environment to implement such an ecological-economic approach. This great diversity may be divided into two major groups of processes. One group includes the societal-environmental interactions that take place regularly as a result of economic activities. These interactions modify landscape systems very slowly and usually produce irreversible and even fundamental transformations only over prolonged time intervals. Examples include century-long cultivation of land, moderate grazing on traditional rangelands, and selective felling of trees.

Emphasis is placed on the present when such transformations are defined. Under rational economic practices, the annual irreversible effect of such transformations is so insignificant that, to some degree, they maintain rather than disrupt the existing anthropogenic structure of landscapes. These gradual transformations should include policies and activities—such as moderate application of fertilizers, forest management, and reforestation—that will work toward the restoration and increase of the natural productive potential.

The second group of transformation processes includes those that result in abrupt and, most often, irreversible changes in the existing landscape patterns. These processes, which create new landscape structures, may be called abrupt or destructive technogenic transformations. In terms of economic origin, they can be classified as (1) pioneer transformations in virgin areas during an initial period of development, (2) transformations that occur when intensively used landscapes are altered for new land uses, and (3) side effects that occur as negative impacts or modifications and result in degradation and pollution of landscapes.

These transformations are not of equal importance for practical ecological-economic regionalization. Contemporary interactions between society and environment are characterized, on the one hand, by expanding economic activity through pioneer or developed areas, and, on the other hand, by intensive economic activity that has lateral or unintended side effects. It follows that the specific regional features of interaction between contemporary society and the environment are reflected most clearly by positive transformations and thus are the principal indicators for identifying ecological-economic regions as well as being the most important predictive factors for forecasting. In contrast, the modificatory transformations, "well adjusted" to the long-term landscape evolution, are poor indicators of an ecological-economic region, although they account, to a great extent, for unintended, side-effect transformations.

The first stage of ecological-economic regionalization is the analysis of mapped anthropogenically modified landscapes (Fig. 5.2). The map is a reduced and generalized version of the 1:15,000,000 base map outlining areas of the major types of human-modified landscapes. Analyses of published reports and cartographic data permit the identification of the following transformations: (1) desertification, (2) erosional destruction of landscapes, (3) deforestation, (4) atmospheric oxidation of landscapes, (5) photochemical smog, (6) activization of cryogenic processes, (7) pollution with oil, (8) pollution of water currents, and (9) total technogenic impact.

Total technogenic impact is a special synthetic indicator used to identify the intensity of an integrated environmental impact by a combination of technogenic processes. The composite indicator—energy equivalent—is determined as the amount of energy generated per unit of area, recalculated into tons of conventional fuel per square kilometer per year. Different map shadings identify five levels of combined technogenic impact, each corresponding to different ranges of values.

The nine types of anthropogenic transformation thus identified do not exhaust all possibilities. Hydrotechnical and other transformations (e.g., salination, soil sinking, urbanization, etc.) have been omitted because of a lack of sufficient information. The classification system for transformations itself needs further development, particularly because of the difficulty in comparing

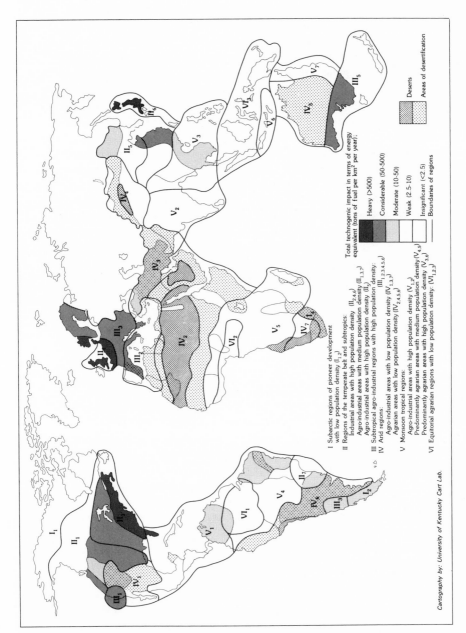

Fig. 5.2 Ecologic-economic regionalization outside the USSR.

Cartography by: University of Kentucky Cart Lab.

I Subarctic regions of pioneer development
with low population density ($I_{1,2}$)
II Regions of the temperate belt and subtropics:
Industrial areas with high population density ($II_{2,4,6}$)
Agro-industrial areas with medium population density (II_5)
Agro-industrial areas with high population density ($II_{1,3,7}$)
III Subtropical agro-industrial regions with high population density:
($III_{1,2,3,4,5,6}$)
IV Arid regions:
Agro-industrial areas with low population density ($IV_{1,2,3,7}$)
Agrarian areas with low population density ($IV_{2,4,5,6}$)
V Monsoon tropical regions:
Agro-industrial areas with high population density ($V_{1,2}$)
Predominantly agrarian areas with medium population density ($V_{4,5}$)
Predominantly agrarian areas with high population density ($V_{3,6}$)
VI Equtonial agrarian regions with low population density: ($VI_{1,2,3}$)

Total technogenic impact in terms of energy
equivalent (tons of fuel per km² per year):

Heavy (>500)

Considerable (50-500)

Moderate (10-50)

Weak (2.5-10)

Insignificant (<2.5)

Boundaries of regions

Deserts

Areas of desertification

the magnitudes of transformations in the preliminary maps presented here. Nevertheless, the available data appear sufficient for preliminary ecological-economic regionalization.

Areas with specific spatial combinations of anthropogenic transformations of the environment were outlined in order to delineate ecological-economic regions on the 1:15,000,000 base map. The boundaries of regions so delineated were then adjusted to those of the natural regions, which are organized in geographical zones divided into provinces. In most cases, when the preliminary ecological-economic boundaries were found to agree with the moderate level of technogenic transformation of a territory, priority was given to the use of natural boundaries (e.g., tropical rain forest regions). In cases of disagreement, priority was given to ecological-economic boundaries (e.g., arid regions) when the degree of total transformation could be identified as important and the region itself had a clear ecological-economic integrity. This resulted in the identification of thirty-two individual ecological-economic regions (Fig. 5.2). Their typology was developed on the basis of general natural-zonal features, economic specialization, and population density.

A more complete understanding of ecological-economic regions requires (1) more thorough analysis of technogenic transformations, with more detailed maps; (2) more detailed studies of the specifics of modificatory transformations in individual areas; and (3) study of the patterns of economic and natural flows of matter and energy that integrate or separate ecological-economic regions. The essence of the landscape-anthropogenic approach is the integration of the maps of landscape regionalization and economic activities to reveal areas of similar response to human-induced changes.

5.2 Red-Zone Maps of Critical Environmental Situations

Areas of Critical Water Problems in the USSR

Areas where ecological processes have created hazards or imminent hazards can be mapped to monitor the rate of environmental deterioration. Using these maps, plans can be devised to stabilize the environment or even restore ecological stability. An example is the map of critically modified landscape systems in the USSR resulting from human impacts on surface and subsurface waters. Figure 5.3 indicates areas with the following types of water problems: (1) stream pollution, (2) soil pollution and salination, (3) significant changes in groundwater levels, (4) pollution or destruction of the biota, (5) depletion of water resources, (6) loss of cultivated areas, and (7) critical problems in terminal water bodies. Other maps identify those territories unaffected or only moderately affected by such problems as well as regions so severely affected that normal land-use activities are no longer possible or are being threatened.

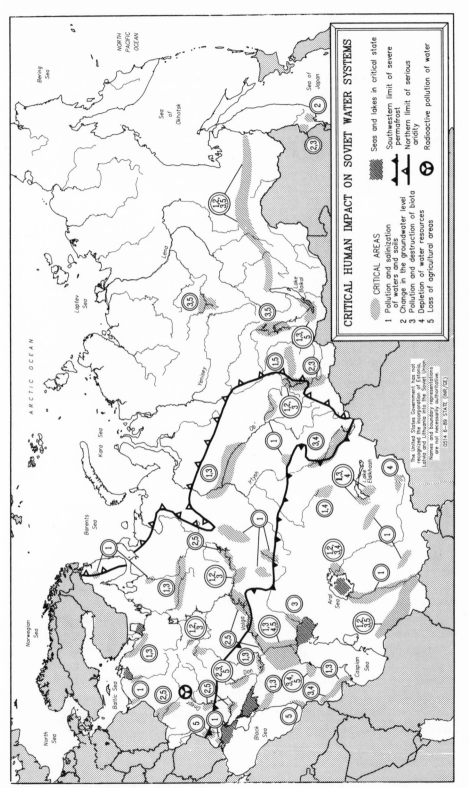

Fig. 5.3 Critical human impact on Soviet water systems. (Compiled by A. N. Krenke, N. I. Koronkevich, and G. P. Medvedeva)

Geochemical data from the hydrometeorological service network were used to identify polluted stream areas, which were then designated "unaffected," "moderately affected," or "severely affected" (the latter considered dangerous for humans). Contamination may result from the presence of phenols and petroleum products or from contamination by toxic agricultural chemicals and defoliants. Soil salination from rising irrigation water levels is considered severe when there is catastrophic soil loss or when the soil is no longer economically useful. Sodium salination occurs in the fairly dense argillaceous lowland soils which originally had groundwater close to the surface (the Kuro-Apoksinsky and Sarlinsky lowlands are the most serious problem areas). If such soils cover more than 50 percent of a region, the whole territory is considered to be in severe danger. In some cases salination is associated with pollution by toxic chemicals, defoliants, and contaminated groundwaters.

Negative groundwater problems may involve water-level increases or decreases. A rise in the water table may result from excess irrigation, water leakage from supply systems, or the return of agricultural water to other water bodies. Lowered water levels may occur in areas of active hydrological activity as well as in areas experiencing drainage changes, and may cause withered plants, loss of peat, and other significant environmental modifications.

Changes in groundwater levels may modify stream flow, change pollution loads, drain fish-spawning areas, remoisten floodplains, block animals' normal migration routes with new channels, and destroy biota. Severely affected areas are those in which the total number of animal species, pasturelands, tidal forests, or other significant areas of natural flora have disappeared or been seriously reduced. Areas where such modifications affect large expanses (hundreds of thousands or millions of hectares) or threaten the existence of an entire important vegetation species have been mapped.

Regions where water consumption or diversion has resulted in negative modifications of the normal natural-anthropogenic systems are identified as areas of depletion of water resources. In particular, such regions are located in floodplains lying within the tailraces of water reservoirs, the lower parts of rivers used for irrigation, hollows, and near-shore areas of lakes where levels have dropped as a result of human activity (the Aral Sea, Lakes Issyk-Kul, Sevan, and Balkhash).

Areas having significant portions (more than tens of thousands of hectares) flooded by water reservoirs and drainage waters or which are no longer economically useful as a result of anthropogenically intensified water erosion are mapped as regions with significant loss of cultivated land. Annual loss of more than forty to fifty tons of topsoil per hectare in a region is identified as a severe erosion problem, while losses of more than fifteen to twenty tons per hectare are labeled moderate. A map of soil loss in the USSR (1:2,500,000) was used to identify these critical areas.

Seas and lakes are classified as critical if the chemical composition of the water has been changed to such a degree that it threatens biotic life, eliminates traditional types of fishing, and seriously limits the possibilities for recreational use of the coast or shore. Areas affected by many of these problems overlap because they are interrelated, resulting in a synergistic territorial impact. Twenty sets of critical modifications, occurring either singly or in combination, were identified.

River and stream pollution is the most widespread type of environmental modification in the USSR, and it has reached a critical state in thirteen areas (Fig. 5.3). Modification of the groundwater levels is also critical in thirteen areas. The map shows that the areas most affected by such modifications are zones of inadequate moisture; these include the main rivers and terminal water bodies which are integrators of hydrotechnical impacts on the river regime and pollution sinks.

Areas of Critical Water Problems in the United States

Similar types of red-zone maps of water problems were published by the U.S. Water Resources Council as part of its second national water assessment (*The Nation's Water Resources 1975–2000*). This report includes figures on projected water supplies and demands and provides a concise summary of critical water problems for the next several decades based on an analysis of a comprehensive water-supply adequacy model applied to 106 water resources subregions across the United States. Ten critical water resources problems were identified. A brief summary of six problems, adopted from Mather (1984), follows.

INADEQUATE SURFACE-WATER SUPPLY

By the year 2000, the Water Resources Council anticipates that the problem of inadequate surface-water supply will be severe in 17 of the 106 subregions, all located in the Great Plains or the southwestern part of the country (Fig. 5.4). Because of the nationwide increase in annual demands for fresh water, there will also be periods during low-flow months in which additional subregions, even some in the more humid East, will have inadequate supplies.

The council suggests that an average in-stream flow of 1035 bgd is entirely adequate for fish and wildlife needs, while the actual average in-stream flow is 1233 bgd. Thus, nationwide, the situation is good, although certain streams are in a relatively unfavorable condition. For example, the lower Colorado region has an average daily flow of 1550 mgd, while some 6864 mgd might be needed for fish and wildlife protection. Thus, in some areas competition for water is a way of life, and trade-offs that will limit future uses and river development must be made. Since surface and subsurface water supplies are

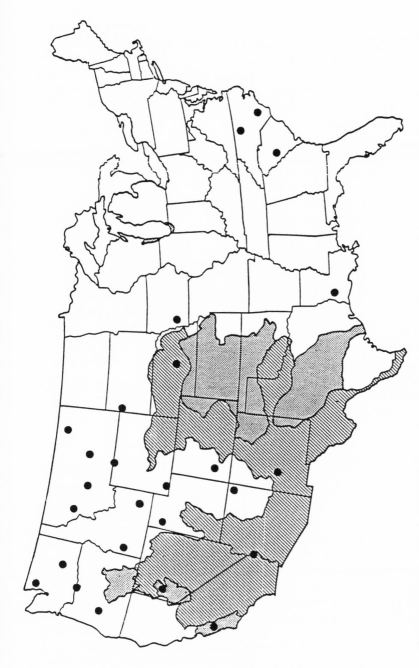

Fig. 5.4 Areas affected by inadequate surface-water supply and related problems. Hatched areas show stream flow 70% depleted in average or dry years, dotted areas stream flow 70% depleted in dry years only. Black dots indicated places with inadequate supply to support conflict between offstream and instream uses. (Source: U.S. Water Resources Council 1978)

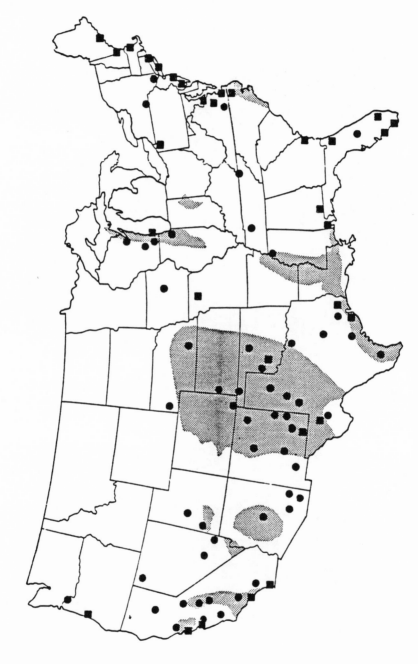

Fig. 5.5 Areas affected by significant groundwater overdraft. Black dots indicate areas of declining groundwater levels while black squares show places where saline water intrusion into fresh water aquifers is occurring. (Source: U.S. Water Resources Council 1978)

interrelated, the surface problem cannot be resolved without concern for related subsurface water problems.

OVERPUMPING OF GROUNDWATER SUPPLIES

A second problem is the localized overpumping of groundwater reserves. Groundwater volumes for the nation as a whole equal about fifty years of surface runoff (well in excess of the total capacity of all the lakes and reservoirs of the nation, including the Great Lakes). Yet, in certain areas, especially in the Great Plains from southern Nebraska to western Texas, parts of central Arizona, and along the southern portion of the Mississippi River valley, significant groundwater overpumping is occurring and will continue into the future (Fig. 5.5). Eight of the 106 water resources subregions have critical overpumping problems at the present time, while 30 have moderate problems and 22 have minor overpumping problems. Thus, more than half of the water resource subregions are experiencing some sort of overpumping problems which may become more serious in the future as demand for fresh water increases.

Clearly, some remedial action may be necessary before critical problems develop in too many areas. Possible solutions include developing additional sources of water, beginning artificial recharge to keep salt or polluted water from entering productive aquifers, reducing water use through water-management techniques, or relocating water-demanding activities. Since irrigation is the single greatest use of groundwater, the results of overpumping will be most clearly seen in agricultural production. In this case, relocation of water-demanding activities may not be possible because of the need for large, arable acreages. A less desirable alternative may be the reduction of irrigation agriculture.

POLLUTION OF SURFACE WATER

For many years, surface water bodies have been used as places to dump waste products. As long as wastes were not very concentrated and were not strongly toxic or nonbiodegradable, few problems developed. However, recent excessive population pressures in certain areas, the introduction of complex industrial wastes, and the rise in other demands for fresh water make it impossible to use surface waters for pollution abatement. Large portions of the nation still suffer from polluted surface waters. Pollution is received into the streams and lakes from both point and nonpoint, or dispersed, sources. Point sources of pollution—generally from factories and municipal treatment systems—can be controlled in time, although control may involve costly treatment programs (Fig. 5.6). However, nonpoint source pollution, which comes largely from runoff from agricultural, forested, and urban areas, and from mining operations, is more difficult to control (Fig. 5.7). The Environmental Protection Agency has estimated that one-third of the oxygen-demanding load on surface water, two-thirds of the phosphorous, and three-fourths of the nitro-

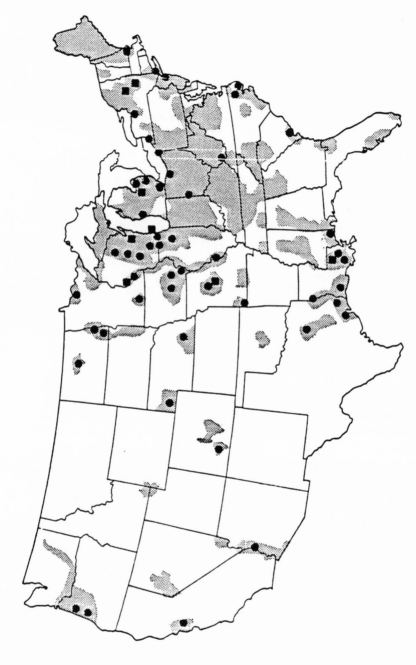

Fig. 5.6 Areas affected by surface-water pollution problems from point sources (municipal and industrial waste) as identified by Federal and state/regional study teams. Black dots indicate areas of pollution from coliform bacteria from municipal wastes or feedlot drainage. Black squares show areas of pollution from PCB, PBB, PVC, and related industrial chemicals. (Source: U.S. Water Resources Council 1978)

gen being discharged into streams come from nonpoint agricultural sources. Storm runoff from urban areas also leads to rapid deterioration of water bodies. Significant amounts of sediment, nutrients, organic material, and trace elements are carried by the storm-water runoff into surface water bodies. As urban areas increase in size in the next few decades, nonpoint-source surface-water pollution will also increase, even though pollution from point sources may decrease. Eutrophication, the growth of algae in receiving waters caused by the presence of an excess supply of nutrients, occurs in all water bodies and has been accelerated recently by human activities. Large areas of the Ohio, Potomac, Mississippi, and Tennessee rivers and portions of Wyoming, Colorado, Utah, Arizona, and New Mexico, along with much of Maine, Wisconsin, Florida, and Louisiana, are problem areas for eutrophication, which results in fish kills and the rapid aging of lake areas.

In a 1975 report to the U.S. Congress, the Office of Water Planning and Standards listed water-quality problems by regions of the country (Table 5.1). The two most widespread problems were health hazards, which existed in the water of forty-five states, and oxygen depletion, which was a problem in forty-six states. Eutrophication potential appeared as a problem in forty-three of the fifty states.

GROUNDWATER POLLUTION

Groundwater supplies can easily be contaminated by drainage from septic tanks, infiltration of waste products from animal feedlots, solid-waste landfills, and subsurface disposal (deep-well injection) of industrial waste products. Saline water inflow in areas of excessive pumping of groundwater aquifers can also result in pollution of groundwater areas.

Groundwater aquifers recover very slowly from pollution. About 40 percent of the population of the United States now obtains its drinking water from groundwater, and increases in population will increase this demand in the future. Figure 5.8 indicates the areas where groundwater pollution is a problem at present. As in the case of many other problems identified by the Water Resources Council, the Southwest is an area with significant groundwater pollution.

DRINKING-WATER QUALITY

The significant advances made in improving the quality of drinking water over the past half century have perhaps created a false sense of security about the safety of the water supply. With the increased ability to detect water-borne disease, more than 4000 cases of water-borne illnesses per year have been reported. The actual number, when the more difficult to detect cases of chemical poisoning are included, may actually be greater by a factor of ten. Only in recent years has consideration been given to the particular effects of combinations of chemicals, whose symptoms might not show up for several decades.

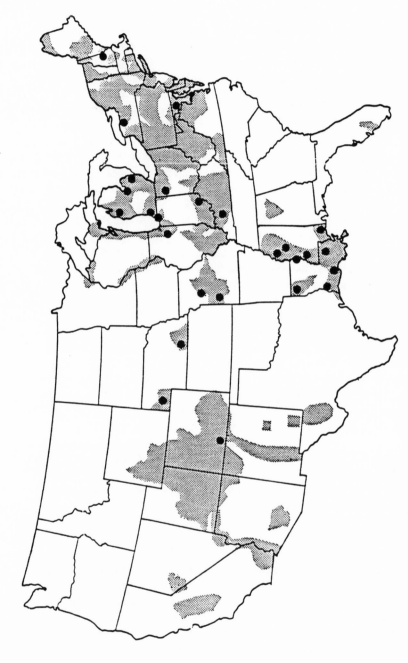

Fig. 5.7 Areas affected by surface-water pollution from nonpoint sources (dispersed) as identified by Federal and state/regional study teams. Black dots show areas where pollution problems are from herbicides, pesticides, and other agricultural chemicals. (Source: U.S. Water Resources Council 1978)

Table 5.1 Water quality problem areas reported by states[a] (number reporting problems/total).

	Middle Atlantic, Northeast[b]	South[c]	Great Lakes[d]	Central[e]	Southwest[f]	West[g]	Islands[h]	Total
Harmful substances	6/13	6/9	5/6	4/8	4/4	2/6	3/6	30/52
Physical modification	7/13	3/9	3/6	8/8	3/4	6/6	5/6	35/52
Eutrophication potential	11/13	6/9	6/6	8/8	2/4	6/6	4/6	43/52
Salinity, acidity, alkalinity	3/13	6/9	2/6	6/8	4/4	4/6	2/6	27/52
Oxygen depletion	11/13	9/9	6/6	6/8	4/4	6/6	4/6	46/52
Health hazards	11/13	8/9	5/6	8/8	3/4	5/6	5/6	45/52

[a]Localized or statewide problems discussed by the states in their reports.
[b]*Middle Atlantic, Northeast*: Conn., Del., D.C., Maine, Md., N.H., N.J., N.Y., Pa., R.I., Vt., Va., W.Va.
[c]*South*: Ala., Ark., Fla., Ga., Ky., La., N.C., S.C., Tenn.
[d]*Great Lakes*: Ill., Ind., Mich., Minn., Ohio, Wis.
[e]*Central*: Colo., Iowa, Kans., Mont., Nebr., N.Dak., S.Dak., Wyo.
[f]*Southwest*: Ariz., N.Mex., Okla., Tex.
[g]*West*: Calif., Idaho, Nev., Oreg., Utah, Wash.
[h]*Islands*: Amer. Samoa, Guam, Hawaii, P.R., Trust Terr., V.I.
Source: Office of Water Planning and Standards (1975).

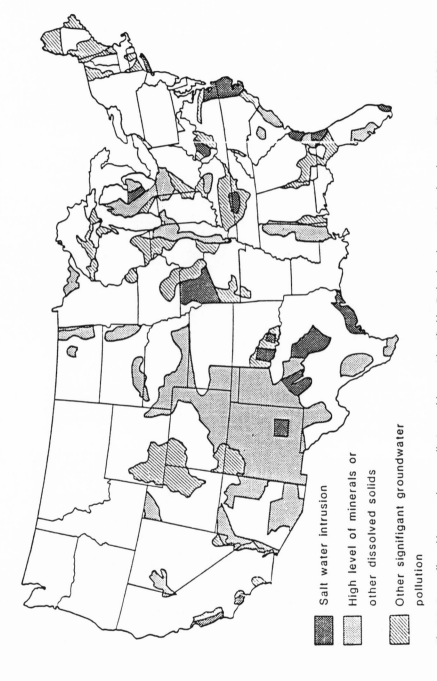

Fig. 5.8 Areas affected by groundwater pollution problems as identified by Federal and state/regional study teams. (Source: U.S. Water Resources Council 1978)

Salt water intrusion

High level of minerals or other dissolved solids

Other signifigant groundwater pollution

Areas where drinking-water quality problems exist now, or may in the near future, are shown in Figure 5.9. The Southwest and the upper Midwest, along with the New York and Mid-Atlantic regions, are the areas of prime concern at the present.

EROSION AND SEDIMENTATION

Natural erosion and sedimentation are significant problems, but when exacerbated by human activity they become critical to the welfare of the country. In 1975 the average cropland loss was 8.6 tons of topsoil per acre, while forest and pastureland loss was about 1 ton per acre. Under accelerated erosion, some cropland areas lost as much as 25 tons per acre, or 0.2 inches per acre. Overgrazing, poor cultural practices, off-road recreational vehicles, and surface mining all increase the opportunity for accelerated erosion. Storm runoff from construction sites results in particularly serious problems of erosion and sediment deposition into water bodies.

Sedimentation can modify stream channels and increase the likelihood of flooding. It must be counteracted by expensive dredging operations, which themselves cause problems because the dredged material must be disposed of as spoil banks that can cover large areas of valuable wetlands and floodplains. Sediments are not only transporters of pollutants such as pesticides and phosphates, but they also cover fish and wildlife habitats and, especially important, nesting and spawning areas.

Other critical problems include flooding, which resulted in the deaths of 107 people and property damage of some $3.4 billion in 1975; wetland drainage, which eliminates a valuable resource for fish and waterfowl use; and the degradation of estuaries and coastal waters through the discharge of domestic and industrial wastes.

Large-Scale Hydrological-Ecological Catastrophes

Probably the best example of a large-scale hydrological-ecological catastrophe is the problem of the Aral Sea and its coastal region in the USSR (Micklin 1988). The problem, which resulted from the overdevelopment of irrigated agriculture in the surrounding area, first became evident in the mid-1970s. From 1961 to 1985, the area of irrigated land in this region increased approximately twofold (by 3–4 million ha). Water inflow to the sea decreased from 55 km^3 yr^{-1} before 1960 to almost 0 in 1985. (The inflow of the Syrdarya waters ceased in mid-1970, while that of the Amudarya waters ceased in the mid-1980s.) This produced a spontaneous drying of the sea, a level drop of 13 m, a dried area exceeding 23,000 km^2 (2.3 million ha), and a water salinity increase from 9 percent to 23 percent. The dried lake area has become a source of dust and salt-laden storms; fishing has practically stopped in the remaining

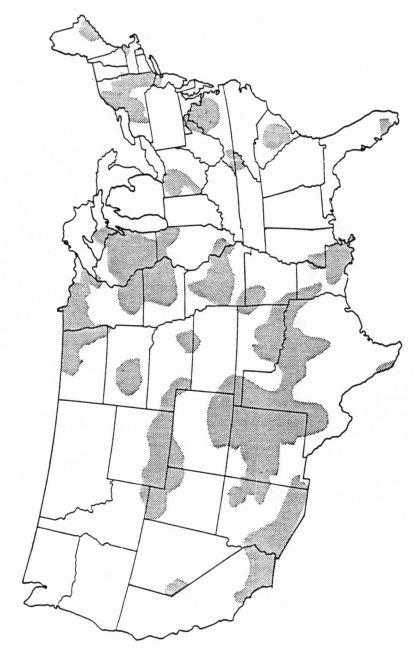

Fig. 5.9 Areas affected by quality of drinking water problems as identified by Federal and state/regional study teams. (Source: U.S. Water Resources Council 1978)

waters of the sea (24×10^6 kg of fish and 2 million muskrats per year were lost, as well as 1.5 million ha of pastureland and meadow).

A great number of delta lakes have disappeared, and the surviving ones are fed not by river waters but by sewer and drainage waters. Some new ponds fed by these waters have appeared, in particular Sarakamyshsky Lake, which has a water surface area of 3000 km^2. Medical and ecological problems have become acute in the lower reaches of the Amudarya and Syrdarya rivers. Sewer and drainage waters are allowed to enter the main bodies of these rivers, which are then used for irrigation and consumption downstream. These waters are strongly mineralized and, more important, are contaminated by toxic chemicals some twenty times more concentrated than they are in the European part of the USSR (per hectare of irrigated land). As a result, hepatitis, problems with pregnancy and childbirth, and dangerous allergic reactions have become widespread. The scale of the ecological catastrophe is comparable in economic, medical, and genetic terms to the accident at Chernobyl. The campaign that has been launched to mitigate the consequences of the ecological disaster is extremely expensive. A radical reconstruction of the economy and changes in land-use patterns are required to prevent further deterioration, including curtailment of cotton cultivation, prohibitions on dumping of toxic chemicals, creation of channels for the disposal of drainage waters into the Aral Sea, construction of extensive pipelines to tap new water supplies, and crop rotations that substitute lucerne and natural pastures for cotton. For the present, the Aral catastrophe is unique, as was the Chernobyl calamity, but it should serve as a caution to limit the widespread use of reservoirs and lakes in other basins (e.g., Balkhash and Isyk-Kul in the USSR and water reservoirs in arid territories in developing countries).

Clearly, a typology of ecologically critical areas can be defined; these include terminal water bodies, tailraces of dams, water reservoirs and their shorelines, ameliorated bogs and marshes, and similar areas. Their scale and prevalence raise the issue to a global scale. The prevention and treatment of problems such as the Aral Sea disaster must be attempted through legislative measures at the international (global) and national levels and environmental protection actions at regional and local levels.

Large-Scale Water Projects and Their Ecological Consequences

We have now reached a stage in technological development in which it is feasible to implement grandiose schemes for the transformation of nature at hemispheric scales. The proposed North American Water and Power Alliance provides one example. In essence, it proposes the transfer of surplus water from Alaska and northwestern Canada to other regions of Canada, thirty-three U.S. states, the Great Lakes, and three northern states in Mexico. In addition to providing a tremendous amount of water power and irrigation water (enough to irrigate 56 million acres [23 million ha] in the United States and Mexico), the plan provides for water to stabilize levels in the Great Lakes, to increase power production at Niagara Falls, and to serve municipal purposes in the southwestern United States. The original estimated cost for this project was over $100 billion. The history of such projects suggests that this price is far too conservative.

Another such project involves the development of the resources of the Amazon River, including the formation of extensive water routes and intensive development of adjacent areas of South America by connecting the headwaters of the Orinoco, Amazon, and Paraná rivers. In Africa there have been suggestions to dam the lower part of the Congo River and direct the water flow through the Sahara Desert to the Mediterranean Sea.

One of the most extreme examples of this type of project involves the plan in the USSR to reverse the flow of rivers flowing to the Arctic Ocean. Two projects were developed to transfer water from rivers and lakes that are now part of the Arctic drainage system southward to the arid regions of the country. Work on both projects was stopped by a decision of the Twenty-seventh Congress of the Communist Party of the Soviet Union in 1986.

The first Soviet project called for the creation of a number of water redistribution systems to transfer stream flow from the northern portion of the European USSR to the Volga River basin. The second project proposed to construct the Sibaral Canal, some 2000 km in length, to transfer water from the basin of the river Ob in Kazakhstan and central Asia to the lower reaches of the Syrdarya and Amudarya rivers. Irrigated agriculture and other types of economic activity were to be the main consumers of the water in both cases. In addition, it was believed that the increase in the Volga runoff would allow the level of the Caspian Sea, which had been falling rapidly since the 1930s, to be regulated. Actually, the level of the Caspian Sea began to rise in 1977 without reversing river flows and had increased by more than a meter by 1985. This rise had been predicted by specialists who had studied the history of cyclic fluctuations in the level of the sea. The Sibaral project was expected to transfer 25 km^3 of water per year initially, with later increases projected up to 60 km^3 per year (Shiklomanov and Markova 1987). The USSR Academy of Sciences Commission, after studying the situation, concluded that great amounts of water could be saved simply by more rational use of the available water resources in the southern portion of the European USSR, Kazakhstan, and central Asia. There appears to be no need to invest enormous quantities of money to implement the "project of the century" at this time. Concern was also expressed regarding possible impacts of a flow reduction into the Arctic Ocean on ice conditions in the Kara-Barents-Laptev seas (Micklin 1988).

F. J. Shipunov suggested an alternative to the river flow reversal project by applying Dukuchayev's principles of soil conservation and fertility enhancement in the chernozem region in Russia to the present situation. Dokuchayev urged the application of more natural land uses in the chernozem region, including compulsory planting of forest belts, creation of ponds, and full use of available soil moisture (including snow retention). Dokuchayev proved the validity of this approach on an experimental farm in the Kamennaya steppe in Voronezh oblast.

According to Shipunov's present estimates, forest belts protect no more than 12–15 percent of the fields in the chernozem region. In order to approach more natural conditions, it would be necessary to plant an additional 4.7–5.5 million ha of forest belts, stabilize sandy areas, and stop the further expansion of ravines. It is estimated that the cost for this work would not exceed 7–8 billion rubles, more than an order of magnitude lower than the expenditures needed to implement the water-reversal project. Planning studies for the development of the river-reversal proposal have already cost up to 1 billion rubles (Zalygin 1987).

Measures based on Dukuchayev's principles, if implemented in the chernozem region, should produce high sustained yields as a result of improved agroecological conditions. Such a program, according to Shipunov, would make it possible to solve the food problem existing in the USSR, remove any question of the need to reverse the flows of northern rivers to the south, and, accordingly, would eliminate the hazards of unpredictable ecological changes that might develop as a result of reversing river flows.

The expediency of any grand-scale project of a macroregional nature must be evaluated not only on the basis of its technical complexity but also in terms of the capital investment required. The possible widespread ecological consequences of such grandiose projects must also be considered, especially because they may be negative or very difficult to predict. The relative advantages of such projects should be compared with those of more conventional projects that may be more efficient in optimizing the use of local resources. Systematic ecological and economic investigations are necessary to achieve the most rational solutions. "If industrial development is planned disregarding ecological security requirements, it is equivalent to choosing solutions which envisage the destruction of the system after a certain period of time. . . . By making such decisions, society does not increase its total wealth, but rather decreases it" (Oldak 1983, 124).

5.3 Management by Natural Biospheric Subdivisions

Physical-Geographical Subdivisions

Prospects for the socioeconomic development of a region depend, in part, on knowledge of the resource-ecological potentials of the biospheric subdivisions. Understanding the state of and the development trends in such natural

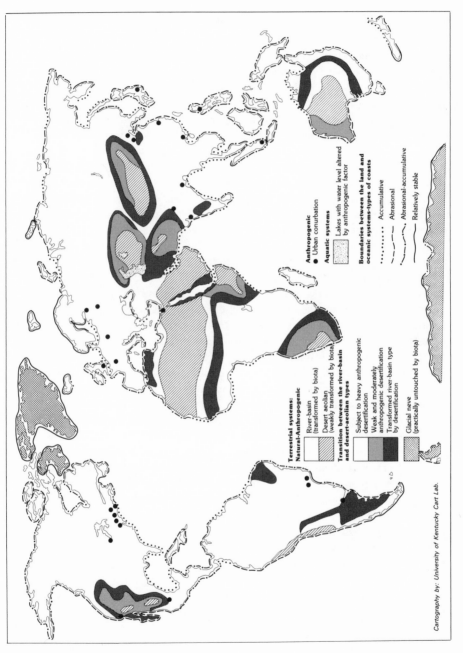

Terrestrial systems:
Natural-Anthropogenic

River-basin
(transformed by biota)

Desert aeolian
(weakly transformed by biota)

**Transition between the river-basin
and desert-aeolian types**

Subject to heavy anthropogenic
desertification

Weak and moderately
anthropogenic desertification

Transformed river-basin type
by desertification

Glacial neve
(practically untouched by biota)

Anthropogenic
● Urban conurbation

Aquatic systems

Lakes with water level altered
by anthropogenic factor

**Boundaries between the land and
oceanic systems-types of coasts**

········· Accumulative

── ─ ─ Abrasional

─··─··─ Abrasional-accumulative

─────── Relatively stable

Cartography by: University of Kentucky Cart Lab.

Fig. 5.10 Contemporary landscape-dynamic (exodynamic) system of the land. (Compiled from S. P. Gorshkov)

subdivisions becomes particularly important when dealing with the task of preserving natural life-supporting systems.

The study and mapping of contemporary landscape complexes and processes should become one of the highest-priority tasks of the current IGBP. The effort should combine and map the scattered data on human-environmental interactions by subdivisions that have been created by similar physical-geographic processes. The land, ocean, and atmosphere constitute the primary subdivisions because the earth's crust is classified into continental elevations and oceanic depressions. The granite-metamorphic layer of the continents, as well as the platform mantle, are largely products of a former biogeochemical transformation. Consequently, the continents are the result of geodynamic processes, including the action of living matter (i.e., they are of biogenic-geodynamic origin), while the oceanic depressions are of earth mantle–geodynamic origin.

At present, the sea is encroaching on the land over much of the world's coastal areas. The coast is retreating at a rate of approximately one meter per year over nearly one-third of this area (Fig. 5.10). Anthropogenic activity aggravates this process in some spots while decreasing it in others. There is no question, however, that the anthropogenic factor increases the instability of the coastal margin.

Three natural zones that differ in the role played by biological activity in physical-geographic processes can be identified as biospheric land areas of secondary rank (Fig. 5.10). Biological activity is practically absent in the first zone, the nival-glacial areas of polar and high-mountain regions, which comprise about 18 million km^2 (11 percent of the land area). The transformation of physical-geographic processes by biological activity is poorly expressed in the second zone, the desert-aeolian areas of tropical, subtropical, and temperate latitudes, which have an area of about 30 million km^2 (18 percent of the land area). The third zone, which can be called humid-biotic, comprises all the other land areas and covers more than 70 percent of the land (120 million km^2). Here, biological activity is the most important participant in physical-geographic processes. An example would be the greatly retarded biogeochemical denudation under a forest canopy as compared with increased soil erosion in areas where the forests are removed.

Of significance in these zones is the role of water runoff in organized river basins in which water from high-mountain nival-glacial areas may also flow. Unlike the humid-biotic zone, deserts and polar-glacial areas lack organized runoff into river basins. Water movement is characterized by floating icebergs in the sea, wandering streams in the periglacial zone, and underground streams in deserts.

There are intermediate transitional zones between the biospheric subdivisions of the land, such as the transitional zone usually found between the humid-biotic and aeolian-desert land subdivisions (Fig. 5.10). In this zone the mechanisms of the two systems conflict. For example, in the humid-biotic subdivision, biogeochemical, deflational, and fluvial processes tend to cause the area to be organized according to the river-basin pattern, while processes of simple disintegration, salt migration, and deflation-accumulation act in a desert-aeolian area (Aristarkhova 1971; Glazovsky 1987). Desertification caused by excessive economic pressure is but the modification of organized humid-biotic systems by more simply organized desert-aeolian biospheric systems under human stimulus. On the whole, the transforming influence of living matter on natural processes is weakening because of a seriously accelerating "abiotization" of the land. The ecological potential of most humid-biotic systems is decreasing.

A physical-geographical approach utilizes natural regional complexes (geosystems) for optimization of human-environment interaction and for geographical analysis of the resistance of geosystems to technogenic impacts (Isachenko 1980). From such analyses the optimal use of each natural complex is determined and a system of activities aimed at the conservation and improvement of the complex is developed. These studies result in a landscape planning map that delineates landscapes possessing potential resources for particular branches of the economy—agriculture, forestry, recreation—as well as for population settlement. The legend for such a map should include the characteristics of landscapes by their natural properties, the method of use, and possible activities for conservation and improvement.

River Basins as Natural Biospheric Subdivisions

Most of the earth's biomass, population, and economic activity are concentrated near rivers. River-basin resources both biotic and abiotic in nature are actively used by humans, and hence their anthropogenic transformation is most important in evaluating the ecological potential of the earth.

Awareness of the specific natural relationships existing within river basins, as well as attempts to control these relationships, was apparent in the north of Italy during the late Middle Ages in the form of activities to counteract floods (American Society of Civil Engineers 1975). The nature conservation decrees of Peter the Great issued at the beginning of the eighteenth century included elements of watershed management (Bannikov et al. 1985). At the beginning of the twentieth century this approach toward land use was adopted in the United States (White 1974), and it is now rather successfully employed, for example, in the watersheds of the Tennessee (North et al. 1980) and Colorado rivers (Gordon 1972).

The need to consider the processes of evapotranspiration, runoff, erosion, and technogenesis in conjunction with the transformation of natural, natural-anthropogenic, and anthropogenic landscapes makes river basins a major subject of study for physical, economic, and social geographers. River basins may be considered to be geological landscape systems. Their lower boundaries are the water table (the river itself or sea level), while their upper boundaries are traditionally delineated by the interface with the atmosphere. Efforts to employ this approach to studies of watersheds permit a new landscape-basin approach along three separate lines. The first involves landscape-geochemical studies based on identification within river basins of landscape-geochemical systems. The concept of the landscape-geochemical system was used by M. A. Glazovskaya (1976) to predict the ecological consequences of oil pollution of landscapes. Soils with their geochemical barriers act as the major buffers and neutralizers of pollutants in landscape-geochemical systems (Perel'man 1975).

Landscape-resource studies constitute a second line of research. They are based on identification within river basins of the so-called functional geosystems; that is, runoff having basin "boundaries" and landscape "contents." The parameters of phytomass and vegetation production, humus resources, biogenic and ash matter, and soil moisture are determined for landscapes with similar relief and vegetation. These data are then recalculated for each functional geosystem, taking into account possible losses of those ecological resources due to economic activities. Such a study has been undertaken for the upper Kolyma Basin (Rakita 1987).

The third line of research is that of landscape dynamics. It is based on subdivision of the river basin into catchments, valley networks, and delta. The catchments, having approximately similar natural landscapes, are treated as the fields of action of exodynamic processes. Within each of those catchments, called a catchment complex, the areas developed by humans are identified along with their inseparable accelerated exodynamic processes.

Catchment complexes having different landscape and geodynamic features are divided by valley networks consisting of large tributaries and the main river system. The specific features of landscapes and exodynamic processes in the valley networks (valley complexes) are, on the one hand, the result of the integrated impact of the drainage basins, and, on the other hand, the reflection of local conditions and anthropogenic pressures. In its landscape and in the character of its exodynamic processes, the river mouth, or delta, reveals the total impact of the catchment and valley units, as well as local conditions, anthropogenic pressures, and specific features of the storage of water in the stream (S. P. Gorshkov 1988).

Mapping the structure and dynamics of the natural, natural-anthropogenic, and anthropogenic subdivisions of river-basin systems is valuable in all three approaches. Cartographic representation of those geographical areas reveals specific functional features of river basins, their ecological potential, and their degree of modification by humans, and offers the opportunity to produce an objective picture of the state of one of the major components of the biosphere. This information is relevant not only for assessing probable past and present ecological potential of the river basin, but also for predicting biospheric changes in future decades.

Expected increases in CO_2 and other trace gases over the next half century may result in a global warming of $3° \pm 1.5°C$ (Antonovsky 1986) and will produce significant changes in the distribution of rainfall over the land surface of the globe. There is a suggestion that this warming might be postponed for several decades because of inertia imposed by ocean mixing (Antonovsky 1986). If this is so, changes in temperature around the globe should stay within normal limits for the next twenty to thirty years, and river-basin systems will be influenced largely by the action of the fertilizing and antitranspiration effects of CO_2; their possible effects on vegetation have been shown through biophysical experiments (Borzenkova et al. 1987). A significantly higher humidity is expected (Aston 1980; Idso and Brazel 1984); this should result in considerable functional transformation of river-basin systems. Thus, human impacts on global conditions should be relevant, first and foremost, for river basins. At the same time, river basins will be undergoing endogenic transformations induced by economic development. An attempt to reveal the overall trend in development of river-basin lands resulting from the complicated interplay of such a variety of events can be implemented most successfully with a landscape-basin approach.

Study of the geological landscape structure and the dynamics of river basins remains a fundamental problem of geography. Such analyses require the use not only of classical geosystems science approaches but also the application of research methods used in geomorphology, hydrology, and hydrogeology. Both classical landscape and landscape-basin approaches are required to manage the environment. Geographers have used both methods (M. A. Glazovskaya 1976; Rakita 1987). The need to develop the landscape-basin approach further in the USSR for purposes of geoecology has been emphasized by many authors (Oldak 1983; Nurmatov 1986).

Plans for the socioeconomic development of any area should be justified on the basis of the natural resource ecological potential of the natural biospheric subdivisions. The river basin is suggested as a unit of resource evaluation because it supplements the traditional physical-geographical landscape approach. It permits determination of the hierarchy of landscapes within the framework of each river basin, and it also solves problems of their change under the influence of anthropogenic pressure (e.g., in the course of movement of pollutants).

Future Challenges

The regional dimension of global change is an important factor that merits more attention as global analyses of current environmental processes and problems increase in number and intensity. The origins of pollutants and processes that are driving environmental alteration must be studied from a spatial-regional perspective. Human perceptions and reactions to environmental impacts will vary regionally and will relate closely to other regional variations over the globe. The spatial processes in the atmosphere, hydrosphere, and over the lithosphere create regional networks and systems that can only be understood fully through a regionally disaggregated set of models. Similarly, the complex combinations of processes that are altering global climate, sea level, and other environmental factors will result in regionally variable change in patterns and impacts over the globe. The list of processes, variables, and impacts associated with global change demand regional analysis, regional theory, and the application of regionalization techniques (Sdasyuk 1987, 1988c; Agranat 1988).

6. MONITORING ENVIRONMENTAL CHANGE

T his chapter uses the perspectives presented in the three preceding chapters to review some of the problems and opportunities presented by geographic experience in data collection. Principally, these are the construction and management of appropriate geographic information systems (GIS) and the harmonization of such systems with monitoring and field studies.

Much of the execution of the IGBP Study of Global Change is premised on the evolving technologies of information processing in computer-based GIS and information gathering with satellite- and aircraft-based remote-sensing systems. Recent successes in operating coarse-resolution general circulation models of the earth's climate on digital computers and the spectacular series of earth images reporting phenomena such as green-leaf density, surface temperature, cloud climatology, and planetary ozone distribution have encouraged many researchers to believe that it is now time to readdress the global dynamics of life processes and related systems on this planet. This is indeed a grand and noble goal for earth scientists in this technological era.

The reality of these technologies is that they are in an early stage of development. To accomplish the goals of the global change project successfully, understanding and use of both GIS and remote-sensing technologies must be advanced beyond their current status. One of the greatest challenges may be finding an appropriate storage medium for the extremely large volumes of data generated by these information technologies. In addition, discrepancies between the capacity of geographic information systems to handle the information structure of remotely sensed data and the capability of those data to provide information compatible with data gathered by more traditional means will require considerable attention.

Field observations—whether of physical parameters or of changes, economic flows, or human perception—provide the needed information not only to build but also to verify models. Geographers have had considerable experience in designing field programs and have also had the benefit of training that opens their minds to integrative studies. They have special skills in modeling and remote-sensing interpretation to bring to the studies that will take place under the IGBP. Yet they will be challenged to design field experiments which mesh these skills in an effective manner on a variety of scales. This challenge is the subject of section 6.2, which covers examples and problems in experimental design, examples of target areas both from a theoretical and a practical viewpoint, a description of scale problems posed by the data, strategies for using available data, and, finally, comments on an inventory and the desirability of permanent networks for continued geographic data monitoring.

6.1 Geographic Information Systems and Remote Sensing

The Concept

The concept of developing a fully integrated numerical model of the earth stems from the great success that has been achieved in numerically modeling atmospheric and oceanic circulation of the planet (Marchuk 1982; Marchuk et al. 1985, 1988; Washington and Parkinson 1986). Global models at resolutions as fine as $1°$ latitude $\times$ $1°$ longitude have been compiled on digital computers to study the evolution of the earth's climate. The significance of land state and dynamics has recently been recognized as a major forcing function in the earth's climate (Shukla and Mintz 1982). Preliminary efforts to address the role of land conditions have taken the form of either static descriptions (e.g., Hummel and Reck 1979; Olson 1982; Matthews 1983; Moiseev et al. 1985) or simple land biospheric energy/mass models which use difficult to obtain spatiotemporal descriptions of the land biosphere to parameterize the model (Sellers et al. 1986; Willmott and Klink 1986; Marchuk et al. 1989). Some progress has been achieved in developing regional models of vegetation dynamics (e.g., Shugart 1984) and hydrologic systems (e.g., Camillo et al. 1987), but no global models of such phenomena have been developed. There is some suggestion that global-scale remotely sensed observations may provide a means to describe land dynamics more effectively, but considerable additional research is required before this potential can be realized (C. J. Tucker et al. 1985a; Goward and Dye 1987). The "best" currently available global models of the biosphere consist of simple extrapolations of limited data through climatic relations (Holdridge 1947; Mather and Yoshioka 1968; Lieth 1978; Box 1981; Rovinsky 1986; Vladimirsky and Kislovsky 1986; Bogaturev et al. 1988). If truly interactive models of land phenomena are to be incorporated into integrated earth models, then considerably more attention must be given to developing analytical descriptions of land processes.

The Problem

Developing dynamic models of land phenomena is difficult because simple concepts of turbulent energy/mass balance do not adequately describe the spatiotemporal evolution of land conditions (Treshnikov and Kondrat'yev 1985; Risser 1986; Unninayer 1988). Discrete and highly contrasting land conditions are maintained in close proximity over long time periods. Landscape heterogeneity varies in space and time not only because of the diurnal, seasonal, and long-term variability of climate but also because of geological events recorded in the topography and stratigraphy of continents. The additional effects of human activity on landscape heterogeneity have a history several centuries long that is insufficiently documented to incorporate into a dynamic land model (Thomas 1956; Marchuk 1982). However, current observed rates of human land modification suggest that human activities are one of the major sources of current short-term land dynamics (Marchuk et al. 1985; Woodwell et al. 1987; Malingreau and Tucker 1988). Deriving such historical descriptions from current point data may be problematic. Derivation of macroscale land parameters through areal averaging or interpolation may introduce serious errors if nonlinear interaction terms are not considered (Becker and Raffy 1987; Rosswall et al. 1988; Tobler 1988). An effective macroscale description of continental biophysical processes is needed before progress can be achieved in studies of global change. The derivation of such a description will be one of the great scientific challenges of the IGBP program. Its accomplishment will require a gathering of data, computation, and intellectual resources not possible until recently.

Toward Solutions

Scientific research in the twentieth century has followed reductionist principles which have produced large quantities of data about the functioning of the earth's physical systems, but rarely at the spatial and temporal scales or in the type of common framework that would permit global-scale synthesis. The advent of earth observations from space and the development of high-speed computers have begun to reverse this tendency. Contemporary technologies are now arriving at a level of sophistication that allows the complexities of the earth's geography to be considered at advanced conceptual and theoretical levels. The "hidden" geographers behind the developing technologies of terrestrial remote sensing, GIS, and global modeling are focusing on these methodologies because they represent real promise in advancing our knowledge of the earth. The calls for studies of global change, earth science systems, and global geosciences in reality represent a realization that, with the influx of contemporary technologies, it is now possible, for the first time in over a century, to advance our knowledge of geography.

Land Processes Research Institutes

A new understanding of the earth's geography will require both a gathering together of currently disparate information sources and a maturation of the technologies by which such integrative research can be undertaken. To date, development of computer-based geographic information technology has been conducted on an ad hoc basis to meet the immediate needs of whatever mission, project, or experiment it supported. If a truly international effort is to be undertaken to pursue studies of global change, centers of expertise that possess the full technical capabilities to conduct "integrative" studies of the earth should be sanctioned to develop the required data systems. Precedents exist in efforts to model the meteorology and climatology of the earth. Research organizations such as the U.S. National Center for Atmospheric Research, NASA's Goddard Institute for Space Studies, and the European Center for Medium-Range Weather Forecasts have been developed and sustained with the purpose of providing sufficient resources to accomplish the complex of tasks needed to achieve progress in predicting the behavior of the earth's atmosphere. Similar centers of expertise are now needed for integrative earth studies.

The IGBP informational infrastructure need not be created from scratch. In the period from 1950 to 1970 the collective efforts of the world scientific community established a considerable network of institutions for observing, collecting, and distributing relevant global data. We can cite here, as an example, the World Data Centers (WDC) established in 1956 by the International Council of Scientific Unions for collection, storage, and distribution of data relative to planetary geophysics obtained while carrying out international observation programs. Two major centers, WDC A in the United States and WDC B in the Soviet Union, and a number of specialized centers (e.g., WDC C) were established. In 1988 a Chinese proposal to establish WDC D was accepted and the Panel on WDCs agreed to broaden the scope of their activities. The activity of these centers is regulated by "Instructions for International Exchange of Data through World Centers of Data," approved by the ICSU *Guide*. The activities of these centers focus on obtaining data for research in two areas: (1) data for hydrologic and meteorologic investigations, and (2) data for geophysical research in solar-earth physics as well as on the internal structure of the earth.

There is a particular need to focus on land processes as a primary research topic at one or more of these centers. The complexities of analytically describing the dynamics and interactions of the biosphere and human activities require a concentrated effort to advance the field (Kaznacheev 1982; Moiseev et al. 1985). One or more international "institutes of land processes" to pursue global-scale studies of the earth's land attributes and dynamics should be sanctioned by the ICSU-IGBP program. These institutes would be responsible for the development of computer-based GIS and accompanying data bases necessary to investigate the global dynamics of the earth's land areas. The basic functions of such institutes would be to provide a repository for relevant data sets, establish and maintain quality standards to ensure the reliability of available data, and develop the capability to produce composite integrated observations from the base data sets.

Beyond this basic requirement, the institutes could serve as focal points for studies that employ such data. Given the computational and technical resources required to maintain such a data system, studies that require integration of large data volumes most logically would be carried out at the repository of such data. Already, the United Nations, NASA, and the U.S. National Science Foundation are pursuing initiatives to develop global-scale geographic information systems (Global Resources Information Database, Pilot Land Data Systems, Geographic Information Systems; see, e.g., Bilingsley and Urena 1984; Estes et al. 1985). Progress in these efforts is hampered by the lack of experts to design and develop the systems. There is a pressing need to employ the well-developed skills of the geography profession to create and handle geographic information as well as to provide a forum in which to educate the next generation of scientists who will ultimately see this work to fruition. The formation and support of one or more research institutes to conduct global land studies would attract and maintain the interests of the geography community.

Research Tasks

The fundamental problems that will be encountered in developing global geographic data systems occur at the interface between computer science, cartography, remote sensing, and geography. Questions concerning data integration, mapping, availability, and global modeling need to be addressed in the near future if progress is to be achieved in studying global change.

THE HUMAN-COMPUTER INTERFACE

The historical tendency for specialist researchers to work in isolation from their interdisciplinary colleagues must be altered in a manner that is mutually beneficial. The concept of one or several data repositories where all researchers can coordinate their data and analyses may be appealing administratively, but it goes counter to the efforts toward self-sufficiency that scientists typically pursue. Computer-based geographic information systems hold promise as a means to coordinate data and analysis, because any investigator with a modem and terminal can access the commonly held data resources. Unfortunately, however, the operation and use of most computer systems are clouded by an arcane technical language that is difficult, if not impossible, for the average (non-computer) scientist to understand. Much progress has been achieved in recent years toward simplifying the human-computer interface. The concepts of artificial intelligence and expert systems, in the presence of the new generation of mega-CPUs (e.g., 100+ megabytes of RAM), hold great promise in this regard (e.g., Coulson et al. 1987). There is every reason to believe that truly "user-friendly" computers will soon be available. Before any effort is made to compile the coordinated global base of information needed for studies of global change, however, the computer system, and particularly its human interface, must be considered, agreed upon, and demonstrated (Kalensky 1988).

INFORMATION STRUCTURE OF REMOTELY SENSED DATA

With the introduction of myriad new sensors, satellite platforms, and computer-based numerical image analyses, the field of remote sensing has been in the midst of a revolution over the last twenty-five years. This revolution has caused fundamental changes in approaches to both data gathering and information extraction that are still in the process of being resolved. The complex of multispectral observations from solar-reflective, terrestrial-emissive, and a variety of artificial (self-generated) electromagnetic radiation sources (ignoring geomagnetic and acoustical sources) has produced an analysis problem that is several orders of magnitude more complex than interpretation of a simple panchromatic aerial photograph. Substantial emphasis has been placed on the development of computer-based image analysis systems to overcome these difficulties.

Considerable attention has been given to statistical pattern recognition as a means of extracting land-cover classes from numerical image data (J. R. Anderson et al. 1976; Swain and Davis 1978; Sukhihk and Sinitsin 1979; Kupriyanov and Usachev 1981; Sagdeev 1981; Jensen 1986). This "signature" model is still widely employed and provides a potentially powerful means to extract nominal information (on land cover) from the data—particularly if the spectral structure of radiant exitance from the landscape as a function of land cover is known beforehand. Pattern recognition has met mixed success, however, because, in individual images, many differing land-cover types (e.g., forest and corn, soils and urban, water and shadow) often produce the same spectral pattern (Todd et al. 1973; Todd 1977; Fitzpatrick-Lins 1978; Gaydos and Newland 1978; Jayroe 1978; Jensen and Toll 1982; Isaev 1984; Andronnikov 1986; Ross 1986; Isaev et al. 1988). Use of the time domain, broadening the spectral coverage of observations, and active incorporation of ancillary information in the classification processes should significantly improve the reliability of this type of information extraction from remotely sensed data (C. J. Tucker et al. 1985a; Crist and Kauth 1986; F. G. Hall and Badwar 1987; Vasiliev 1987; Marble 1988). Accurate, reliable extraction of land-cover information from numerical remotely sensed data remains today as much an art as a science. If land-cover analysis (at least from numerical remotely sensed data) is to be a major element of any study of global change, considerable further research will be needed to establish consistent, reliable means to accomplish this task (e.g., D. L. Williams et al. 1984; Wharton 1987).

Efforts to improve the reliability of land-cover mapping through computer-processed remotely sensed data have revealed the limited understanding that exists concerning the geographic variability and temporal dynamics of radia-

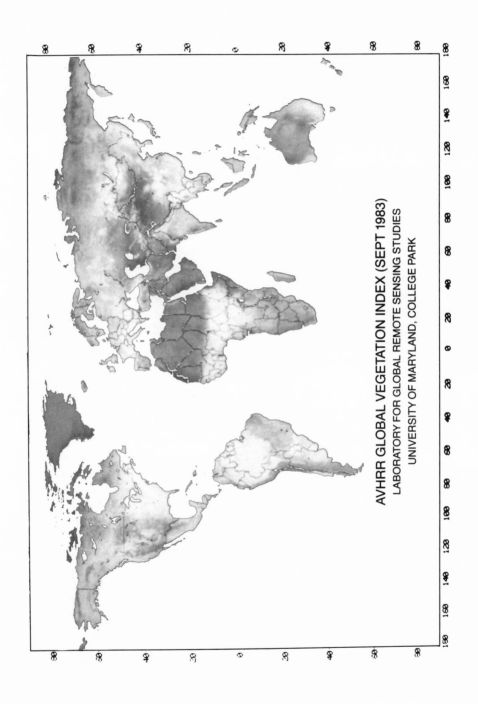

AVHRR GLOBAL VEGETATION INDEX (SEPT 1983)
LABORATORY FOR GLOBAL REMOTE SENSING STUDIES
UNIVERSITY OF MARYLAND, COLLEGE PARK

tively active landscape elements. A new focus in terrestrial remote sensing research, biophysical remote sensing, has been stimulated by this problem (Malila and Wagner 1972; R. W. Pease et al. 1976; Goward and Oliver 1977; Burtsev and Tishchenko 1978; Jensen 1983; Justice et al. 1985; Li and Strahler 1985; N. A. Armand 1986; Feoktistov 1986; A. H. Strahler et al. 1986; Breast and Goward 1987; Choudhury et al. 1987; Goward 1989b). The primary distinguishing attribute of this approach to the analysis of remotely sensed data is that land-cover attributes such as albedo, percentage green foliage, and soil moisture are extracted directly from the measurements without intervening land-cover classification (Fig. 6.1). This approach to information extraction from remotely sensed data is not new. It is the basis of the photogrammetric side of aerial photography interpretation. What *is* new is the type of land-cover information now being extracted (e.g., albedo, surface temperature, and biomass). These measurements have not traditionally been derived from photography, although examples can be found in the literature (S. R. Pease and Pease 1972; J. E. Jones 1977; Kondrat'yev et al. 1982). The advent of computer processing and advanced sensor systems has significantly advanced this aspect of terrestrial remote sensing.

As an example, the inherent limitations found in land-cover interpretation from visible and near-infrared observations—only green foliage, water, and soils can be distinguished—have been converted into a major strength in biophysical remote sensing. A general measure of the "greenness" of a landscape provides a new, vitally important, environmental indicator (e.g., photosynthetic capacity, green foliage density; see Sagdeev 1981; Goward et al. 1985, 1987; Fung et al. 1987; G. Johnson et al. 1987; Vasiliev 1987; Kakhru 1988; A. S. Hope et al. 1988; Goward 1989b). However, this shift to "remotogrammetry" (to coin a term) has produced a new class of geographic data which consists of contiguous but discrete measurements. These measurements can neither be contoured (isoline) nor classified (choropleth) without a loss of

Fig. 6.1 An example of the type of discrete, contiguous measurements that are being derived from numerical remotely sensed data. Measurements of visible (VIS) and near infrared (NIR) spectral reflectance, collected by the advanced very high resolution radiometer (AVHRR) on the NOAA-7, polar orbiting, meteorological satellite have been combined, in the form of the normalized difference vegetation index (i.e., [NIR − VIS]/ [NIR + VIS]) to produce an estimate of the global distribution of green foliage present (see Goward, 1989 for further discussion), the lighter the gray tone the greater the amount of green foliage. This particular image is a composite of one month (Sept. 1983) of daily observations. Compositing, a process of selecting clear views by comparison of daily measurements, is carried out to reduce the obscuring effect of cloud cover. Note the high contrast in the observations that occurs in many regions of the globe. For example, the steep gradient in NDVI measurements south of the Sahara Desert in Africa, caused by climate and the heterogeneity of the measurements in the southwestern region of the United States, produced by climate-topography interactions. Contouring or classification of these data would subsantially reduce the inherent precision of these measurements.

information and precision (Fig. 6.1) because discrete land-cover conditions can and do exist in close proximity over long periods of time. Preservation of the radiometric and spatial integrity of the original measurements, as well as the derived parameters, is critically important to evaluating landscape state and dynamics. Using biophysical remote-sensing data sets with ancillary (e.g., GIS map-type) information has not yet been given much attention outside the remote-sensing community. However, the early results of biophysical analyses have been fundamentally responsible for the great interest earth scientists have expressed for a remote-sensing role in any study of global change (National Research Council 1986; Rasool 1987; Mounsey and Tomlinson 1988). The remote-sensing and GIS communities need to revisit questions of data storage and retrieval with an appreciation that the discrete-continuous nature of the remotely sensed observations needs to be preserved.

Although the terrestrial remote-sensing community appears relatively mature when viewed from a distance, closer inspection reveals a research community just beginning to grasp the basic significance of the acquired measurements. Remote-sensing research is currently creating a new approach to earth sciences based on a knowledge of the radiatively active elements of landscapes. This perspective has produced a number of interesting scientific and technical questions which will need answers before the more pressing issues of global change can be adequately addressed with remotely sensed observations.

DATA STORAGE AND ANALYSIS IN COMPUTER-BASED GIS

A geographic information system, at its simplest, is a means to store and easily retrieve geographic data. A well-organized map cabinet is a good example of a simple GIS, and some of the early work in automated cartography and computer-based GIS was not far removed from the concept of an electronic map case (Tomlinson 1972). A more sophisticated GIS allows cross-referencing between maps, compilation of new maps from composite information, and comparison with nonmap (e.g., remotely sensed) data (Bryant and Zobrist 1976). The most sophisticated GIS operations currently being considered would have the capacity to integrate the available information and make logical deductions as well as predictions from the available information (T. R. Smith et al. 1987). This latter type of GIS is the most desirable for the types of problems that will be addressed in studies of global change. Already, some strides have been made in this direction in the form of global general circulation models (GCM) of the earth's atmosphere (Kondrat'yev 1983, 1988; Moiseev et al. 1985; Washington and Parkinson 1986; Marchuk 1988, 1989). However, these predictive GIS operations tend to be quite primitive and coarse when compared with the stated needs of the IGBP Study of Global Change.

Much of the research to date on geographic information systems has focused on local and regional scales and concentrated on vector data structures (Marble and Peuquet 1983; Merchant and Ripple 1987; Merchant 1988). This concentration represents the realities of the marketplace and the capabilities of previous generations of computers (T. R. Smith et al. 1987; Goodchild 1988a). Because of conflicts in data storage structures (image rasters versus map vectors), there have been only limited examples of geographic information systems that can interact fully with remotely sensed observations (e.g., the Image-based Information System [IBIS] at Jet Propulsion Laboratory; see Bryant and Zobrist 1976; Marble and Peuquet 1983; T. R. Smith et al. 1987; Simonett 1988). In general, either the remotely sensed data must be classified into nominal categories before entry into the GIS (so it can be "vectorized"), or the vector geographic information must be "rasterized" before it is overlain, as another "image," in the image-processing system. There is a loss of information, either precision of measurement or precision of location, in either direction (Fig. 6.2; see Tobler 1988).

The current generation of mainframe supercomputers, minicomputers, workstations, and potentially even microcomputers now has such a large capacity to store and handle data that the previous conflict of vector versus raster is becoming moot. There is much evidence to suggest that there are real analytical advantages to hybrid GISs in which a range of data structures is permitted and encouraged (Peuquet 1983; T. R. Smith et al. 1987). Once such systems are widely available, the distinctions between numerical image processing and GISs are likely to disappear. The development of such a hybrid, high-capacity GIS is a basic requirement for any study of global change because any single source of information, including remote sensing, is incapable of answering the complex of questions that such a study creates (Mounsey and Tomlinson 1988). In addition, in order to extract the maximum information possible from remotely sensed observations, a fully interactive GIS environment is still needed in which complex, "expert" inquiries may be constructed for information extraction (Estes and Bredakamp 1988).

DATA INTEGRATION

Location. The realization of global, integrative earth-system studies assumes that all the disjunctive data sources can be brought to some common framework that will permit interactive analysis. The GIS concept has excited considerable attention as a means to accomplish this feat. Storage of any data on a computer requires some common frame of reference to facilitate retrieval and analysis. For earth studies, Ptolemy provided such a common reference system: latitude and longitude. Any point on the earth can be uniquely located in this reference system. Thus a computer-based GIS is, at its simplest, a computer data-base management system that uses latitude and longitude as its reference frame. Precise location of observations on the earth based on information provided by the observer is a difficult task. Large expenditures on

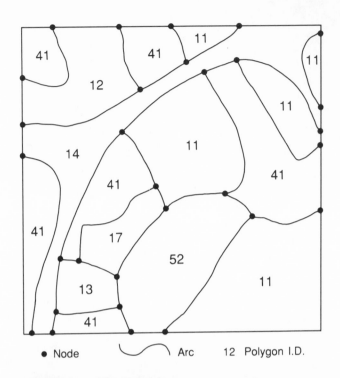

● Node ⁓ Arc 12 Polygon I.D.

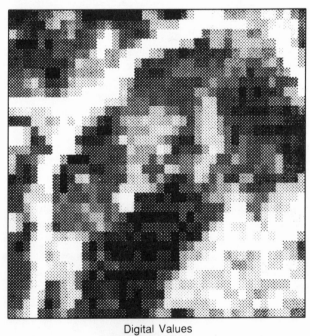

Digital Values

low   high

satellite-geopositioning systems clearly indicate the difficulties encountered in determining location. The quality of locational information inherent in available data needs to be studied and documented.

Scale. The types of point observations typically acquired by ground observers cause problems in map production. Interpolation and/or extrapolation between locations implies that the manner in which the particular observed phenomenon changes in space (and time) between the observation points is understood. Any effort to map point information without this knowledge introduces unknown errors which may increase rapidly away from the point of observation. Remotely sensed observations have introduced a new set of location problems because the sensors instantaneously and integratively observe large surface areas (Woodcock and Strahler 1987). The relation between these remotely sensed area observations and the traditional point observations of the field scientist is uncertain for the same reasons that it is difficult to extrapolate and interpolate point measurements.

There is a need to investigate the manner in which biophysical and human-dominated land attributes vary in time and space (e.g., Kaznacheev 1982;

Fig. 6.2 An example of the contrast between raster and vector representations of the same 10 km² of United States suburban landscape to the west of Hartford, Connecticut. Figure (top) is a "node and arc" vector representation of this landscape, derived by the U.S. Geological Survey from visual analysis of high-altitude color infrared photograph (Anderson et al. 1976). The symbol codes are land use/land cover categories, as defined by the usgs (i.e., 11-residential, 12-commercial and services, 13-industrial, 14-transportation, 17-other urban, 41-deciduous forest, 52-lake). Fig. (bottom) is a visible wavelength (0.5 − 0.5 μm) measurement set of the same landscape, acquired by the Landsat Multispectral Sensor System (mss) at approximately the same time (season and year) as the photography used for the land cover analysis in Fig. (top). The approximate size of each image picture element (pixel) is 80 × 80 meters. This gray tone representation, in which variations in reflected spectral radiance are displayed as a set of 7 gray tones, is nearly a factor of 10 reduction in the actual measurement precision of the mss data (64 gray tone difference). This gray tone display is provided because the human visual system is not able to handle the radiometric complexity of the raw measurements. Note the high within-class variance in this simplified representation of the mss data. This variance relates to variable vegetation/non-vegetated surfaces with each land cover category (except the lake water, where differences in depth and turbidity cause the observed variations). This variance information provides valuable insights concerning land conditions, within each of the usgs land cover categories, that affect the geography of surface energy balances, regional hydrology, and photosynthetic processes in this location. This information is lost once the remote sensing data are classified into land cover categories, as in Fig. (top). However, the high level of precision with which the boundaries of the lake, highways, and other land cover features are identified in Fig. (top), would be lost if this vector representation of landscape were converted to rasters of 80 meters, equivalent to the Landsat mss data. Each datum presents unique aspects of the observed landscape which are of value in analysis of terrestrial phenomena. A geographic information system that is capable of handling both data representations is a fundamental requirement for effective analysis of the sources and processes of global change.

Kharin and Babaev 1982; Risser 1986; Rosswall et al. 1988; Tobler 1988; Vinogradov 1988). The combination of remotely sensed observations and ground measurements provides the potential to study these patterns, but carefully designed experiments carried out over several years will be required to extract the answers. Preliminary experiments of this type are now being carried out under the International Satellite Land Surface Climatology Project (ISLSCP; see Schmugge et al. 1985; Kondrat'yev 1986). Similar studies are needed to evaluate other types of land phenomena. In each case, a major focus of such research should be the question of scaling; that is, how do local phenomena aggregate to produce continental to global descriptions of land conditions and dynamics?

CARTOGRAPHY

The conversion of observations from the surface of a sphere to any other nonspherical reference surface produces problems in analytical geometry which, if not properly handled, can create serious errors in interpolation (e.g., Knizhnikov et al. 1980; Willmott et al. 1985b; Legates and Willmott 1986; Peuquet 1988; Tobler 1988). The question of true commonality must be resolved before any serious efforts are undertaken to incorporate a wide range of global geographical information into a common computer data base. The degree to which mapped information can be made compatible depends both on the reliability of the original information sources and the manner in which these observations have been projected onto a map base. The cartographic complexities of meshing divergent data sources cannot be ignored.

Map projections. There is a wide range of mathematical approaches for converting three-dimensional information (e.g., earth descriptions) for display on two-dimensional surfaces (e.g., maps). These mapping projections have evolved from antiquity to provide a range of solutions to a basically unsolvable problem. Each projection introduces certain distortions in either relative areal extent or location that bias the relative significance of phenomena across the earth. Failure to account for these distortions and adjust for such "errors" will seriously jeopardize the integrity of geographic information extracted from mapped sources. Any computer-based GIS for global research must have the capacity to ingest data from a range of map sources and resolve the map projection of the source data explicitly. This implies a capacity to conduct "inverse" mapping numerically; that is, the recovery of precise geographic location from projection information. This is apparently not yet possible in all cases (Marble and Peuquet 1983).

Remote-sensing image geometry. Remote-sensing instruments, from cameras to charged-coupled devices, produce implicit projected two-dimensional maps of the earth's surface. Only in recent years has sufficient attention been given to this problem (e.g., Bernstein 1983). Precision mapping of remotely sensed observations of the earth's surface requires detailed knowledge of sensor platform attitude with respect to the earth's geoid. In general, this information is not currently observed at the level of precision necessary to locate a single sensor observation accurately within the two-dimensional area of that observation without ancillary independent (e.g., map) information. This produces a level of ambiguity with respect to the phenomena observed that significantly reduces the spatial precision of the observations below sensor instantaneous field of view. Better approaches to tracking aircraft and spacecraft trajectories relative to the earth's surface are needed to resolve this problem. Perhaps the technology developed for military targeting could be employed for this purpose.

Modeling requirements. Researchers want to incorporate as much detail into their observations as possible. Much of the mapped and remotely sensed data available are at scales or resolutions that significantly exceed the capacity of contemporary computer storage and processing systems. Current global models of the earth's atmosphere operate, at their finest resolutions, at levels of 1° latitude × 1° longitude. There is every reason to believe that finer-resolution land data may be needed to evaluate the effects of heterogeneity in land processes. However, the information that can ultimately be ingested into global computer models to evaluate possible future worlds must be capable of reduction in spatial detail to scales that the computer models can handle. There is a need to develop a theoretical and analytical basis for generalizing highly detailed land data to scales that can be used in computer models of the globe.

REFERENCE DATA LIBRARIES

The nature of scientific information has begun to change substantially in recent years. Development of low-cost, portable instruments has caused a move away from static, descriptive, categorical information to process-related interval and ratio data. This has produced a situation in which categorical geographic information such as vegetation distributions and soils maps has served as the basis for determining such attributes as surface albedo and hydraulic conductivity. The most dramatic shift of this type has been in the interpretation of remotely sensed observations. Previous efforts to conduct categorical analysis have, for the most part, given way to interval and ratio interpretations of terrestrial biophysical information. This shift in research approach reflects the growing awareness in the earth sciences that this planet can be understood only on the basis of process dynamics. As forces are gathered to compile a global data base by which to study global change, the necessity of providing process-related information must be the primary criterion for inclusion in such a system.

Data types. Basic information is needed on a range of terrestrial phenomena in order to conduct analyses of global processes. First-order division of the earth's physical systems into categories such as the lithosphere, biosphere, atmosphere, and hydrosphere is relatively easy, but the question of which attributes of these subsystems should be sought and included in a global data base is likely to create considerable disagreement. The initial tendency to call for inclusion of all "relevant" information will lead to an unwieldy data base which neither data managers nor researchers will find usable. For example, remotely sensed observations, if stored in all possible forms—from raw telemetry to derived biophysical measurements—will quickly exceed the electronic and physical storage capacity of most research organizations. Terms such as albedo, productivity, evaporation, and salinity may be of general interest or confined to the particular needs of an isolated investigation. Before large sums of money are expended on the acquisition and active storage of any data file, its relevance for global change analysis requires consideration.

The basic informational content and structure of any proposed data base need to be defined, and contributors to such a data base must be solicited. It seems reasonable to expect that individual expert teams would acquire, process, and produce the final product data, which would be stored in a composite data base in the fashion of the International Satellite Cloud Climatology Project (ISCCP; see Kondrat'yev 1986; Rasool 1987). Before this data search is undertaken, however, there is a need to identify which terrestrial information must be known to accomplish defined research objectives. The approach based on energy/mass balance calculations of earth processes has produced substantial progress in this century in understanding the earth (e.g., Budyko 1974a, 1974b; P. C. Miller 1980). A complex range of rate and state variables such as runoff, albedo, and canopy conductance must be known as a function of space and time in order to proceed with energy/mass balance analyses of the globe. If this approach is the underlying method by which global change studies are to be pursued, then a full accounting of information needs and possible sources must be conducted.

Basic documentation. The quality of any data source is dependent on maintaining an accurate history of its origins. Most current maps of terrestrial phenomena are composites of myriad sources (e.g., J. S. Olson and Watts 1982; Matthews 1983). Qualitative and quantitative assessments of these information sources should be possible to evaluate the precision of the resultant information. A substantial library of documentation will be needed to support any data source included in a global data base. All primary and secondary source materials should be acquired and maintained where possible.

When developing geographic information systems it is important to foresee facilities for storage, accumulation, and processing of information presented in a variety of forms and in different media. It seems reasonable to have in mind at least four major forms of information representation: digital, textual, cartographic, and video images; as well as three kinds of media: paper, photographic, and magnetic. The priority of digital forms of information presentation cannot be absolute because of practical considerations. Similarly, there cannot be any universal medium for information, especially when dealing with the question of satisfying the needs of users. All of this raises the problem of convertibility of information both in forms and in media.

Calibration and validation. Measured data such as those acquired by field instruments and remote-sensing devices require ancillary information about their characteristics that permits inter- and intracalibration. Insufficient knowledge of some sensors' performance characteristics prevents simple technical calibration; for example, the AVHRR sensors on the NOAA meteorological satellites contain no internal calibrator on the solar reflected radiance measurements. In these cases, it may be necessary to develop postobservational calibration procedures to increase confidence in the measurements. In any case, information that permits cross comparison of measurements must be identified and included before data are ingested into a common global data base. The potential for drawing unwarranted conclusions (in space and time) through use of uncalibrated information is great, and every necessary step to prevent this error must be taken.

A second level of data verification that should be undertaken is validation. In this case, two or more independent sources of information on the same phenomenon are compared. The resultant data are verified if the independent sources confirm the same results. Single-source analyses are subject to error because of uncertainties in data sources and calibration. Validation removes much of this uncertainty. Procedures to conduct validation need to be defined and developed within the framework of a global change data system.

Data formats. The unfortunate reality of current computer systems is that each one has its own (often several) "universal" data formats. These include physical storage media (e.g., magnetic tapes, floppy disks, cassettes, cartridges, optical disks) and numerical encoding of data (e.g., byte length and order, real versus integer, header length and content). It is now time to move toward universal standards that allow data transfers to occur between all computer-based data systems. The tyranny of computer technology must be overcome by the needs of a complex, international research community. Adequate standardization of data storage must be accomplished to prevent wasteful activity on data reformatting for resident computers. This issue is perhaps best addressed by computer scientists, but they seem unwilling to pursue this task on their own. Some means must be found to force a solution. An international computer data standards commission seems warranted. Such activity, currently being pursued by the U.S. National Committee for Digital Cartographic Standards of the American Congress of Surveying and Mapping, and equivalent activities at the international level, should be encouraged and supported by the ICSU-IGBP (Morrison 1988).

DATA STORAGE

There is a tendency to forget that the volume of data likely to be produced by global change research can be expected to substantially exceed the current capacity of electronic storage media. Peuquet (1988) effectively points out that a one-look remote-sensing image of the earth, collected at a 10-m (10 × 10) resolution will produce 1.5×10^{13} data points. If this were a multispectral (more than one band sensor, or more than one image needed), that number would be multiplied by the number of additional bands or images required. One earth image at this resolution would require 15 terabytes (1.5×10^{13} bytes) of storage. A current 2400-foot, 6250 bytes-per-inch magnetic tape stores about 1.4×10^8 bytes (140 megabytes). It would therefore require in excess of 10^5 tapes to store one image. Magnetic tape, the most widely used storage medium today, is notoriously unreliable; it has a shelf life of less than five years and must be exercised about once every six months. Magnetic tape is not the solution for storing a data set collected for global change studies. Basic data storage technology appears to be on the threshold of major breakthroughs, with laser-based optical storage media showing the most immediate promise. Before any massive effort is undertaken to collect comprehensive global data sets, a solution to this data storage and handling problem must be found (Mounsey and Tomlinson 1988; Goward 1989a).

Current Status of GIS

The concept of developing a global-scale geographic information system to address the questions posed under the ICSU Study of Global Change presents a major challenge to the proponents of computer-based GIS technology. A true twenty-first-century understanding of the earth is possible, particularly in light of recent progress in interpreting satellite observations of the earth. Success in this endeavor is dependent on surmounting fundamental technological, ergonometric, and analytical barriers. Current computer technologies are not fully capable of achieving the desired goals because of limited data capacities, arcane operating systems, and a lack of data standards. Basic concepts of earth systems are still defined, for the most part, in discipline-specific terminology and methods. The compilation of a global earth systems model will require substantial cross-disciplinary cooperation and communication, which implies that a common framework for this research can be found. The implementation of a truly user-friendly computer network—where computer operations are invisible to the user—should help significantly in accomplishing this feat.

Geographic information systems are key links in the IGBP informational infrastructure. Such systems should retain their significance well beyond the end of the IGBP. The experience already acquired in developing GISS shows that, within the context of the IGBP, it is expedient to establish not a single massive GIS but rather a network of smaller, problem-oriented, interconnected GISS, which, taken together, can be regarded as a problem-oriented system. Such an approach to GIS development should greatly aid in achieving clear direction in the system's purpose and how it should function to increase operational usefulness.

Before such a GIS can be realized, a number of substantive issues must be resolved. These issues center on data quality and integration. The answers lie in the fields of geography, cartography, remote sensing, and computer science. Much activity is currently under way to address many, if not all, of these problems. However, these activities are generally being carried out in isolation in order to meet the specific needs of particular projects or investigations. The motivation of the ICSU International Geosphere-Biosphere Program may be sufficient to encourage collaboration, but a more formal effort under the auspices of the IGBP is likely to be required before such a high-quality data system is realized.

GIS Analysis of Land-Use Changes in the European USSR

A geocartographic data base from the European USSR has been created to analyze the regional dynamics of natural resource management problems. One level of this data base includes information about changes in land-use characteristics from 1860 to 1960 based on a dense network of operational territorial units (OTU; see Fig. 6.3). In this case, the size of the OTUs (1° longitude × 1.5° latitude) was determined by the level of accessible data (mainly for 1860). This data base provides the possibility of analyzing changes in different land-use characteristics by regions, estimating relations between them, and designing scenarios of possible future change. Another part of the data base includes a wide range of different aspects of environmental management problems and basic information about landscapes on a more detailed OTU network covering the last thirty years.

Estimates of rates of change can be determined from the maps of percentage change in arable lands and grasslands over the total area of OTUs (Figs. 6.4 and 6.5). The location of every OTU is determined by the latitude-longitude scale shown. For arable lands, there is a wide region of increase covering the south Ukraine, the Don River basin, and the middle part of Volga River basin. Grassland regions have been decreasing in the south Ukraine and Don River basin while increases have occurred in the southeastern part of the region around the Caspian Sea and in a broad region in the western and northern portions of the mapped area.

6.2 Surface Measurements and Field Studies

Experimental Design

In order to build or verify the models discussed previously, we are ultimately forced to rely on field observations of physical parameters or changes, economic flows, or even human perceptions to provide the basic data. Following the quantitative revolution in geography in the 1960s, many field experi-

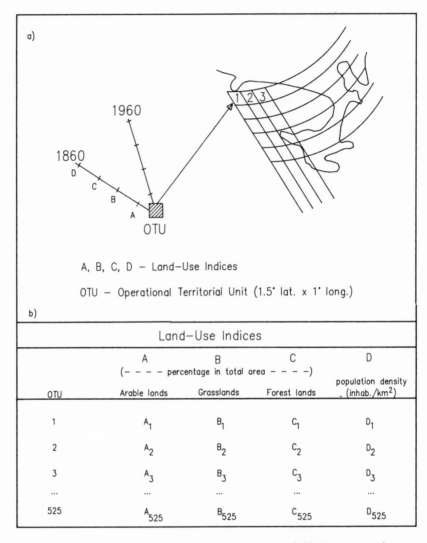

A, B, C, D — Land—Use Indices

OTU — Operational Territorial Unit (1.5° lat. x 1° long.)

b)

	Land—Use Indices			
	A	B	C	D
	(− − − − percentage in total area − − − −)			
				population density
OTU	Arable lands	Grasslands	Forest lands	(inhab./km²)
1	A_1	B_1	C_1	D_1
2	A_2	B_2	C_2	D_2
3	A_3	B_3	C_3	D_3
...	...	...	...	...
525	A_{525}	B_{525}	C_{525}	D_{525}

Fig. 6.3 The scheme of the map data-base preparation. (Compiled by H. H. Kazansky)

ments were established, especially in geomorphology and surface climatology. However, the experiments tended to focus on one of the subdisciplines. They also tended to be on a rather small scale—several kilometers or less. Another characteristic, demonstrated for the United States by Graf (1984), was a spatial bias of such sites, at least in geomorphology studies, which tended to concentrate in New England, Colorado, the Mid-Atlantic states, the Rio Grand Valley of New Mexico, and the Sierra Nevada of California.

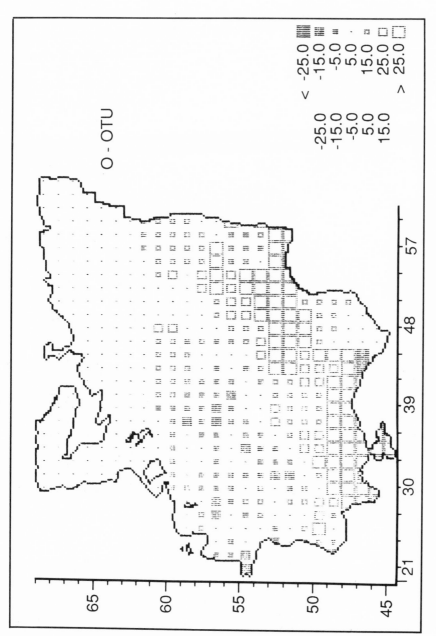

Fig. 6.4 Percent change in arable lands, European Russia, 1860–1960. (Compiled by H. H. Kazansky)

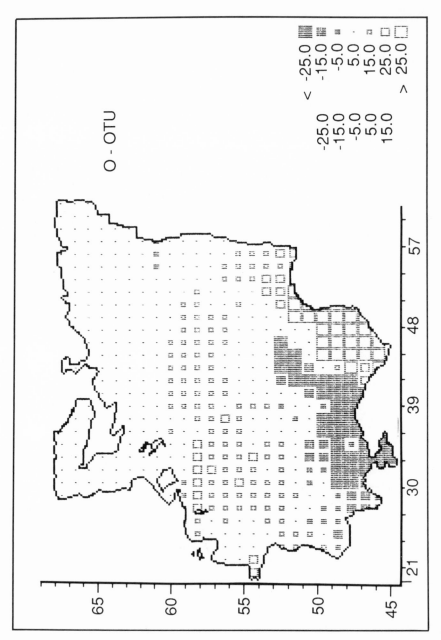

Fig. 6.5 Percent change in grasslands, European Russia, 1860–1960. (Compiled by H. H. Kazansky)

Modern technology has made possible a much more integrated approach, even though certain representative areas may still have to be selected. From the outset, the experiments should include the following: (1) a clear, though relatively simple, conceptual model of the surface system being investigated—a model that aids identification of the key geologic, pedologic, hydrologic, biospheric, and atmospheric variables; (2) recognition of the types of process-response models that will be applied to the system and the input data required for such models; (3) how the model data, both input and output, are related to remote-sensing technology; (4) the frequency and accuracy level of observations; and (5) the type of GIS that will be used to monitor and archive the collected data.

A truly experimental approach would best be couched in a hypothesis-testing framework using a hypothesis of the following type: no important change can be detected in the ecosystem of the site, over the annual to decadal time scale, that will affect its present value as a human resource. Examples of completed work may show how we can achieve this requirement, although it is nearly impossible to accomplish at an individual geographic site.

The Alpine Geosystem Model (French 1986) is a good example of the kind of conceptual model that could be employed. This model consists of four hierarchical levels or subsystems: geomorphology-paleoecology, soil and vegetation community, biotic production–population decomposition, and physiology-behavior. The four levels interact with the additional subsystems of climate and hydrology-geochemistry.

Physical geographers are probably on their firmest ground with a varied suite of well-tested physical process-response models from which to choose, at least as far as a mesoscale or smaller is concerned. Outcalt's (1972) digital climate simulator and Dozier's (1980) radiation model for a snow surface in complex terrain are but two examples. One significant problem that will need to be addressed on a site basis is the interface between models of the various physical spheres. That this is not insurmountable is shown by modeling approaches that compromise between area-specific, data-based regression models and complex energy/mass exchange models along the lines suggested by the WATER model (Burt et al. 1981) for monitoring spatial agricultural water consumption.

The relationship of input and output model data to remote-sensing technology is a more difficult area to address. It is technologically feasible to interrogate a wide variety of variables remotely only for a relatively limited time. This has recently been achieved in topoclimatic investigations of the Amazon rain forest by the National Center for Atmospheric Research (NCAR) Portable Automated Mesomet (PAM) system, whose data were telemetered via GOES (Geostationary Operational Environmental Satellite) satellite to North American bases (NCAR 1987). IGBP studies will require long-term observations such as those provided by the Landsat or other systems but at much less frequent time intervals. This requires matching the physical models to the satellite data-collection frequency. An example of how this can be done has been provided by Carlson et al. (1981), who used such data to study urban surface heat–energy exchanges and the creation of urban heat islands.

The choice of human geographic impact or change indicators will be critical to making our studies geographic as opposed to purely biogeophysical. Greenland (1983) has suggested that, in the context of resource management, a large variety of indicators may be developed, limited only by the imagination and innovation of the investigator. In the kind of IGBP studies we are considering here, however, there is somewhat more restraint if studies are based solely on those parameters which can be monitored from space or air. Nevertheless, there is still considerable choice, ranging from the obvious ones such as vegetation change (as, for example, in Frank's [1984b] study on erosion, vegetation, and albedo in Utah) to more esoteric (at least in the context of physical geography) variables such as urban population density, which was estimated from space by Watkins and Morrow-Jones (1985). The criteria for the selection of these variables will be their potential availability for monitoring on a continuous basis and their ease of fit with the physical models. There is no a priori reason why only remotely sensed data should be used for the purpose of monitoring socioeconomic indicators except that it might lead to a greater degree of consistency.

The frequency and accuracy of observations may be determined by a number of factors. The frequency and accuracy of satellite-derived observations are reaching such a relatively high level that a more likely restraining factor will be the type of process-response models selected and the social impact indicators chosen. Once these choices have been made, it remains to ensure that the available technology will be consistent over the decadal time period envisioned in the IGBP studies.

Many different types of geographic information systems are becoming available. Guidance in the selection of one of these for monitoring, archiving, and analyzing data should be made on the principle of choosing the simplest considering the site and the models involved. Practically speaking, GIS software is frequently updated, and the cost of updates and operator retraining over a ten-year period would be more manageable for simple systems than for highly sophisticated ones. An investigating group might have to forgo certain kinds of analyses to gain simplicity, but the time and space scales of the investigation must always be held in focus when selection of a GIS is made.

Representative Target Areas

The selection of target areas for the application of geographic methodology is critical. Geographers in the USSR have given considerable thought to theoretical aspects of site selection. American geographers have relied more on already existing sites. The two approaches are described below.

THEORETICAL: FACTORS OF THE GEOGRAPHIC SPHERE STRUCTURES

The IGBP documents give considerable attention to the development of a network of biospheric stations for complete monitoring of interactions at the earth-atmosphere interface. Each such station is, or would be, an extremely expensive facility designed for observation purposes during (at least) the forthcoming period of the IGBP study. That is why it is necessary to define criteria for choosing areas that reveal some fundamental properties of the biosphere together with the most important features of human-nature interaction.

Historically, this is not a new way of stating the problem. At the beginning of this century, N. I. Vavilov attempted to determine the botanical-agronomical basis for selecting significant areas. He suggested the importance of making an "exhaustive as possible collection of the world's major high quality species of cultural plants in order to study the composition of the species as an initial material for practical selection" (Vavilov [1930] 1967, 99). By contemporary standards, that work has been done by a very small number of researchers. Expeditions were sent to just those places where one might expect to find the maximum intraspecific variability both in cultured plants and in their wild ancestors—i.e., to the "center of world variety" and "the centers of formation."

A systematic-geographical method for determining the centers of formation was accepted as the theoretical basis for that work, which demanded "the establishment of the hereditary variety distribution of forms of any given species over regions and countries" and the determination of geographic centers of the concentration of varieties, since the "areas of the maximum variety . . . will usually be the centers for the creation of new forms" (Vavilov [1926] 1967, 99).

Vavilov related the existence of the maximum variety of forms with the maximum variety of environmental conditions and the age of the land. He believed that the maximum environmental variation should be expected in mountainous regions located near the boundaries of climatic zones, but they should be geologically ancient mountain systems. Moreover, Vavilov showed that mountain areas were precisely the breeding ground for agriculture. This theory suggests that the greatest variety in conditions will be observed in areas where there are marked natural (physical-geographical) divisions in combination with climatic boundary zones (e.g., oceanic and continental, sea and temperate-continental, temperate-continental, and continental). The centers of the greatest variety in environmental conditions—and, accordingly, the anticipated greatest variety in ecosystems and the gene pool corresponding to the biospheric level—should occur in such boundary areas (Fig. 6.6).

The spatial differentiation of environmental conditions at a global level occurs as a result of air mass differences, which determine the division into climatic zones, and the peculiarities of land and ocean interaction, which cause longitudinal heterogeneity of moisture conditions. Lithologic-orographic heterogeneity of the land surface modifies the climate and ensures geochemical

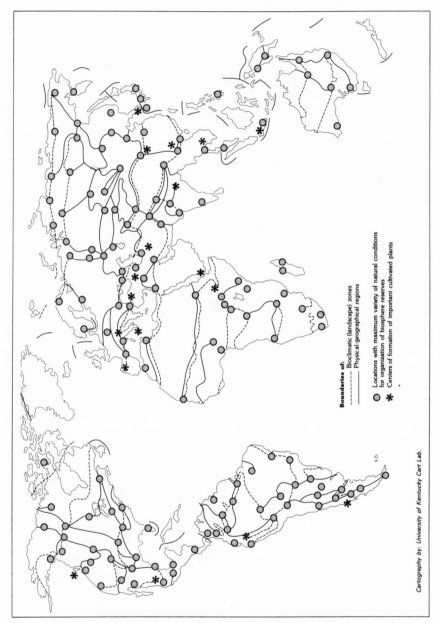

Boundaries of:
- - - - - Bioclimatic (landscape) zones
—— Physical-geographical regions
◉ Locations with maximum variety of natural conditions for organization of biosphere reserves
∗ Centers of formation of important cultivated plants

Cartography by: University of Kentucky Cart Lab.

Fig. 6.6 Locations potentially suitable for organization of biosphere reserves. (Compiled by V. E. Sokolov, P. D. Gunin, A. V. Drozdov, and Yu. G. Puzachenko)

variety. This heterogeneity is the result of global tectonics, which is of a relatively discrete nature and is responsible for the development of large continental masses. Even if climatic boundaries are not distinct, geologic-geomorphological boundaries are usually discrete.

Hence the two factors, climate and geology, are the independent foundations of territorial subdivisions. Sorting and differentiation are performed first by the former and then by the latter. These general considerations have been clearly expressed in the system of representation of physical-geographical division of the planet's surface worked out by Soviet geographers (Lukasheva and Ignat'yev 1964).

In order to justify the choice of territories with the greatest variety of environmental conditions and possessing the most important properties of the biosphere, one could determine the individual units that are naturally formed into continents or subcontinents. Earlier, the choice of such units might have been related to lithospheric plates, but they themselves have a complicated structure about which no clear understanding exists at present.

Empirical analysis of satellite photographs shows that prevailing sizes of units on the earth's surface relating to successive hierarchic levels differ from each other linearly by a factor of three, and thus in terms of area by a factor of nine to ten. This regularity is confirmed by physical theories describing fluctuation processes. As a rule, left to their own devices, complex fluctuation spectra form a discrete set of frequencies with a threefold difference in periods. This regularity manifests itself in different spatiotemporal features of the geographic sphere (Puzachenko 1986).

Based on the linear dimensions of continents, one can assume that the number of regions on the biospherical level should be about 10 to 15 on every continent. According to Soviet geographers, such regions correspond to the earth's largest physical-geographic subdivisions. They are distinguished by (1) similarity of the geostructure (morphostructure)—ancient plates, shields, orogenic areas, etc., determining the similarity in the history of their development; and (2) common features in the macrorelief—large lowlands, plateaus, and plains (Lukasheva and Ignat'yev 1964). Based on the *Physical-Geographic Atlas of the World*, 13 such areas (or regions) are distinguished in North America, 11 in South America, 8 in Africa, 6 in Australia, and 36 in Eurasia, including 9 on the European subcontinent and 11 in the Asian part bordering on the Indian Ocean basin. Physical-geographical areas consist of regions that are differentiated primarily on the basis of specific features of the most recent stages in their geological development, particularly in the Quaternary. Regional boundaries have a secondary significance for singling out territories with the greatest variety of environmental conditions.

Stations should be placed in spots where it will be possible to distinguish change factors. For example, by locating observation points in regions having maximum gradients of precipitation in both western and eastern parts of conti-

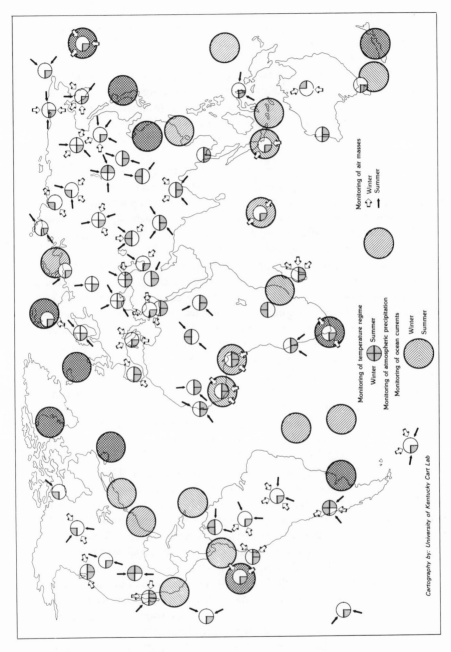

Fig. 6.7 Optimum locations for monitoring and for biosphere reserves. (From Sokolov and Puzachenko 1986)

Monitoring of air masses
↔ Winter
→ Summer

Monitoring of temperature regime
Winter Summer

Monitoring of atmospheric precipitation

Monitoring of ocean currents
Winter Summer

Cartography by: University of Kentucky Cart Lab

nents, influenced by air masses with quite different moisture conditions, we can help identify the factor(s) responsible for the observed precipitation changes.

The same principle can be used to distinguish regions within which the highest sensitivity to temperature changes can be expected. However, in order to exclude any possible influence of temperature changes due to variations in the latent heat of evaporation, it is preferable to choose continental areas with small variations of precipitation and maximum temperature gradients. Consequently, monitoring stations selected for precipitation observations may not correspond to the stations selected for observing temperature variations.

In accordance with the general principles, it is more expedient to locate stations for global monitoring of atmospheric pollution in regions having significant air mass interaction because it is possible to observe air masses of various origins having different gas and aerosol composition. Such locations ensure the maximum amount of data along with an economy of observations. As a rule, such regions correspond to fairly large climatic regions—in particular, to the zones of prevailing precipitation coming from different oceans. They may or may not coincide with the optimal areas for the location of temperature and moisture monitoring stations.

Figure 6.7 shows a suggested distribution of observation stations. It may be enriched in detail and specified on the basis of more rigorous quantitative estimates; however, its genetic basis makes it possible to assume that even the present version reflects the fundamental spatial layout for observation stations.

In addition to the conditions considered above, the choice of regions for the establishment of biospheric stations requires that these regions have a particularly great diversity of ecosystem species as well as lithological-geomorphological conditions. Under such conditions, one relatively small observation site will ensure the control and protection of a great variety of biospheric conditions. Since sites with enhanced variability can be regarded, in most cases, as ecotones of different origins, it is there that the highest degree of instability of the ecosystems and greatest sensitivity of their components to various forms of anthropogenic pressures can be expected. That instability is due to the fact that most elements of ecosystems under the conditions of ecotones are found in the vicinity of their ecological boundaries, and thus possess enhanced sensitivity to external influences. Territories characterized by the highest diversity of ecosystems with diverse lithological-geomorphological conditions are most suitable for carrying out complex scientific research. In Figure 6.7 such areas are marked with a special sign. At those points the diversity of ecosystems is primarily determined not by climatic but by lithological-geomorphological factors.

PRACTICAL SUGGESTIONS

If such theoretical detail as outlined above proves to be impractical in establishing new monitoring stations, then already existing networks and individual studies might be used to formulate ideas and achieve the deployment of representative target areas. We suggest as examples in the United States: (1) the existing field areas of some completed and ongoing geographic studies, (2) Long-Term Ecological Research (LTER) sites, and (3) sites belonging to the International Satellite Land Surface Climatology Project (ISLSCP). National Atmospheric Deposition Program (NADP) sites might also be considered. Some sites might fall into more than one of these categories.

Typical of established geographic field sites are the Niwot Ridge alpine tundra site in the Colorado Front Range and the two Sierra Nevada sites of the University of California, Santa Barbara, investigative group. One of the California sites is at Mammoth Mountain, and the other is part of the Integrated Watershed Study of the California Air Resources Board. Both the Colorado and the California sites have been the subject of intensive studies over a long period of time. Halfpenny et al. (1986) list the large number of works completed at the Niwot site, while a good description of the Sierra Nevada site is given by Davis et al. (1984). In Colorado, a wide variety of ecosystem studies are under way, while investigations in California focus on electromagnetic properties of snow, remote sensing of snow characteristics, snow hydrology, and snow chemistry. Both sites have the necessary requirements for IGBP studies in that they (1) have a relatively long history of study, (2) are representative of the type of surface surrounding them, (3) have human impacts that are not so great as to be uninterpretable, and (4) have studies that fit into other portions of the overall IGBP programs. Another field site for geographers in the United States might include Chitistone Pass, Alaska (Brazel and Outcalt 1973; Dozier and Outcalt 1979).

The LTER program is an attempt to establish coherence in ecological research over the long term (Callahan 1984). It recognizes that many parts of ecosystems operate over a long time scale and show directionality and periodicity. Studies that have recognized this (e.g., Hubbard Brook) have made fundamental contributions to ecology. Consequently, in 1988 there were fifteen LTER sites established in varying biomes throughout the coterminous United States.

Within these sites, it was recognized that human-derived (as well as natural) perturbations also act over a long time period (e.g., air pollution, acidification, CO_2). Studies at the sites are organized around five core themes: (1) pattern and control of primary production; (2) spatial and temporal distribution of populations selected to represent trophic structure; (3) pattern and control of organic matter accumulation in surface layers and sediments; (4) patterns of inorganic input and movement through soils, groundwater, and surface waters; and (5) patterns and frequency of disturbance to the research site. The LTER sites (Table 6.1 shows the first eleven sites established) are funded for five-year renewable periods and overseen by a central coordinating committee consist-

Table 6.1 The LTER sites: Ecosystem and climate.

Site	Ecosystem	Climate
H. J. Andrews Experimental Forest (Oregon)	coniferous forest	marine west coast
Cedar Creek Natural History Area (Minnesota)	hardwood forest/ tall-grass prairie	humid continental
Central Plains Experimental Range (Colorado)	high plains grassland	mid-latitude steppe
Coweeta Hydrology Lab (North Carolina)	deciduous forest	humid subtropical
Illinois & Mississippi rivers (Illinois)	temperate freshwater	humid continental
Jornada (New Mexico)	desert	subtropical desert
Konza Prairie (Kansas)	tall-grass prairie	mid-latitude steppe
Niwot Ridge/Green Lakes Valley (Colorado)	alpine tundra	highland
North Inlet (South Carolina)	coastal marine	humid subtropical
Northern Lakes (Wisconsin)	N temperate lake mixed forest	humid continental
Okefenokee National Wildlife Refuge (Georgia)	freshwater wetland	humid subtropical

ing of all site principal investigators; they operate under normal NSF peer-review procedures.

The descriptions of the climates of the LTER sites (Greenland 1987; Figs. 6.8 and 6.9) suggest two related concepts which should be considered when selecting target areas for IGBP geographical study sites. First, the site should be representative of its biome; second, it should be able to fit into a recognized environmental gradient (e.g., from wet to dry or from high temperature to low temperature). This second idea parallels the similar suggestion included in the Soviet site discussion above. Several gradients of this kind can be seen in Figures 6.8 and 6.9.

Many of the LTER sites also belong to the National Atmospheric Deposition Program (NADP) and thus have NADP samplers. This is another potentially important link with other IGBP programs and their biogeochemical components. Weekly samples of wet deposition are taken in each of the approximately two hundred NADP sites in the United States. Samples are analyzed by the Illinois Water Survey for pH, conductivity, and concentrations of Ca, Mg, K, Na, NH_4 (ammonium), NO_3 (nitrate), Cl, SO_4 (sulfate), PO_4 (phosphate), H^+, and cation/anion ratios. Field measurements of pH and conductance are made.

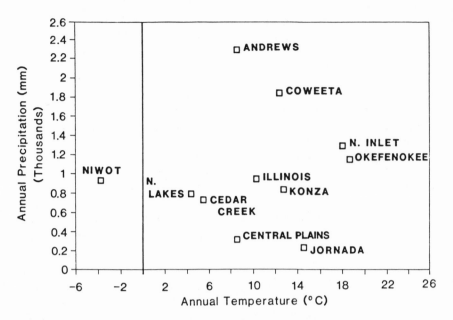

Fig. 6.8 Annual temperature and precipitation conditions for Long-Term Ecological Research sites. (From Greenland 1987)

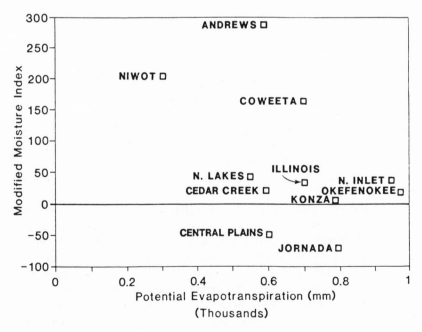

Fig. 6.9 Moisture relations between the Long-Term Ecological Research sites. (From Greenland 1987)

Another important program that may be used as a model for choosing IGBP study sites is the International Satellite Land Surface Climatology Project (Ruttenberg 1983). This project is part of the World Climate Program and has two objectives. First, it seeks to use time series of satellite data to monitor seasonal and long-term variations in land use and vegetation cover in order to assess quantitative surface-structure changes resulting from human action and/or climate variability. Second, it aims to utilize satellite imagery to derive quantities needed to improve on the parameterization of land surface–atmosphere interactions in climate models and/or to provide input for the models.

Interesting criteria were established for the selection of ground sites for the ISLSCP. These included the need for locations (a) where regional climates are potentially sensitive to actual or anticipated changes, (b) that have undergone large-scale anthropogenic surface modification or would be likely to do so, (c) that are in regions of high climatic variability, (d) that would provide a variety of surface types, (e) that would be agriculturally important, and (f) that have established research facilities and project support. Factors a and c correspond to the selection criteria used by the Soviets. Five project sites were proposed to provide detailed validation of land-surface parameterizations within numerical models. These included the general areas of the southern Great Plains of North America, the northern Great Plains (in Canada), central Niger, the Sonoran Desert, and an Amazon rain forest location.

The first representative ISLSCP target area was chosen at the Konza prairie near Manhattan, Kansas, which exemplifies the tall-grass prairie biome of the southern Great Plains of North America. Since Konza is also an LTER site, the ISLSCP and the LTER programs are integrated by such a selection. During the summer of 1987 this site was the focus of the First ISLSCP Field Experiment (FIFE), where spatially and temporally intense field observations of the surface energy budget and other atmospheric variables were made at the same time as satellite observations of a 10 × 10 km area. Energy budget models are being employed to merge satellite-derived data sets, meteorological observations, and surface measurements to calculate parameters describing the condition of the land surface and how these parameters affect the transfer of mass and energy between the surface and the atmosphere (Schmugge and Sellers 1986).

These programs and their study sites give examples of the kinds of target sites that geographical IGBP studies could identify. Indeed, a strong case can be made for the association of geographers with these sites. Also, funding agencies are often more open to the idea of research that complements already existing programs. Funding agencies that have geography sections should be encouraged to earmark funds for such associated research. In addition, sites from these programs already represent most major biomes, soils, and climatic regimes, with the possible exception of the tropical rain forest. An interesting contrast exists between LTER sites, which mostly represent a particular biome with a minimum of human impact, and ISLSCP sites, which are chosen for the high degree of impact they have experienced.

Scale Problems

Geographers have traditionally sought to address problems of scale. IGBP studies will have scale problems of at least two kinds. First, there is the scale problem imposed by the limitations of the remote-sensing hardware—in both time and space. Second, there is the scale problem of interfacing or nesting of different size scales and/or information densities; this may be related to the problem of extrapolation outward from points of ground-based measurements.

As a simple example of the former problem, time and space resolutions of three (of the many available) systems can be examined. The NOAA geostationary GOES satellite monitors visible and thermal infrared light on a continuous basis with spatial resolutions of 1, 2, and 4 km. The Landsat-4 (TM) monitors in 7 spectral bands with a spatial resolution of 30–120 m and passes once every 16 days. The French SPOT satellite can monitor 1 or 3 spectral bands at a resolution of 10 or 20 m with a frequency of once every 26 days.

Clearly, it is a major research problem for physical geography and other physical sciences to specify the size of the land areas to be studied, and to select, adapt, or develop models of the physical system that can utilize the combined information from the above (and other) satellites. Within IGBP studies, the problem is reduced a little by the fact that the focus is on relatively long-term changes, and infrequency of satellite passage is not a problem.

Research is also needed on the interfacing of different scale sizes. In some physical fields, such as numerical modeling of the atmosphere, this has been approached by nesting of grids of varying sizes. Thus there might be a very high density array of data points existing within a sparser network. This approach often works for the atmosphere because of its commonly smooth gradients (except near frontal areas) in the values of the variables being treated. It might work in some earth surface problems but not in others. It would not work in cases in which there is great heterogeneity of land cover and distinct changes are occurring over a short distance (e.g., the urban-rural boundary). Other problem cases include some of the very areas identified by the Soviets as being in need of special study. Geographers need to develop new methods of varying grid size—methods that do not necessarily treat the problem as linear in time or space. In mental or perceptual maps, for example, we have not been constrained by linearity. Nor should there be need for constraint in the present context, save only for the constraint of consistency and the adherence to physical and geometric laws.

Such new directions will build on traditional approaches. These have included making two-dimensional models driven by input data from one or a limited number of input data points. One example of this is the simulation by Dozier and Outcalt (1979) of temperature and radiation budget values on a grid for the Chitistone Pass area. Another example is the use of the WINDS model, which estimates wind velocity and direction field over complex terrain given only the wind velocity and direction values at one point (Fosberg et al. 1976).

The ISLSCP program has identified two scales of investigation. The first scale treats point and limited-area measurements. This is aimed at the collection of ground truth to interpret satellite imagery, and the collections at different sites may be made independently. The second scale considers large-area experiments that would be conducted over a large region using a wide range of technical equipment. The proposed regions for this scale of the study were listed above. Little attention was paid in the initial ISLSCP plans for coordination between these two scales. This is the kind of problem that geographers could usefully explore.

IGBP planners are well aware of the scale problem. Initial documents (e.g., National Research Council 1986) talk of a hierarchy of levels ranging from global to regional (macrocells) to ecosystems (microcells) and suggest that where biophysical models linking the levels do not exist, they must be developed. A special meeting on the subject of scale (Risser 1986) identified hierarchy theory as a point of departure. Hierarchy theory directs attention to the level of explanation required for specific questions and searches for the specific variables that interface the hierarchical levels in question. Risser reported that, in theory, interactive variables should change only in extent (size and time scale) and grain (detail of observation) in coupling levels (T.F.H. Allen and Hoekstra 1984). The meeting also suggested developing general principles of aggregation and desegregation of processes across scales based on experience in certain cases where it has been successfully achieved, such as in some atmospheric processes. The scale problem may be one in which geographers can make a fundamental contribution to the IGBP.

Use of Available Data

The huge cost of data collection for IGBP projects behooves all investigators, not just geographers, to attempt to make effective use of existing data. Study sites might indeed be selected partially on the strength of their existing data, which could be used for ground confirmation. Even if no data were collected for the IGBP, there would still exist almost fifteen years of Landsat data as well as a great deal of other satellite data for shorter periods or with less resolution.

There are at least two areas where geographers might make important contributions to the IGBP through the use of techniques not commonly applied in other fields. The first area involves the use of repeat photography from the

ground. This is increasingly employed by geographers—with great effectiveness—to shed light on changes in vegetation and/or land use. Veblen and
Lorenz (1986) employed the technique to document human-induced vegetation
change in the Front Range of Colorado. Byers (1987) used a similar method in
the Himalayas to demonstrate that human-induced changes were not nearly as
great as conventional wisdom had made them out to be.

A second technique of growing importance is the use of geographic information systems. These will play a major role in IGBP studies because of the large
quantities of data to be manipulated and the fact that many of these data will
be spatial in nature. Perhaps more important, however, is the challenge for
geographers to use GISs to solve some of the problems mentioned above, such
as the incompatibility of spatial resolution of data. Of course, traditional techniques for extrapolating variable values at unevenly spaced locations to regular
grid points will have to be used. But beyond this, developments in GIS technology may be able to address specific issues such as data arrays of varying
density, the nesting of different-density data sets, and their subsequent manipulation in, for example, the case of overlaying higher-resolution Landsat/SPOT-
type information onto lower-resolution GOES data.

Inventory and Establishment of Permanent Monitoring Networks

Networks for monitoring geographic data may be highly variable in geographic scale and political organization. They may be global and international,
national, statewide, or local. The ISLSCP and LTER are examples of international and national programs, respectively. Most states and many local governments operate their own networks to monitor some kind of geographic data
varying from air quality to land use and population.

It is not proposed that geographers spend a great deal of time setting up new
observational networks; the cost alone would be prohibitive. Rather, it is
suggested that geographers make use of existing observational networks, sup-
plementing observations where necessary, and introduce modeling and GIS
tools to bridge the scales.

Research in the discipline of physical geography has tended to move from
the global scale of the last century to a microscale following the quantitative
revolution and the recognition of the importance of process. One of the more
fruitful areas in which geographers have recently been working is that of the
meso-, or subregional, scale. Examples include the work of Vale (1977) in
investigating the forest changes in the Warner Mountains of California, and
Trimble's (1981) examination of the changes in sediment storage in the Coon
Creek basin of Wisconsin. It is suggested that rather than establishing completely new monitoring networks, some geographers, besides piggybacking
on the national and international networks, would be better served to identify

areas of county or multicounty size that have already been studied in some way. These areas could then become the focus of experiments using the previously discussed experimental designs. The whole suite of technological tools, especially an appropriate GIS, could be used to address a hypothesis and some of the specific research problems noted above. In this manner geographers might make an important contribution to the IGBP that is unlikely to be made by the geophysicists and biologists working in other parts of the program.

7. CONCLUSIONS AND FUTURE WORK

This book is a first effort by some Soviet and American geographers to describe geographical research applicable to the development of the International Geosphere-Biosphere Program. It also outlines areas for further work. Its authors have made an attempt to point out some geographical approaches to the IGBP, although they make no claim to have provided a full coverage of the problem. Nor have they limited themselves to the strict IGBP framework, which has so far emphasized the importance of recognizing the anthropogenic constituents of global changes while omitting them from the field of its planned studies. Human activity is now the most powerful dynamic factor in global change; it affects both geosphere and biosphere systems. At the same time, human society is being affected by the negative consequences of its own actions. This is expressed in a whole range of natural-anthropogenic and anthropogenic processes. We can cite as examples the decrease in stratospheric ozone, acid precipitation, the degradation of soils, deforestation, desertification, and pollution of the urban environment, the ocean, and many water reservoirs. All these are phenomena that sum up the interaction of human activity and natural forces.

A realistic evaluation of the present state of the biosphere or any look toward future prospects requires an examination of its evolution over a long period. Paleoclimatic and paleolandscape spatial reconstructions help in understanding regularities in the trends of development of the landscape shell and in determining contemporary "coordinates" on this curve. They can also establish regularities and ranges of climatic fluctuations over time and reveal the changeability or stability of various components of the landscape system during those fluctuations. The historical approach to spatial reconstructions creates a basis for predicting ecological and climatic scenarios of the future.

Projections of orbital forcing of incoming solar radiation show that the long-term trend of global climate is moving toward a glacial interval. However, anthropogenic influences over the past few decades and projections of their effects over the next fifty to one hundred years have convinced many that we are facing a trend toward warming, possibly at an increasing rate.

The scenarios based on paleogeographic reconstructions need to consider two time scales. The components of the landscape systems affected by natural climatic changes need to be considered over thousands of years, while the role of anthropogenic factors should be considered in decades. Construction of future scenarios is made considerably more difficult by the propensity of human actions to influence the zonal structure of the landscape. This accounts, in large measure, for an acceleration in the degradation processes, changes in productivity, and a decrease in the ability of natural resources to regenerate themselves. If we are to understand such complex systems as landscapes and predict their future state, it is necessary to consider the following general concepts.

First, the metabolism of landscape systems includes absorption, redistribution, and discharge of fluxes of energy, water, geochemical elements, and other substances (for example, biogenic material containing living matter such as pollen and spores). The most important characteristics of a landscape are the continuous renewal of biomass and the biogeochemical change of inanimate matter during the processes of metabolism. At the same time, flows of migrating people, goods, and information are affecting these processes. Some fluxes (e.g., energy fluxes) are mostly vertical; others (e.g., water, air, goods, and pollution) are mostly horizontal. The study of horizontal flows is of special interest to geographers.

Second, landscape systems include not only heterogeneous areas and their borders but also various internal networks such as river systems, transportation networks, and migrational routes of animals. Streams of movement along those networks are related not only to the corresponding potentials but also to the functional distances of exchange. Flows circulating in the landscape establish new states of spatial heterogeneity, which in turn create new forms of streams and new states.

Third, the boundaries of spatially heterogeneous areas of various hierarchical types differ as to the ease with which they may be crossed by horizontal flows. Thus they can exert an influence on the spread of various phenomena, serving not only as barriers to the movement of certain properties but also as zones of attraction or accumulation of particular phenomena.

On the basis of these conceptual approaches, ecological policy should consider the impact of society on (1) components of the surface, (2) geographical boundaries, and (3) geographical networks.

The dynamic balance of the earth is supported by the specific and unique role of the landscape cover. One of the major directions of geographic investigations of global change is a study of the dynamics of the landscape cover under the impact of the interaction of geospheric, biospheric, and anthropogenic processes of different scales. The quasi balance of the earth's state is apparently determined by its proximity to one of its stable states. Rapid changes in types of weather and conditions of the biota, swings from glacial to nonglacial conditions, and the nonlinearity of the earth's system indicate the existence of such metastable states (Butzer 1975). In this case, even a minor change in the earth's state (including an anthropogenic one) can transfer it from the vicinity of one stable state to the vicinity of another, which will lead to an irreversible transfer of the system into a new state. Changing areas of polar ice, tropical forest, and desert may prove to be triggers for change. This possibility should be taken into account when considering global changes.

Work is progressing on the integration of models of the global biosphere, atmosphere, and geosphere into one single model for the planet. The most active of the spheres is the biosphere, which acts, to a great degree, as a regulator of the earth's processes—in particular, the process of the exchange of matter and energy between spheres. The regulating function of the biota is determined by both its dynamism and its location on the boundaries between the atmosphere and either the ocean or the land.

We need to develop three-dimensional models of landscape structure and change if we are to create dynamic geographies that can be coupled with atmospheric and oceanic models. This means that we must investigate and specify the morphology of landscape, especially the aspects of landscape that greatly influence exchanges of energy and mass with the atmosphere, and horizontal flows of energy, mass, and the agents of landscape change. For example, spatial fluxes of water and fossil fuels through pipeline networks need to be understood, and numerical models of the flow processes need to be developed. Structures of landscapes, such as Rowe's (1988) three-dimensional preliminary representation of natural vegetation, which was developed to study plant-canopy influences on large-scale albedo, also need to be compiled for a variety of other important problems. The inherently three-dimensional structure of the built and agricultural environs, for example, should be parameterized. Topography and soils also await specification at a large scale, as does the seasonal snow cycle and its interaction with the built, agricultural, and natural environs. The structure and dynamics of landscape, in short, must be modeled if we are ever to understand or predict the role that terrestrial systems play in global change. Since humanity plays a key role in landscape dynamics, human activities must be an integral part of such models.

A systematic study of humans as both generators and victims of disturbances in the landscape cover and in the biosphere as a whole is needed. The essence of the present global changes can be discovered through analysis of the factors and mechanisms of the anthropogenic changes of landscapes and their socioeconomic consequences. That gives rise to the task of studying the landscapes involved in different aspects of resource cycles—extraction, processing, consumption, and return of substances to nature. High-priority research problems include the following: a study of the anthropogenic effect on the resources of natural systems; the influence of changes in atmospheric composition on landscapes; quantitative and qualitative depletion of fresh water; and the threat of destruction of landscapes as a result of irreversible unstable processes.

One of the major tasks of the IGBP is the study and preservation of natural life-supporting systems. This should include study of the natural-anthropogenic processes and the breakdown of the cycles of restoration of natural resources, including the causes, dynamics, and spread of deforestation, erosion, degradation of the natural fertility of soils, desertification, and the decrease in the genetic diversity of the earth.

Deforestation, desertification, and soil degradation pose three major challenges for geographers. First, the present inadequacy of spatial data bases is a significant constraint on progress in testing hypotheses about the implications of deforestation, desertification, and soil degradation. Second, the spatial data sets need to be integrated with global and regional scale models through characterization of regional variation of properties of interest and their significance to the energy balance, the hydrologic cycle, and global elemental cycles. Third, the empirical testing of geographic theories (both descriptive and normative) needs to be continued and intensified.

A vast amount of work is needed to improve the quality of spatial data bases, especially in the less developed areas of Africa, Asia, and Latin America that are undergoing the most rapid transformations in land use. Present knowledge of the spatial distribution of soils and vegetation, to mention only two factors, is clearly inadequate for a valid characterization of these areas and their likely behavior when subjected to change. The missing information must be collected by field surveys that use standard methods of sampling and classification. Accurate characterization of the spatial location of sampling sites and the collection of multivariate data from each site are essential.

Spatial data sets require valid analysis if they are to be useful in the understanding of deforestation, desertification, and soil degradation. Hypotheses must be generated that relate local data to regional and global processes, and statistical tests must attempt to confirm or deny the importance of any given study site or data set to its surrounding region, and the validity of the units by which it is characterized. Many techniques already exist for aggregating landscape data; for example, land evaluation (Beek 1984; Breeuwsma et al. 1986; Buringh 1986; Nortcliff 1987), fertility capability classification (Sanchez et al. 1982), soil potential ratings (McCormack and Stocking 1986), and other methods (Manrique 1985; King et al. 1986) are promising ways to aggregate landscape information into homogeneous units for planning agriculture, forestry, and other land-use activities. Offori et al. (1986) have attempted to develop criteria to identify land suitable for clearing, while Young (1986) has attempted to identify land suitable for agroforestry. But more attention needs to be given to the problems inherent in spatial statistical analyses, such as spatial autocorrelation and the general lack of true independence or normality inherent in most geographical data sets (Anselin 1988).

Apart from energy, water, and elemental budgets or regional cycles, a number of specific geographic theories provide the basis for improved testing of hypotheses regarding the processes of deforestation, desertification, and soil degradation. The theory of island biogeography and its relevance to the design of nature reserves, for example, has been hotly debated in the geographic literature (Diamond 1975; Margules et al. 1982; East 1983; Boecklen and Gotelli 1984; Opsdam et al. 1985; Wilcox and Murphy 1985; Boecklen 1986; Freemark and Merriam 1986; Zimmerman and Bierregard 1986). A consensus on the applicability (or lack thereof) is beginning to emerge (R. L. Jones 1988), but more tests of revised expressions of this theory are necessary.

A less well articulated theory is also promising. Landscape ecology, which relates patterns and processes of spatial diffusion of organisms and their response to disturbance, provides the basis for testable hypotheses (Forman and Godron 1986). If landscape units with predictable characteristics can, in fact, be elucidated, they may provide a physically valid format for aggregation and characterization of landscape response to deforestation, desertification, and soil degradation.

Determination of the causes of anthropogenic changes in the major landscape parameters can help to predict where and for how long these changes have prevailed and suggest possible actions to rectify negative situations. The social consequences of the changed environment also deserve analysis to determine which events should be considered calamities and how society should fight these dangers. Evaluations by geographers can be improved if they are based on studies of the landscape system and the reactions of society, as well as on the resource systems of different geographical areas.

Simulations of the impact of environmental changes on human society usually reveal the following weaknesses: (1) forecasts of environmental changes may prove to be unrealistic, (2) the level of capital investment and management assumed in models may change in the future, and (3) models may prove to be quite unreliable if they are used for evaluation of the impact of ecological factors that differ considerably from those assumed in the original model.

Estimations of humans' impacts on the environment tend to be limited to evaluations of separate effects. So far, attention has been focused on forecasting possible influences of specific projects but not on measuring the real signs (signals) of the impact. For this reason, only a few empirical studies have been carried out for monitoring operating projects. Experience gained from investigations being carried out in the Kursk "modeling" area by the Institute of Geography of the USSR Academy of Sciences has proven to be valuable. Recommendations from the Kursk study concerning methods of economic and noneconomic evaluation of the anthropogenic impact on the environment suggest investigation of the following processes: (1) the influence of human activities as trigger mechanisms for interactions, (2) the changes that take place in nature under the influence of those impacts, and (3) the consequences of environmental changes on human health and economic activity (Preobrajensky and Vorachek 1985).

Analysis of the consequences of human activity and the evaluation of risks arising from various decisions are indispensable prerequisites for regulating the anthropogenic impact on nature, and for preventing or mitigating negative ecological consequences. One of the unfortunate tendencies of our time is the growing economic impact of natural disasters. So far, the IGBP, which is directed toward promoting long-term management of the environment on a global scale, does not even mention the problem of fighting against natural calamities and the task of using accumulated scientific information in that fight.

What can geographers do to assist the process of global environmental risk assessment? Many possibilities exist, but only one example is introduced here. It is proposed that the global community of geographers undertake a project to assess risks associated with burgeoning environmental changes in coastal areas. Rapid increases in coastal populations and development activities are occurring throughout the world. Major investments in development projects for agriculture, fishing, and offshore resources are commonplace in less developed nations, while industrial, residential, and recreational growth dominates in the coastal zones of developed nations. Coasts are exposed to a wide range of locally existing natural risks (Are 1980; Popov et al. 1987; Zenkovich 1987, 1988). In addition, the prospect of rising sea levels and other long-term changes that are outcomes of interaction among diverse universal and local risks suggests that worse is to come. Potentially hazardous storage and manufacturing facilities are also springing up on near-shore sites in most maritime nations. In short, coastal changes reflect the operation of a wide range of increasing local and universal risks. They comprise a dynamic risk mosaic that provides a suitable test of global risk-assessment approaches and methods.

As a first step toward this goal, collaborative teams of Russian and American geographers might undertake a pilot version of the coastal risk-assessment project that would focus on natural and human environmental changes in one or more maritime sites in each country. The initial objective would be to produce risk information useful to decision makers and other user groups in both countries. The pilot project would also be designed to permit comparative data gathering and comparative testing of different approaches and methods of risk assessment with a view to providing guidance for a general analysis of global environmental risks.

American geographers have made progress in studying how people react to natural calamities as individuals and as groups. The major innovation consists of an integrated evaluation of the effect of natural calamities on areas, inhabitants, and the economy, and an analysis of response actions. According to recent research, optimum adjustment is seldom reached. Decisions reached without adequate planning may increase the scale of damages or prolong the emergency situation. This is especially dangerous in view of the rapidly growing technological capacity of society, and with it the increased risk of technological catastrophes.

One major product of geographical studies of natural calamities proposed by Soviet geographers is the compilation of an atlas containing maps of natural factors, maps of important types of natural calamities (dangerous natural phenomena), and maps of the socioeconomic significance of dangerous natural phenomena expressed as indexes of economic risks and costs of protecting against them. An integral part of this research should be the location of areas that are dangerous from the viewpoint of technological and socioeconomic calamities as well as a survey of areas of natural and technological risks to human life and health.

One suggestion is the creation of *red-zone maps of critical ecological situations* (analogous to the red books for protection of flora and fauna) that reflect locations where we might be approaching the threshold of irreversible change that will result in a loss of resources and the regenerative capacity of the environment (Puzachenko 1989). The red-zone maps would pinpoint areas that require priority attention for research programs, monitoring, and detailed evaluation of the impact of human activity. This will help to suggest alternative ways of development that may lead to a more stable ecological and economic state—a change from "red-zone" maps of danger to "green" maps of stability.

This volume contains examples of preliminary red-zone maps reflecting the location of critical situations in both the Soviet Union and the United States that have resulted from anthropogenic modifications of water. Work needs to be started on the production of landscape-dynamic maps reflecting unfavorable evolution in which the ecological situation shifts from a satisfactory state to an unsatisfactory one. With further degeneration, such areas may reach first a critical and then a catastrophic state. Red-zone maps would raise a warning flag about such dangers. The concept of red-zone maps is related to the idea of the ecological potential and stability of both land and water systems, which includes evaluation of the potential of "self-purification" of soils, water reservoirs, and air masses.

Special attention should be given to evaluation of the impact of human activity on areas of extreme natural conditions and on fragile ecosystems such as high mountains, the polar zone, coastal wetlands, and arid areas. The situation is especially complicated in many developing countries, where direct anthropogenic pressure on fragile ecosystems continues to grow. In these regions, socioeconomic problems almost guarantee the destruction of the life-supporting natural systems. This destruction threatens the stability of the biosphere and the effectiveness of its most important ecological mechanisms for self-regulation. It is necessary to mobilize international efforts to solve these problems in the developing countries.

A territorial basis for managing natural-anthropogenic processes is provided by different heterogeneous regional systems which exist in close interrelation and with some unfavorable interaction. Because of the regional "area" base, and as a result of society's activity, it is necessary to take into account the influence of geographical boundaries and geographical networks. In a period of rapid scientific and technological progress, with a marked increase in the flows of information, goods, people, innovations, and so on, there is also a sharp increase in the need for mutual dependence, a subject worthy of separate study. Any ecological violation (such as a technogenic disaster) in one region or place may affect other areas and even the world as a whole.

The traditional concepts of regional development must be reconsidered in terms of ecological safety. Fundamental should be the concept of management of the natural-anthropogenic systems as a whole rather than their separate components (e.g., water resources, soils, economy, or demography). Any attempt to manipulate one of the components separately more often than not leads to ecological disaster despite the seemingly optimum use of that particular component.

The development of a series of models of global change requires, foremost, the collection and dissemination of biospheric, atmospheric, and oceanic data to serve as inputs to any modeling efforts. An urgent task is the improvement of methods for modeling the dynamics of the geosystems and the formation of a new generation of geoinformational systems. To solve that task it is necessary (1) to develop the scientific foundations for and extend a global network of geosystem "monitoring," and (2) to create scientific and technical bases for an informational infrastructure for geographical studies.

Geographers should undertake specific GIS-based studies on two scales. The first scale should be a mesoscale (about 50 km × 50 km), which corresponds to the "practical" sites considered in the section on Target Areas in section 6.2. The second scale should be a larger, subcontinental, scale (discussed under Theoretical: Factors in the same section). In both studies an appropriate GIS grid should be selected. Topographic data would be basic. Then, using ten-year intervals, data on land use, vegetation and faunal densities, and appropriate ecological impact indicators should be archived. Detailed studies on surface climate changes (e.g., in albedo, absorbed shortwave radiation, etc.) should then be undertaken. Depending on the degree of land-use data available, more detailed studies on such items as atmospheric emissions and transport around the grid might be made. In addition, the grids will lend themselves to studying the effect and importance of corridors. Analysis of results from each of the two scales will help to identify the most appropriate scale to use for overall IGBP purposes.

In the area of environmental measurements and detection of global changes, several key problems of interest to geographers can be identified. First, there is a need for substantive analysis of satellite-derived data in order to calibrate such measurements against surface observations. This validation is crucial in several respects. It is required for algorithm development in mapping environmental variables such as vegetation cover, soil moisture, cloud cover, sea ice, snow cover, and so on. The choice of the appropriate spatial scale of observations of these variables, as viewed by surface observers and by satellite, is an eminently geographical one. It is also essential for interpretive purposes where previous surface measurements are being superseded by satellite measurements; this is the case for sea surface temperatures and upper air soundings, for example.

A second and related problem is the necessity for maintaining long-term baseline data at sites representative of major biomes (D. H. Miller 1988). Such programs are in place at a few LTER sites in the United States, and these could form a nucleus for the proposed geosphere-biosphere observations. However, we must ensure that comprehensive, consistent, and sustained measurement programs are carried out. Attention needs to be given to designing and implementing these observations.

A third aspect of the data problem for global change studies is the need to develop integrated, interdisciplinary data sets. The great variety of measurement techniques and scales of observation, and the disparate nature of the variables (continuous, discrete) makes this a research problem that will require expertise in geographical information systems, remote sensing, data analysis, and modeling.

The major task of geographers in the elaboration of the IGBP is the study of changes in the components and mechanisms of the geosphere and biosphere that are affected by both natural and anthropogenic factors. An important characteristic is the direct introduction of the anthropogenic link as well as a systematic approach to the study of natural and natural-anthropogenic processes and structures of various scales.

The major criterion for determining the priority of research themes is their importance in solving problems of the survival of humanity and the preservation of the earth as a living system. Thus it becomes imperative that we understand the interaction of the major parameters existing in the narrow ecological corridor for life support on the earth. Special efforts should be made to predict possible changes of the biosphere in the coming century. Research should be carried out at all three major levels of spatial organization—local, regional, and global.

BIBLIOGRAPHY

Abler, R. 1987. What shall we say? To whom shall we speak? *Annals of the Association of American Geographers* 77:511–24.

Abramov, L. S. 1988. Znachenie idey V. I. Vernadskogo dlya sovremennoy geografii (Ideas of V. I. Vernadsky in modern geography). *Izvestiya USSR Academy of Sciences, Series Geography* 4:5–15.

Agranat, G. A. 1988. Territiriya: povyshenie roly v jizni obshchestva (k postanovke problemy) (Territory: An increase of its role in the life of society [toward the formulation of the problem]). *Izvestiya USSR Academy of Sciences, Series Geography* 2:5–16.

Ahlcrona, E. 1988. The impact of climate and man on land transformation in central Sudan: Applications of remote sensing. *Meddelanden fran Lunds Universitets Geografiska Institutioner, Avhandlinger* 103.

Alegre, J. C., and D. K. Cassel. 1986. Effect of land-clearing methods and post-clearing management on aggregate stability and organic carbon content of a soil in the humid tropics. *Soil Science* 142:289–95.

Alegre, J. C., D. K. Cassel, and D. E. Bandy. 1986a. Reclamation of an ultisol damaged by mechanical land clearing. *Soil Science Society of America Journal* 50:1026–31.

Alegre, J. C., D. K. Cassel, D. E. Bandy, and P. A. Sanchez. 1986b. Effect of land clearing on soil properties of an ultisol and subsequent crop production in Yurimaguas, Peru. In *Land clearing and development in the tropics*, ed. R. Lal, P. A. Sanchez, and R. W. Cummings, Jr., 167–77. Rotterdam: A. A. Balkema.

Alexander, E. B. 1985. Rates of soil formation from bedrock or consolidated sediments. *Physical Geography* 6:25–42.

Alexandrov, V. V., P. L. Arkhipov, V. N. Parkhomenko, and T. P. Stenchikov. 1983. Global'naya model' systemy okean-atmosfera i issledovanie ee chuvstvitel'nosti k izmeneniyu kontsentratsii CO_2 (Global model of the ocean-atmosphere system and investigation of its sensitivity to CO_2 concentration change). *Izvestiya USSR Academy of Sciences, Series Physics of the Atmosphere and Ocean* 19(5):451–58.

Alexandrov, V. V., and Yu. M. Svirezhev. 1985. Ecological and demographic consequences of a nuclear war. In *Mathematical models of ecosystems*. Moscow: Moscow Computer Center, USSR Academy of Sciences.

Allen, J. C. 1985. Soil response to forest clearing in the United States and the tropics: Geological and biological factors. *Biotropica* 17:15–27.

———. 1986. Soil properties and fast-growing tree species in Tanzania. *Forest Ecology Management* 16:127–47.

Allen, J. C., and D. F. Barnes. 1985. The causes of deforestation in developing countries. *Annals of the Association of American Geographers* 75:163–84.

Allen, T.F.H., and T. W. Hoekstra. 1984. Interlevel relations in ecological research and management: Some working principles from hierarchy theory. Department of Agriculture, U.S. Forest Service, General Technical Report RM-110. Rocky Mountain Forest and Range Experiment Station, Fort Collins, Colo.

American Farmland Trust. 1984. *Soil conservation in America: What do we have to lose?* Washington, D.C.: American Farmland Trust.

American Society of Civil Engineers. 1975. *Sedimentation engineering—Manuals and reports on engineering practice.* ASCE Task Committee for the Preparation of the Manual on Sedimentation of the Sedimentation Committee of the Hydraulics Division, No. 54. New York: American Society of Civil Engineering.

Anderson, J. R., E. E. Hardy, J. T. Roach, and R. E. Witmer. 1976. *A land use and land cover classification system for use with remote sensor data.* U.S. Geological Survey Professional Paper 964. Washington, D.C.: U.S. Government Printing Office.

Anderson, M. R. 1987. Snowmelt on sea ice surfaces as determined from passive microwave satellite data. In *Large-scale effects of seasonal snow cover,* ed. B. E. Goodison, R. G. Barry, and J. Dozier. International Association of Hydrological Sciences, Publication No. 166, 329–42. Wallingford, U.K.: IAHS Press.

Andre, J.-C., J.-P. Goutorbe, and A. Perrier. 1986. HAPEX-MOBILHY: A hydrologic atmospheric experiment for the study of water budget and evaporative flux at the climatic scale. *Bulletin of the American Meteorological Society* 67:138–44.

Andrianov, B. V., and A. G. Doskach. 1983. Khozyaystvenno-kul' turnaya differentsiatsiya narodov mira i geograficheskaya sreda (Economic and cultural differentiation of nations and geographical environments). *Nature* (Moscow) 4:44–53.

Andronnikov, V. L. 1986. Biosfera i klimat po dannym kosmicheskikh issledovanii (Biosphere and climate according to the data of space studies). *Proceedings of All-Union Conference.* Baku, 141–56.

Annenkov, V. V. 1980. O teoreticheskikh voprosakh istoriko-geograficheskikh issledovaniy prirodopol' zovaniya (On theoretical aspects of historic-geographical studies of the use of nature). In *Geografoekologocheskie aspekty ekonomicheskogo i sotsial 'nogo planirovaniya (Geographical and ecological aspects of economic and social planning),* 144–53.

Anselin, L. 1988. *Spatial econometrics: Methods and models.* Dordrecht: Kluwer Academic.

Anthes, R. A. 1984. Enhancement of convective precipitation by mesoscale variations in vegetative covering in semiarid regions. *Journal of Climate and Applied Meteorology* 23:541–54.

Anthony, R. W. 1978. Dust storm—severe storm characteristics of 10 March 1977. *Monthly Weather Review* 106:1219.

Antonovsky, M. Ya. 1986. Sovremennaya otsenka roli CO_2 i drugih malyh gazov v izmenenii klimata (Assessment of CO_2 and other trace gases in climate change). In *Kompleksniy global'niy monitoring sostoyaniya noosfery (Complex global monitoring of noosphere),* 2:201–10. Proceedings of International Conference, Austria, 1985. Leningrad: Gidrometeoizdat.

Arakawa, A. 1972. Design of the UCLA general circulation model. In *Numerical simulation of weather and climate*. Technical Report 4, Department of Meteorology, University of California, Los Angeles.

Are, F. E. 1980. *Termoabraziya morskih beregov* (*Thermo-abrasion of sea coasts*). Moscow: Nauka.

Aristarkhova, L. V. 1971. *Protsessy aridnogo rel'efoobrazovaniya* (*Processes of relief formation in arid lands*). Moscow: Moscow State University Press.

Armand, A. D. 1984. *Sovremenniye problemy ecosystem* (*Modern problems of ecosystems*). Moscow: Institute of Geography, USSR Academy of Sciences.

———. 1988. *Samoorganizatsiya i samoregulirovanie geograficheskikh sistem* (*Self-organization and self-regulation of geographical systems*). Moscow: Nauka.

Armand, D. L. 1975. *Nauka o landshafte* (*Landscape science*). Moscow: Mysl'.

Armand, N. A., ed. 1986. *Aerokosmicheskie metody izucheniya prirodnykh usloviy pustyn'* (*Aerospace methods of nature study of deserts*). Ashkhabad: Ylym.

Aston, A. 1980. The effect of doubling atmospheric CO_2 on streamflow: a simulation. *Journal of Hydrology* 67(1–4):273–80.

Aubreville, A. 1949. *Climates, forets, et desertification de l'Afrique tropicale* [in French]. Paris: Société d'Editions Geographiques, Maritimes et Coloniales.

Australian Centre for International Agricultural Research. 1984. *Proceedings of the International Workshop on Soils*. Townsville, Queensland: Australian Centre for International Agricultural Research.

Avakyan, A. B., V. P. Saltankin, and V. A. Sharapov. 1987. *Vodokhranilishche* (*Water reservoirs*). Moscow: Mysl'.

Babaev, A. G., N. S. Orlovsky, and N. G. Kharin. 1985. Complex desert development and desertification control in the USSR. In *Arid lands today and tomorrow*, ed. E. W. Whitehead, C. F. Hutchinson, B. N. Timmerman, and R. C. Varady, 825–39. Boulder, Colo.: Westview Press.

Bach, W. A. 1976. Global air pollution and climatic change. *Review Geophysics Space Physics* 14:429–74.

Bach, W. A., J. Pankrath, and J. Williams, eds. 1980. *Interactions of energy and climate*. Dordrecht: Reidel.

Bannikov, A. G., A. K. Rustamov, and A. A. Vakhulin. 1985. *Okhrana prirody* (*Nature protection*). Moscow: Agropromizdat.

Barazangi, M., and B. Rouhban. 1983. Evaluating and reducing earthquake risk in Arab countries. *Nature and Resources* 19(4):2–6.

Bardinet, C., J.-M. Monget, and M. Poisson. 1978. *Land use mapping in the Sahel zone using Landsat*. Reading, U.K.: Remote Sensing Society.

Barnes, D. F., and J. C. Allen. 1982. *Social forestry in developing countries*. Research Paper D-73F. Washington, D.C.: Resources for the Future.

Barrett, E. C., and D. W. Martin. 1981. *The use of satellite data in rainfall monitoring*. London: Academic Press.

Barron, E. J. 1985. Explanations of the Tertiary global cooling trend. *Palaeogeography, Palaeoclimatology, and Palaeoecology* 50:17–40.

Barry, R. G. 1981. *Mountain weather and climate*. London: Methuen.

———. 1983. Late-Pleistocene climatology. In *Late Quaternary environments of the United States*. Vol. 1: *The late Pleistocene*, ed. S. C. Porter, 390–407. Minneapolis: University of Minnesota Press.

————. 1985a. The cryosphere and climate change. In *Detecting the effects of increasing carbon dioxide*, ed. M. C. MacCracken and F. M. Luther, 109–48. Washington, D.C.: U.S. Department of Energy, DOE/ER-0735.

————. 1985b. Snow and ice data. In *Paleoclimate analysis and modeling*, ed. A. D. Hecht, 259–90. New York: John Wiley and Sons.

————. 1986a. The sea ice data base. In *The geophysics of sea ice*, ed. N. Untersteiner, 1099–1134. New York: Plenum Press.

————. 1986b. Snow cover data: Status and future prospects. In *Snow watch 1985*, ed. G. Kukla, R. G. Barry, A. D. Hecht, and D. Wiesnet, 127–39. Glaciological Data Report GD-18. Boulder: University of Colorado, Data Center-A for Glaciology.

————. 1988. Permafrost data and information: Status and needs. In *Permafrost*. 3 vols., ed. K. Senneset, 1:119–22. Fifth International Conference Proceedings. Trondheim: Tapir Publishers.

————. In press. Observational evidence of changes in global snow and ice cover. In *Workshop on greenhouse gas–induced climatic change: A critical appraisal of simulations and observations*, ed. M. E. Schlesinger. Amsterdam: Elsevier.

Barry, R. G., A. Henderson-Sellers, and K. P. Shine. 1984. Climate sensitivity and the marginal cryosphere. In *Climate processes and climate sensitivity*, ed. J. E. Hansen and T. Takahashi, 221–37. Geophysical Monograph 29. Washington, D.C.: American Geophysical Union.

Bartlein, P. J., and T. Webb III. 1985. Mean July temperature at 6000 yr B.P. in eastern North America: Regression equations for estimates from fossil pollen data. *Syllogeous* 55:301–42.

Bartlett, E. C., and M. G. Hamilton. 1986. Potentialities and problems of satellite remote sensing with special reference to arid and semiarid regions. *Climatic Change* 9:167–89.

Basilevich, N. I., L. E. Rodin, and N. N. Rosov. 1970. *Geograficheskie aspekty izucheniya biologicheskoi produktivnosti* (*Geographical aspects of a study of biological productivity*). Leningrad.

Baulin, V. V. 1985. *Permafrost in oil- and gas-bearing regions of the USSR* [in Russian]. Moscow: Nauka.

Becker, F., and M. Raffy. 1987. Problems related to the determination of land surface parameters and fluxes over heteorogeneous media from satellite data. *Advances in Space Research* 7(11):45–58.

Beek, K. J. 1984. Summary and conclusions. In *Progress in land evaluation*, ed. J.C.F.M. Haans, G.G.L. Steur, and G. Heide, 279–85. Rotterdam: A. A. Balkema, 1984.

Belotserkovsky, M. Yu., et al. 1985. Geograficheskie problemy zashchity pocho of erozii i regulirotaniya rechny rusel v svete nauchno-tekhnicheskogo progressa (Geographical problems of soil erosion protection and river basin regulation in view of scientific progress). *Vestnik of Moscow State University Press, Series 5, Geography* 3:9–15.

Belousov, V. V., ed. 1987. *Mejdunarodnaya geosferno-biosfernaya programma "Global'nye izmeneniya" Ofitsial'nye materialy* (*International Geosphere-Biosphere Programme "Global Change"*). *Vestnik of USSR Academy of Sciences* (Moscow).

Berkovsky, L. 1976. The effect of variable surface albedo on the atmospheric circulation in desert regions. *Journal of Applied Meteorology* 15:1139–44.

Bernstein, R. 1983. Image geometry and rectification. In *The manual of remote sensing*. 2d ed., ed. R. N. Colwell, 1:875–81. Falls Church, Va.: American Society of Photogrammetry.

Berry, L. 1985. Desertification in the Sudan-Sahelian zone: The first years since the 1977 desertification conference. In *Arid lands today and tomorrow*, ed. E. W. Whitehead, C. F. Hutchinson, B. N. Timmerman, and R. C. Varady, 577–82. Boulder, Colo.: Westview Press.

Bilingsley, F. C., and J. L. Urena. 1984. Concepts for a global resources information system. In *Precora 9 Proceedings, Spatial information technologies for remote sensing today and tomorrow*, 123–31. Sioux Falls, S.D.

Bird, E.C.F. 1985. *Coastline changes: A global review*. Chichester, U.K.: John Wiley and Sons.

Bird, E.C.F., and M. L. Schwartz, eds. 1985. *The world's coastline*. New York: Van Nostrand Reinhold.

Bjutner, E. K. 1986. *Planetarnyi gazoobmen O_2 i CO_2 (Planetary gas exchange of O_2 and CO_2)*. Leningrad: Gidrometeoizdat.

Blackie, J. R., K. A. Edwards, and R. T. Clarke. 1979. Hydrological research in East Africa. *East African Agriculture and Forestry Journal* 43:1–313.

Blaikie, P. M. 1985. *The political economy of soil erosion*. London: Longman.

Blaikie, P. M., and H. Brookfield. 1987. *Land degradation and society*. London: Metheun.

Bochkareva, T. V. 1987. Issledovaniya i resheniya ekologicheskikh problem gorodskikh aglomeratsiy (Study and environmental problem decisions in urban areas). In *Problemy izucheniya gorodskikh aglomeratsiy (Problems in the analysis of urban areas)*. Moscow: Institute of Geography, USSR Academy of Sciences.

————. 1988. *Ekologicheskiy "jin" urbanizatsii (Environmental consequences of urbanization)*. Moscow: Mysl'.

Boecklen, W. J. 1986. Effects of habitat heterogeneity on the species-area relationships of forest birds. *Journal of Biogeography* 13:59–68.

Boecklen, W. J., and N. J. Gotelli. 1984. Island biogeographic theory and conservation practice: Species-area or specious area relationships? *Biological Conservation* 29:63–80.

Boer, G. J., and N. A. McFarlane. 1979. The AES atmospheric general circulation model. In *Report of the JOC study conference on climate models*. GARP Publication Series 22, 1:409–60. Geneva: World Meteorological Organization.

Bogaturev, B. G., A. P. Kirilenko, and A. M. Tarko. 1988. *Prostransrvenno-raspredelennye modeli biosfery (Spatial distributive models of the biosphere)*. Moscow: Moscow Computer Center, USSR Academy of Sciences.

Bohloon, B., D. C. Coleman, and G. Uehara, eds. 1989. *Dynamics of soil organic matter in tropical ecosystems*. New York: Springer Verlag.

Bolin, B. 1986. Greenhouses, gases, and climate change—Report from Villach. *World Resources Institute Journal* 19–24.

Bolin, B., and R. B. Cook, eds. 1983. *The major biogeochemical cycles and their interactions*. Scientific Committee on Problems of the Environment, Report 21. Chichester, U.K.: John Wiley and Sons.

Bolin, B., B. R. Dubos, J. Jäger, and R. A. Warrick. 1986. *The greenhouse effect, climate change and ecosystems*. Scientific Committee on Problems of the Environment, Report 29. Chichester, U.K.: John Wiley and Sons.

Bolle, H. J., and S. I. Rasool. 1985. *Development of the implementation plan for the International Satellite Land-Surface Climatology Project (ISLSCP). Phase I.* No. WWCP-94. Geneva: World Meteorological Organization.

Bonderev, L. G. 1987. Ecologicheskie problemy rannikh tsivilizatsiy (Ecological problems of the earliest civilizations). In *Teoreticheskie i metodicheskie problemy paleogeografii (Theoretical and methodological problems of paleogeography)*, 108–27. Moscow: Moscow University Press.

Booth, W. 1989. Monitoring the fate of the forests from space. *Science* 243:1428–29.

Borisenkov, E. P., and K. Ya. Kondrat'yev. 1988. *Krugovorot ugleroda i klimat (Carbon cycle and climate)*. Leningrad: Gidrometeoizdat.

Borzenkova, I. I., M. I. Budyko, E. K. Bjutner, et al. 1987. *Antropogemmiye izmeneniya klimata (Anthropogenic climatic changes)*. Leningrad: Gidrometeoizdat.

Bosch, J. M., and J. D. Hewlett. 1982. A review of catchment experiments to determine the effect of vegetation changes on water yield and evapotranspiration. *Journal of Hydrology* 55:3–23.

Bovill, E. W. 1921. The encroachment of the Sahara on the Sudan. *Journal of the African Society* 20(79):174–85; 20(80):259–69.

Box, E. O. 1981. *Macroclimate and plant forms: An introduction to predictive modeling in phytogeography, tasks in vegetation science*. Vol. 1. The Hague: Junk.

Bradley, R. S. 1985. *Quaternary paleoclimatology. Methods of paleoclimatic reconstruction*. Boston: Allen and Unwin.

Bradley, R. S., H. F. Diaz, J. K. Eischeid, P. D. Jones, P. M. Kelly, and C. M. Goodess. 1987. Precipitation fluctuations over Northern Hemisphere land areas since the mid-19th century. *Science* 237:171–75.

Bradley, R. S., P. M. Kelly, P. D. Jones, C. M. Goodess, and H. F. Diaz. 1985. *A climatic data bank for Northern Hemisphere land areas, 1851–1980*. Technical Report 017. Washington, D.C.: U.S. Department of Energy.

Brady, N. C. 1984. *The nature and properties of soils*. 9th ed. New York: Macmillan.

Brazel, A. J., and S. I. Outcalt. 1973. The observation and simulation of diurnal evaporation contrast in an Alaskan alpine pass. *Journal of Applied Meteorology* 12(7):1134–43.

Breast, C. L., and S. N. Goward. 1987. Deriving surface albedo measurements from narrow band satellite data. *International Journal of Remote Sensing* 8(3):351–67.

Breeuwsma, A., J.H.M. Wosten, J. J. Vleeshouwer, A. M. Van Slobbe, and J. Bouma. 1986. Derivation of land qualities to assess environmental problems from soil surveys. *Soil Science Society of America Journal* 50:186–90.

Brooks, H. 1986. The typology of surprises in technology, institutions, and development. In *Sustainable development of the biosphere*, ed. W. C. Clark and R. E. Munn, 325–48. Cambridge: Cambridge University Press.

Brown, S., and A. Lugo. 1984. Biomass of tropical forests: A new estimate based on forest volumes. *Science* 223:1290–93.

Bryant, N. A., and A. L. Zobrist. 1976. IBIS: A geographic information system based on digital image processing and image raster data type. *Proceedings of the Sym-*

posium on Machine Processing of Remotely Sensed Data. West Lafayette, Ind.: Laboratory for Applied Remote Sensing, Purdue University.

Bryson, R. 1974. A perspective on climate change. *Science* 184:753–60.

Budagovsky, A. I. 1986a. Metody otsenki parametrov modeley ispareniya pochvennykh vod (Evaluation of parameters in models of soil water evaporation). *Vodnye Resursy* A(6):3–15.

―――. 1986b. Utochnenie modeley ispareniya pochvennykh vod (Specification of models of soil water evaporation). *Vodnye Resursy* B(5):5–58.

Budyko, M. I. 1956. *Teplovoy balanse zemnoy poverkhnosti (Heat balance of earth's surface)*. Leningrad: Gidrometeoizdat. (English translation, U.S. Department of Commerce, 1963.)

―――. 1972. *Vliyanie cheloveka na klimat (Human influence on climate)*. Leningrad: Gidrometeoizdat.

―――. 1974a. *Climate and life*. New York: Academic Press.

―――. 1974b. *Izmenenie klimata (Climate changes)*. Leningrad: Gidrometeoizdat.

―――. 1979. *Problema uglekislogo gaza (Problems of carbonic acid)*. Leningrad: Gidrometeoizdat.

―――. 1980. *Klimat v proshlom i budushchem (Climate in the past and future)*. Leningrad: Gidrometeoizdat.

Budyko, M. I., and Yu. A. Izrael, eds. 1987. *Man-induced climatic changes* [in Russian]. Leningrad: Hydrometeoizdat.

Budyko, M. I., and M. D. MacCracken. 1987. US-USSR meeting of experts on causes of recent climatic change. *Bulletin of the American Meteorological Society* 68:237.

Bunting, T. E., and L. Guelke. 1979. Behavioral and perception geography: A critical appraisal. *Annals of the Association of American Geographers* 69:448–62.

Buringh, P. 1986. Land evaluation for agriculture in the tropics: A comparison of some new methods. In *Land clearing and development in the tropics*, ed. R. Lal, P. A. Sanchez, and R. W. Cummings, 29–36. Rotterdam: A. A. Balkema.

Burrough, P. A. 1986. *Principles of geographical information systems for land resources assessment*. Oxford: Clarendon Press.

Burt, J. E., J. T. Hayes, P. A. O'Rourke, W. H. Terjung, and P. E. Todhunter. 1981. A parametric crop water use model. *Water Resources Research* 17(4):1095–1108.

Burton, I., R. W. Kates, and G. F. White. 1978. *The environment as hazard*. New York: Oxford University Press.

Burtsev, A. I., and A. P. Tishchenko, eds. 1978. *Kosmicheskaya geofizika (Outer-space physics)*. Leningrad: Gidrometeoizdat.

Butzer, K.W. 1975. *Environment and archeology: An ecological approach to prehistory*. 2d ed. Chicago: Aldine, Atherton.

Byers, A. 1987. Man-induced changes near the Mt. Everest National Park. Ph.D. dissertation, University of Colorado, Boulder.

Byrne, G. F., and P. F. Crapper. 1980. Land cover change detection by principal component analysis. *Proceedings of the Fourteenth Symposium on Remote Sensing of the Environment*, 3:1375–82. Ann Arbor, Mich.: Environmental Research Institute of Michigan.

Byrne, G. F., P. F. Crapper, and K. K. Mayo. 1980. Monitoring land cover change by principal component analysis of multitemporal Landsat data. *Remote Sensing of the Environment* 10:175–84.

Cairns, J., Jr., K. L. Dickson, and E. E. Harricks. 1975. Recovery and restoration of damaged ecosystems. *Proceedings of the International Symposium on the Recovery of Damaged Ecosystems*. Virginia Polytechnic Institute and State University, Blacksburg, Va., March 23–25.

Callahan, J. T. 1984. Long-term ecological research. *BioScience* 34(6):363–67.

Camillo, P. J., R. J. Gurney, and T. J. Schmugge. 1987. A soil and atmospheric boundary layer model for evapotranspiration and soil moisture studies. *Water Resources Research* 19:371–80.

Cannell, M.G.R. 1982. *World forest biomass and primary production data*. New York: Academic Press.

Carleton, A. 1987. Satellite-derived attributes of cloud vortex systems and their application to climate studies. *Remote Sensing of the Environment* 22:271–96.

Carlson, T. N. 1979. Atmospheric turbidity in Saharan dust outbreaks as determined by analyses of satellite brightness data. *Monthly Weather Review* 107:322.

Carlson, T. N., J. K. Dodd, S. G. Benjamin, and J. N. Cooper. 1981. Satellite estimation of the surface energy balance, moisture availability and thermal inertia. *Journal of Applied Meteorology* 20(1):67–87.

Carson, D. 1982. Current parameterization of land-surface processes in atmospheric general circulation models. In *Land surface processes in atmospheric general circulation models*, ed. P. S. Eagleson, 67–108. New York: Cambridge University Press.

Carter, G. C., and T. Dale. 1974. *Topsoil and civilization*. Rev. ed. Norman: University of Oklahoma Press.

Chalov, R. S. 1979. *Geograficheskie issledovaniya ruslovych protsessov (Geographical study of riverbed processes)*. Moscow: Moscow University Press.

Chang, Jen-Hu. 1958. *Ground temperature*. 2 vols. Milton, Mass.: Harvard University, Blue Hill Meteorological Observatory.

Charney, J. C., W. J. Quirk, S. H. Chew, and J. Kornfield. 1977. A comparative study of the effects of albedo change on drought in semi-arid regions. *Journal of Atmospheric Science* 34:1366–88.

Charney, J. C., P. H. Stone, and W. J. Quirk. 1975. Drought in the Sahara: A biogeophysical feedback mechanism. *Science* 187:434–35.

Chen, R. S., E. Boulding, and S. H. Schneider, eds. 1983. *Social science research and climate change*. Dordrecht: D. Reidel.

Chernavskaya, M. M., A. N. Krenke, M. E. Lyakhov, V. V. Popova, and A. N. Zolotokrylin. 1986. Izmeneniya klimata vostochnoi Evropy v istoricheskom proshlom (Climate changes in the history of eastern Europe). *Izvestiya USSR Academy of Sciences, Series Geography* 11:5–16.

Chistov, S. V. 1987. Ingenerno-geograficheskoe rayonirovanie severa SSSR. (Engineering-geographical regionalization of the north of the USSR). In *Opasnye prirodnye yavleniya (Dangerous natural phenomena)*, 156–75. Moscow: VINITI.

Chorley, R. J., ed. 1969. *Water, earth and man*. London: Methuen.

Choudhury, B. J., M. Owe, S. N. Goward, R. E. Golus, J. P. Ormsby, A. T. Chang, and J. R. Wang. 1987. Spatial and temporal variability of microwave brightness over the southern Great Plains. *International Journal of Remote Sensing* 8(2):177–91.

Christiansson, C. 1981. *Soil erosion and sedimentation in semi-arid Tanzania: Studies of environmental change and ecological imbalance*. Stockholm: Scandinavian

Institute of African Studies and Department of Physical Geography, University of Stockholm.

Church, R., and D. Migereko. 1986. Optimizing energy costs in the Ugandan coffee cooperative marketing system. Paper presented at Thirty-third North American Meeting of the Regional Science Association, November 1986, Columbus, Ohio.

Clapp, R. B., and G. M. Hornberger. 1978. Empirical equations for some soil hydraulic properties. *Water Resources Research* 14:601–4.

Clark, W. C. 1986. On the practical implications of the greenhouse question. In *Report of the International Conference on the Assessment of the Role of Carbon Dioxide and of Other Greenhouse Gases in Climate Variations and Associated Impacts*, 24–29. World Meteorological Organization, Publication WMO 661. Geneva: World Meteorological Organization.

Clark, W. C., and R. E. Munn, eds. 1986. *Sustainable development of the biosphere.* Cambridge: Cambridge University Press.

CLIMAP Project Members. 1976. The surface of the ice-age earth. *Science* 191:1131–37.

Coakley, J. A., Jr., and R. D. Cess. 1985. Response of the NCAR community climate model to the radiative forcing by the naturally occurring tropospheric aerosol. *Journal of the Atmospheric Sciences* 42:1677–92.

Cohen, S. J. 1986. Impacts of CO_2-induced climatic change on water resources in the Great Lakes basin. *Climatic Change* 8:135–53.

COHMAP Members. 1988. Climatic changes of the last 18,000 years: Observations and model simulations. *Science* 241:1043–52.

Coiner, J. C. 1980. Using Landsat to monitor changes in vegetation cover induced by desertification processes. *Proceedings of the Fourteenth Symposium on Remote Sensing of the Environment*, 3:1341–51. Ann Arbor, Mich.: Environmental Research Institute of Michigan.

Colhoun, E. A., and J. A. Peterson. 1986. Quaternary landscape evolution and the cryosphere: Research progress from the Sahel to Australian Antarctica. *Australian Geographical Studies* 24:145–67.

Colwell, J. E. 1981. Forest change detection. *Proceedings of the Fifteenth Symposium on Remote Sensing of the Environment*, 2:839–52. Ann Arbor, Mich.: Environmental Research Institute of Michigan.

Committee on Scientific and Technical Cooperation. 1986. *Vliyanie khozyastva na prirodu: Otshenki, modeli, karty (Economy impact upon nature: Assessment, models, maps).* Budapest: Council of Mutual Economic Assistance.

Corby, G. A., A. Gilchrist, and P. R. Rowntree. 1977. United Kingdom Meteorological Office five-level general circulation model. *Methods in Computational Physics* 17:67–110.

Coulson, R. N., L. J. Folse, and D. K. Loh. 1987. Artificial intelligence and natural resource management. *Science* 237:262–67.

Courel, M. F., R. S. Kandel, and S. I. Rasool. 1984. Surface albedo and the Sahel drought. *Nature* (London) 307:528–31.

Covello, V. T., and J. Mumpower. 1985. Risk analysis and risk management: An historical perspective. *Risk Analysis* 5(2):103–20.

Crane, R. G., and R. G. Barry. 1988. Comparison of the MSL synoptic pressure patterns of the Arctic as observed and simulated by the GISS general circulation model. *Meteorology and Atmospheric Physics* 39(3–4):169–83.

Crist, E. P., and R. J. Kauth. 1986. The tasseled cap de-mystified. *Photogrammetric Engineering and Remote Sensing* 50:343–52.

Crosson, P. R. 1986. Soil erosion and policy issues. In *Agriculture and the environment*, ed. T. T. Phipps, P. R. Crosson, and K. A. Price, 35–73. Washington, D.C.: Resources for the Future.

Cuny, F. 1983. *Disasters and development*. New York: Oxford University Press.

Curran, P. J. 1982. Multispectral photographic remote sensing of green vegetation biomass and productivity. *Photogrammetric Engineering and Remote Sensing* 48(2):243–50.

Cutter, S. L. 1988. Geographers and nuclear war: Why we lack influence on public policy. *Annals of the Association of American Geographers* 78(1):132–43.

Dale, V., ed. 1989. Draft report of a workshop on using remote sensing to estimate land-use changes. Prepared for the Carbon Dioxide Research Program of the Environmental Sciences Division, Oak Ridge National Laboratory, Oak Ridge, Tenn.

Darby, H. C. 1956. Clearing of the woodland in Europe. In *Man's role in changing the face of the earth*, ed. W. L. Thomas. Chicago: University of Chicago Press.

Darmstadter, J., J. Dunkerley, and J. Alterman. 1977. *How industrial societies use energy*. Resources for the Future. Baltimore: Johns Hopkins University Press.

Davis, R. E., J. Dozier, and D. Marks. 1984. Micrometeorological measurements and instrumentation in support of remote sensing observations of an alpine snow cover. *Proceedings of the Western Snow Conference* 51:161–64.

Degefu, W. 1987. *Drought and hunger in Africa*. Cambridge: Cambridge University Press.

Delcourt, H. R., and W. F. Harris. 1980. Carbon budget of the southeastern U.S. biota: Analysis of historical change in trend from source to sink. *Science* 210:321–23.

Denmead, O. T. 1984. Plant physiological methods for studying evapotranspiration: Problems of telling the forest from the trees. *Agricultural Water Management* 8:167–89.

Dennett, M., J. Elston, and J. A. Rodgers. 1985. A reappraisal of rainfall trends in the Sahel. *Journal of Climatology* 5:353–61.

Dewey, K. F. 1977. Daily maximum and minimum temperature forecasts and the influence of snow cover. *Monthly Weather Review* 98:399–401.

———. 1987a. Satellite-derived maps of snow cover frequency for the Northern Hemisphere. *Journal of Climate and Applied Meteorology* 26:1210–29.

———. 1987b. Snow cover—atmospheric interactions. In *Large-scale effects of seasonal snow cover*, ed. B. E. Goodison, R. G. Barry, and J. Dozier, 27–42. International Association of Hydrological Sciences, Publication No. 166. Wallingford, U.K.: IAHS Press.

Diamond, J. M. 1975. The island dilemma: Lessons of modern biogeography studies for the design of nature reserves. *Biological Conservation* 7:129–46.

Diaz, H. F. 1986. An analysis of twentieth-century climate fluctuations in northern North America. *Journal of Climate and Applied Meteorology* 25:1625–57.

Dickinson, R. E. 1980. Effects of deforestation on climate. In *Blowing in the wind: Deforestation and long-range implications*, 411–41. Studies in Third World Societies No. 14. Williamsburg, Va.: Department of Anthropology, College of William and Mary.

———. 1983. Land surface processes and climate—Surface albedos and energy balance. In *Theory of climate*, ed. by B. Saltzman, 305–53. London: Academic Press.

———. 1985. Climate sensitivity. *Advances in Geophysics* 28A:99–129.

———, ed. 1987. *The geophysiology of Amazonia*. New York: John Wiley and Sons.

Dickinson, R. E., J. Jaeger, W. M. Washington, and R. Wolski. 1981. Boundary subroutine for the NCAR global climate model. National Center for Atmospheric Research, Technical Note 0301/78-01. National Center for Atmospheric Research, Boulder, Colo.

Dobrodeev, O. P., and I. A. Suetova. 1976. The earth's living matter (mass, production, geography, chemical significance and probable effect upon climates and the earth's glaciation) [in Russian]. In *Problems of general physical geography and paleography*, 26–58. Moscow: Moscow State University Press.

Dobrovolsky, G. V., and I. S. Urusevskaya. 1984. *Soil geography* [in Russian]. Moscow: Moscow State University Press.

Douglas, I. 1988. Review of *Human activity and environmental change*, by K. J. Gregory and D. E. Walling. *Progress in Physical Geography* 12:308–9.

Downing, T. E., and R. W. Kates. 1982. The international response to the threat of chlorofluorocarbons to atmospheric ozone. *American Economic Review* 72(2): 267–72.

Dozier, J. 1980. A clear-sky spectral solar radiation model for snow-covered mountainous terrain. *Water Resources Research* 16:709–18.

———. 1986. Remote sensing of snow properties in mountainous terrain. In *Snow watch 1985*, ed. G. Kukla, R. G. Barry, A. Hecht, and D. Wiesnet, 193–204. Glaciological Data Report GD-18. Boulder: University of Colorado, WDC-A for Glaciology.

———. 1987. Remote sensing of snow characteristics in the southern Sierra Nevada. In *Large-scale effects of seasonal snow cover*, ed. B. E. Goodison, R. G. Barry, and J. Dozier, 305–14. International Association of Hydrological Sciences, Publication No. 166. Wallingford, U.K.: IAHS Press.

Dozier, J., and S. I. Outcalt. 1979. An approach toward energy balance simulation over rugged terrain. *Geographical Analysis* 11(1):65–85.

Dregne, H. E. 1976. *Soils of arid regions*. Amsterdam: Elsevier Scientific.

———. 1983. *Desertification of arid lands*. Advances in desert and arid land technology and development. Vol. 4. New York: Harwood Academic Publishers.

———. 1984. Desertification—present and future. *International Journal for Development Technology* 2:255–59.

Dregne, H. E., and C. J. Tucker. 1988. Desert encroachment. *Desertification Control Bulletin* 16:16–19.

Drozdov, A. V. 1984. Maps of environmental pollution. In *Problems of the environment in urbanized regions*, 123–35. Moscow.

———. 1989. Karty zagryazneniya okruzhayushchey sredy (Maps of environmental pollution). In *Problemy okruzhayushchey sredy v urbanizirovannykh regionakh* (*Problems of the environment in urbanized regions*), 123–35. Moscow: Institute of Geography, USSR Academy of Sciences.

Dukuchayev, V. V. 1892. *Nashi ctepi prejdi i teper* (*Our steppes past and present*). Moscow.

Dulov, A. V. 1983. *Geograficheskaya sreda i istoriya Rossii/konets XV– seredina XIX v* (*Geographical environment and history of Russia/the end of the fifteenth to the middle of the nineteenth century*). Moscow: Nauka.

Dunne, T., and W. E. Dietrich. 1980a. Experimental study of Horton overland flow on hillslopes. 1. Soil condition, infiltration, and frequency of runoff. *Zeitschrift für Geomorphologie*, suppl. bd. 35:40–59.

———. 1980b. Experimental study of Horton overland flow on hillslopes. 2. Hydraulic characteristics and hillslope hydrographs. *Zeitschrift für Geomorphologie*, suppl. bd. 35:60–80.

———. 1982. *Soil erosion and conservation in the tropics*. American Society of Agronomy, Special Publication Number 43, 41–55. Madison, Wisc.: American Society of Agronomy.

Dunne, T., W. E. Dietrich, and M. J. Brunengo. 1978. Recent and past erosion rates in semiarid Kenya. *Zeitschrift für Geomorphologie N. F.*, suppl. bd. 29:130–40.

Dunne, T., and L. B. Leopold. 1978. *Water in environmental planning*. San Francisco: W. H. Freeman.

Dyunin, A. K. 1963. *Mekhanika meteley* (*Snowstorm mechanics*). Novosibirsk: USSR Academy of Sciences Press.

Dzerdzievsky, B. L. 1975. K metodike izucheniya fluktuatsii klimata raznykh maschtabov vremeni (Different methods to study time-scale fluctuations of climate). In *Obshchaya tsirkulyatsiya atmosfery i klimat* (*General circulation of the atmosphere and climate*), 185–202. Moscow: Nauka.

Dzyuba, V. V., M. N. Laptev, and S. M. Myagkov. 1984. Prognoz stikhiynorazrushitel'nykh ekzogennykh protsessov v slaboizuchennykh gornych raionakh (Forecasting of spontaneous destructive exogenic processes in poorly studied mountain regions). In *Inzhenernaya geografiya gornykh stran* (*Engineering geography of mountainous regions*), 119–33. Moscow: Moscow University Press.

Eagleson, P. S., ed. 1982. *Land surface processes in atmospheric general circulation models*. Cambridge: Cambridge University Press.

East, R. 1983. Application of species area curves to African savanna reserves. *African Journal of Ecology* 21:123–28.

El-Baz, F. 1983. A geological perspective of the desert. In *Origin and evolution of deserts*, ed. S. G. Wells and D. R. Haragan, 163–83. Albuquerque: University of New Mexico Press.

Eliason, P. T., L. A. Soderblom, and P. S. Chavez. 1981. Extraction of topographic and spectral albedo information from multispectral images. *Photogrammetric Engineering and Remote Sensing* 11:1571–79.

Ellsaesser, H. W., M. C. MacCracken, G. L. Potter, and F. M. Luther. 1976. An additional model test of positive feedback from high desert albedo. *Quarterly Journal of the Royal Meteorological Society* 102:655–66.

El-Swaify, S. A., and E. W. Dangler. 1982. Rainfall erosion in the tropics: A state of the art. In *Soil erosion and conservation in the tropics*, ed. W. Kussow, S. A. El-Swaify, and J. Mannering, 1–25. American Society of Agronomy, Special Publication No. 43. Madison, Wisc.: American Society of Agronomy.

Eriksson, K. G. 1979. Saharan dust sedimentation in the western Mediterranean Sea. In *Scientific Committee on Problems of the Environment, Report 14*, ed. C. Morales, 197–209. Washington, D.C.: National Academy Press.

Ermakov, Yu. G., and A. M. Ryabchikov. 1980. Prognozirovanie sostoyaniya okruzha-yushchey sredy v razvitykh kapitalisticheskikh stranakh (Environmental prognosis in developed capitalistic countries). *Vestnik of Moscow State University, Series 5, Geography* (Moscow) 2:17–25.

Ermakov, Yu. G., and V. A. Uledov. 1976. Izmeniniye prizednoy sredy v SSHA (Environmental changes in the USA). In *Aktual'nye problemy izmeneniya prirodnoi sredy za rubejom (Contemporary problems of environmental changes abroad)*, 115–39. Moscow: Moscow University Press.

Estes, J. E., and J. H. Bredakamp. 1988. Activities associated with global data bases in the National Aeronautics and Space Administration. In *Building databases for global science*, ed. H. Mounsey and R. Tomlinson, 251–69. International Geographical Union. London: Taylor and Francis.

Estes, J. E., J. L. Star, P. J. Cressy, and M. Dervirian. 1985. Pilot land data system. *Photogrammetric Engineering and Remote Sensing* 15(6):703–9.

Farhar-Pilgrim, B. 1985. Social analysis. In *Climate impact assessment: Studies of the interaction of climate and society*, ed. R. W. Kates, J. H. Ausubel, and M. Berberian, 323–50. New York: John Wiley and Sons.

Faure, H., and J. Y. Gac. 1981. Will the Sahelian drought end in 1985? *Nature* (London) 291:475–78.

Fearnside, P. M. 1982. Deforestation in the Brazilian Amazon: How fast is it occurring? *Interciencia* 7:82–88.

Fejgel'son, E. M. 1982. Oblachnye i aerozolnye effekty v luchistom teploobmene (Cloud and aerosol effects in radiant heat exchange). In *Rasprostranenie sveta v dispersnoi srede (Dissemination of light in a dispersed medium)*, 176–86. Minsk: Nauka i Tekhnika.

Feoktistov, A. A. 1986. Vozmozhnosti issledovaniya dannykh IK-diapazona dlya otsenki evapotranspiratsii posevov sel'skokhozyaystvennykh kul'tur (Possibilities of using IR data in investigation of evapotranspiration from agricultural crops). In *Earth study from outer space*, 3:94–99. Moscow.

Finsterbusch, K., and C. P. Wolf. 1977. *Methodology of social impact assessment*. Stroudsburg, Pa.: Dowden, Hutchinson, and Ross.

Fischoff, B., S. Lichtenstein, P. Slovic, S. L. Derby, and R. L. Keeney. 1981. *Acceptable risk*. Cambridge: Cambridge University Press.

Fisher, P. F. 1988. Knowledge-based approaches to determining and correcting areas of unreliability in geographic databases. Paper presented to the First Specialist Meeting of Research Initiative One, National Center for Geographical Information and Analysis, Montecito, Calif.

Fitzpatrick-Lins, K. 1978. Accuracy and consistency comparisons of land use and land cover maps made from high-altitude photographs and Landsat multispectral imagery. *Journal of Research, U.S. Geological Survey* 6:169–73.

Flejshman, S. M., and V. F. Petrov, eds. 1976. *Seleopasnye rajony SSSR (Regions of dangerous mudslides in the USSR)*. Moscow: Moscow University Press.

Forman, R.T.T., and M. Godron. 1986. *Landscape ecology*. New York: John Wiley and Sons.

Fosberg, M. A., W. E. Marlatt, and L. Krupnak. 1976. *Estimating airflow patterns over complex terrain*. USDA, Forest Service Research Paper RM-162. Washington, D.C.: U.S. Department of Agriculture.

Foster, H. D. 1980. *Disaster planning: The preservation of life and property.* New York: Springer Verlag.

———. 1984. Reducing vulnerability to natural hazards. *The Geneva Papers on Risk and Insurance* 9(30).

Fournier, M. 1973. Stilisation des bassin-versants d'investigation hydrologue par l'étude de l'erosion du sol. *Bulletin Association Global Dustfall during the Quaternary as Related to Environments—Soil Sciences* 116(3).

Frank, T. D. 1984a. Assessing the change in the surficial character of a semiarid environment with Landsat residual images. *Photogrammetric Engineering and Remote Sensing* 50:471–80.

———. 1984b. The effect of change in vegetation cover and erosion patterns on albedo and texture of Landsat images in a semi-arid environment. *Annals of the Association of American Geographers* 74:393–407.

Freemark, K. E., and H. G. Merriam. 1986. Importance of area and habitat heterogeneity to bird assemblages in temperate forest fragments. *Biological Conservation* 36:433–44.

French, H. M. 1976. *The periglacial environment.* London: Longman.

———. 1986. Hierarchical conceptual model of the Alpine geosystem. *Arctic and Alpine Research* 18(2):133–46.

Frenkiel, F. N., and D. W. Goodall, eds. 1978. *Simulation modelling of environmental problems.* Scientific Committee on Problems of the Environment, Report 9. New York: John Wiley and Sons.

Frey, H. T., and H. W. Dill, Jr. 1971. *Land use changes in the southern Mississippi valley, 1959–1969.* Economic Research Service, USDA, Agricultural Economic Report 215. Washington, D.C.: U.S. Department of Agriculture.

Friedman, D. G. 1984. Natural hazard risk assessment for an insurance program. *The Geneva Papers on Risk and Insurance* 9(30):57–128.

Fung, I. Y., C. J. Tucker, and K. C. Prentice. 1987. Application of very high resolution radiometer vegetation index to study atmosphere-biosphere exchange of CO_2. *Journal of Geophysical Research* 92(D3):2999–3015.

Garelik, Is., A. M. Grinberg, and A. N. Krenke. 1975. Ispol'zovanie materialov s'yomok so sputnikov dlya glyatsiologicheskikh issledovanii (The use of outer-space observations for glaciological study). *Izvestiya USSR Academy of Sciences, Series Geography* (Moscow) 1:93–101.

Gates, W. L., and M. E. Schlesinger. 1977. Numerical simulation of the January and July global climate with a two level atmospheric model. *Journal of Atmospheric Sciences* 34:36–76.

Gaydos, L., and W. L. Newland. 1978. Inventory of land use and land cover of the Puget Sound region using Landsat digital data. *Journal of Research, U.S. Geological Survey* 6:807–14.

Gee, G. W., D. Rai, and R. J. Serne. 1983. Chemical mobility and reactivity in soil systems. In *SSSA Special Publication Number 11*, 203–28. Madison, Wisc.: American Society of Agronomy.

Gentry, A. H., and J. Lopez-Parodi. 1980. Deforestation and increased flooding of the Upper Amazon. *Science* 210:1354–56.

Gerasimov, I. P. 1985. *Ecological problems in the past, present, and future world geography* [in Russian]. Moscow: Nauka.

Gerasimov, I. P., and A. A. Velitchko, eds. 1982. *Paleogeography of Europe during the last 100,000 years* [in Russian]. Moscow: Nauka.

Giddens, A. 1984. *The constitution of society.* Cambridge: Polity Press.

Gildea, M. P., and B. Moore. 1987. FAOSOL—A global soils archive. Durham, N.H.: University of New Hampshire Press.

Gilmer, D. S., E. A. Work, J. E. Colwell, and D. L. Rebel. 1980. Enumeration of prairie wetlands with Landsat and aircraft data. *Photogrammetric Engineering and Remote Sensing* 56:631–34.

Glantz, M. H., and R. W. Katz. 1985. Drought as a constraint to development in sub-Saharan Africa. *Ambio* 6:334–39.

Glantz, M. H., and N. Orlovsky. 1983. Desertification: A review of the concept. *Desertification Control Bulletin* 9:15–22.

Glazovskaya, M. A. 1976. Landshaftnye geokhimicheskie sykstemy i ikh ustoychivost' k tekhnogenezu (Landscape geochemical systems and their stability against technogenesis). In *Biogeokhimicheskie tsykly v biosfere* (*The biogeochemical cycles in the biosphere*), 99–118. Moscow.

Glazovskaya, T. G., and E. S. Troshkina. 1987. Noveyshie karty lavinnoy opasnosti SSSR i mira (The newest maps of avalanche danger in the USSR and the world). In *Opasnye prirodnye yavleniya* (*Dangerous natural phenomena*), 195–204. Moscow: VINITI.

Glazovsky, N. F. 1975. Sovremennye problemy kompleksnykh issledovani migratsionnykh protsessov (Modern problems of conjugate study of migration processes). *Vestnik of Moscow State University, Series 5, Geography* (Moscow) 2:27–35.

————. 1982. Tekhnogennye potoki veshchestva v biosfere (Technogenous flows of material in the biosphere). In *Dobycha poleznykh iskopaemykh i geokhimiya prirodnykh geosystem* (*Mineral output and geochemistry of natural ecosystems*), 7–28. Moscow: Moscow University Press.

————. 1985. Geograficheskoe raspredelenie tekhnogennogo geokhimicheskogo vozdeystviya na landshafty (Geographical distribution of technogenic geochemical impact on landscapes). In *Materialy VII vsesoyuznogo s'ezda pochvovedov* (*Proceedings Seventh All-Union Congress of Soil Scientists*). Vol. 6. Tashkent.

————. 1987. *Sovremennoe solenakoplenie v aridnykh oblastyakh* (*Contemporary salt accumulation in arid areas*). Moscow: Nauka.

————. 1988. Structura noosfery i zadachi geografii (Structure of the noosphere and tasks of geography). *Izvestiya USSR Academy of Sciences, Series Geography* 1:38–48.

Gleick, P. H. 1986. Regional water resources and global climatic change. In *Effects of changes in stratospheric ozone and global climate*, ed. J. G. Titus. Washington, D.C.: U.S. Environmental Protection Agency.

————. 1987. Regional hydrologic consequences of increases in atmospheric CO_2 and other trace gases. *Climatic Change* 10(2):137–61.

Gold, J. R., and B. Goodey. 1984. Behavioral and perceptual geography: Criticisms and response. *Progress in Human Geography* 8:544–50.

Golitsyn, G. S., and A. S. Ginsburg. 1985. Natural analogs of a nuclear catastrophe. In *Climatic and biological consequences of a nuclear war*, 83–98. Moscow: Mir.

Gonin, T. B. 1982. *Metody i resul-taty otsenok estestvennoy i antropogenno-izmenen-noy prirodnoy sredy po materialam kosmicheskikh syemok* (*Methods and results of assessment of human-changed natural environment through outer-space survey*). Leningrad: Nauka.

Gonzalez-Enrico, E., E. J. Kamprath, G. C. Naderman, and W. V. Soares. 1979. Effect of lime incorporation on the growth of corn on an oxisol of central Brazil. *Soil Science Society of America Journal* 43:1155–58.

Goodchild, M. F. 1988a. A spatial analytical perspective on geographical information systems. *International Journal of Geographic Information Systems* 1(4):327–34.

———. 1988b. Stepping over the line: Technological constraints and the new cartography. *American Cartographer* 15:311–20.

Goodland, R., and H. S. Irwin. 1975. *Amazon jungle. Green hell to red desert? An ecological discussion of the environmental impact of the highway construction project in the Amazon basin.* New York: Elsevier.

Gorbunov, A. P. 1984. Nekotorye itogi i zadachi izucheniya kriolitozony gornykh stran (Some results and tasks of studies in cryolitic mountain zones). In *Inzhenernaya geografiya gornykh stran* (*Engineering geography of mountainous regions*), 160–77. Moscow: Moscow University Press.

Gordon, J. 1972. The inter-relationship of water quantity and quality as a determinant of water management policy. *Water Research* 6:1501–8.

Gornitz, V. 1985. A survey of anthropogenic vegetation changes in West Africa during the last century—climate implications. *Climatic Change* 7:285–326.

Gorshkov, S. P. 1986. Problema CO_2: peresmotr idey (CO_2 problem: Review of ideas). *Izvestiya USSR Geographical Society* (Leningrad) 118(4):297–305.

———. 1987. Dinamicheskie aspecty fizicheskoi geografii (Dynamic aspects of physical geography). In *Geografiya v sisteme nauk* (*Geography in the system of sciences*), 102–16. Leningrad: Nauka.

———. 1988. Sovremennye ekzodinamicheskie systemy i protsessy (Contemporary exodynamic systems and processes). In *Global'nye problemy sovremennosti i kompleksnoe zemlev edenie* (*Modern global problems and complex land survey*), 57–63. Leningrad: V 90.

Gorshkov, S. P., Yu. G. Ermakov, L. I. Kurakova, and A. M. Pyabchikov. 1980. Nekotorye aspekty antropogennogo izmeneniya krugovorota veshchestva (Some aspects of anthropogenic changes in the cycle of matter). *Vestnik of Moscow State University, Series 5, Geography* (Moscow) 4:27–34.

Gorshkov, V. G. 1981. Raspredelenie biosfernykh potokov energii (Distribution of biosphere energy flows). *Voprosy ekologii i okhrany prirody* (Leningrad) 1:21–31.

Goward, S. N. 1989a. Experiences and perspective in compiling long-term remote sensing data sets on landscapes and biospheric processes. *GeoJournal.* Special issue on Global Change: Geographical Approaches.

———. 1989b. Satellite bioclimatology. *Journal of Climate* 7(2):710–20.

Goward, S. N., and D. G. Dye. 1987. Evaluating North American net primary productivity with satellite observations. *Advances in Space Research* 7(11):165–74.

Goward, S. N., A. Kerber, D. G. Dye, and V. Kalb. 1987. Comparison of North and South American biomes from AVHRR observations. *Geocarto* 2(1):27–40.

Goward, S. N., and J. E. Oliver. 1977. The application of remote sensing techniques in microscale climatology. *Proceedings of the Indiana Academy of Sciences* 86:326–37.

Goward, S. N., C. J. Tucker, and D. G. Dye. 1985. North American vegetation patterns observed with the NOAA-7 advanced very high resolution radiometer. *Vegetation* 64:3–14.

Graf, W. L. 1984. The geography of American field geomorphology. *Professional Geographer* 36:78–82.

Grainger, A. 1982. *Desertification: How people can make deserts. How people can stop and why they don't*. London: Earthscan.

———. 1983. Improving the monitoring of deforestation in the humid tropics. In *Tropical rain forest: Ecology and management*, ed. S. L. Sutton, T. C. Whitmore, and A. C. Chadwick, 387–95. Oxford: Blackwell Scientific.

Greenland, D. 1983. *Guidelines for modern resource management*. Columbus, Ohio: Charles Merrill.

———. 1987. The climates of long-term ecological research sites. *Occasional Papers of the Institute of Arctic and Alpine Research* 44, ed. D. Greenland, 1–81. Boulder: University of Colorado.

Gregory, K. J., and D. E. Walling. 1987. *Human activity and environmental change*. Chichester, U.K.: John Wiley and Sons.

Grichuk, V. P. 1989. *History of flora and vegetation of the Russian Plain during the Pleistocene* [in Russian]. Moscow: Mysl'.

Griffiths, G. H. 1988. Monitoring urban change from Landsat TM and SPOT satellite imagery by image differencing. In *Remote sensing: Moving towards the 21st century*, 493–97. International Geoscience and Remote Sensing Symposium, Edinburgh.

Griffiths, G. H., and W. G. Collins. 1981. Landsat imagery for mapping and monitoring vegetation in northern Kenya. *Proceedings of the Ninth Annual Conference of the Remote Sensing Society*. Reading, U.K.: Remote Sensing Society.

Grigoryev, A. A. 1970. *The subarctic: Selected theoretical works* [in Russian]. Moscow: Mysl'.

Gulakyan, K. A., V. V. Kunttsel', and G. P. Postoev. 1977. *Prognozirovanie opolznevykh protsessov* (*Forecasting landslides*). Moscow: Nedra.

Halem, M., et al. 1979. Comparisons of observed seasonal climate features with a winter and summer numerical simulation produced with the GLAS general circulation model. In *Report of the JOC study conference on climate models*. GARP Publication Series 22, 1:207–53. Geneva: World Meteorological Organization.

Halfpenny, J. C., K. P. Ingraham, J. Mattysse, and P. C. Lehr. 1986. Bibliography of alpine areas of the Front Range, Colorado. *Occasional Papers of the Institute of Arctic and Alpine Research* 43. Boulder: University of Colorado.

Hall, D. K., A.T.C. Chang, and J. L. Foster. 1987. Distribution of snow extent and depth in Alaska as determined from Nimbus-7 SMMR Maps (1982–83). In *Large-scale effects of seasonal snow cover*, ed. B. E. Goodison, R. G. Barry, and J. Dozier, 403–14. International Association of Hydrological Sciences, Publication No. 166. Wallingford, U.K.: IAHS Press.

Hall, D. K., and J. Martinec. 1985. *Remote sensing of snow and ice*. New York: Chapman and Hall.

Hall, F. G., and G. D. Badwar. 1987. Signature-extendable technology: Global space-based crop recognition. *IEEE Transactions of Geoscience and Remote Sensing*, GE-25, 1:93–103.

Hamilton, L. S., and P. N. King. 1983. *Tropical forested watersheds: Hydrologic and soils response to major uses or conversions.* Boulder, Colo.: Westview Press.

Hammer, T. 1982. *Reforestation and community development in the Sudan.* Discussion Paper D-73 M. Washington, D.C.: Resources for the Future.

Hansen, J., G. Russell, D. Rind, P. Stone, A. Lacis, S. Lebedeff, R. Ruedy, and L. Travis. 1983. Efficient three-dimensional global models for climate studies: Models I and II. *Monthly Weather Review* 111:609–62.

Hare, F. K. 1977. Connections between climate and desertification. *Environmental Conservation* 4:81–90.

––––––. 1983. *Climate and desertification. A revised analysis.* World Climate Program WCP-44. Geneva: WMO/UNEP.

Hartshorne, R. 1939. The nature of geography. *Annals of the Association of American Geographers* 29:173–658.

Harwell, M. A., and T. C. Hutchinson, Jr., eds. 1985. *Environmental consequences of nuclear war.* Chichester, U.K.: John Wiley and Sons.

Hashimoto, T., et al. 1982. Reliability, resiliency, and vulnerability criteria for water resource system performance evaluation. *Water Resources Research* 18:14–20.

Hawley, D. L. 1979. Forest inventory of clearcuts utilizing remote sensing techniques. *Proceedings of the Thirteenth Symposium on Remote Sensing of the Environment*, 2:1385–1407. Ann Arbor, Mich.: Environmental Research Institute of Michigan.

Heathcote, R. L. 1985. Extreme event analysis. In *Climate impact assessment*, ed. R. W. Kates, J. H. Ausubel, and M. Berberian, 369–401. New York: John Wiley and Sons.

Heede, R. 1983. *A world geography of recoverable carbon resources in the context of possible climatic change.* Cooperative Thesis No. 72. Boulder: University of Colorado and NCAR.

Heijnen, J., and R. W. Kates. 1974. Drought in northeast Tanzania: Comparative observations along a moisture gradient. In *Natural hazards: Local, national, global*, ed. G. F. White, 105–14. New York: Oxford University Press.

Hellden, U. 1984. Drought impact monitoring: A remote sensing study of desertification in Kordofan, the Sudan. *Lunds Universitets Naturgeografiska Institution Rapporter och Notiser*, No. 61. Lund, Sweden.

Hellden, U., and K. Olsson. 1982. The potential of Landsat MSS data for wood resources monitoring—A study in arid and semi-arid environment in Kordofan, the Sudan. *Lunds Universitets Naturgeografiska Institution Rapporter och Notiser*, No. 52. Lund, Sweden.

Hellden, U., and M. Stern. 1980. Monitoring land degradation in southern Tunisia. A test of Landsat imagery and digital data. *Lunds Universitets Naturgeografiska Institution Rapporter och Notiser*, No. 48. Lund, Sweden.

Henderson-Sellers, A. 1987. Effects of change in land use on climate in the humid tropics. In *The geophysiology of Amazonia. Vegetation and climate interactions*, ed. R. E. Dickinson, 463–93. New York: John Wiley and Sons.

Henderson-Sellers, A., and V. Gornitz. 1984. Possible climatic impacts of land cover transformations, with particular emphasis on tropical deforestation. *Climatic Change* 6:231–58.

Henderson-Sellers, A., and N. Hughes. 1982. Albedo and climate theory. *Progress in Physical Geography* 6:1–44.

Henderson-Sellers, A., and M. F. Wilson. 1983. Surface albedo data for climate modeling. *Review Geophysics and Space Physics* 21:1743–78.

Henderson-Sellers, A., M. F. Wilson, G. Thomas, and R. E. Dickinson. 1986. *Current global land-surface data sets for use in climate-related studies.* Boulder, Colo.: National Center for Atmospheric Research (NCAR/TN-272 + STR).

Herrera, R., C. F. Jordan, E. Medina, and H. Klinge. 1981. How human activities disturb the nutrient cycles of a tropical rain forest in Amazonia. *Ambio* 10:109–14.

Hewitt, K., ed. 1983a. *Interpretations of calamity.* Boston: Allen and Unwin.

————. 1983b. Place annihilation: Area bombing and the fate of urban places. *Annals of the Association of American Geographers* 73:257–84.

Holdgate, M. W., and G. F. White. 1977. *Environmental issues.* New York: John Wiley and Sons.

Holdridge, L. R. 1947. Determination of world plant formations from simple climatic data. *Science* 105:367–68.

Holloway, J. L., Jr., and S. Manabe. 1971. Simulation of climate by a global general circulation model. I. Hydrological cycle and heat balance. *Monthly Weather Review* 99:335–70.

Hope, A. S., S. N. Goward, and D. E. Petzold. 1988. TERSAIL: A numerical model for combined analysis of canopy bidirectional reflectance and thermal emissions. *Remote Sensing of the Environment* 26:287–300.

Hope, G. 1984. Australian environmental change: Timing, directions, magnitudes, rates. In *Quaternary extinctions: A prehistoric revolution,* ed. P. S. Martin and R. G. Klein, 681–90. Tucson: University of Arizona Press.

Hopkins, D. M., J. V. Matthews, Jr., C. E. Schweger, and S. B. Young, eds. 1982. *Paleoecology of Beringia.* New York: Academic Press.

Houghton, R. A., J. E. Hobbie, J. M. Melillo, B. Moore, B. J. Peterson, G. R. Shaver, and G. M. Woodwell. 1983. Changes in the carbon content of terrestrial biota and soils between 1860 and 1980: A net release of CO_2. *Ecological Monographs* 53:235–62.

Houghton, R. A., and G. M. Woodwell. 1981. Biotic contributions to the global carbon cycle: The role of remote sensing. *Proceedings of the Symposium on Machine Processing of Remotely Sensed Data,* 593–600. West Lafayette, Ind.: Laboratory for Applied Remote Sensing, Purdue University.

Howarth, P. J., and G. M. Wickware. 1981. Procedures for change detection using Landsat digital data. *International Journal of Remote Sensing* 2:277–91.

Hsu, K. J., L. Montadert, D. Bernoulli, M. B. Cita, A. Erickson, R. E. Garrison, R. B. Kidd, F. Melieres, C. Muller, and R. Wright. 1977. History of the Mediterranean salinity crisis. *Nature* (London) 267:399–403.

Hummel, J. R., and R. A. Reck. 1979. A global surface albedo model. *Journal of Applied Meteorology* 18:239–53.

Huntley, B., and I. C. Prentice. 1988. July temperatures in Europe from pollen data, 6000 years before present. *Science* 241:687–90.

Huntley, B., and T. Webb III. 1988. *Vegetation history.* Dordrecht: Kluwer Academic Publishers.

Hutchinson, C. F. 1986. Land remote sensing technology and methodology. *Climatic Change* 9:149–66.

Hutchison, B. A., and B. B. Hicks. 1985. *The forest-atmosphere interaction.* Boston: D. Reidel.

Idso, S. B. 1984. The case for carbon dioxide. *Environment Science* (May–June): 19–22.

Idso, S. B., and A. Brazel. 1984. Rising atmospheric carbon concentrations may increase streamflow. *Nature* (London) 312:51–53.

Idso, S. B., R. D. Jackson, B. Kimball, and F. Nakayama. 1975. The dependence of bare soil albedo on soil water content. *Journal of Applied Meteorology* 14:109–13.

Imbrie, J., and J. Z. Imbrie. 1980. Modeling the climatic response to orbital variations. *Science* 207:943–53.

Ingebritsen, S. E., and R.J.P. Lyon. 1985. Principal components analysis of multitemporal image pairs. *International Journal of Remote Sensing* 6:687–96.

International Board for Soil Research and Management. 1987. *Land development and management of acid soils in Africa.* Proceedings of the IBSRAM Session of the First Regional Seminar on Lateritic Soils, Minerals and Ores, Douala, Cameroon, 1987.

International Council of Scientific Unions. 1986. *The International Geosphere Biosphere Programme: A study of global change.* Prepared for the ICSU Twenty-first General Assembly, 14–19 September, Berne, Switzerland.

International Federation of Institutes of Advanced Study. 1987. *Human response to global environmental change.* Toronto Ad Hoc Preparatory Group Meeting, June 10–13, 1987. Toronto: International Federation of Institutes of Advanced Study.

Isachenko, A. G. 1980. *Optimizatsiya prirodnoy sredy (Optimization of natural environment).* Moscow: Mysl'.

Isaev, A. S., ed. 1984. *Aerokosmicheskie metody issledovaniya lesov (Aerospace methods in forest studies).* Krasnoyarsk: ILiD.

Isaev, A. S., and V. Ya. Ryapolov. 1988. Distantsionnye metody kontrolya i prognoza lesoentomologicheskogo sostoyaniya taezhnykh territoriy (Distance methods for control and forecasting of forest entomological conditions in taiga areas). In *Earth study from outer space,* 1:48–55. Moscow.

Izrael', Yu. A. 1984. *Ekologiya i kontrol' sostoyaniya prirodnoy sredy (Ecology and control of natural environment).* Leningrad: Hydrometeoizdat.

Jackson, R. D., and S. B. Idso. 1975. Surface albedo and desertification. *Science* 189:1012–13.

Jaeger, L. 1976. Monatskarten des Niederschlagesr für die ganze Erde. *Berichte Deutscher Wetterd,* NR 139. Offenback.

———. 1983. Monthly and areal patterns of mean global precipitation. In *Variations in the global water budget,* ed. A. Street-Perrott et al., 129–40. Dordrecht, The Netherlands: D. Reidel.

Jaenicke, R. 1981. Atmospheric aerosols and global climate. In *Climatic variations and variability: Facts and theories,* ed. A. Berger, 577–97. Dordrecht: D. Reidel.

Jäger, J. 1983. *Climate and energy systems. A review of their interactions.* New York: John Wiley and Sons.

————. 1986. Climatic change: Floating new evidence in the CO_2 debate. *Environment* 28(7):6–9, 38–41.

Jayroe, R. R., Jr. 1978. Some observations about Landsat digital analysis. NASA Technical Memo 78184. NASA Marshall Space Flight Center, Alabama.

Jensen, J. R. 1981. Urban change detection mapping using Landsat data. *American Cartographer* 8:127–47.

————. 1983. Biophysical remote sensing. *Annals of the Association of American Geographers* 73:111–32.

————. 1986. *Introductory digital image processing: A remote sensing perspective.* Englewood Cliffs, N.J.: Prentice-Hall.

Jensen, J. R., and D. L. Toll. 1982. Detecting residential land-use development at the urban fringe. *Photogrammetric Engineering and Remote Sensing* 48:629–43.

Johnson, D. 1977. The human dimension of desertification. *Economic Geography* 53:317–21.

Johnson, G., E. Barthmaier, T.W.D. Gregg, and R. E. Aulds. 1979. Forest stand classification in western Washington using Landsat and computer-based resource data. *Proceedings of the Thirteenth Symposium on Remote Sensing of the Environment,* 2:1681–95. Ann Arbor, Mich.: Environmental Research Institute of Michigan.

Johnson, G., A. van Dijk, and C. M. Sakamoto. 1987. The use of AVHRR data in operational agricultural assessment in Africa. *Geocarto* 2(1):41–60.

Jones, J. A. 1990. Termites, soil fertility and carbon cycling in dry tropical Africa: A hypothesis. *Journal of Tropical Ecology* 6:291–305.

Jones, J. E. 1977. *Calculation of evapotranspiration using color infrared photography, Gila River Phreatophyte Project.* U.S. Geological Survey, Report GP01977-791-786. Reston, Va.: U.S. Geological Survey.

Jones, R. L. 1988. Biogeography. *Progress in Physical Geography* 12:103–13.

Jouzel, J., et al. 1987. Vostok ice core: A continuous isotope record over the last climatic cycle (160,000 years). *Nature* (London) 329:403–8.

Joyce, A. T., J. H. Ivey, and G. S. Burns. 1980. The use of Landsat MSS data for detecting land use changes in forestland. *Proceedings of the Fourteenth Symposium on Remote Sensing of the Environment,* 2:979–88. Ann Arbor, Mich.: Environmental Research Institute of Michigan.

Justice, C. O., J.R.G. Townshend, B. N. Holben, and C. J. Tucker. 1985. Analysis of the phenology of global vegetation using meteorological satellite data. *International Journal of Remote Sensing* 6:1271.

Kakhru, M. M. 1988. Statisticheskiy analiz pripoverkhnostnykh raspredeleniy poley khlorofilla i temperatury po sputnikovym izobrazheniyam skanerov CZCS i AVHRR (Statistical analysis of distribution of chlorophyll and temperature fields near the earth's surface according to Sputnik's output of scanners CZCS and AVHRR). In *Earth study from outer space,* 2:36–43. Moscow.

Kalensky, D. 1988. Some views on digital databases. In *Building databases for global science,* ed. H. Mounsey and R. Tomlinson, 307–14. International Geographical Union. London: Taylor and Francis.

Kalnay, E., R. Balgovind, et al. 1983. *Documentation of the GLAS Fourth Order General Circulation Model.* Vol. 1: *Model documentation.* Technical Memo 86064. Greenbelt, Md.: NASA.

Kaplina, T. N. 1965. *Kriogennye sklonovye protsessy* (*Cryogenic slope processes*). Moscow: Nauka.

Karl, T. R. 1983. Some spatial characteristics of drought duration in the United States. *Journal of Climate and Applied Meteorology* 23:1356–66.

Karl, T. R., and A. J. Koscielny. 1982. Drought in the United States: 1895–1981. *Journal of Climatology* 2:313–21.

Karol', I. P., V. V. Rozanov, and Yu. M. Timofeev. 1983. *Gazovye primesi v atmosfere* (*Gaseous admixtures in the atmosphere*). Leningrad: Hydrometeoizdat.

Kasperson, R. E., and J. X. Kasperson, eds. 1988. *Nuclear risk analysis in comparative perspective*. Winchester, Mass.: Allen and Unwin.

Kasperson, R. E., and K. D. Pijawka. 1985. Societal responses to hazards and major hazard events: Comparing natural and technological hazards. *Public Administration Review* 45, Special Issue (January) 19:7–18.

Kates, R. W. 1971. Natural hazards in human ecological perspective: Hypotheses and models. *Economic Geography* 47:438–51.

———. 1978. *Risk assessment of environmental hazard*. Scientific Committee on Problems of the Environment, Report 8. New York: John Wiley and Sons.

———. 1985. The interaction of climate and society. In *Climate impact assessment: Studies in the interaction of climate and society*, ed. R. W. Kates, J. H. Ausubel, and M. Berberian, 3–36. Scientific Committee on Problems of the Environment, Report 27. New York: John Wiley and Sons.

Kates, R. W., J. H. Ausubel, and M. Berberian, eds. 1985. *Climate impact assessment: Studies in the interaction of climate and society*. Scientific Committee on Problems of the Environment, Report 27. New York: John Wiley and Sons.

Kates, R. W., and J. X. Kasperson. 1983. Comparative risk analysis of technological hazards (A review). *Proceedings of the U.S. National Academy of Sciences* 80: 7027–38.

Katz, R. W. 1988. Statistics of climate change: Implications for scenario development. In *Societal response to regional climate change*, ed. M. H. Glantz, 95–112. Boulder, Colo.: Westview Press.

Kauth, R. J., and G. S. Thomas. 1976. The tasseled cap—a graphic description of agricultural crops as seen by Landsat. *Proceedings of the Symposium on Machine Processing of Remotely Sensed Data*. West Lafayette, Ind.: Laboratory for Applied Remote Sensing, Purdue University.

Kaznacheev, V. L., ed. 1982. *Prognoz antropoekologicheskikh situatsii s pomoshch'yu kosmicheskikh sredstv* (*The forecasting of anthroecological situations by means of outer-space measurements*). Leningrad: Nauka.

Kellogg, C. E. 1938. Soil and society. In *Soils and men. Yearbook of agriculture 1938*, ed. U.S. Department of Agriculture, 863–86. Washington, D.C.: U.S. Government Printing Office.

Kellogg, W. W. 1987. Mankind's impact on climate: The evolution of an awareness. *Climatic Change* 10:112–36.

Kershaw, A. P. 1986. Climatic change and aboriginal burning in northeast Australia during the last two glacial/interglacial cycles. *Nature* (London) 322:47–49.

Kessler, A. 1985. Heat balance climatology. In *General Climatology*, ed. O. M. Essenwanger, 1–224. World Survey of Climatology, Vol. 1A. Amsterdam: Elsevier.

Kharin, N. G., and A. Babaev. 1982. *Izuchenie i prognoz protsessov opustynivaniya po materialam aerokosmicheskikh s'yimok* (*Study and forecasting of processes of desertification based on aerospace surveys*), 121–30. Leningrad: Nauka.

Khotinskiy, N. A. 1977. *The Holocene of northern Eurasia* [in Russian]. Moscow: Nauka.

―――. 1989. *Problems of reconstruction and correlation of the Holocene climates* [in Russian], 12–17. Moscow: Nauka.

Khotinskiy, N. A., and S. S. Savina. 1985. Paleoklimatcheskie skhemy territorii SSSR v boreal'nom, atlanticheskom i subboreal'nom periodakh golotsena (Paleoclimatic schemes of the USSR territory in boreal, atlantic and sub-boreal periods of the Holocene). *Izvestiya USSR Academy of Sciences, Series Geography* 4.

Khrisanova, E. N. 1987. Sovremennye etapy gominizatsii (Modern stages of gominization). In *Stanovlenie i evolyutsiya cheloveka* (*Formation and evolution of man*), 2:5–92. Series Anthropology. Moscow: VINITI.

Kimes, D. S., and J. A. Kirchner. 1982. Radiative transfer model for heterogeneous 3-D scenes. *Applied Optics* 21:4119–29.

King, D., J. Daroussin, P. Bonneton, and B. Nicoullaud. 1986. An improved method for combining soil map data. *Soil Use and Management* 140–45.

Klige, R. K. 1985. *Izmeneniya globalnogo vodoobema*. Moscow: Nauka.

Klimanov, V. A. 1978. Paleoklimaticheskie usloviya ravniny v klimaticheskiy optimum Golotsena (Paleoclimatic conditions of the Russian plain in the climatic maximum of the Holocene). *Doklady USSR Academy of Sciences* (Moscow) 242(4):902.

―――. 1989a. Climates of east Europe in the Holocene optimum based on palynological data [in Russian]. In *Razvitie prirody territorii SSSR v pozdnem pleistotsene i golotsene*, 251–58. Moscow: Nauka.

―――. 1989b. Cyclicity and quasi-periodicity of climatic oscillations during the Holocene [in Russian]. In *Paleoklimaty pozdnelednikovya i golotsena*. Moscow: Nauka.

Knapp, B. 1979. *Soil processes*. London: Allen and Unwin.

Knizhnikov, Yu. F., V. I. Kravtsova, I. A. Labutina, et al. 1980. *Kosmicheskaya s'yimka i tematicheskoe kartografirovanie* (*Outer-space survey and thematic cartography*). Moscow: Moscow University Press.

Knox, J. C. 1983. Responses of river systems to Holocene climates. In *Late Quaternary environments of the United States*. Vol. 2: *The Holocene*, ed. H. E. Wright, Jr., 26–41. Minneapolis: University of Minnesota Press.

Kolars, J. 1982. Earthquake vulnerable populations in modern Turkey. *Geographical Review* 72(1):20–35.

Kolosovsky, N. N. 1958. *Osnovy ekonomicheskogo rayonirovaniya* (*Foundation of economic regionalization*). Moscow: GosKomIzdat.

Komar, I. V. 1975. *Ratsional'noe ispol'zovanie prirodnykh resursov i resursnye tsycly* (*Rational usage of natural resources and resource cycles*). Moscow: Nauka.

Kondrat'yev, K. Ya. 1976. Aerozol' i klimat (Aerosols and climate). *Trudy Glavnoy geofizicheskoy observatorii* (*Proceedings of the Central Geophysical Observatory*) 381:3–66.

―――. 1980. *Radiatsionnye faktory sovremennykh izmeneniy global'nogo klimata* (*Radiational factors in recent changes in global climate*). Leningrad: Hydrometeoizdat.

————. 1982. Vsemirnaya issledovatel'skaya klimaticheskaya programma: sostoyanie, perspectivy i rol' kosmicheskikh sredstv nabludeniy (International scientific climate programme: Status, perspectives and role of outer-space monitoring). *Science and Technology Review, Series Meteorology and Climatology* 8:274. Moscow: VINITI.

————. 1983. *Sputnikovaya klimatologiya (Sputnik's climatology)*. Leningrad: Hydrometeoizdat.

————. 1986. Vliyanie protsessov na poverkhnosti sushi na izmeneniya klimata i mezhdunarodnyy proekt po sputnikovoy klimatologii poverkhnosti sushi (The influence of land surface processes on climate changes and the international project on Sputnik's climatology of land surface). In *Earth study from outer space*, 3. Moscow.

————. 1988. *Prirodnye i antropogennye izmeneniya klimata (Natural and anthropogenic climate changes)*. Leningrad: Nauka.

Kondrat'yev, K. Ya., V. I. Kozzov, V. V. Mukhenberg, and L. N. Dyachenko. 1982. The shortwave albedo and surface emissivity. In *Land surface processes in atmospheric general circulation models*, 463–515. Cambridge: Cambridge University Press.

Koshin, V. S., and S. M. Myagkov. 1986. Engineering-geographic problems of a mining enterprise (with reference to the apatite mines of the Kola Peninsula). *Soviet Geography* 27(1):43–50.

Kotlov, F. V., I. A. Brashnina, and I. K. Sipyagina. 1967. *Gorod i geologicheskie protsessy (City and geological processes)*. Moscow: Nauka.

Kotlyakov, V. M. 1968. *Snejniy pokrov Zemli i ledniki (Snow cover and glaciers of the earth)*. Moscow: Gidrometeoizdat.

————. 1981. Stanovlenie i perspektivy kosmicheskoi glyatsiologii (Formation and perspectives of glaciology from outer space). In *Earth study from outer space*, 1:7–15. Moscow.

————. 1987. Global'naya klimaticheskaya rol' snezhnogo pokrova (Global climatic role of snow cover). In *Vzaimodeystvie oledeneniya s atmosferoy i okeanom (Interaction of freezing with atmosphere and ocean)*, 34–65. Moscow: Nauka.

————. 1988. Mezhdunarodnaya geosferno-biosfernaya programma "Global'nye izmeneniya" (International Geosphere-Biosphere Programme "Global Change"). *Vestnik of USSR Academy of Sciences* (Moscow) 1:92–102.

Kotlyakov, V. M., J. R. Mather, G. V. Sdasyuk, and G. F. White. 1988a. Global change: Geographical approaches (A review). *Proceedings of the U.S. National Academy of Sciences* 85:5986–91.

Kotlyakov, V. M., G. F. White, J. R. Mather, and G. V. Sdasyuk. 1988b. Menyayushchiysya mir: geograficheskiy podkhod k izucheniyu. Sovetsko-amerikanskiy proekt (The changing world: A geographical approach. A Soviet-American project). *Izvestiya USSR Academy of Sciences, Series Geography* 3:128–35.

Kotlyakov, V. M., et al. 1988c. Global'nye atlasy: novyi etap geografo-kartograficheskogo izucheniya prirody i resursov (Global atlases: A new stage of geographic-cartographical study of nature and resources). *Izvestiya USSR Academy of Sciences, Series Geography* 3:22–30.

Kovda, V. A. 1976. Biogeokhimicheskye tsykly prirody i vtorzhenie cheloveka v nikh (Biogeochemical cycles of nature and human intervention in them). In *Biogeo-*

khimicheskie tsykly biosfery (*Biogeochemical cycles of the biosphere*), 19–98. Moscow: Nauka.

———. 1977. *Aridizatsiya sushi i bor'ba s zasukhoy* (*Land aridization and drought fighting*). Moscow: Nauka.

———. 1981. *Pochvenny pokrov, ego uluchshenie, upravlenie i okhrana* (*The soil cover, its improvement, management and conservation*). Moscow: Nauka.

———. 1983. Loss of productive land due to salinization. *Ambio* 12:121–23.

———. 1984. *Problemy bor'by s opustynivaniyem i zasoleniyem oroshaemykh zemel'* (*Problems of struggle against desertification and salination of irrigated lands*). Moscow: Nauka.

Kozlowski, T. T. 1978. *Physiology of woody plants*. New York: Academic Press.

Kozshukhov, Yu. S. 1981. Stoimostnaya otsenka prirodnykh usloviy gradostoitel'stva na territorii SSSR (Value assessment of natural conditions for city building in the USSR). *Vestnik of Moscow State University, Series 5, Geography* (Moscow) 1:20–26.

———. 1982. Cost evaluation of environmental conditions for urban construction in the USSR. *Soviet Geography: Review and Translation* 22(8):591–98.

Krenke, A. N. 1974. Sushchestvuyushchie predstavleniya o bystrykh podvizhkakh lednikov (Contemporary notions of rapid glacial motions). *Materialy glyatsiologichesikikh issledovaniy Khronika obsuzhdeniya* (*Proceedings of glaciological study/Chronicle of discussion*) 29:274–89.

———. 1980. O vliyanii pereraspredeleniya rechnogo stoka na ledovoy rezhim severnogo ledovitogo okeana (On the influence of the redistribution of river runoff on the annual regime of the polar ocean). *Materialy glyatsiologicheskikh issledovaniy* 38:287–92.

———. 1982. *Massoobmen lednikovykh system na territorii SSSR* (*Mass change in glacial systems in the USSR*). Leningrad: Gidrometeoizdat.

Krenke, A. N., and E. M. Loktionova. 1989. Rol'tayaniya snezhnogo pokrovy v formirovanii temperaturnago polya nad kontinentam (The role of snow-cover melting in temperature field formation above continents). In *Materialy glyatsiologicheskikh* 66:43–52.

Krenke, A. N., and V. M. Menshutin. 1984. Podobie poley akkumulyatsii i ablyatsii lednikov i raschyet ikh vodno-ledovogo balansa po kosmicheskim snimkam (The similarity of glacial accumulation and ablation fields and estimation of their water balance according to outer-space observations). In *Sbornik distantsionnoy otsenki obshey uvlazhnyonnosti territorii* (*Collection of outer-space estimates of general humidity of territories*), 66–74. Moscow.

Krenke, A. N., and A. Yu. Mikhailov. 1986. Vzaimosvyaz' tsirkulyatsii atmosfery, rel'efa i oledeneniya na severo-vostoke SSSR v nastoyashchem i proshlom soglasno glyatsiologicheskim raschyotam (Interaction between atmosphere circulation, relief, and freezing in present-day northeastern USSR and in the past based on glaciological and hydrodynamical estimates). *Materialy meteorologicheskikh issledovaniy* (*Proceedings of meteorological studies*) (Moscow) 10:7–17.

Krenke, A. N., and G. V. Sdasyuk. 1987. Nauka teknika i mir: geograficheskie aspekty (Science, technology and peace: Geographical aspects). *Izvestiya USSR Academy of Sciences, Series Geography* 2.

Krenke, A. N., and A. N. Zolotokrylin. 1984. Issledovanie roli tipov rastitel'nosti vo vzaimodeystvii podstilayushchey poverkhnosti i atmosfery (Study of the role of different types of vegetation in fluxes between the surface and atmosphere). *Izvestiya USSR Academy of Sciences, Series Physics of Atmosphere and Ocean* 11:1081–89.

Krestovskiy, O. I. 1986. *Vliyanie vyrubok i vosstanovleniya lesov na vodnost' rek (Impact of forest cutting and reforestation on river water balance)*. Leningrad: Gidrometeoizdat.

Kupriyanov, V. V., and V. F. Usachev, eds. 1981. *Aerokosmicheskie metody pri issledovanii vodnykh resursov i ikh zagryazneniya (Aerospace methods for the study of water resources and water pollution)*. Leningrad: Hydrometeoizdat.

Kushkarev, A. B., and V. A. Karakin. 1987. *Regionalnue geoinformatsionnye sistemu (Regional geoinformation systems)*. Moscow: Nauka.

Kutzbach, J. E., and A. Street-Perrott. 1985. Milankovitch forcing of fluctuations in the level of tropical lakes from 18 to 0 kyr BP. *Nature* (London) 317:130–39.

Kuvshinova, K. V., ed. 1987. *Tsirkulyatsionnye mekhanizmy sovremennykh kolebanii klimata (Circular mechanisms of modern climate fluctuations)*. Moscow: Nauka.

Kuz'min, P. P. 1937. Staivanie lednikov i teplovoy balans (Glacier melting and the energy balance). *Geophysics* 7(4):272–83.

Kyunttsel', V. V. 1980. *Zakonomernosti opolznevogo protsessa na evropeyskoy territorii SSSR i ego regional'nyy prognoz (Regularities in landslide processes in European USSR and their regional forecasting)*. Moscow: Nauka.

Lal, R. 1987. Management of acid tropical soils for sustainable agriculture. In *Proceedings of an International Board for Soil Research and Management Inaugural Workshop*, Bangkok, Thailand, 167–77.

Lal, R., and D. Greenland, eds. 1979. *Soil physical properties and crop production in the tropics*. New York: John Wiley and Sons.

Lamb, H. H. 1977. *Climate: Present, past and future*. Vol. 2: *Climatic history and the future*. London: Methuen, 339–40, 380–86.

Lamb, P. J. 1982. Persistence of sub-Saharan drought. *Nature* (London) 299:46–48.

———. 1987. On the development of regional climatic scenarios for policy-oriented climate impact assessment. *Bulletin of the American Meteorological Society* 68:1116–23.

Lamprey, H. F. 1975. Report on desert encroachment reconnaissance in northern Sudan, 21 October to 10 November. UNESCO/UNEP, Paris (mimeograph).

Land, K. C., and S. H. Schneider. 1987. Forecasting in the social and natural sciences. *Climatic Change*, Special Issue 11(1–2).

Landsberg, H. H. 1979. *Energy: The next twenty years*. Report sponsored by the Ford Foundation. Cambridge, Mass.: Ballenger.

Langdale, G. W., and W. D. Schrader. 1982. Soil erosion effects on soil productivity of cultivated cropland. In *Determinants of soil loss tolerance*, ed. B. L. Schmidt, R. R. Allmaras, J. V. Mannering, and R. I. Papendick, 41–51. Special Publication No. 45. Madison, Wisc.: American Society of Agronomy.

Lanly, J. P. 1982. *Tropical forest resources*. FAO Forestry Paper 30. Rome: UN Food and Agriculture Organization.

Lanly, J. P., and J. Clement. 1982. *Forest resources of tropical Africa. Part I. Regional synthesis*. Rome: UNFAO.

Larionov, G. A., L. F. Litvin, and R. S. Chalov. 1984. Eroziya pochv i ruslovye protsessy v gornykh stranakh (Soil erosion and channel processes in mountainous areas). In *Inzhrenernaya geografiya gornykh stran (Engineering geography of mountainous areas)*, 67–100. Moscow: Moscow University Press.

Latham, J. S. 1981. Monitoring the areal extent of irrigated lands of the Gefara plain, Libya. *Proceedings of the Ninth Annual Conference of the Remote Sensing Society.* Reading, U.K.: Remote Sensing Society.

Laval, K. 1986. General circulation model experiments with surface albedo changes. *Climatic Change* 9:91–102.

Lavrov, S. B., V. V. Pokshishevskiy, and G. V. Sdasyuk, eds. 1985. *Regionalization for planning in the USSR: Concepts, methods and practice.* UNCRD Monograph. Nagoya, Japan: UN Centre for Regional Development.

Lavrov, S. B., and G. V. Sdasyuk. 1988. *Concepts of regional development.* Moscow: Progress Publishers.

Legasov, V. A., L. P. Feoktistov, and I. I. Kuz'min. 1985. Yadernaya energetika i mezhdunarodnaya bezopasnost' (Atomic energy and international safety). *Nature* (Moscow) 6:6–16.

Legasov, V. A., I. I. Kuz'min, and A. N. Chernopleniv. 1984. Vliyanie energetiki na klimat (Power industry impact on climate). *Izvestiya USSR Academy of Sciences, Series Physics of the Atmosphere* 20(11):1089–1103.

Legates, D. R. 1988. A climatology of global precipitation. Ph.D. dissertation, University of Delaware.

Legates, D. R., and C. J. Willmott. 1986. Interpolation of point values from isoline maps. *American Cartographer* 13(4):308–23.

Le Houerou, H. N. 1976. The nature and causes of desertification. *Arid Lands Newsletter* 3:1–7.

————. 1980. *Browse in Africa: The current state of knowledge.* Addis Ababa: International Livestock Center for Africa.

Lemeshev, M. Ya. 1986. Aktual'nye voprosy prirodopol'zovaniya (Contemporary problems of nature management). *Human Sciences* 5:34–49.

Lemeshev, M. Ya., N. V. Chepurnykh, and N. P. Yurina. 1986. *Regional'noe prirodopol'zovanie: na puti k garmonii (Regional use of natural resources: On the path to harmony).* Moscow: Mysl'.

Leontief, W. 1977. Structure of the world economy: Outline of a simple input-output formulation. *American Economic Review* (December): 823–34.

Lettau, H. H. 1969. Note on aerodynamic roughness parameter estimation on the basis of roughness element description. *Journal of Applied Meteorology* 8:828–32.

Lettau, H. H., K. Lettau, and L.C.B. Molion. 1979. Amazonia's hydrologic cycle and the role of atmospheric recycling in assessing deforestation effects. *Monthly Weather Review* 107:227–38.

Li, X., and A. H. Strahler. 1985. Geometric-optical modeling of a conifer forest canopy. *IEEE Transactions of Geoscience and Remote Sensing,* GE-23, 5:705–21.

Lieth, H. 1975. Primary productivity of the major vegetation units of the world. In *Primary productivity of the biosphere*, ed. H. Lieth and R. H. Whittaker, 203–15. Berlin: Springer Verlag.

————, ed. 1978. *Primary production in the biosphere.* Benchmark Papers in Ecology 8. Stroudsberg, Pa.: Dowden, Hutchinson, and Ross.

Likens, G. E., F. H. Bormann, and N. M. Johnson. 1981. Interactions between major biogeochemical cycles in terrestrial ecosystems. In *The major biogeochemical cycles and their interactions*. Scientific Committee on Problems of the Environment, Report 21. Chichester, U.K.: John Wiley and Sons.

Lipatov, G. L. 1977. *O vliyanii bol'shogo goroda na intensivnost' osadkov (On the impact of a large city on precipitation intensity)*. Moscow.

Lissitsin, A. P. 1974. *Sludge formation in oceans* [in Russian]. Moscow: Nauka.

Liu, K.-b., and P. A. Colinvaux. 1985. Forest changes in the Amazon basin during the last glacial maximum. *Nature* (London) 318:556–57.

Liverman, D. M. 1983. The use of a global simulation model in assessing the impact of climate on food systems. Ph.D. dissertation, University of California, Los Angeles.

———. 1987. Forecasting the impact of climate on food systems: Model testing and model linkage. *Climatic Change* 11:267–85.

Livingstone, D. A., and T. Van der Hammen. 1978. Paleography and paleoclimatology. In *Tropical forest ecosystems: A state of knowledge report*, 61–90. Paris: UNESCO/UNEP/UNFAO.

Lockwood, J. G. 1987. Changing atmospheric carbon dioxide. *Progress in Physical Geography* 11:581–611.

Lodwick, G. D. 1979. A computer system for monitoring environmental change in multitemporal Landsat data. *Canadian Journal of Remote Sensing* 7:24–33.

Logan, T. J. 1982. Improved criteria for developing soil loss tolerances on cropland. In *Determinants of soil loss tolerance*, ed. B. L. Schmidt, R. R. Allmaras, J. V. Mannering, and R. I. Papendick, 131–38. Special Publication No. 45. Madison, Wisc.: American Society of Agronomy.

Lopes, A. S., T. J. Smyth, and N. Curi. 1987. Management of acid tropical soils for sustainable agriculture. In *Proceedings of an International Board for Soil Research and Management Inaugural Workshop*, Bangkok, Thailand, 147–65.

Losev, K. S. 1988. Sotsial'no-ekonomicheskie posledstviya ispol'zovaniya vody: vozmozhnye puti razvitiya (Socioeconomic and ecological consequences of water usage: Possible trends). *Izvestiya USSR Academy of Sciences, Series Geography* 6:44–50.

Lowenthal, D., ed. 1965. *Man and nature*, by George Perkins Marsh. Cambridge, Mass.: Harvard University Press.

Lowrance, W. W. 1976. *Of acceptable risk: Science and the determination of safety*. Los Altos, Calif.: William Kaufmann.

Ludwig, J. A., and W. G. Whitford. 1981. Short-term water and energy flow in arid systems. In *Arid land ecosystems: Structure, functioning, and management*, ed. D. W. Goodall and R. A. Perry, 2:271–99. International Biological Program. Cambridge: Cambridge University Press.

Lugo, A. E. 1988. Estimating reduction in the diversity of tropical forest species. In *Biodiversity*, ed. E. O. Wilson and F. M. Peter, 58–70. Washington, D.C.: National Academy Press.

Lukasheva, L. I., and G. M. Ignat'yev. 1964. Landshafty sushi i fiziko-geograficheskoe rayonirovanie materikov (Landscapes and the physical-geographical division of continents). In *Fiziko-geograficheskiy atlas mira/poyasnitel'nyy tekst/ (Physical geographical atlas of the world/reference/)*. Moscow.

Lukashov, A. A. 1987. Geomorfologicheskiy analiz i otsenka territorii pri osvoenii mestorozhdeniy poleznykh iskopaemykh v gornykh rayonakh (Geomorphological analysis and evaluation of the region during development of mineral deposits in mountainous areas). In *Otsenka i dolgosrochnyy prognoz izmeneniya prirody gor (Evaluation and long-term forecasting of nature changes in mountains)*, 4–13. Moscow: Moscow University Press.

L'vovich, M. I. 1945. *Elementy regima rek zemnogo shara (Rivers of the earth: Elements of regime)*. Moscow: Sverdlovsk.

―――. 1972. World water balance (general report). *Symposium on World Water Balance* 2:3–21. IASH Publication No. 93.

―――. 1974. *Mirovye vodnye resursy i ikh budushchee (World water resources and their future)*. Moscow: Mysl'.

―――. 1986. *Voda i jhizn' (Water and life)*. Moscow: Mysl'

L'vovich, M. I., and A. V. Belyaev. 1982. Metodika geograficheskikh issledovaniy vodnogo balansa territorii i kartografirovaniya ee elementov (Geographic and cartographic methods of water balance study of the earth). *Vodnye Resursy* (Moscow) 3.

L'vovich, M. I., and N. I. Koronkevich. 1974. Orientirovochniy prognoz ispol'zovaniya i okhrany vodnykh resursov SSSR na uriovne 2000 g (Preliminary forecast of water usage and water resources protection in the USSR for the year 2000). *Izvestiya USSR Academy of Sciences, Series Geography* 2.

L'vovich, M. I., and G. White. In press. Anthropogenic changes of fresh water resources during the last 300 years. In *The earth transformed by human action*, ed. B. L. Turner and R. W. Kates. Cambridge: Cambridge University Press.

Mabbutt, J. A., and C. Floret, eds. 1980. *Case studies on desertification*. Paris: UNESCO/UNEP/UNDP.

McAvaney, B. J., W. Bourke, and K. Puri. 1978. A global spectral model for simulation of the general circulation. *Journal of Atmospheric Sciences* 35:1557–83.

McCormack, D. E., and M. A. Stocking. 1986. Soil potential ratings. I. An alternative form of land evaluation. *Soil Survey and Land Evaluation* 6:37–41.

McCormack, D. E., K. K. Young, and L. W. Kimberlin. 1982. Current criteria for determining soil loss tolerance. In *Determinants of soil loss tolerance*, ed. B. L. Schmidt, R. R. Allmaras, J. V. Mannering, and R. I. Papendick, 95–111. Special Publication No. 45. Madison, Wisc.: American Society of Agronomy.

MacDonald, G. M., and J. C. Ritchie. 1986. Modern pollen spectra from the western interior of Canada and the interpretation of late Quaternary vegetation development. *New Phytologist* 103:245–68.

McDowell, P. F., T. Webb III, and P. J. Bartlein. In press. Long-term environmental change. In *The earth transformed by human action*, ed. B. L. Turner and R. W. Kates. Cambridge: Cambridge University Press.

McNaughton, K. G., and P. G. Jarvis. 1983. Predicting the effects of vegetation changes on transpiration and evaporation. In *Water deficits and plant growth*, ed. T. T. Kozlowski, 7:1–47. New York: Academic Press.

Malaisse, F. P. 1978. The Miombo ecosystem. In *Tropical forest ecosystems: A state of knowledge report*, 589–606. Paris: UNESCO.

Malila, W. A. 1980. Change vector analysis: An approach for detecting forest changes with Landsat. *Proceedings of the Symposium on Machine Processing of Remotely*

Sensed Data, 10:326–35. West Lafayette, Ind.: Laboratory for Applied Remote Sensing, Purdue University.

Malila, W. A., and T. W. Wagner. 1972. Multispectral remote sensing of elements of water and radiation balances. *Proceedings of the Eighth International Symposium on Remote Sensing of the Environment*, 1:639–64. Ann Arbor, Mich.: Environmental Research Institute of Michigan.

Malingreau, J. P., G. Stephens, and L. Fellows. 1985. Remote sensing of forest fires: Kalimantan and North Borneo in 1982–83. *Ambio* 14(6):314–21.

Malingreau, J. P., and C. J. Tucker. 1988. Large-scale deforestation in the southeastern Amazon basin of Brazil. *Ambio* 17(1):49–55.

Malone, T. F. 1986. Mission to planet earth: Integrating studies of global change. *Environment* 28:6–11, 39–42.

Manabe, S., and R. J. Stouffer. 1980. Sensitivity of a global climate model to an increase of CO_2 concentration in the atmosphere. *Journal of Geophysical Research* 85:5529–54.

Manrique, L. R. 1985. A soil taxonomy based land assessment for food crop production. *Soil Taxonomy News* 10:3–5.

Marble, D. F. 1988. Approaches to the efficient design of spatial databases at a global scale. In *Building databases for global science*, ed. H. Mounsey and R. Tomlinson, 49–65. International Geographical Union. London: Taylor and Francis.

Marble, D. F., and D. J. Peuquet, eds. 1983. Geographic information systems and remote sensing. In *Manual of remote sensing*. 2d ed., ed. R. N. Colwell, 1:923–58. Falls Church, Va.: American Society of Photogrammetric Engineering.

Marchuk, G. I. 1982. *Matematicheskoe modelirovanie v probleme okruzhayushchey sredy (Mathematical modeling in environmental problems)*. Moscow: Nauka.

Marchuk, G. I., et al. 1979. Numerical simulation of the global circulation of the atmosphere. In *Report of the JOC study conference on climate models*. GARP Publication Series 22, 1:318–70. Geneva: World Meteorological Organization.

Marchuk, G. I., K. Ya. Kondrat'yev, O. A. Avaste, et al. 1985. Mezhgodovaya izmenchivost' komponentov radiatsionnogo balansa zemli po dannym sputnikovykh izmereniy (Interannual changeability of the components in the earth's radiation balance based on Sputnik measurements). *Doklady USSR Academy of Sciences* 280(1):65–70.

Marchuk, G. I., K. Ya. Kondrat'yev, and V. V. Kozoderov. 1988. Klyuchevye aspekty issledovaniy radiatsionnogo balansa zemli (Main aspects in the study of the radiation balance of the earth). In *Issledovaniya zemli iz kosmosa (Earth study from outer space)*, 5:3–10. Moscow.

———. 1989. Analiz dannykh nablyudeniy radiatsionnogo balansa zemli (Analysis of data on the earth's radiation balance). In *Earth study from outer space*, 1:3–16. Moscow.

Margules, C., A. J. Higgs, and R. W. Rafe. 1982. Modern biogeographic theory: Are there any lessons for nature reserve design? *Biological Conservation* 24:115–28.

Markham, B. L., and J. L. Barker. 1987. Radiometric properties of U.S. processed Landsat MSS data. *Remote Sensing of the Environment* 22:39–71.

Markham, B. L., and J.R.G. Townshend. 1981. Land cover classification accuracy as a function of sensor spatial resolution. *Proceedings of the Fifteenth Symposium on*

Remote Sensing of the Environment, 3:1075–90. Ann Arbor, Mich.: Environmental Research Institute of Michigan.

Markov, K. K. 1960. *Paleography* [in Russian]. Moscow: Moscow University Press.

Marland, G. 1988. The prospect of solving the CO_2 problem through global reforestation. Report TRO 39. U.S. Department of Energy, Environmental Sciences Division of Oak Ridge National Laboratory, Oak Ridge, Tenn.

Marsh, G. P. 1864. *Man and nature; or, physical geography as modified by human action*. New York: Charles Scribner. Reprint. Belknap Press of Harvard University Press, 1965.

Marshall, S. E., and S. G. Warren. 1987. Parameterization of snow albedo for climate models. In *Large-scale effects of seasonal snow cover*, ed. B. E. Goodison, R. G. Barry, and J. Dozier, 43–50. International Association of Hydrological Sciences, Publication No. 166. Wallingford, U.K.: IAHS Press.

Mashbits, Ya. G. 1974. Osobennosti i problemy geografii prirodnykh resursov i khozyaistva razvivayushchikhsya stran (Peculiarities and problems of the geography of natural resources and economy of developing countries). *Voprosy Geografii* (Moscow) 95:174–92.

Mather, J. R. 1969. The average annual water balance of the world. *Proceedings of the Symposium on Water Balance in North America*. American Water Resources Association Proceedings Series No. 7, June 23–26. Banff, Canada.

———. 1974. *Climatology: Fundamentals and applications*. New York: McGraw-Hill.

———. 1978. *The climatic water budget in environmental analysis*. Lexington, Mass.: D. C. Heath and Company.

———. 1984. *Water resources: Distribution, use and management*. New York: John Wiley and Sons.

Mather, J. R., and G. A. Yoshioka. 1968. The role of climate in the distribution of vegetation. *Annals of the Association of American Geographers* 58(1):29–41.

Matthews, E. 1983. Global vegetation and land use: New high-resolution data bases for climate studies. *Journal of Climate and Applied Meteorology* 22:474–87.

Meckelein, W. 1980. *Desertification in extremely arid environments*. Stuttgarter Geographische Studien, Band 95. Stuttgart.

Melillo, J. M., C. A. Palm, R. A. Houghton, G. M. Woodwell, and N. Myers. 1985. A comparison of two recent estimates of destruction of tropical forests. *Environmental Conservation* 12:37–40.

Mensching, H. G. 1985. Land degradation and desertification in the Sahelian zone. In *Arid lands today and tomorrow*, ed. E. W. Whitehead, C. F. Hutchinson, B. N. Timmerman, and R. C. Varady, 605–13. Boulder, Colo.: Westview Press.

Merchant, J. W., ed. 1988. Special GIS issue. *Photogrammetric Engineering and Remote Sensing* 54(11):1545–1628.

Merchant, J. W., and W. J. Ripple, eds. 1987. Special GIS issue. *Photogrammetric Engineering and Remote Sensing* 53(10):1359–1445.

Micklin, P. F. 1988. Desiccation of the Aral Sea: A water management disaster in the Soviet Union. *Science* 241:1170–75.

Miller, D. H. 1978. The factor of scale: Ecosystem, landscape mosaic, and region. In *Sourcebook on the environment*, ed. K. A. Hammond, G. Macinko, and W. B. Fairchild, 63–88. Chicago: University of Chicago Press.

————. 1981. *Energy at the surface of the earth: An introduction to the energetics of ecosystems*. New York: Academic Press.

————. 1988. Needed: Climate research stations. *EOS* 69(14):193.

Miller, P. C. 1980. *Carbon balance in northern ecosystems and the potential effect of carbon dioxide–induced climate change*. Washington, D.C.: U.S. Department of Energy.

Milne, A. K. 1986. The use of remote sensing in mapping and monitoring vegetational change associated with bushfire events in eastern Australia. *Geocarto* 1:25–32.

Mintz, Y. 1982. *Influence of the vegetation structure of the atmosphere on the thermal forcing of the atmosphere*. World Meteorological Organization, Publication No. WCP-47. Geneva: WMO.

————. 1984. The sensitivity of numerically simulated climates to land-surface boundary conditions. In *The global climate*, ed. J. T. Houghton, 79–105. London: Cambridge University Press.

Mintz, Y., P. J. Sellers, and C. J. Willmott. 1983. *On the design of an interactive biosphere for the GLAS general circulation model*. Technical Memo 84973. Greenbelt, Md.: NASA.

Mirovoi vodnyi balans i vodnye resursy Zemli. 1974. (*World water balance and water resources of the earth*). Leningrad: Hydrometeoizdat.

Mitchell, C. W. 1981. Soil degradation mapping from Landsat imagery in North Africa and the Middle East. *Proceedings of the Eighth Annual Conference of the Remote Sensing Society*. Reading, U.K.: Remote Sensing Society.

Mitchell, J. K. 1984. Hazard perception studies: Convergent concerns and divergent approaches during the past decade. In *Environmental perception and behavior: An inventory and prospect*, ed. T. F. Saarinen et al., 33–69. Department of Geography Research Paper No. 209, University of Chicago.

————. 1988. Confronting natural disasters. *Environment* 30(3):25–29.

————. 1990. Human dimensions of environmental hazards: Complexity, disparity, and the search for guidance. In *Nothing to fear: An examination of the risks and hazards in American society*, ed. Andrew Kirby. Tucson: University of Arizona Press.

Moiseev, N. N., V. V. Alexandrov, and A. M. Tarko. 1985. *Chelovek i biosfera. Opyt systemnogo analiza i eksperimenty s modelyami* (*Man and biosphere. Systems analysis approach to modeling: Some experience*). Moscow: Nauka.

Morrison, J., ed. 1988. The proposed standard for digital cartographic data. *American Cartographer*, Special Issue 15(1):9–144.

Mounsey, H., and R. Tomlinson, eds. 1988. *Building databases for global science*. International Geographical Union. London: Taylor and Francis.

Munn, R. E., ed. 1980. *Environmental impact assessment*. Scientific Committee on Problems of the Environment, Report 5. Chichester, U.K.: John Wiley and Sons.

Musick, H. B. 1986. Temporal change of Landsat MSS albedo estimates in arid rangeland. *Remote Sensing of the Environment* 20:107–20.

Myagkov, S. M. 1984. Opyt dolgosrochnogo izmeneniya prirody gor k 2005 g (The experience of long-term change of nature in mountains to 2005). In *Inzhenernaya geografiya gornych stran* (*Engineering geography of mountainous areas*), 190–226. Moscow: Moscow University Press.

―――. 1986. Problemy geografii razrushitel'nykh yavleniy v svete zadachi uskoreniya nauchno-tekhnicheskogo progressa (Geography of destructive nature processes). *Vestnik of Moscow State University Press, Series 5, Geography* 1:9–15.

―――. 1989a. *Antarktida: proshloe i budushchee oledeneniya (Antarctica: Past and the future of the freezing process)*. Moscow: Moscow University Press.

―――. 1989b. Neblagopriyatnye i opasnye prirodnye yavleniya v izmenyayushchemsya mire (Nonfavorable and dangerous natural phenomena in the changing world). *Vestnik of Moscow State University Press, Series 5, Geography* 3.

―――. 1990. Geografisheskie problemy sokreshcheniya ushcherba ot stikhiynykh bedstviy (Geographical problems of natural hazards damage reduction). *Vestnik of Moscow State University, Series 5, Geography* 4:3–6.

Myers, N. 1980. *Conversion of tropical moist forest*. Report prepared for the Committee on Research Priorities of the National Research Council. Washington, D.C.: National Academy Press.

―――. 1984. *The primary source: Tropical forests and our future*. New York: W. W. Norton.

―――. 1988. Tropical forests and their species: Going, going . . . ? In *Biodiversity*, ed. E. O. Wilson and F. M. Peter, 28–35. Washington, D.C.: National Academy Press.

Nakano, T., T. Mochizuki, I. Matsuda, and I. Nakabayashi. 1986. Basic studies on earthquake disaster prevention for Tokyo district. *International Seminar on Regional Development Planning for Disaster Prevention: Tokyo Seminar, September 29, 1986*. Nagoya, Japan: UN Centre for Regional Development.

National Center for Atmospheric Research. 1987. PAM in the rainforest. National Center for Atmospheric Research, Staff Notes, July 9.

National Geographic Society. 1988. *Endangered earth*. Map supplement to *National Geographic* 174:910A.

National Research Council. 1983. *Changing climate*. Report of the Carbon Dioxide Assessment Committee. Board on Atmospheric Sciences and Climate. Washington, D.C.: National Academy Press.

―――. 1985. *A strategy for earth science from space in the 1980's and 1990's*. Part II. *Atmosphere and interactions with the solid earth, oceans and biota*. Washington, D.C.: National Academy Press.

―――. 1986. *Global change in the geosphere-biosphere: Initial priorities for an IGBP*. U.S. Committee for IGBP, Commission on Physical Sciences, Mathematics, and Resources, National Research Council. Washington, D.C.: National Academy Press.

―――. 1987a. *Confronting national disasters: An International Decade for Natural Hazard Reduction*. Advisory Committee on the International Decade for Natural Hazard Reduction. Washington, D.C.: National Academy Press.

―――. 1987b. *River and dam management: A review of the Bureau of Reclamation Glen Canyon environmental studies*. Washington, D.C.: National Academy Press.

Neilson, R. P. 1986. High-resolution climatic analysis and southwest biogeography. *Science* 232:27–34.

Nelson, R. 1985. Sensor-induced temporal variability of Landsat MSS data. *Remote Sensing of the Environment* 18:35–48.

————. 1988. *Dryland management: The desertification problem*. Working Paper No. 8. Washington, D.C.: World Bank.

Nelson, R., N. Horning, and T. A. Stone. 1987. Determining the rate of forest conversion in Mato Grosso, Brazil, using Landsat MSS and AVHRR data. *International Journal of Remote Sensing* 8:1767–84.

Nicholson, S. E. 1979. Revised rainfall series for the West African subtropics. *Monthly Weather Review* 107:473–87.

————. 1983. Sub-Saharan rainfall in the years 1976–1980: Evidence of continued drought. *Monthly Weather Review* 111:1646–54.

————. 1985. Sub-Saharan rainfall 1981–1984. *Journal of Climate and Applied Meteorology* 24:1388–91.

————. 1988. Land surface atmosphere interaction: Physical processes and surface changes and their impact. *Progress in Physical Geography* 12:36–65.

Nix, H. A. 1985. Agriculture. In *Climate impact assessment: Studies in the interaction of climate and society*, ed. R. W. Kates, J. Ausubel, and M. Berberian, 105–30. Scientific Committee on Problems of the Environment, Report 27. New York: John Wiley and Sons.

Nortcliff, S. 1987. Developments in soil and land evaluation. *Progress in Physical Geography* 11:283–91.

North, R. M., L. B. Dworsky, and D. J. Allee. 1980. *Unified river basin management*. Proceedings of a Symposium, American Water Resources Association, Gatlinburg, Tenn., May 4–7. American Water Resources Association, TPS 81-83.

Norton, C. C., R. F. Mosher, and B. Hinton. 1979. An investigation of surface albedo variations during the recent Sahel drought. *Journal of Applied Meteorology* 18:1252–62.

Nosseir, M. K. 1983. Construction of a dynamic model of land use/land cover from sequential remote sensing data. *Proceedings of the Seventeenth Symposium on Remote Sensing of the Environment*, 1:629–36. Ann Arbor, Mich.: Environmental Research Institute of Michigan.

Nualchawee, K., L. D. Miller, C. H. Tom, and S. Wacharakitti. 1981. Monitoring forest land cover alteration in Thailand with the analysis of ancillary and digital Landsat data. *Proceedings of the Thirteenth Symposium on Remote Sensing of the Environment*, 3:1163–72. Ann Arbor, Mich.: Environmental Research Institute of Michigan.

Nurmatov, K. M. 1986. Basseinoviy printsip upravleniya protsessami prirodopol'zovaniya (Nature management processes and basin principles). In *Optimizatsiya ispol'zovaniya, okhrany i vosproizvodstva prirodnykh resursov: na primare vozobnovlyaemykh vidov (Optimization of usage, protection, and rehabilitation of natural resources)*, 129–37. Moscow.

Oeschger, H., et al. 1985. Variations of the CO_2 concentration of occluded air and of anions and dust in polar ice cores. In *The carbon cycle and atmospheric CO_2: Natural variations, archean to present*, ed. E. T. Sundquist and W. S. Broecker, 132–42. Geophysical Monograph 32. Washington, D.C.: American Geophysical Union.

Office of the United Nations Disaster Relief Coordinator [UNDRO]. 1979. *Natural disasters and vulnerability analysis*. Report of Expert Group Meeting, 9–12 July 1979. Geneva: UNDRO.

Office of Water Planning and Standards. 1975. *National water quality inventory.* Report to Congress, Washington, D.C.

Offori, C. S., G. M. Higgins, and M. F. Purnell. 1986. Criteria for choice of land suitable for clearing for agricultural production. In *Land clearing and development in the tropics,* ed. R. Lal, P. A. Sanchez, and R. W. Cummings, 19–28. Rotterdam: A. A. Balkema.

Oke, T. R. 1978. *Boundary layer climates .* London: Methuen.

Okolov, V. F., and S. M. Myagkov. 1987. Metodika dolgosrochnogo prognoza klimaticheski obuslovlennykh opasnykh yavleniy (na primere lavin) (Methods of long-term forecasting of dangerous phenomena dependent on climate: An example based on avalanches). In *Otsenka i dolgosrochnyy prognoz izmeneniya prirody gor (Assessment and long-term forecasting of nature change in mountains),* 104–19. Moscow: Moscow University Press.

Oldak, P. G. 1983. *Ravnovesnoe prirodopol'zovanie. Vzglyad ekonomista (Stable nature protection from an economic point of view).* Novosibirsk: Nauka.

O'Loughlin, C. J., and A. J. Pearce, eds. 1984. *Symposium on effects of forest land use on erosion and slope stability.* Honolulu, Hawaii: East-West Center.

Olson, J. S. 1982. Earth's vegetation and atmospheric carbon dioxide. In *Carbon dioxide review, 1982,* ed. W. C. Clark, 388–98. New York: Oxford University Press.

Olson, J. S., and J. A. Watts. 1982. Map of major world ecosystem complexes. In *Carbon dioxide review, 1982,* ed. W. C. Clark, map insert. New York: Oxford University Press.

Olson, P. E. 1986. A 40-million-year lake record of early Mesozoic orbital climatic forcing. *Science* 234:842–48.

Olsson, L. 1983. Desertification or climate? *Lund Studies in Geography, Series A:60* (Gleerup, Sweden).

———. 1985. An integrated study of desertification. *Meddelanden fran Lunds Universitets Geografiska Institution Avhandlingar,* No. 98. Lund, Sweden.

Opasnye prirodnye yavleniya. 1982. *(Dangerous natural phenomena).* Moscow: VINITI.

Opsdam, P., G. Rijsdijk, and F. Hastings. 1985. Bird communities in small woods in an agricultural landscape: Effects of area and isolation. *Biological Conservation* 34:333–52.

O'Riordan, T. 1986. Coping with environmental hazards. In *Geography, resources and environment,* ed. R. W. Kates and I. Burton, 2:272–309. Chicago: University of Chicago Press.

———. 1988. The earth as transformed by human action: An international symposium. *Environment* 30(1):25–28.

Osborne, F. 1953. *The limits of the earth.* Boston: Little, Brown.

Otterman, J. 1974. Baring high albedo soils by overgrazing: A hypothesized desertification mechanism. *Science* 186:531–33.

———. 1975. Reply to R. D. Jackson and S. B. Idso, "Surface albedo and desertification." *Science* 189:1013–15.

———. 1977. Anthropogenic impact on the albedo of the earth. *Climatic Change* 1:137–57.

———. 1981. Satellite and field studies of man's impact on the surface in arid regions. *Tellus* 33:68–77.

Otterman, J., and R. S. Fraser. 1976. Earth-atmosphere system and surface reflectivities in arid regions from Landsat MSS data. *Remote Sensing of the Environment* 5:247–66.

Otterman, J., and C. J. Tucker. 1985. Satellite measurements of surface albedo and temperatures in semi-desert. *Journal of Climate and Applied Meteorology* 24:228–34.

Outcalt, S. I. 1972. The development and application of a simple digital surface climate simulator. *Journal of Applied Meteorology* 11:629–36.

Palm, R. I. 1990. *Natural hazards: An integrative framework for research and planning*. Baltimore: Johns Hopkins University Press.

Pankhurst, A. 1984. Vulnerable groups. *Disasters* 8(3):206–13.

Parmenter, C., and D. W. Folger. 1974. Eolian biogenic detritus in deep sea sediments: A possible index of equatorial ice age aridity. *Science* 184:695–97.

Parry, M. L. 1986. Some implications of climate change for human development. In *Sustainable development of the biosphere*, ed. W. C. Clark and R. E. Munn, 378–406. Cambridge: Cambridge University Press.

Parry, M. L., T. R. Carter, and N. T. Konijn, eds. 1988. *The impact of climate variations on agriculture*. 2 vols. Dordrecht: Kluwar Academic Publishers.

Pease, R. W., J. E. Lewis, and S. I. Outcalt. 1976. Urban terrain climatology and remote sensing. *Annals of the Association of American Geographers* 66:1367.

Pease, S. R., and R. W. Pease. 1972. *Photographic films as remote sensors for measuring albedos of terrestrial surfaces*. Technical Report, U.S. Geological Survey Contract 14-08-0001-11914. Riverside, Calif.: U.S. Geological Survey.

Peltier, L. C. 1950. The geographical cycle in periglacial regions as it is related to climatic geomorphology. *Annals of the Association of American Geographers* 40:214–36.

Pereira, H. C. 1973. *Land use and water resources in temperate and tropical climates*. Cambridge: Cambridge University Press.

Perel'man, A. I. 1972. Geochimiya noosfery (Geochemistry of the noosphere). *Nature* (Moscow) 1:20–26.

———. 1975. *Geochimiya landshaftov (Geochemistry of landscapes)*. Moscow: High School Publishers.

Persson, R. 1974. *World forest resources: Review of the world's forests in the early 1970's*. Research Notes No. 17. Stockholm, Sweden: Royal College of Forestry, Department of Forest Survey.

Petak, W. J., and A. A. Atkisson. 1982. *Natural hazard assessment and public policy: Anticipating the unexpected*. New York: Springer Verlag.

Peuquet, D. J. 1983. A hybrid structure for the storage and manipulation of very large spatial data sets. *Computer Vision, Graphics and Image Processing* 24:14.

———. 1988. Cartographic inputs to global database. In *Building databases for global science*, ed. H. Mounsey and R. Tomlinson, 66–78. International Geographical Union. London: Taylor and Francis.

Pielou, E. C. 1988. Slow change in large areas: Where biogeography takes over from ecology. *Canadian Geographer* 32:46–50.

Pla, L. E. 1980. Desertification-generating hypotheses from aerial photographs. *Proceedings of the Fourteenth Congress of the International Society of Photogrammetry*, Hamburg, FRG, 772–82.

Ponce, S. L., ed. 1983. The potential for water yield augmentation through forest and range management. *Water Resources Bulletin* 19:351–419.

Popov, B. A., B. N. Novikov, and V. A. Sovershaev. 1987. Terroabraziya—razrushitel'nyy protsess v beregovoy zone arkticheskikh morey (Earth abrasion—an erosive process in the coastal zone of Arctic seas). In *Opasnye prirodnye yavleniya (Dangerous natural phenomena)*, 88–99. Moscow: VINITI.

Porter, S. C., ed. 1983. *Late-Quaternary environments of the United States.* Vol. 1: *The late Pleistocene*. Minneapolis: University of Minnesota Press.

Posey, J. W., and P. F. Clapp. 1964. Global distribution of normal surface albedo. *Geofisica International* 4:33–48.

Post, W. M., W. R. Emanuel, P. J. Zinke, and A. G. Stangenberger. 1982. Soil carbon pools and world life zones. *Nature* (London) 298:156–59.

Potter, G. L., H. W. Ellaesser, M. C. MacCracken, and F. M. Luther. 1975. Possible climatic impact of tropical deforestation. *Nature* (London) 258:697–98.

Preobrajensky, V. S., and V. Vorachek, eds. 1985. *Otsenka vliyaniya khozyaistva na prirodu. Vozdeystvie—izmeneniya—posledstviya (Assessment of industry's impact on nature. Impact—changes—consequences).* 2 vols. Brno.

Privalovskaya, G. A. 1985. Utilization of natural resources and territorial division of labor at the present stage of the USSR's socioeconomic development. In *Regionalization for planning in the USSR: Concepts, methods and practice*, 54–72. Nagoya, Japan: UN Centre for Regional Development.

Privalovskaya, G. A., and T. G. Runova. 1980. *Territorial'naya organizatsiya promyshlennosti i prirodnye resursy SSSR (Spatial organization of industry and natural resources in the USSR).* Moscow: Nauka.

Prospero, J. M., and T. N. Carlson. 1972. Vertical and aerial distribution of Saharan dust over the western equatorial North Atlantic ocean. *Journal of Geophysical Research* 77:2255–2565.

Prospero, J. M., and R. T. Nees. 1977. Dust concentration in the atmosphere of the equatorial North Atlantic: Possible relationship to the Sahelian drought. *Science* 196:1196–98.

Puzachenko, Yu. G. 1986. Ptostranstvenno-vremennaya i erarkhiya geosystemy s pozitsiy teorii kolebaniy (Time-space hierarchy of a geosystem in relation to a theory of fluctuations). In *Questions of geography* 127:96–111. Moscow: Mysl'

———, ed. 1989. *Ekosistemy v kriticheskikh sostoyaniyakh (Ecosystems in critical stages).* Moscow: Nauka.

Raich, J. W. 1983. Effects of forest conversion on the carbon budget of a tropical soil. *Biotropica* 15:177–84.

Rakita, S. A. 1975. Inzhenerno-geograficheskoe rayonirovanie i kolichestvennaya otsenka vliyaniya prirodnykh usloviy na proizvodstvo (Engineering-geographical regionalization and quantity evaluation of the impact of natural conditions on industrial production). *Voprosy geografii* (Moscow) 89:75–90.

———. 1983. Vzaimodejstvie prirody i khozyajstva v krupnykh regionakh severa: metodika i resul'taty geograficheskogo izucheniya (Nature and economic interaction in large regions of the north: Methods and results of geographical study). In *Priroda i khozyaistvennoe osvoenie Severa (Nature and industrial development of the north).* Moscow: Moscow State University Press.

————. 1987. In *Sistemno-konstruktivnoe izuchenie prirodnikh usloviy i resursov (Systems approach to the study of natural conditions and resources)*, 112–36. Moscow: Moscow State University Press.

Rapp, A. 1986. Introduction to soil degradation processes in drylands. *Climatic Change* 9:19–31.

Rapp, A., L. Berry, and P. H. Temple, eds. 1972. Studies of erosion and sedimentation in Tanzania. *Geografiska Annaler* 54A(3–4).

Rapp, A., and U. Hellden. 1979. Research on environmental monitoring methods of land-use planning in African drylands. *Lunds Universitets Naturgeografiska Institution Rapporter och Notiser*, No. 42. Department of Physical Geography, University of Lund, Sweden.

Rasool, S. I., ed. 1987. Potential of remote sensing for the study of global change. *Advances in Space Research* 7:1–90.

Rauner, Yu. L. 1972. *Teplovoi balans rastitel'nogo pokrova (Heat balance of vegetation)*. Leningrad: Gidrometeoizdat.

Raven, P. H. 1988. On diminishing tropical forests. In *Biodiversity*, ed. E. O. Wilson and F. M. Peter, 119–22. Washington, D.C.: National Academy Press.

Reining, P. 1978. *Handbook on desertification indicators based on the Sciences Associations' Nairobi Seminar on Desertification*. Washington, D.C.: American Association for the Advancement of Science.

Richards, J. A. 1984. Thematic mapping from multi-temporal image data using principal components transformation. *Remote Sensing of the Environment* 16:35–46.

Richards, J. F., and R. P. Tucker, eds. 1985. *World deforestation in the twentieth century*. Durham, N.C.: Duke University Press.

Riebsame, W. E., and L. Dillard. 1987. The nature of climate perception. Natural Hazards Center, University of Colorado, Boulder (unpublished manuscript).

Risser, P. G. 1986. *Report of workshop on Spatial and Temporal Variability of Biospheric and Geospheric Processes: Research needed to determine interactions with global environmental change*. Paris: International Council of Scientific Unions Press.

Robinove, C. J., P. S. Chavez, D. Gehring, and R. Holmgren. 1981. Arid land monitoring using Landsat albedo difference images. *Remote Sensing of the Environment* 11:133–56.

Robinson, A. R. 1979. Sediment yield as a function of upstream erosion. In *Universal soil loss equation: Past, present and future*, ed. A. E. Peterson and J. B. Swan, 7–16. Special Publication No. 8. Madison, Wisc.: American Society of Agronomy.

Robinson, D. A., and G. Kukla. 1984. Albedo of a dissipating cover. *Journal of Climate and Applied Meteorology* 23:1626–34.

————. 1985. Maximum estimated surface albedo of seasonally snow-covered lands in the Northern Hemisphere. *Journal of Climate and Applied Meteorology* 24:402–11.

Robinson, J. 1985. Global modeling and simulations. In *Climate impact assessment: Studies in the interaction of climate and society*, ed. R. W. Kates, J. H. Ausubel, and M. Berberian, 469–92. Scientific Committee on Problems of the Environment, Report 27. New York: John Wiley and Sons.

Rockwood, A. A., and S. K. Cox. 1978. Satellite-inferred surface albedo over northwestern Africa. *Journal of Atmospheric Sciences* 35:513.

Rodoman, B. B. 1974. Polyaizatsiya landshafta kak sredstvo sokhraneniya biosfery i rekreatsionnykh resursov (Polarization of the landscape as a means for preserving biosphere and recreation resources). In *Resursy, sreda, rasselenie (Resources, environment, settlement)*, 150–63. Moscow.

Romankevich, E. A. 1977. *Geochimiya organicheskogo veshchestva v okeane (Geochemistry of organic matter in the ocean)*. Moscow: Nauka.

Romanovsky, N. N. 1977. *Ice wedge polygon formation* [in Russian]. Novosibirsk: Nauka.

Rosensweig, C. 1985. Potential CO_2-induced climate effects on North American wheat-producing regions. *Climatic Change* 7:367–89.

Rosensweig, C., and R. E. Dickinson. 1986. *Climate-vegetation interactions*. Office of Interdisciplinary Earth Studies, Report OIES-2. Boulder, Colo.: University Corporation for Atmosphere Research.

Ross, Yu. K., ed. 1986. *Aerokosmicheskie metody issledovaniya sel'skokhozyaystvennykh ugodii (Aerospace methods for study of agricultural lands)*. Leningrad: Gidrometeoizdat.

Rosswall, T., R. G. Woodmansee, and P. G. Risser, eds. 1988. *Scales and global change*. Scientific Committee on Problems of the Environment, Report 35. New York: John Wiley and Sons.

Ross-Wight, J., and F. H. Siddoway. 1982. Determinants of soil loss tolerance for rangelands. In *Determinants of soil loss tolerance*, ed. B. L. Schmidt, R. R. Allmaras, J. V. Mannering, and R. I. Papendick, 67–74. Special Publication No. 45. Madison, Wisc.: American Society of Agronomy.

Rotty, R. 1986. Estimates of CO_2 from wood fuel based on forest harvest data. *Climatic Change* 9:311–25.

Rouse, W. R., and R. L. Bello. 1983. The radiation balance of typical terrain units in the low Arctic. *Annals of the Association of American Geographers* 73:538–49.

Rovinsky, F. Ya. 1986. Kompleksny global'ny monitoring sostoyaniya biosfery (Complex global monitoring of the biosphere). *Meteorologiya i gidrologiya* 6:108–14.

Rowe, C. M. 1988. Modeling land-surface albedos from plant canopy structure. Ph.D. dissertation, University of Delaware.

Rowntree, P. R., and P. B. Vose. 1983. Simulation of the atmospheric response to soil moisture anomalies over Europe. *Quarterly Journal of the Royal Meteorological Society* 109:501–26.

Rozanov, B. G. 1984. Aridizatsiya sushi i antropogennoe opustynivanie (Land aridization and anthropogenic desertification). *Soil Science* (Moscow) 12.

Rozhkov, A. G. 1981. *Bor'ba s ovragami (The struggle against ravines)*. Moscow: Kolos.

Ruddiman, W. F., and H. E. Wright, Jr., eds. 1987. *North America and adjacent oceans during the last glaciation*. Geology of North America, K-3. Boulder, Colo.: Geological Society of America.

Runova, T. G. 1985a. Ecological regionalization for spatial planning: Present and future tasks. In *Regionalization for planning in the USSR: Concepts, methods and practice*, 96–112. Nagoya, Japan: UN Centre for Regional Development.

———. 1985b. Ratsional'noe prirodopol'zovaniye kak obyekt ekonomiko-geograficheskogo izucheniya (Rational environmental management as an object of economic-geographical studies). *Izvestiya USSR Academy of Sciences, Series Geography* 8:46–59.

————. 1987. Territorial'naya organizatsiya prirodopol'zovaniya kak geografiches-kaya problema (Spatial organization of environmental management as a geo-graphical problem). *Izvestiya USSR Academy of Sciences, Series Geography* 5:15–23.

Ruttenberg, S. 1983. Draft workshop report on the International Satellite Land-Surface Climatology Project (ISLSCP). IAMAP and COSPAR. UCAR/NCAR, Boulder, Colo.

Ryabchikov, A. M. 1972. *Structure and dynamics of the biosphere*. Moscow: Mysl'.

————, ed. 1980. *Krugovorot veshchestva v prirode i ego izmenenie khozyaistvennoi deyatel'nost'yu cheloveka* (*The cycle of matter in nature and its change by economic activity*). Moscow: Moscow University Press.

————. 1983. Problems of natural land conservation (global scale). *Vestnik of Moscow State University, Series Geography* 2:3–13.

Saarinen, T. F., et al., eds. 1984. Environmental perception and behavior: An inventory and prospect. Department of Geography Research Paper No. 209, University of Chicago.

Saf'yanov, G. A. 1978. *Reregovaya zona okeana v XX veke* (*The ocean coastline in the year 2000*). Moscow: Mysl'.

Sagan, C., O. B. Toon, and J. B. Pollack. 1979. Anthropogenic albedo changes and the earth's climate. *Science* 206:1363–68.

Sagdeev, R. Z., ed. 1981. *Mnogozonal'nye aerokosmicheskie s'yomki zemli* (*Multizonal aerospace survey of the earth*). Moscow: Nauka.

Saker, N. J. 1975. An 11-layer general circulation model. In *Report of Meteorological Office 20*. Technical Note II/30. Bracknell, U.K.: U.K. Meteorological Office.

Salati, E., and P. B. Vose. 1983. Depletion of tropical rain forests. *Ambio* 12:67–71.

————. 1984. Amazon basin: A system in equilibrium. *Science* 225:129–38.

Sanchez, P. A. 1976. *Properties and management of soils in the tropics*. New York: John Wiley and Sons.

————. 1982. Amazon basin soils: Management for continuous crop production. *Science* 216:821–27.

Sanchez, P. A., and J. R. Benites. 1987. Low-input cropping for acid soils of the humid tropics. *Science* 238:1521–27.

Sanchez, P. A., W. Couto, and S. W. Buol. 1982. The fertility capability classification system: Interpretation, applicability and modification. *Geoderma* 27:283–309.

Sapunov, V. N. 1985. Vodosnezhnye potoki i ikh mesto v ryadu skhodnykh razrushi-tel'nykh yavleniy (Snowmelt water flows rank with similar destructive phenom-ena). *Vestnik of Moscow State University, Series 5, Geography* (Moscow) 6:31–36.

Sauer, C. O. 1925. The morphology of landscape. *University of California Publications in Geography* 2(2):19–54.

Schantz, H. L., and B. L. Turner. 1958. *Photographic documentation of vegetational changes in Africa over a third of a century*. College of Agriculture Report 169. University of Arizona, Tucson.

Scharfen, G., R. G. Barry, D. A. Robinson, G. Kukla, and M. C. Serreze. 1987. Large-scale patterns of snow melt on Arctic Sea ice mapped from meteorological satellite imagery. *Annals of Glaciology* 9:200–205.

Schiffer, R. A., and W. B. Rossow. 1983. The International Satellite Cloud Climatol-ogy Project (ISCCP), the first project of the World Climate Research Programme'. *Bulletin of the American Meteorological Society* 64:779–84.

Schlesinger, M. E., and W. L. Gates. 1979. Performance of the Oregon State University two-level atmospheric general circulation model. In *Report of the JOC study conference on climate models*. GARP Publication Series 22, 1:139–206. Geneva: World Meteorological Organization.

Schlesinger, M. E., and J.F.B. Mitchell. 1985. Model projection of the equilibrium climatic response to increased carbon dioxide. In *Projecting the climate effects of increasing carbon dioxide*, ed. M. C. MacCracken and F. M. Luther. Washington, D.C.: U.S. Department of Energy, DOE/ER-0237.

Schlesinger, W. H. 1977. Carbon balance in terrestrial detritus. *Annual Review of Ecology and Systematics* 8:51–81.

Schmugge, T. J., and P. J. Sellers. 1986. The First International Satellite Land Surface Climatology Project (ISLSCP) Field Experiment—FIFE. In *Proceedings of an ISLSCP Conference*, 567–71. Rome, Italy, 2–6 December 1985. ESA SP-248.

Schmugge, T. J., P. J. Sellers, and R. J. Gurney. 1985. First International Satellite Land Surface Climatology field experiment. *Proceedings of the Nineteenth Symposium on Remote Sensing of the Environment*, Ann Arbor, Mich.

Schneider, S. H. 1986. A goddess of the earth? The debate on the Gaia hypothesis—An editorial. *Climatic Change* 8:1–4.

———. 1987. An international program on "Global Change": Can it endure?—An editorial. *Climatic Change* 10(3):211–18.

Schneider, S. R., D. F. McGinnis, Jr., and G. Stephens. 1985. Monitoring Africa's Lake Chad basin with Landsat and NOAA satellite data. *International Journal of Remote Sensing* 6:59–73.

Schumm, S. A., and M. D. Harvey. 1982. Natural erosion in the USA. In *Determinants of soil loss tolerance*, ed. B. L. Schmidt, R. R. Allmaras, J. V. Mannering, and R. I. Papendick, 15–22. Special Publication No. 45. Madison, Wisc.: American Society of Agronomy.

Scientific Committee on Problems of Environment. 1975. *Nitrogen, phosphorus and sulphur: Global cycle*. Report 7. Chichester, U.K.: John Wiley and Sons.

———. 1979. *Global carbon cycle*. Report 13. Chichester, U.K.: John Wiley and Sons.

Sdasyuk, G. V. 1987. *Regional imperatives in utilization and management of resources. India and USSR*. New Delhi: Concept Publishing House.

———. 1988a. Ot spetsializatsii po predmetam k spetsializatsii po problemam (From subject specialization to problem specialization). *Izvestiya USSR Academy of Sciences* 5:54.

———. 1988b. Pereosmyslit' traditsionnye kontseptsii, razrabotat' novye podkhody (Reexamination of traditional concepts and development of new approaches). *Izvestiya USSR Academy of Sciences* 6:81–82.

———. 1988c. Problemy otstalosti: peremeshchenie tsentratyajesti global'nykh problem v razvivayushchiesya strany (Problems of underdevelopment: A shift of global problems to developing countries). In *Global'nye problemy sovremennosti i kompleksnoe zemlevedenie (Global problems and complex earth's study)*, 87–94. Leningrad: Geographical Society, USSR Academy of Sciences.

Seiler, W., and P. J. Crutzen. 1980. Estimates of gross and net fluxes of carbon between the biosphere and atmosphere. *Climatic Change* 2:207–47.

Sellers, P. J., Y. Mintz, Y. C. Sud, and A. Dalcher. 1986. A simple biosphere (SiB) model for use within general circulation models. *Journal of Atmospheric Sciences* 43(6):505–31.

Sevruk, B., ed. 1986. *Correction of precipitation measurements*. ETH/IAHS/WMO Workshop on the Correction of Precipitation Measurements. Zurich: ETH Geographisches Institut.

Shackleton, N. J., R. G. West, and D. Q. Bowen, eds. 1988. *The past three million years: Evolution of climatic variability in the North Atlantic region*. London: Royal Society.

Sher, A. V. 1976. *Significance of the Beringian land bridge for formation of the Holarctic mammal fauna in the Cenozoic* [in Russian]. Valdivostok: Far East Scientific Center Press, 227–41.

Shiklomanov, I. A., and O. L. Markova. 1987. *Problemy vodoobespecheniya i perebroski rechnogo stoka v mire* (*Problems of water maintenance and river water transfer in the world*). Leningrad: Gidrometeoizdat.

Shugart, H. H. 1984. *A theory of forest dynamics*. New York: Springer Verlag.

Shugart, H. H., et al. 1986. CO_2, climate change and forest ecosystems. In *The greenhouse effect, climatic change, and ecosystems*, ed. B. Bolin et al., 475–521. New York: John Wiley and Sons.

Shukla, J., and Y. Mintz. 1982. Influence of land-surface evapotranspiration on the earth's climate. *Science* 215:1498–1501.

Simberloff, D. 1986. Are we on the verge of a mass extinction in tropical rain forests? In *Dynamics of extinction*, ed. D. K. Elliott, 165–80. New York: John Wiley and Sons.

Simonett, D. S. 1988. Considerations on integrating remote sensing and geographic information systems. In *Building databases for global science*, ed. H. Mounsey and R. Tomlinson, 105–28. International Geographical Union. London: Taylor and Francis.

Sioli, H. 1985. The effects of deforestation in Amazonia. *Geographical Journal* 151: 197–203.

Skidmore, E. L. 1982. Soil loss tolerance. In *Determinants of soil loss tolerance*, ed. B. L. Schmidt, R. R. Allmaras, J. V. Mannering, and R. I. Papendick, 87–93. Special Publication No. 45. Madison, Wisc.: American Society of Agronomy.

———. 1986. Wind erosion control. *Climatic Change* 9:209–18.

Skutsch, M. 1982. *Why people don't plant trees: The socioeconomic impact of existing woodfuel programs. Village case studies, Tanzania*. Discussion Paper D-73P. Washington, D.C.: Resources for the Future.

Smith, N.J.H. 1981. Colonization lessons from a tropical forest. *Science* 214:755–61.

Smith, T. R., S. Menon, J. L. Star, and J. E. Estes. 1987. Requirements and principles for the implementation and construction of large-scale geographic information systems. *International Journal of Geographical Information Systems* 1(1):13–31.

Sokolov, M. S., and M. A. Glazovskaya. 1979. Compiling methods for land reclamation schematic maps showing application areas and detoxication conditions of pesticides [in Russian]. In *Methods and problems of ecotoxicological modelling and prediction*, 22–30. Pushchino.

Sokolov, V. E., and Yu. G. Puzachenko. 1986. In Kompleksnyi global'nyi monitoring sostoyaniya biosfery (Complex global monitoring of the biosphere). *Proceedings of Third International Symposium*, Leningrad, 2:20–26.

Solntsev, V. N. 1981. *Sistemnaya organizatsiya landshaftov* (*Organization of landscape systems*). Moscow: Mysl'.

Solomon, A. M., J. R. Trabalka, D. E. Reichle, and L. D. Voorhees. 1985. The global cycle of carbon. In *Atmospheric carbon dioxide and the global carbon cycle*, ed. J. Trabalka, 1–13. Washington, D.C.: U.S. Department of Energy, DOE/ER-0239.

Sommer, A. 1976. Attempt at assessment of the world's tropical moist forests. *Unasylva* 28:112–13.

Soulé, M. E. 1986. *Conservation biology. The science of scarcity and diversity.* Sunderland, Mass.: Sinauer Associates.

Sovershaev, V. A. 1987. Rol' shtormovykh nagonov redkoy povtoryaemosti v dinamike morskikh beregov (The role of storm waves of rare recurrence in the dynamics of sea coasts). In *Prirodnye osnovy beregozashchity* (*Natural foundation of coastal protection*), 131–38. Moscow: Nauka.

Spangler, W.M.L., and R. L. Jenne. 1984. *Reference manual: World monthly surface station climatology.* Boulder, Colo.: National Center for Atmospheric Research.

Spaulding, W. G., and L. J. Graumlich. 1986. The last pluvial climatic episodes in the deserts of southwestern North America. *Nature* (London) 320:441–44.

Spooner, B., and H. S. Mann. 1982. *Desertification and development: Dryland ecology in a social perspective.* London: Academic Press.

Stebbing, E. P. 1935. The encroaching Sahara. *Geographical Journal* 86:509–10.

Steinhauser, F. (Technical Supervisor). 1979. *Climatic atlas of North and Central America.* Vol. I: *Maps of mean temperature and precipitation.* Geneva: WMO (also UNESCO and Cartographia).

Stenchikov, G. L. 1985. Climatic consequences of nuclear war: CCAS model. In *Climatic and biological consequences of a nuclear war*, 53–82. Moscow: Mir.

Stonehouse, B., ed. 1986. *Arctic air pollution.* Cambridge: Cambridge University Press.

Stow, D. A., L. R. Tinney, and J. E. Estes. 1980. Deriving land use/land cover change statistics from Landsat: A study of prime agricultural land. *Proceedings of the Fourteenth Symposium on Remote Sensing of the Environment*, 2:1227–37. Ann Arbor, Mich.: Environmental Research Institute of Michigan.

Strahler, A. H., C. E. Woodcock, and J. A. Smith. 1986. On the nature of models in remote sensing. *Remote Sensing of the Environment* 21:311–32.

Strahler, A. N., and A. H. Strahler. 1987. *Modern physical geography.* 3d ed. New York: John Wiley and Sons.

Street-Perrott, F. A., and S. P. Harrison. 1985. Temporal variations in lake levels since 30,000 yr B.P.—An index of the global hydrological cycle. In *Climate processes and climate sensitivity*, ed. J. E. Hansen and T. Takahashi, 118–29. Geophysical Monographs 29. Washington, D.C.: American Geophysical Union.

Sud, Y. C., and M. Fennessy. 1982. A study of the influence of surface albedo on July circulation in semi-arid regions. *Journal of Climatology* 2:105–25.

Sukhikh, V. I., and S. T. Sinitsin, eds. 1979. *Aerokosmicheskie metody v okhrane prirody i v lesnom khozyaystve* (*Aerospace methods in environmental protection and the forest industry*). Moscow: Lesnaya Promyshlennost'.

Susman, P., P. O'Keefe, and B. Wisner. 1983. Global disasters, a radical interpretation. In *Interpretations of calamity*, ed. K. Hewitt, 263–83. Boston: Allen and Unwin.

Swain, P. H., and S. M. Davis. 1978. *Remote sensing: The quantitative approach.* New York: McGraw-Hill.

Switzer, P., and S. E. Ingebritsen. 1986. Ordering of time-difference data from multi-spectral imagery. *Remote Sensing of the Environment* 20:85–94.

Tarasova, G. A., and E. M. Fejgel'son. 1982. Vliyanie troposfernogo aerozolya na integral'nye al'bedo sistemy atmosfera podstilayushchaya poverkhnost' (Tropospheric aerosol impact on the albedo of the atmosphere-earth surface system). *Izvestiya USSR Academy of Sciences, Series Physics of Atmosphere and Ocean* 11:1199–1206.

Terjung, W. H. 1976. Climatology for geographers. *Annals of the Association of American Geographers* 66:199–222.

Terwindt, J.H.J. 1983. Prediction of earthquake damage in the Toyko Bay area—A literature survey. *GeoJournal* 7(3):215–27.

Thomas, W. L., Jr., ed. 1956. *Man's role in changing the face of the earth.* Chicago: University of Chicago Press.

Thompson, L. G., et al. 1984. Tropical glaciers: Potential for ice core paleoclimatic reconstructions. *Journal of Geophysical Research* 89(D3):4638–46.

Thornthwaite, C. W. 1954. Topoclimatology. *Proceedings of the Toronto Meteorological Conference, 1953,* 227–32. London: Royal Meteorological Society.

Thornthwaite, C. W., and B. Holzman. 1939. The determination of evaporation from land and water surfaces. *Monthly Weather Review* 67:4–11.

Timmerman, P. 1986. Mythology and surprise in the sustainable development of the biosphere. In *Sustainable development of the biosphere,* ed. W. C. Clark and R. E. Munn, 435–53. Cambridge: Cambridge University Press.

Tobler, W. R. 1988. Resolution, resampling and all that. In *Building databases for global science,* ed. H. Mounsey and R. Tomlinson, 129–37. International Geographical Union. London: Taylor and Francis.

Todd, W. J. 1977. Urban and regional land use change detected using Landsat data. *Research Journal, U.S. Geological Survey* 5:529–34.

Todd, W. J., P. Mausel, and M. F. Baumgardner. 1973. An analysis of Milwaukee County land use from ERTS data. *LARS Information Note* 022773. West Lafayette, Ind.: Laboratory of Applied Remote Sensing, Purdue University.

Tolba, M. K. 1984. For all people, by all people's efforts . . . *Energy: Economics, Technology, Environment.* Moscow: Nauka, 12:2–5.

Tomlinson, R. F., ed. 1972. *Geographical data handling.* Ottawa: IGU Commission on Geographical Data Sensing and Processing.

Tooley, M. J., and I. Shennan, eds. 1987. *Sea-level changes.* Oxford: Basil Blackwell.

Trabalka, J., ed. 1985. *Atmospheric carbon dioxide and the global carbon cycle.* Washington, D.C.: U.S. Department of Energy, DOE/ER-0239.

Treshnikov, A. F., and K. Ya. Kondrat'yev. 1985. Klyuchevye problemy issledovaniy geograficheskoy sredy (Main problems in geographical environmental study). *Izvestiya USSR Geographical Society* 2:89–96.

Trimble, S. W. 1981. Changes in sediment storage in the Coon Creek basin, driftless area, Wisconsin. *Science* 214:181–83.

Troll, C. 1944. Strukturboden, Solifluktion, Frostklimat der Erde. *Geologische Rundschau* 34:545–695. (Trans. *U.S. Army Snow, Ice, Permafrost Research Establishment Transactions* 43 [1958].)

————. 1968. Landschaftsokolgie. In *Pflanzensoziologie und Landschaftsokologie*, ed. R. Tuxen, 1–21. The Hague: Junk (quoted in R.T.T. Forman and M. Godron, *Landscape ecology* [1986]).

Tucker, C. J. 1979. Red and photographic infrared linear combinations for monitoring vegetation. *Remote Sensing of the Environment* 8:127–50.

Tucker, C. J., I. Y. Fung, C. D. Keeling, and R. H. Gammon. 1986. Relationship between atmospheric CO_2 variations and a satellite-derived vegetation. *Nature* (London) 319:169–74.

Tucker, C. J., B. N. Holben, and E. Goff. 1984. Intensive forest clearing in Rondonia, Brazil, as detected by satellite remote sensing. *Remote Sensing of the Environment* 15:255–61.

Tucker, C. J., and C. O. Justice. 1986. Satellite remote sensing of desert spatial extent. *Desertification Control Bulletin* 13:2–5.

Tucker, C. J., and L. D. Miller. 1977. Soil spectra contributions to grass canopy spectral reflectance. *Photogrammetric Engineering and Remote Sensing* 43(6): 721–26.

Tucker, C. J., J. R. G. Townshend, and T. E. Goff. 1985a. African land-cover classification using satellite data. *Science* 227:369–75.

Tucker, C. J., C. L. Vanpraet, M. J. Shearman, and G. Van Ittersum. 1985b. Satellite remote sensing of the total biomass production in the Senegalese Sahel: 1980–1984. *Remote Sensing of the Environment* 17:233–49.

Tucker, R. P., and J. F. Richards, eds. 1983. *Global deforestation in the nineteenth-century world economy*. Durham, N.C.: Duke University Press.

Tushinsky, G. K., ed. 1970. *Lavinoopasnye rajony Sovetskogo Soyuza (Areas of the USSR subject to avalanche hazard)*. Moscow: Moscow University Press.

————, ed. 1971. *Inzhenernaya glyatsiologiya (Engineering glaciology)*. Moscow: Moscow University Press.

UNESCO. 1978. *World water balance and water resources of the earth*. UNESCO Series Studies and Reports in Hydrology, No. 25. Leningrad.

United Nations Conference on Desertification. 1977a. *Desertification, its causes and consequences*. Compiled and edited by the Secretariat of the UN Conference on Desertification. New York: Pergamon Press.

————. 1977b. Plan of action to combat desertification. Document A/Conference 74/36. UN Environment Program, Nairobi, Kenya.

————. 1977c. World map of desertification. UN Conference on Desertification Document A/Conference 74/2. UN Environment Program, Nairobi, Kenya.

United Nations Environment Program. 1982. *The world environment, 1972–1982*. Dublin: Tycooly International.

————. 1987. *The greenhouse gases*. Nairobi: UNEP/GEMS Environment Library No. 1.

United Nations Food and Agriculture Organization. 1962. *Forest influences: An introduction to ecological forestry*. UNFAO Forestry Series No. 9. Rome: UNFAO.

————. 1966–1989. *Production yearbooks 1966–1988*. Rome: UNFAO.

————. 1979. *A provisional methodology for soil degradation assessment*. Rome: UNFAO.

————. 1981. *Map of fuelwood scarcity in developing countries*. Rome: UNFAO.

United Nations Food and Agriculture Organization and UNEP. 1982a. Projecto de evaluacion de los recursos forestales tropicales (en el marco de SIMUVIMA)—los recursos forestales de la America tropical. Primera parte: Sintesis regional. Prepared by J. P. Lanly. Rome: Food and Agriculture Organization.

———. 1982b. Tropical forest resources assessment (in the framework of GEMS)—forest resources of tropical Asia. Part I: Regional synthesis. Prepared by J. P. Lanly and Y. S. Rao. Rome: Food and Agriculture Organization.

———. 1986. Tropical forest resources assessment project (in the framework of GEMS)—forest resources of tropical Africa. Part I: Regional synthesis. Prepared by J. P. Lanly and Y. S. Rao. Rome: Food and Agriculture Organization.

United Nations Food and Agriculture Organization, UNEP, and UNESCO. 1980. *Provisional map of present degradation rates and present state of soil*. Rome: UNFAO.

United Nations Food and Agriculture Organization and UNESCO. 1974. *Soil map of the world, 1:5,000,000*. Paris: UNFAO.

U.S. Council on Environmental Quality. 1985. *Environmental quality 1984: The fifteenth annual report of the Council on Environmental Quality*. Washington, D.C.: U.S. Government Printing Office.

U.S. Department of Agriculture. 1938. *Soils and man*. USDA Yearbook of Agriculture. Washington, D.C.: U.S. Government Printing Office.

U.S. Department of Agriculture, Soil Conservation Service. 1981. Soil, water, and related resources in the United States: Status, condition and trends. *1980 RCA Appraisal. Part 1*. Washington, D.C.: U.S. Government Printing Office.

U.S. Department of Commerce. 1973a. *A study of earthquake losses in the Los Angeles, California, area*. Washington, D.C.: National Oceanic and Atmospheric Administration.

———. 1973b. *A study of earthquake losses in the San Francisco Bay area*. Washington, D.C.: National Oceanic and Atmospheric Administration.

U.S. Water Resources Council. 1978. *The nation's water resources 1975–2000*. Vol. 1: *Summary. Second National Water Assessment*. Washington, D.C.: U.S. Government Printing Office.

Unninayer, S. 1988. The global system, observing and monitoring change, data problems, data management and databases. In *Building databases for global science*, ed. H. Mounsey and R. Tomlinson, 357–77. International Geographical Union. London: Taylor and Francis.

Ushakov, S. A., and N. A. Yasamanov. 1984. *Dreif materikov i klimat zemli (Continental drift and earth's climate)*. Moscow: Mysl'.

Vale, T. R. 1977. Forest changes in the Warner Mountains, California. *Annals of the Association of American Geographers* 67:28–45.

Vashalova, T. V. 1987. Paleogeograficheskiy podkhod k rekonstruktsii aktivnosti snezhnykh lavin v tselyakh dolgosrochnogo prognoza (Paleogeographical approach to the reconstruction of avalanche activity for the purpose of long-term forecasting). In *Otsenka i dolgosrochnyi prognoz izmeneniya prirody gor (Evaluation and long-term forecasting of nature change in mountainous areas)*, 120–27. Moscow: Moscow University Press.

Vashalova, T. V., L. P. Vinnikov, and Yu. V. Semekhin. 1984. Tekhnogennye geomorfologicheskie protsessy kak ob'yekt inzhenernoy geografii gornykh stran (Technogenic geomorphological processes as an object of engineering geography in mountainous areas). In *Inzhenernaya geografiya gornykh stran (Engineering geography of mountainous areas)*, 178–89. Moscow: Moscow University Press.

Vasiliev, L. N., ed. 1987. *Mezhdunarodnyy aerokosmicheskiy eksperiment "Kursk-85"* (*International aerospace experiment "Kursk-85"*). Moscow: VINITI.

————, ed. 1988a. Geograficheskaya interpretatsiya aerokosmicheskoy informatsii (Geographic interpretation of aerospace information). In *Sovremennye problemy biosfery* (*Modern problems of the biosphere*). Moscow: Nauka.

————. 1988b. Sistemnye kosmicheskie issledovaniya prirodnoy sredy (Study of natural environments from outer-space systems). In *Geograficheskaya interpretatsiya aerokosmicheskoy informatsii* (*Geographic interpretation of aerospace information*), 6–12. Moscow.

Vavilov, N. I. 1967. *Izbrannye proizvedeniya* (*Selected works*). 2 vols. Moscow: Nauka.

Veblen, T. T., and D. C. Lorenz. 1986. Anthropogenic disturbance and recovery patterns in montane forests, Colorado Front Range. *Physical Geography* 7:1–24.

Velitchko, A. A. 1973. *Natural process in the Pleistocene* [in Russian]. Moscow: Nauka.

————. 1980. Latitudinal asymmetry of natural components during ice ages in the Northern Hemisphere [in Russian]. *Izvestiya USSR Academy of Sciences, Series Geography* 2:5–23.

————. 1983. Elementy geoekologicheskogo prognoza dlya territorii SSSR na nachalo XXI stoletiya (Elements of geoecological prognosis for the beginning of the 21st century in the USSR). *Izvestiya USSR Academy of Sciences* 11:68–78.

————, ed. 1984. *Late Quaternary environments of the Soviet Union*. Minneapolis: University of Minnesota Press.

————. 1985a. Evolyutsionnaya geografiya (Evolutionary geography). *Izvestiya USSR Academy of Sciences* 6:25–35.

————. 1985b. Nature at the cradle of mankind [in Russian]. *Priroda* 3:35–45.

————. 1987a. Relationship of climatic changes in high and low latitudes of the earth during the late Pleistocene and Holocene. In *Paleography and loess*, 9–25. Budapest: Akademiai Kiado Press.

————. 1987b. Structure of thermal changes in the Meso-Cenozoic climates based on data from East Europe [in Russian]. In *Klimaty zemli v geologicheskom proshlom*, 5–41. Moscow: Nauka.

————. 1988. Problems of human impact on environments. Paleographic aspects of ecological scenarios of the future [in Russian]. In *Globalnye problemy geographecheskoi nauki*, 35–44. Moscow: Nauka.

————. 1989a. Evolutionary analysis of the contemporary landscape sphere of the earth and prognosis. *Quaternary International* 1:1–8.

————. 1989b. The Holocene as an element of global natural process [in Russian]. In *Paleoklimaty pozdneleonikovya i golotsena*, 8–12. Moscow: Nauka.

Velitchko, A. A., M. S. Bara, V. P. Grichuk, et al. 1982. Paleoklimaticheskie rekonstruktsii dlya optimuma mikulinskogo mejlednikov'ya na territorii Evropy (Paleoclimatic reconstructions for the optimum of Mikulin's interglacial period over Europe). *Izvestiya USSR Academy of Sciences, Series Geography* 2:5.

Vernadsky, V. I. 1967. *Biosfera* (*Biosphere*). Moscow: Mysl'.

————. 1973. Razmyshleniya naturalista (A naturalist's reflection). *Nature* (Moscow) 6:30–41.

————. 1981. *Isbrannii trydi po istorii nauki* (*Selected works on the history of science*). Moscow: Nauka.

————. 1987. *Chimicheskoe stroenie biosphery zemli i ee okrejeniya* (*Chemical structure of the earth's biosphere and its environment*). Moscow: Nauka.

Verstraete, M. M. 1986. Defining desertification: A review. *Climatic Change* 9:5–18.

Vianello, R. L. 1985. Vertical velocity forced by topography in the Southern Hemisphere. *Journal of Climatology* 5:213–20.

Vinogradov, B. V. 1982. Distantsionnye izmereniya fitomassy (Evaluation of phytomass from a distance). In *Issledovaniya zemli iz kosmosa* (*Earth study from outer space*), 5:36–45. Moscow.

————. 1983. Aerokosmicheskiy monitoring vosstanovitel'nykh suktsessiy i ego primenenie v biosfernykh zapovednikakh (Monitoring of rehabilitative successions from outer space and its use in biosphere reserves). In *Prikladnye aspekty programmy "Chelovek i biosfera"* (*Aspects of application in the Man and the Biosphere Programme*), 167–81. Moscow.

————. 1984. *Aerokosmicheskiy monitoring ekosistem* (*Aerospace monitoring of ecosystems*). Moscow: Nauka.

————. 1988. Aerokosmicheskiy monitoring gumusovogo sostoyaniya pochv (Aerospace monitoring of soil humus). *Pochvovedenie* 4:38–48.

Vladimirov, V. V. 1982. *Rasselenie i okruzhayushchaya sreda* (*Settlement and environment*). Moscow: Construction Publishing House.

Vladimirov, V. V., E. M. Mikulina, and Z. N. Yargina. 1986. *Gorod i landshaft* (*A city and the landscape*). Moscow: Mysl'.

Vladimirsky, B. M., and L. D. Kislovsky. 1986. Kosmicheskiye vozdeistviya i evolyutsiya biosfery (Outer-space impact and evolution of the biosphere). In *Novoe v zhizni i nauki tekhniki. Kosmonavtika i astronomiya* (*News in science and techniques. Cosmonautics and astronomy*). Moscow: Nauka, 1–64.

Vogt, W. 1948. *Road to survival*. New York: William Sloane Associates.

Voitkevich, G. V. 1983. *Earth genesis and chemical evolution* [in Russian]. Moscow: Nauka.

Volkov, I. I., V. A. Gronenko, M. V. Ivanov, et al. 1983. *Global'nyi biogeokhimicheskiy tsykl sery* (*Global biogeochemical sulfur cycle*). Moscow: Nauka.

Volkova, V. S. 1977. *The stratigraphy and history of vegetation in west Siberia in the late Cenozoic* [in Russian]. Moscow: Nauka.

Voskresensky, K. S., V. E. Zemchikhin, and S. V. Chistov. 1987. Otsenka i prognoz termoerozionnogo ovragoonrazovaniya na severe zapadnoi Sibiri (Assessment and prognosis of thermo-abrasive formation of ravines in northwestern Siberia). In *Opasnye prirodnye yavleniya* (*Dangerous natural phenomena*), 37–87. Moscow: VINITI.

Walker, A. S., and C. J. Robinove. 1981. *Annotated bibliography of remote sensing methods for monitoring desertification*. U.S. Geological Survey Circular 851. Reston, Va.: U.S. Geological Survey.

Walker, J., and P. R. Rowntree. 1977. The effect of soil moisture on circulation and rainfall in a tropical model. *Quarterly Journal of the Royal Meteorological Society* 103:29–46.

Walsh, J. E. 1987. Large-scale effects of seasonal snow cover. In *Large-scale effects of seasonal snow cover*, ed. B. E. Goodison, R. G. Barry, and J. Dozier, 3–14. International Association of Hydrological Sciences, Publication No. 166. Wallingford, U.K.: IAHS Press.

Walsh, J. E., M. B. Richman, and D. W. Allen. 1982. Spatial coherence of monthly precipitation in the United States. *Monthly Weather Review* 110:272–86.

Walsh, R.P.D., M. Hulme, and M. D. Campbell. 1988. Recent rainfall changes and their impact on the hydrology and water supply in the semi-arid zone of the Sudan. *Geographical Journal* 154:181–97.

Walsh, S. J. 1987. Relationship of selected biophysical variables to soil moisture and soil temperature variability. *Physical Geography* 8:287–97.

Wang, W. C., D. J. Wuebbles, W. M. Washington, R. G. Isaacs, and G. Molnar. 1986. Trace gases and other potential perturbations to global climate. *Reviews of Geophysics* 24:110–40.

Warren, A., and C. Agnew. 1988. *An assessment of desertification and land degradation in arid and semi-arid areas*. International Institute for Environment and Development, Paper No. 2. London.

Warren, P. L., P. A. Knapp, C. F. Hutchinson, M. C. Parton, and R. A. Schowengerdt. 1985. Monitoring arid land vegetation change with remote sensing: An example from southern Arizona. In *Arid lands today and tomorrow*, ed. E. W. Whitehead, C. F. Hutchinson, B. N. Timmerman, and R. C. Varady, 251–59. Boulder, Colo.: Westview Press.

Warrick, R. A., and M. J. Bowden. 1981. The changing impacts of droughts in the Great Plains. In *The Great Plains: Perspectives and prospects*, ed. M. P. Lawson and M. E. Baker, 111–37. Lincoln: University of Nebraska Press.

Warrick, R. A., and W. E. Riebsame. 1983. Societal response to CO_2-induced climate change: Opportunities for research. In *Social science research and climate change: An interdisciplinary appraisal*, ed. R. S. Chen, E. Boulding, and S. H. Schneider, 20–60. Dordrecht: D. Reidel.

Warrick, W. A.; R. M. Gifford, and M. L. Parry. 1986. CO_2, climatic change and agriculture. In *The greenhouse effect, climatic change, and ecosystems*, ed. B. Bolin et al., 393–473. New York: John Wiley and Sons.

Washington, W. M., and C. L. Parkinson. 1986. *An introduction to three-dimensional climate modeling*. Mill Valley, Calif.: University Science Books.

Washington, W. M., and D. L. Williamson. 1977. A description of the NCAR global circulation models. *Methods in Computational Physics* 17:111–72.

Watkins, J., and H. Morrow-Jones. 1985. Small area population estimates using aerial photography. *Photogrammetric Engineering and Remote Sensing* 51(12):1933–35.

Watts, M. 1983. *Silent violence: Food, famine and peasantry in northern Nigeria*. Berkeley: University of California Press.

Webb, T. III, E. J. Cushing, and H. E. Wright, Jr. 1983. Holocene changes in the vegetation of the midwest. In *Late Quaternary environments of the United States*. Vol. 2: *The Holocene*, ed. H. E. Wright, Jr., 142–65. Minneapolis: University of Minnesota Press.

Weismuller, R. A., S. J. Kristof, D. K. Scholz, P. E. Anuta, and S. A. Momin. 1977. Change detection in coastal environments. *Photogrammetric Engineering and Remote Sensing* 43:1533.

Wendler, G., and F. Eaton. 1983. On the desertification of the Sahel zone. *Climatic Change* 5:365–80.

Wernstedt, F. L. 1972. *World climatic data*. Lemont, Pa.: Climatic Data Press.

Western, D., and C. Van Praet. 1973. Cyclical changes in the habitat and climate of an East African ecosystem. *Nature* (London) 241:104–6.

Westman, W. E. 1985. *Ecology, impact assessment and environmental planning.* New York: John Wiley and Sons.

Wharton, S. W. 1987. A spectral-knowledge-based approach for urban land-cover discrimination. *IEEE Transactions of Geoscience and Remote Sensing*, GE-25, 3:272–82.

White, G. F. 1974. *Natural hazards: Local, national, global.* New York: Oxford University Press.

Whitford, W. G., V. Meentmeyer, T. R. Seastedt, K. Cromack, D. A. Crossley, Jr., P. Santos, R. L. Todd, and J. B. Waide. 1981. Exceptions to the AET model: Deserts and clearcut forest. *Ecology* 62:275–77.

Whittaker, R. H., and G. E. Likens. 1973. Carbon in the biota. In *Carbon in the biosphere*, ed. G. M. Woodwell and E. V. Pecan, 281–302. US-AEC Conference-720510. Springfield, Va.: National Technical Information Service.

Whyte, A.V.T. 1985. Perception. In *Climate impact assessment: Studies in the interaction of climate and society*, ed. R. W. Kates, J. H. Ausubel, and M. Berberian, 469–92. Scientific Committee on Problems of the Environment, Report 27. New York: John Wiley and Sons.

———. 1986. From hazard perception to human ecology. In *Geography, resources, and environment*, ed. R. W. Kates and I. Burton, 2:240–71. Chicago: University of Chicago Press.

Whyte, A.V.T., and I. Burton, eds. 1980. *Environmental risk assessment.* Scientific Committee on Problems of the Environment, Report No. 15. New York: John Wiley and Sons.

Wijkman, A., and L. Timberlake. 1984. *Natural disasters: Acts of God or acts of man?* Washington, D.C.: Earthscan.

Wilcox, B. A., and D. D. Murphy. 1985. Conservation strategy: The effects of fragmentation on extinction. *American Naturalist* 125:879–87.

Williams, D. L., J. R. Irons, B. L. Markham, R. F. Nelson, D. L. Toll, R. S. Latty, and M. L. Stauffer. 1984. A statistical evaluation of the advantages of Landsat thematic mapper in comparison to multispectral scanner data. *IEEE Transactions of Geoscience and Remote Sensing*, GE-22.

Williams, G.D.V., R. A. Fautley, K. H. Jones, R. B. Stewart, and E. E. Wheaton. 1988. Estimating the impacts of climatic change on agriculture in the Canadian prairies: The Canadian case study. In *Assessment of climate impacts on agriculture.* Vol. 1: *In high latitude areas*, ed. M. L. Parry, T. R. Carter, and N. T. Konijn. Dordrecht: Kluwar Academic Publishers.

Williams, J. 1979. The effects of different energy strategies on the atmospheric CO_2 concentration in climate. In *Carbon dioxide, climate and society*, ed. J. Williams, 239–48. Oxford: Pergamon Press.

Williams, J., G. Krömer, and A. Gilchrist. 1979. The impact of waste heat release on climate: Experiments with a general circulation model. *Journal of Applied Meteorology* 18:1501–11.

Williamson, D. L. 1983. *Description of the NCAR Community Climate Model (CCM0B).* NCAR Technical Report NCAR/TN-210 + STR. Boulder, Colo.: National Center for Atmospheric Research.

Willmott, C. J. 1984. A primer on the representation of the terrestrial seasonal snow cycle within GCMs. *Modeling and Simulation* 15:327–32.

Willmott, C. J., and K. Klink. 1986. A representation of the terrestrial biosphere for use in global climate studies. *Proceedings of the ISLSCP Conference in Rome, Italy.* European Space Agency (ESA SP-248), 109–12.

Willmott, C. J., J. R. Mather, and C. M. Rowe. 1981. Average monthly and annual surface air temperature and precipitation data for the world. Part 1: The Eastern Hemisphere. Part 2: The Western Hemisphere. *Publications in Climatology* 34.

Willmott, C. J., C. M. Rowe, and Y. Mintz. 1985a. Climatology of the terrestrial seasonal water cycle. *Journal of Climatology* 5:589–606.

Willmott, C. J., C. M. Rowe, and W. D. Philpot. 1985b. Small-scale maps: A sensitivity analysis of some common assumptions associated with grid-point interpolation and contouring. *American Cartographer* 12(1):5–16.

Wilm, H. G., C. W. Thornthwaite, et al. 1944. Report of the Committee on Transpiration and Evaporation, 1943–44. *Transactions of the American Geophysical Union* 25:683.

Wilson, E. O. 1988. The current state of biological diversity. In *Biodiversity*, ed. E. O. Wilson and F. M. Peter, 3–20. Washington, D.C.: National Academy Press.

Wilson, E. O., and F. M. Peter, eds. 1988. *Biodiversity.* Washington, D.C.: National Academy Press.

Wilson, M. F. 1984. Construction and use of land surface information in a general circulation model. Ph.D. dissertation, University of Liverpool.

Wilson, M. F., and A. Henderson-Sellers. 1985. A global archive of land cover and soils data for use in general circulation climate models. *Journal of Climatology* 5:119–43.

Wilson, R., and E.A.C. Crouch. 1987. Risk assessment and comparisons: An introduction. *Science* 236:267–70.

Winstanley, D. 1976. Climatic changes and the future of the Sahel. In *The politics of natural disaster*, ed. M. Glantz, 189–213. New York: Praeger.

Wong, C. S. 1978. Atmospheric input of carbon dioxide from burning wood. *Science* 200:197–200.

Woodcock, C. E., and A. H. Strahler. 1987. The factor of scale in remote sensing. *Remote Sensing of the Environment* 21:311–32.

Woods, J. C., M. K. Wood, and J. M. Trumble. 1987. Important factors influencing water and sediment production on arid lands in New Mexico. *Journal of Arid Environments* 12:111–18.

Woodwell, G. M., J. E. Hobbie, R. A. Houghton, J. M. Melillo, B. Moore, B. J. Peterson, and G. R. Shaver. 1983a. Global deforestation: Contribution to atmospheric carbon dioxide. *Science* 222:1081–86.

Woodwell, G. M., J. E. Hobbie, R. A. Houghton, J. M. Melillo, B. J. Peterson, G. R. Shaver, T. A. Stone, B. Moore, and A. B. Park. 1983b. *Deforestation measured by Landsat: Steps toward a method.* Washington, D.C.: U.S. Department of Energy, DOE/EV/10468-1.

Woodwell, G. M., R. A. Houghton, T. A. Stone, R. F. Nelson, and W. Kovalick. 1987. Deforestation in the tropics: New measurements in the Amazon Basin using Landsat and NOAA advanced very high resolution radiometer imagery. *Journal of Geophysical Research* 92(2):2157–63.

Woodwell, G. M., R. H. Whittaker, W. A. Reiner, G. E. Likens, C. C. Detwicke, and D. B. Botkin. 1978. The biota in the world carbon budget. *Science* 199: 141–46.

World Meteorological Organization. 1986. *Report of the International Conference on the Assessment of the Role of Carbon Dioxide and of Other Greenhouse Gases in Climate Variations and Associated Impacts*. Publication No. 661. Geneva: WHO.

Wright, H. E., Jr. 1971. Late Quaternary vegetation history of North America. In *The late Cenozoic glacial ages*, ed. K. Turekian, 425–64. New Haven: Yale University Press.

———, ed. 1983. *Late Quaternary environments of the United States*. Vol. 2: *The Holocene*. Minneapolis: University of Minnesota Press.

Yaalon, D., and E. Ganor. 1973. The influence of dust on soils during the Quaternary. *Soil Science* 116:146–55.

Yates, H. W., J. D. Tarpley, S. R. Schneider, D. F. McGinnis, and R. A. Scofield. 1984. The role of meteorological satellites in agricultural remote sensing. *Remote Sensing of the Environment* 14:219–33.

Yermakov, Yu. G., and A. M. Ryabchikov. 1980. Prognozirovanie sostoyaniya okruzhayushchey sredy v razvitykh kapitalisticheskikh stranakh (Environmental prognosis in developed capitalist countries). *Vestnik of Moscow State University, Series 5, Geography* (Moscow) 2:17–25.

Yermakov, Yu. G., A. M. Ryabchikov, and V. N. Solntsev. 1982. Geograficheskie aspekty prognozirovaniya sostoyaniya okruzhayushchey sredy zarubezhnykh territoriy (Geographical aspects of forecasting of environments in foreign countries). *Izvestiya Moscow State University Press, Series Geography* 3:12–19.

Yermakov, Yu. G., and V. A. Uledov. 1976. Izmeneniye prirodnoy sredy v SSHA (Environmental changes in the USA). In *Aktual'nye problemy izmeneniya prirodnoy sredy za rubejom (Contemporary problems of environmental changes abroad)*, 115–39. Moscow: Moscow University Press.

Yost, R. S., E. J. Kamprath, E. Lobato, and G. Naderman. 1979. Phosphorus response of corn on an oxisol as influenced by rates and placement. *Soil Science Society of America Journal* 43:338–43.

Young, A. 1986. Evaluation of agroforestry potential in sloping areas. In *Land evaluation for land use planning and conservation in sloping areas*, ed. W. Siderius, 106–32. Wageningen: International Livestock Research Institute.

Zalygin, S. P. 1987. Povorot (A transfer). *New World* (Moscow) 1:3–18.

Zeigler, D. J., J. H. Johnson, and S. D. Brunn. 1983. *Technological hazards*. Washington, D.C.: Association of American Geographers.

Zenkovich, V. P., ed. 1987. *Prirodnye osnovy beregozashchity (Natural basis for bank protection)*. Moscow: Nauka.

———. 1988. Nekotorye voprosy izucheniya beregovoi zony (Some aspects of coastal zone study). *Izvestiya USSR Academy of Sciences, Series Geography* 2:132–35.

Zimmerman, B. L., and R. O. Bierregard. 1986. Relevance of the equilibrium theory of island biogeography and species-area relations to conservation, with a case from Amazonia. *Journal of Biogeography* 13:133–43.

Zolotarev, G. S. 1983. *Inzhenernaya geodinamika (Engineering geodynamics)*. Moscow: Moscow University Press.

Zolotarev, G. S., et al., eds. 1987. *Formirovanie opolzney, selei i lavin: Inzhenernaya zashchita territoriy (Landslide, mudflow, and avalanche formation: Protection of areas of engineering works)*. Moscow: Moscow University Press.

Zolotokrylin, A. N. 1986. Svyaz' al'bedo i temperatury povrkhnosti sushi v aridnykh oblastyakh (A connection between albedo and land surface temperature). *Proceedings Meteorological Investigations* (Moscow) 10:39–45.

Zon, R., and W. N. Sparhawk. 1923. *Forest resources of the world*. 2 vols. New York: McGraw-Hill.

Zvonkova, T. V. 1987. *Geograficheskoe prognozirovanie (Geographical forecasting)*. Moscow: High School Publishing House.

Zvonkova, T. V., L. A. Semenova, and K. S. Samoilova. 1985. *Geograficheskoe obosnovanie ekologicheskikh ekspertiz (Geographical foundation of environmental impact assessment)*. Moscow: Moscow University Press.

INDEX